Families That Work:
Children in a Changing World

Sheila B. Kamerman and Cheryl D. Hayes, *Editors*

Panel on Work, Family, and Community
Committee on Child Development Research
and Public Policy
Commission on Behavioral and Social Sciences
and Education
National Research Council

National Academy Press
Washington, D.C. 1982

NOTICE: The project that is the subject of this report was approved by the Governing Board of the National Research Council, whose members are drawn from the Councils of the National Academy of Sciences, the National Academy of Engineering, and the Institute of Medicine. The members of the committee responsible for the report were chosen for their special competences and with regard for appropriate balance.

This report has been reviewed by a group other than the authors according to procedures approved by a report review committee consisting of members of the National Academy of Sciences, the National Academy of Engineering, and the Institute of Medicine.

The National Research Council was established by the National Academy of Sciences in 1916 to associate the broad community of science and technology with the Academy's purposes of furthering knowledge and of advising the federal government. The Council operates in accordance with general policies determined by the Academy under the authority of its congressional charter of 1863, which established the Academy as a private, nonprofit, self-governing membership corporation. The Council has become the principal operating agency of both the National Academy of Sciences and the National Academy of Engineering in the conduct of their services to the government, the public, and the scientific and engineering communities. It is administered jointly by both Academies and the Institute of Medicine. The National Academy of Engineering and the Institute of Medicine were established in 1964 and 1970, respectively, under the charter of the National Academy of Sciences.

Library of Congress Cataloging in Publication Data
Main entry under title:

Families that work.
  Bibliography: p.
  Contents: Introduction—Dimensions of change,
  Work and family through time and space / Urie
Bronfenbrenner and Ann C. Crouter [etc.]
  1. Family—Addresses, essays, lectures.
  2. Mothers—Employment—Addresses, essays, lectures.
  3. Parents—Employment—Addresses, essays, lectures.
  4. Children of working parents—Addresses, essays,
lectures. 5. Child development—Addresses, essays,
lectures. I. Kamerman, Sheila B. II. Hayes,
Cheryl D. III. National Research Council (U.S.).
Panel on Work, Family, and Community.
HQ734.F228 1982   306.8'7   82-81829
ISBN 0-309-03282-2

Available from

NATIONAL ACADEMY PRESS
2101 Constitution Avenue, N.W.
Washington, D.C. 20418

Printed in the United States of America

PANEL ON WORK, FAMILY, AND COMMUNITY

SHEILA B. KAMERMAN (*Chair*), School of Social Work, Columbia University
JOAN S. BISSELL, Employment Development Department, State of California
URIE BRONFENBRENNER, Department of Human Development and Family Studies, Cornell University
CLAIR B. BROWN, Department of Economics, University of California, Berkeley
JOHN P. DEMOS, Department of History, Brandeis University
LEOBARDO ESTRADA, School of Architecture and Urban Planning, University of California, Los Angeles
E. MAVIS HETHERINGTON, Department of Psychology, University of Virginia
LAURENCE E. LYNN, JR., John F. Kennedy School of Government, Harvard University
ELLIOTT A. MEDRICH, Children's Time Study, University of California, Berkeley
KRISTIN A. MOORE, Program of Research on Women and Family Policy, The Urban Institute, Washington, D.C.
LEE RAINWATER, Department of Sociology, Harvard University
MARSHALL S. SMITH, Wisconsin Research and Development Center for Individualized Schooling, University of Wisconsin
HAROLD W. WATTS, Department of Economics, Columbia University

CHERYL D. HAYES, Study Director
SALLY BLOOM-FESHBACH, Research Associate/Consultant

iii

iv

Contents

v

Preface

Children are the future citizens, the future labor force, and the future parents of our society. For many of us who are ourselves parents, children are our stake in history, part of our own future support system, our personal joy—and sometimes pain. How children develop, and the factors that affect their development, for better or for worse, are of major concern to us as individuals and to the society at large. When there are intimations of problems for children, we become concerned. When there is evidence of harm to children, we become aroused. When there are indications of social turmoil and change with unclear consequences for children, we become apprehensive.

One change that has occurred with dramatic suddenness during the past two decades has been the extraordinary growth in the number of women entering the labor force and remaining there despite marriage, pregnancy, maternity, and the demands of child care. Single women (unmarried, divorced, separated) with children have always tended to have a high labor force participation rate. Now, however, not only has their number increased substantially, but also the number of married mothers at work has grown even more.

Children, now and for the foreseeable future, are likely to grow up in families with a single parent or two parents who are working. What are the consequences?

Many people are convinced that one consequence is an observable and significant increase in the problems children are experiencing: learning problems, behavioral problems, emotional problems. Some teachers, for example, are certain that children growing up in a working family are undisciplined, that they fail to develop good work habits and have difficulty at school. There are some who believe that even if children's problems are not yet visible or not yet clearly attributable to mothers' working outside the home, they will emerge over time. Some parents worry that children growing up without constant parental supervision and guidance may not learn proper parenting skills. Still others are sure that, on the contrary, the change in maternal roles can only have positive effects, helping children to become more responsible and more independent. Although the Panel on Work, Family, and Community was not established in order to make a definitive finding on whether maternal employment has positive, negative, or neutral effects on children, clearly this was a latent question.

It is in this context of changes in family work patterns and relationships, and out of the concerns regarding the consequences for children, that the panel was established in 1980 by the Committee on Child Development Research and Public Policy, with the support of the National Institute of Education, U.S. Department of Education. Our charge was to carry out a scholarly review of what is known about the outcomes of changes in parental employment as they affect children directly or as they affect them indirectly, through their interactions with other changes in families and in the other institutions (schools, community services, the workplace) that affect families and children in their daily lives. The task was to learn more about what is happening; to identify what problems, or benefits, seem to be emerging for children as a consequence; and to determine how and why they occur. Of particular concern was how these developments affect the ways in which children are socialized and educated and what the outcomes are likely to be. Ultimately, our objective was to be able to suggest a course of action designed to reduce the problems (or enhance the benefits) or to indicate what additional knowledge would be needed in order to propose such actions.

We have completed our initial task. Our conclusion is that the phenomenon itself is far too complex to identify any simple causal nexus between parental employment and effects on children. Work, by itself, is not a uniform condition experienced in the same way by all adults who are themselves parents. Parents are not the same; nor are their children; nor are the communities in which children live, the schools they attend, their neighbors and friends. In effect, if we have any message to communicate after the extensive efforts we have made, it would be to tell parents, teachers, and professionals: "Don't ask if working parents are good or bad for kids because the answer is 'It depends.' It depends on the parents, on the child, on the circumstances, and so forth."

Some children live in families in which parents need to work for economic reasons; some children live in families in which parents want to work for nonpecuniary reasons; and some children live in families in which both monetary and nonmonetary values are involved in the decision to work or not to work. The outcomes for children vary and are not clearly ascribable to any single factor.

Everything we know suggests that the changes occurring in parental work patterns will not disappear. In some way, a variety of responses will occur in the society, either haphazardly or deliberately. Parents will adapt; schools will adapt; neighborhoods will adapt and so will children, or at least, so will most children. Thus, we are left instead with a new question: *Under what circumstances do the children of working parents develop well and under what circumstances do they have problems? Which are the characteristics of parents, work, children, school, and neighborhood that enhance the positive development of children—and which exacerbate or attenuate negative development?*

It is in addressing this question that we offer recommendations and suggest a research agenda. Our task has not been easy. There is no defined body of knowledge at the interface of child-family-work-community. There is no agreed-on field of research. Each issue we raised required a different world view and raised new questions. Existing research is carried out by discipline or conventional topical definitions. Data are often not available or are of poor quality. Not all of our efforts were successful. For example, neither existing school research nor community research addresses the questions we were raising. As a result, we urge new conceptualizations of these institutions.

We conclude with a plea, therefore, not for more studies but for different studies, studies which focus more directly on children, what happens to them and why; and studies that acknowledge the complexity of the environment in which children are reared. We end up reaffirming that if the goal is to understand how children develop well, then they must be studied in their living environment, an environment that increasingly includes working parents. Indeed, growing up with working parents has become a normal, ordinary condition for children and therefore is one more factor that must be integrated into the context of children's lives. Whether it will be, and how, remains to be seen.

We would note here that our efforts focused on parental employment; it was not our purpose to assess the consequences for children of parental unemployment. Obviously, if there is concern with how children develop and with their well-being, the consequences of parental unemployment should receive major attention. Although this was not our purpose here, much of what we say has implications for such study as well.

Our panel members represent a variety of disciplines; most are themselves parents and even working parents. Each panel member deserves a special acknowledgment; each worked hard. For many, this was an issue of personal as well as professional concern. Inevitably, there were differences, but they were differences that exist in the large society, too. As a consequence, we were forced to confront and to resolve some of the value conflicts that pervade this subject.

We acknowledge, especially, the support of Marc Tucker, who at the outset of the study was the assistant director for educational policy and organization of the National Institute of Education. He and his staff consistently encouraged us in our work. It was Marc Tucker's view of how children are educated that made the project possible. Convinced that one of the failures of educational research has been a narrow focus on schools and a concomitant lack of study of the roles played by families, peers, neighbors, and community, he supported us in the direction we chose to follow: an exploration of what is happening to children as a consequence of the major changes occurring in family structures and family functioning, and how these changes relate to other institutions—school, workplace, community.

Laurence E. Lynn, Jr., who chaired the Committee on Child Development Research and Public Policy when the panel was first established and who has been an active member of the panel, and Alfred J. Kahn, who chaired that committee for the past year, have both provided support and encouragement.

Of particular importance has been the role played by Cheryl D. Hayes, study director for our panel as well as executive officer for the parent committee. As a staff member of the Academy and as a colleague, she was largely responsible for the committee's undertaking this study and has made a major contribution to the work of the panel and to this report. Her sensitivity and organizational skills are legion. Both the substance and the style of the report owe much to her. Her investment, too, has been both personal and professional. I hope our report answers some of her questions.

Special thanks are due to Sally Bloom-Feshbach, research associate/consultant to the panel, who coauthored one of the review chapters in Part II of this volume and who assumed major responsibility for the panel's background survey of existing data sources. Her assistance throughout this project has been invaluable.

In addition, we wish to acknowledge the significant contribution of those who prepared the review chapters that are the heart of this report. Their conscientiousness in undertaking the task and their responsiveness to the panel's concerns in the numerous revisions have made this an important study that we hope will influence researchers and those who support research in this area during the years ahead.

Ginny Peterson, administrative assistant to the Committee on Child Development Research and Public Policy, assumed major responsibility for the myriad administrative details associated with the panel's work and supervised the production of the report. Irene Martinez typed and retyped the several versions of the document. Their roles have been essential to the successful completion of this project, and we are grateful to them for the time and energy they devoted.

Finally, thanks are also due to David Goslin, executive director of the Commission on Behavioral and Social Sciences and Education, for his support and encouragement, and to Barbara Armstrong, editor, who prepared this manuscript for publication.

SHEILA B. KAMERMAN
Chair, Panel on
Work, Family, and Community

PART I
A Time of Transition

1
Introduction

The past decade has witnessed significant changes in American society. The traditional family with a husband-father who is the provider and a wife-mother who maintains the home and cares for the children is no longer the norm. The form of the family is changing and with it the roles and relationships among family members. Increasingly during the past 10 years, women, including women with children, are working or looking for work outside the home, while the proportion of men in the labor force has actually fallen somewhat.[1] Changes in patterns of labor force participation have been accompanied by dramatic changes in family structure. Families are smaller now than in the past. A rapidly rising divorce rate has spurred a significant increase in the number and proportion of families with only one parent, most of these female-headed. Simultaneously, there has been a sharp decline in the fertility rate and in the average number of children born per woman. Taken together, these changes in work and family affect virtually all of our social, cultural, and economic arrangements. Most importantly, they affect the environments in which children are reared and the experiences they have in growing up.

This book is about the implications of changing patterns of work for

[1] We define work as paid employment outside the home. Although home maintenance tasks and housework are clearly work, we do not include them in our definition unless they are performed in connection with paid employment by an employer outside one's own household.

3

children's socialization and education. It is not an assessment of whether mothers should or should not work. Instead, it provides an account of what is known and what remains to be known about how this and related social phenomena affect children both directly and indirectly through the various institutions in our society with which they interact daily. The task of the Panel on Work, Family, and Community was to review the state of knowledge about the dimensions and consequences of change in children's lives, in particular those associated with shifting patterns of work and family structure. Our objective was to map the domain— to define the significant linkages between and among work, family, and formal and informal community institutions as they affect children's daily experiences. We believe that recent trends in labor force participation will very likely continue. Accordingly, the ultimate goal of our study was to develop a strategy for research to inform the future public- and private-sector decision makers who will establish policies and practices affecting the well-being of children whose parent or parents work

THE FOCUS OF THE STUDY

Although they are not traceable to any abrupt shift or single cataclysmic event, changes in patterns of work and related shifts in family structure have been dramatic in the past two decades, and the pace of change has accelerated during the past ten years. The course of these changes, however, has been difficult to predict. Repeatedly in the past, projections of future growth in the labor force participation of mothers and fathers, as well as rates of divorce, have seriously underestimated the number and proportion of the U.S. population that would be affected. Undoubtedly, the decades of the 1980s and the 1990s will witness a slowing in the pace of change. Nevertheless, for better or worse, everything we know suggests that these patterns are established and will continue. Some have described them as the most significant social changes of the twentieth century. At the very least, as researchers at The Urban Institute suggest, we are experiencing a "subtle revolution" (Smith, 1979).

These trends have far-reaching implications for a variety of formal and informal institutions, most of which are still predicated on the notion of a society dominated by traditional two-parent, single-earner families. As the roles and responsibilities of mothers and fathers have shifted, so have expectations for institutions that provide support and services. The workplace is no longer a man's world, and employers are increasingly being called upon to provide benefits that will assist employees in meeting their work and family responsibilities. The home is no longer solely the domain of women. Some evidence suggests that the division of labor for household tasks and child rearing may be changing somewhat, as are consumption patterns, living standards, and the responsibility for household decision making, although researchers disagree about the extent and significance of such trends. Public and private community institutions, including schools, churches, recreation and social service centers, and the marketplace, are also under pressure to adapt to the changing needs of families.

Most importantly, however, the "subtle revolution" has significant implications for children. Of all issues associated with changing patterns of labor force participation and changes in family structure, those concerning the care and nurture of future generations have caused the most controversy.

Children's development is in part influenced by the environments in which they grow up, the individuals with whom they interact, and the experiences they have. Socialization and education take place in a variety of settings, including homes, schools, and neighborhoods. How children perform in one setting is significantly affected by what goes on in the other settings in which they spend time. Children's home life, for example, affects their performance in school, and conversely, their classroom experiences affect behavior at home. Inevitably, questions are being raised about the consequences of changing patterns of work and family life on the well-being of children—on their academic achievement; on their attitudes toward education, work, and family formation; on their interactions and relationships with parents, siblings, peers, teachers, and other adults; on their personality development; and on the incidence of problems such as delinquency, teenage pregnancy, drug abuse, and alcoholism. Are children of working parents better or worse off than children in traditional two-parent families in which the father spends his days at the workplace and the mother spends hers at home? Which children are more or less likely to have problems?

There is no simple answer. Current understanding of the relationship between social change and child outcomes is limited at best. Conflicting value orientations significantly influence any assessment of available evidence. On the one hand, there are many who regard the labor force participation of women as a liberating step that can only increase the productive capacity of the nation as a whole. According to this viewpoint, children benefit from the presence of a mother as well as a father who has a strong sense of independence and from the increased income that results from her employment. On the other hand, there are those who regard changing patterns of work and family as a threat to traditional values and as a needless burden on a labor market that is already unable to provide enough jobs. This group argues that children suffer a lack of essential personal attention from parents, especially mothers, who are struggling to integrate outside employment with household responsibilities. Such children, they would suggest, are especially adversely affected in families where the father is absent. The debate over the effects of these changing life-styles remains largely unresolved.

What seems clear, however, is that no social change takes place in isolation or has a single, universal effect. The consequences for children of shifting patterns of labor force participation and related changes in family structure depend in large part on how a variety of institutions in our society adapt—including the family, formal and informal community institutions, the workplace, and the marketplace—and the relationships that exist between and among them.

If there is only one message that emerges from this study, it is that *parental employment in and of itself—mothers' employment or fathers' or both parents'—is not necessarily good or bad for children.* Evidence suggests that children of different ages in families of different types living in different locations and circumstances may fare differently. Some may be better off, some worse off, and some may not be influenced at all. How children are affected depends on the ways in which other social, cultural, ideological, and economic factors mediate these changes. It also depends on the extent to which other institutions in our society provide needed supports to children and their families. The effectiveness of institutions such as the schools, for example, in performing their designated function of educating children greatly depends on what occurs in children's lives outside these institutions—where they spend their time, with whom, and engaged in what kinds of activities.

MAPPING THE DOMAIN: OUR APPROACH TO THE STUDY

The Panel on Work, Family, and Community was established to review the current state of knowledge about how families, various formal and informal community institutions, the workplace, and the marketplace have adapted to changing patterns of labor force participation and related changes in family structure and with what consequences for children. In order to accomplish this objective, the panel undertook several related tasks. The first was to develop a conceptual framework that would serve as a basis for understanding how interrelationships among work, family, and community influence children's education and socialization. Then the panel commissioned several reviews, each of which surveyed work, family, and community interrelationships from a different perspective. The authors were asked to review and assess the literature and to suggest an agenda for future research. Both of these tasks—conceptualization and literature review—have contributed in an essential way to the conclusions and recommendations presented in this report.

The Conceptual Framework

We began with the premise that recent widespread changes in labor force participation and family structure are likely to have far-reaching implications in our society for the future of both its institutions and its children. As a first step in identifying and understanding these implications, the panel developed a conceptual framework that relates changes in the workplace, in family life, and in the roles of formal and informal community institutions to the status of children living in different circumstances in our society. The panel's framework is designed to highlight how current adaptations in work, family, and community affect the way children spend their time; the kinds of adult and peer interactions they have; their school performance; their development of personality characteristics, attitudes, and values; and their transition to adult roles. It is also intended to highlight the interactions between and among the systems that affect children's development and daily experiences. Indeed, our primary concern was to chart the myriad ways in which work, family life, and the roles of community institutions affect and are affected by each other and result in a variety of adaptations and outcomes for children.

The panel's conceptual framework has five major categories of variables that affect one another both directly and indirectly (see Table 1-1):

(1) *Government Policies* This category of variables includes numerous federal, state, and local policies and programs regarding income transfer, fiscal matters, employment, housing, community development, transportation, health, education, child care, and personal social services.

(2) *Workplace Policies and Practices* This category of variables includes workplace conditions, employment policies and practices, and the organization and structure of work, as well as the benefits and services provided by employers.

TABLE 1-1 Conceptual Framework: Work, Family, and Community[a]

Government Policies (1)	Workplace Policies and Practices (2)	Community Institutions (3)	The Family System (4)	Child Outcomes in Different Settings (5)
Characteristics[b] Types of actions; level of grant—federal, state, or local; legislation; regulations; guidelines; administrative practices, etc.	*Characteristics*[b] Types of employment; nature of job, employer, industry; size; extent of unionization; proportion of women in labor force, etc.	*Characteristics*[b] Formal and informal; public, private; not-for-profit, for-profit.	*Characteristics*[b] Of family, of children.	*Settings* Family/home; school; child care/preschool; peer group; neighborhood; workplace.
Relevant Policies Tax; income transfer; employment; housing and community development; health; education; personal social services; child care; transportation.	*Relevant Policies* Organization of work; structure of work; work conditions; work hours; fringe benefits, including released time with pay, time without pay, services, etc.	*Relevant Institutions* Workplace and employment policies and practices (including fringe benefits); school and other educational institutions; public and private social service agencies; churches; social and recreational organizations; child-care facilities; other formal resources; neighborhood associations; kin networks; other informal resources; marketplace goods and services.	*Relevant Relationships* Husband-wife relationships; parent-child relationships; child-sibling relationships; (all examined in terms of time spent together/apart, activities, attitudes, etc.).	*Relevant Outcome* Physical and mental health; cognitive development; personality characteristics; attitudes and values; vocational aspirations and outcomes; educational level; fertility; deviant behavior; types of activities (play and tasks).

[a] Table developed at panel meeting, subsequently revised.
[b] Characteristics specified here are a partial listing only, provided for illustration purposes.

(3) *Community Institutions*   This category of variables refers to the variety of formal and informal arrangements and resources that are available at the local neighborhood level to provide needed supports and services to children and their families. Included are publicly and privately run organizations and neighborhood and kin networks—for example, schools, churches, social service agencies, social organizations, recreational facilities, and neighborhood associations—as well as the marketplace.

(4) *The Family System*   This category of variables includes both working and nonworking families of different structures (e.g., single-parent or two-parent families); varying ethnic, racial, and cultural backgrounds; varying social and economic characteristics; and children of different sexes, ages, and numbers. We note here the significance of household as well as family and the important distinction between the two. The natural parents of some children may live in different households. Some children may experience multiple and complex familial relationships (stepparents, half-siblings) while living within one household. In addition, attention is focused on functioning within the family, including parent-child relationships (e.g., shared activities, interactions, and attitudes), husband-wife relationships, and child-sibling relationships, all of which affect the socialization of children.

(5) *Child Outcomes in Different Settings*   This last category of variables includes the variety of physical, social, and emotional effects (e.g., physical and mental health outcomes, cognitive gains and school achievement, personality characteristics, attitudes and values, vocational aspirations, fertility) that result from children's experiences in the different settings in which they spend time (e.g., family/home, school, day care/preschool, peer groups, neighborhood, workplace).

The panel's focus is on how each of the above categories of variables has responded to changes in work patterns as well as to interactions between and among the variables. Therefore, for example, we are concerned with the employer's provision of fringe benefits and services insofar as it has implications for the functioning of employees' families and the well-being of their children. We are concerned with the availability and access of working parents and their children to the public and/or private community services and supports, schools, service agencies, and neighborhood groups that combine to meet the everyday needs of working families with children. We are concerned with how home-school relations affect children's cognitive and social development. We are concerned with the attitudes, achievement, relationships, and aspirations of children whose parents work in different occupations. These are but a few of the many interesting questions that arise when considering how the various dimensions of people's lives interrelate. Our conceptual framework provides a means of organizing the very complex relationships that determine outcomes for children and families. It has served as a basis for ordering what we know already, for evaluating the results of existing research, and for charting a course for future research and policy efforts.

The Review Topics

The panel identified several topics for review that focus on various dimensions of the conceptual framework linking work, family, and community. Each review begins from a different entry point in the framework, taking as its dependent variable a selected element within one of the five categories of variables (for example, workplace adaptations or children's school achievement) and treating the other dimensions as intervening or independent variables. The authors, charged with the dual tasks of reviewing the literature and developing a research agenda, highlighted the interactions between the categories of variables whenever possible.

In summary, the authors were asked to (1) conceptualize their topic, paying special attention to linkages among dimensions of the framework; (2) review the state of knowledge on their topic; (3) identify and critique existing data sets that are relevant to their topic; (4) point out gaps in existing knowledge; and (5) suggest salient research issues and directions for future data collection and analysis.

The following topics are examined in five chapters in Part II of this report:

• the impact of parental work on the family as a socialization system and as an economic system
• adaptations to a changing work force by employers in different-sized firms and different types of organizations
• the relationship between parental work and child outcomes, including achievement and attainment in school settings, as well as children's perceptions of themselves and the world in which they live.

We made several efforts to commission papers on adaptations by schools and other formal and informal community institutions (e.g., churches, social service agencies, neighborhood groups). In the process, however, we discovered that the lack of conceptualization of the relationship between changing work patterns and the roles of these organizations and the lack of relevant data made it difficult to assemble information on the nature, extent, and consequences of their responses.

THE ORGANIZATION OF THE REPORT

Part I of this volume documents established and emerging trends in labor force participation, family structure, income, and how children spend their time. It also presents a brief sketch of the policy and research issues that have arisen from changing patterns of work. In Part II the existing data and research on the ways in which the workplace, families, and community institutions are responding to these social phenomena and their consequences for children are reviewed in a series of papers. Finally, Part III presents our conclusions concerning the current state of knowledge and our recommendations for future research.

REFERENCE

Smith, R., ed. (1979) *The Subtle Revolution: Women at Work.* Washington, D.C.: The Urban Institute.

2
The Dimensions of Change: Trends and Issues

The experience of growing up in the United States is likely to be different for children in the 1980s than it was for children several decades ago. Although a significant proportion still live in a traditional two-parent family (including natural and stepparent families) in which the father is the breadwinner and the mother is the homemaker (36 percent in 1980), most do not. Since 1970, patterns of labor force participation and family structure have shifted markedly, with consequent effects on children's experiences and on the settings in which they live and spend time. Today, there are significantly fewer children under 18 years of age than there were 10 years ago, and they constitute a smaller proportion of the U.S. population as a whole. Despite their declining numbers, however, in the 1980s more children than at any time since World War II will live for some time during their formative years (0 to 18) in a single-parent family, usually female-headed. And more children than ever before will have two parents who work or a sole parent who is working outside the home. Children do and will continue to constitute a large portion of the poverty population. Those in single-parent, female-headed families are especially likely to be poor, particularly if their mothers are not employed. Moreover, a greater number of children will spend more time each day in the care and company of individuals other than their parents.

In the remainder of this chapter, we present data concerning changes during the past decade in labor force participation—especially among women with children—changes in family structure, changes in family income, and changes in the settings where children spend time. Although

12

clearly these trends are related, there is little definitive evidence of causal links. Undoubtedly, a complex variety of social, economic, cultural, and ideological factors contributed to these phenomena and are not easily separated. Therefore, our purpose is not to present these trends as direct causes and effects of one another, but instead to describe them as significant associated patterns of change in our society during the past decade and to suggest some of the relevant emerging issues.

CHANGES IN LABOR FORCE PARTICIPATION AND WORK STATUS

Despite the declining population of young people, the number and proportion of children with working mothers rose steadily during the past decade. In 1979, for the first time more U.S. children lived in families with a mother in the labor force than in families with a mother who was a full-time homemaker. By 1980 about 53 percent of all children under 18 years of age had mothers who were employed or seeking employment outside the home. Although school-age children are still more likely than preschool-age children to have mothers in the labor force, the proportion of very young children (under 3 years) with working mothers has increased most dramatically since 1970, to more than 40 percent (see Table 2-1). Among school-age and preschool-age children in the United States, those in female-headed families are more likely to have working mothers than those in two-parent families (see Table 2-1). This likelihood, however, varies by race: Black and Hispanic children under the age of 18 living in families maintained by women are *less* likely than white children to have working mothers (see Table 2-2). Of special interest is that, although more children in single-parent families have working mothers, the percentage of increase during the past decade was twice as great for children with married mothers.

Indeed, the most dramatic change in labor force participation has been among mothers in two-parent families. Between 1960 and 1980 this proportion nearly doubled. Today more than half of all married women with children under 18 years of age are in the labor force. Many women in this group who in another era would have stopped working when they married or had children are now continuing to work. Those with school-age children are more likely to be working than those with preschool-age children; however, the rate of increase in labor force participation by women has been far greater for mothers of preschool-age children. Following the historic pattern, however, black mothers with husbands present, unlike their single-parent counterparts, are more likely to be in the labor force than white or Hispanic mothers in this category (Bureau of Labor Statistics, 1980).

TABLE 2-1   Children by Age, Type of Family, and Labor Force
Status of Mother: 1970 and 1980[a] (Numbers in Thousands)

	1970		1980		Change from 1970 to 1980	
	Number	Percent	Number	Percent	Number	Percent
All children under 18 years	65,755	100.0	58,107	100.0	− 7,648	—
Mother in labor force	25,554	38.9	30,663	52.8	5,108	35.7
Mother not in labor force	39,550	60.1	26,493	47.2	− 13,057	− 38.1
Children in married-couple families	58,399	100.0	46,829	100.0	− 11,570	—
Mother in labor force	21,982	37.6	24,218	51.7	2,236	− 37.5
Mother not in labor force	36,417	62.4	22,611	48.3	− 13,806	− 19.4
Children in families maintained by women	6,695	100.0	10,327	100.0	3,632	—
Mother in labor force	3,562	53.2	6,445	62.4	2,883	17.3
Mother not in labor force	3,133	46.8	3,882	37.6	749	− 19.6
All children 6–17 years	46,149	100.0	40,688	100.0	− 5,461	—
Mother in labor force	19,954	43.2	23,196	57.0	3,242	31.9
Mother not in labor force	25,627	56.8	16,722	43.0	− 8,905	− 24.3
Children in married-couple families	40,479	100.0	32,150	100.0	− 8,329	—
Mother in labor force	17,035	42.1	18,032	56.1	997	33.2
Mother not in labor force	23,444	57.9	14,118	43.9	− 9,326	− 24.2
Children in families maintained by women	5,102	100.0	7,768	100.0	2,666	—
Mother in labor force	2.919	57.2	5,164	66.5	2,245	16.2
Mother not in labor force	2,183	42.8	2,604	33.5	421	− 21.7
All children under 6 years[b]	19,606	100.0	17,418	100.0	− 2,188	—
Mother in labor force	5,590	28.5	7,467	42.9	1,877	50.5

TABLE 2–1 (*Continued*)

	1970		1980		Change from 1970 to 1980	
	Number	Percent	Number	Percent	Number	Percent
Mother not in labor force	13,923	71.5	9,771	57.1	− 4,152	− 20.1
Children in married-couple families	17,920	100.0	14,679	100.0	− 3,241	—
Mother in labor force	4,947	27.6	6,186	42.1	1,239	52.5
Mother not in labor force	12,973	72.4	8,493	57.9	− 4,480	− 20.0
Children in families maintained by women	1,593	100.0	2,559	100.0	966	—
Mother in labor force	632	40.4	1,281	50.0	638	23.8
Mother not in labor force	950	59.6	1,278	50.0	328	− 16.1

a Excludes children under 18 years old who were maintaining their own families or subfamilies or who were living in institutions or with family members other than parents or stepparents.
b Statistics for children under 3 years old cannot be computed separately.

SOURCES: Special Labor Force Reports (1981), Bureau of Labor Statistics (1980).

In recent years, as the number of single-parent families has increased, the number of single mothers in the labor force has also risen rapidly. In 1979 approximately one of every nine women in the work force, five million in all, was maintaining her own family. Single mothers are even more likely to be working or looking for work outside the home if their children are of school age than if they are preschoolers (Bureau of Labor Statistics, 1980). Moreover, white mothers in this group are far more likely than black or Hispanic mothers to be in the labor force (Bureau of Labor Statistics, 1980).

Although the proportion of single-parent families headed by fathers has increased only slightly during the past decade, the labor force participation rate among men in this group has declined somewhat. In 1970 more than 91 percent of single-parent fathers with children under 18 years of age were in the labor force; in 1979 only 86 percent of them were (unpublished data, Bureau of Labor Statistics, 1981). This decline has followed the general pattern of male labor force participation during the past decade. The decrease is largely attributable to longer education, earlier retirement, and longer life spans (Smith, 1979b).

TABLE 2-2   Children by Age, Type of Family, Labor Force Status of Mother, and Race and Hispanic Origin: 1980[a] (Numbers in Thousands)

	White		Black		Hispanic	
	Number	Percent	Number	Percent	Number	Percent
All children under 18 years[b]	49,057	100.0	7,815	100.0	4,674	100.0
Mother in labor force	25,510	52.0	4,485	57.4	2,064	44.2
Mother not in labor force	22,780	46.4	3,172	40.6	2,540	54.3
Children in married-couple families	49,915	100.0	3,864	100.0	3,657	100.0
Mother in labor force	21,235	50.7	2,395	62.0	1,611	44.1
Mother not in labor force	20,680	49.3	1,470	38.0	2,046	55.9
Children in families maintained by women	6,376	100.0	3,792	100.0	947	100.0
Mother in labor force	4,275	67.0	2,090	55.1	453	47.8
Mother not in labor force	2,100	32.9	1,702	44.9	494	52.2
All children 6–17 years[b]	34,295	100.0	5,562	100.0	3,012	100.0
Mother in labor force	19,380	56.5	3,326	59.8	1,447	48.0
Mother not in labor force	14,280	41.6	2,121	38.1	1,510	50.1
Children in married-couple families	28,767	100.0	2,683	100.0	2,323	100.0
Mother in labor force	15,891	55.2	1,714	63.9	1,107	47.7
Mother not in labor force	12,876	44.8	968	36.1	1,216	52.3
Children in families maintained by women	4,894	100.0	2,764	100.0	634	100.0
Mother in labor force	3,490	71.3	1,613	58.3	340	53.6
Mother not in labor force	1,404	28.7	1,152	41.7	295	46.5

TABLE 2-2   (*Continued*)

	White		Black		Hispanic	
	Number	Percent	Number	Percent	Number	Percent
All children under 6 years[c]	14,762	100.0	2,253	100.0	1,662	100.0
Mother in labor force	6,130	41.5	1,159	51.4	617	37.1
Mother not in labor force	8,500	57.6	1,051	46.6	1,030	62.0
Children in married-couple famlies	13,148	100.0	1,182	100.0	1,334	100.0
Mother in labor force	5,344	40.6	681	57.6	504	37.8
Mother not in labor force	7,804	59.4	501	42.4	830	62.2
Children in families maintained by women	1,482	100.0	1,028	100.0	313	100.0
Mother in labor force	786	53.0	478	46.5	113	36.1
Mother not in labor force	697	47.0	550	53.5	200	63.9

[a] Excludes children under 18 years old who were maintaining their own families or subfamilies or who were living in institutions or with family members other than parents or stepparents.
[b] Percentage in this cell do not total 100 because they do not account for children living in single-parent families maintained by fathers.
[c] Data for children under 3 years old cannot be computed separately.

SOURCE: Unpublished data from Bureau of Labor Statistics.

Of the total number of employed mothers in 1980 (about 31 million), approximately 73 percent worked full time. The remaining 26 percent worked part time, either fewer hours every day or fewer weeks during the year. A significantly greater proportion of single-parent mothers who work than of mothers with husbands present were employed full time. In addition, women with school-age children are somewhat more likely to work full time than women with preschoolers. From available data, however, it appears that marital status rather than the age of the child plays a larger role in determining whether a mother who is employed will work full time or part time (see Table 2-3).

As more and more women have joined the labor force in the past

TABLE 2–3   Employed Mothers by Full-Time or Part-Time Work Status, Marital Status, and Age of Children: 1980 (Numbers in Thousands)

	With Children Under 18 Years			
	Total	6–17 Years	3–5 Years	Under 3 Years
Total employed mothers	18,578	12,365	3,009	3,204
Worked full time[a]	13,522	9,247	2,166	2,108
Worked part time[a]	5,056	3,118	843	1,096
Employed mothers in married-couple families	12,677	8,017	2,009	2,651
Worked full time	8,502	5,491	1,335	1,676
Worked part time	4,175	2,526	674	975
Employed mothers maintaining their own families[b]	5,901	4,348	1,000	553
Worked full time	5,020	3,756	831	432
Worked part time	881	592	169	121

[a] Full-time workers are those who worked 35 or more hours per week; part-time workers are those who worked 1 to 34 hours per week.
[b] Includes married mothers whose husbands were absent, and divorced, widowed, and never-married mothers.

SOURCE: Unpublished data from Bureau of Labor Statistics.

decade, more have also become unemployed. Although official unemployment data are subject to error, they suggest that in 1980 the annual unemployment rate for all women with children under 18 years of age was 6.9 percent compared to 5.9 percent in 1970. Women with preschool children are more likely to be unemployed than are those with school-age children. This suggests that although they do not leave the labor force as they might have a decade ago, many working women become unemployed for some period of time after the birth of a child. Unemployment among single-parent mothers is higher than among those with a husband present (6.8 percent compared to 5.7 percent). It is highest, 10.2 percent, among single-parent mothers with children under 3 years (unpublished data, Bureau of Labor Statistics, 1981). Unemployment is also significantly higher among blacks and somewhat higher among Hispanics than among whites (unpublished data, Bureau of Labor Statistics). This does not suggest that mothers with husbands present are better able or more likely to get and hold a job. Instead, it probably reflects racial, age, and education differences among the different groups (see Table 2-4).

The shifting pattern of U.S. labor force participation during the past decade, most notably the dramatic increase in the number of mothers who are working outside the home, represents a fundamental change in the activities of many American women. It is attributable in part to the population growth and in part to the dramatic increase during the 1960s and the 1970s in the proportion of women who chose (or were obliged) to seek paid work. This change is undoubtedly linked to broader changing social, cultural, ideological, and economic conditions in this nation. The economic growth of the 1960s, increases in the number of available jobs, growing legal pressures to assure women equal access to the workplace, the spread of the women's movement, and rising rates of inflation that significantly increased the cost of living have all provided major incentives for women to enter the job market and to stay in it. Factors such as the declining income of young men and the mechanization of the household have also undoubtedly contributed (O'Neill, 1980). Regardless of the motivation for mothers to go to work, however, their employment has been accompanied by changes in family structure, and their earnings have brought about changes in patterns of family income.

TABLE 2-4   Unemployment of Mothers in the Labor Force, by Marital Status and Age of Children: 1980 (Numbers in Thousands)

	With Children Under 18 Years			
	Total	6–17 Years	3–5 Years	Under 3 Years
Total mothers	30,927	17,347	5,311	8,269
In labor force	17,493	11,168	2,880	3,445
Labor force participation rate	56.6	64.4	54.2	41.7
Unemployment rate	6.9	5.3	8.1	10.9
Mothers in married-couple families	24,829	13,561	4,201	7,067
In labor force	13,447	8,381	2,161	2,906
Labor force participation rate	54.2	61.8	51.4	41.1
Unemployment rate	5.7	4.3	7.0	8.8
Mothers maintaining their own families[a]	9,463	6,277	1,672	1,513
In labor force	6,541	4,711	1,120	710
Labor force participation rate	69.1	75.1	67.0	46.9
Unemployment rate	6.8	5.8	7.2	10.2

[a] Includes married mothers whose husbands were absent, and divorced, widowed, and never-married mothers.

SOURCE: Unpublished data from Bureau of Labor Statistics.

CHANGES IN FAMILY STRUCTURE

Although almost all U.S. children live in families, the form of the family is changing. Today, nearly one of every five children lives with only one parent, a proportion that has increased significantly since 1970 when about one child of every nine lived solely with either a mother or a father. Most of these children live in families that are maintained by mothers. Only a small proportion live in families maintained by fathers, and that proportion has remained relatively constant during the past 10 years (see Table 2-5). While most white and Hispanic children live with two parents, nearly half of all black children do not (see Table 2-6).

The increasing number of children in single-parent families largely reflects a rapidly rising divorce rate, although rising illegitimacy, particularly among teenage mothers, also contributes. Nearly one of every three marriages in the United States now ends in divorce. Current estimates suggest that between 40 and 50 percent of children born in the 1970s will live for at least some period of time in a single-parent family while they are growing up (Bureau of the Census, 1979). Children are also increasingly likely to live in households in which one parent is not the natural parent, since most mothers who divorce become remarried within five years. In 1977 an estimated 10 percent of all children under 18 years of age in two-parent families were living with one natural parent and one stepparent. If current trends continue, more than 30 percent of all children in the United States will be living in such families by the end of the century (personal communication with Arthur Norton, Bureau of the Census).

There were 7.7 million fewer children under 18 years of age in 1980 than there were in 1970, which represents a 12 percent reduction in the size of the cohort. As a proportion of the total population, the decline was even more significant—from about one-third to one-quarter. The rate of decline during the past 10 years among both the school-age (6 to 17 years) and the preschool-age (under 6 years) groups was approximately the same. In the year ending March 1980, however, the number of children under age 6 registered its first increase since 1970. Nevertheless, because this growth was more than offset by a greater drop in the school-age group, there was a net decline in the total population under 18 years of age during the decade (see Table 2-7).

Not only will there be fewer children in the 1980s, but those children will likely have fewer siblings. The lifetime fertility rate (the average number of lifetime births expected by women), which peaked at 3.8 in 1957, has declined steadily since then. By 1970 it had dropped to 2.5 and by 1979 to approximately 1.7, reflecting a growing preference for

TABLE 2-5   Living Arrangements and Age of Children Under 18 Years Old: 1970 and 1980[a] (Numbers in Thousands)

Living Arrangements and Age of Child	1970 Number	1970 Percent	1980 Number	1980 Percent	Change from 1970 to 1980 Number	Change from 1970 to 1980 Percent
All children under 18 years	65,755	100.0	58,107	100.0	– 7,648	—
Living with:						
Two parents	58,399	88.8	46,829	80.6	– 11,570	– 9.2
Mother only	6,695	10.2	10,327	17.8	3,632	74.5
Father only	661	1.0	951	1.6	290	60.0
All children 6–17 years	46,149	100.0	40,688	100.0	– 5,461	—
Living with:						
Two parents	40,479	87.8	32,150	79.0	– 8,329	– 10.0
Mother only	5,102	11.0	7,768	19.1	2,666	73.6
Father only	568	1.2	771	1.9	203	58.3
All children under 6 years	19,606	100.0	17,418	100.0	– 2,188	—
Living with:						
Two parents	17,920	91.4	14,679	84.3	– 3,241	7.7
Mother only	1,593	8.1	2,559	14.7	966	81.5
Father only	93	0.5	180	1.0	87	100.0
All children under 3 years	8,389[b]	100.0	8,839	100.0	450[c]	—
Living with:						
Two parents	7,473[b]	89.1	7,660	86.7	187[c]	– 2.7
Mother only	884[b]	10.5	1,085	12.3	201[c]	17.1
Father only	31[b]	0.4	93	1.1	62	70.0

[a] Excludes children under 18 years old who were maintaining their own families or subfamilies or who were living in institutions or with family members other than parents or stepparents.
[b] Data are from 1975, the first available year when data were collected specifying children under 3 years old.
[c] Change from 1975 to 1980.

SOURCES: Special Labor Force Reports (1981), Bureau of Labor Statistics (1980), unpublished data from Bureau of Labor Statistics.

smaller families as well as an increasing number of women who remain childless or delay childbearing. In 1979, according to Bureau of the Census (1980a) data, 6 percent of married women between 18 and 34 years of age expected to have no children and another 10 percent expected to have only one child.

To some extent this trend may be the result of a growing tendency among young women to postpone marriage and childbearing. The median age at first marriage has risen steadily during the past two decades. By 1979 it had reached 22.1 years, compared with 20.8 in 1970. Significantly, the rise in median age at first marriage in this period represents the largest change in any 10-year period since records were first kept in 1890 (Bureau of the Census, 1980c). The average period of time from first marriage to first birth and between second-, third-, and fourth-order births has also increased and was greater in the 1970s than in the preceding 15 to 20 years. Young women who had their first child between 1975 and 1978 did so an average of two years after marriage, about nine months later than women who married a decade earlier. This recent increase in spacing is observed among births to both black and white women (Bureau of the Census, 1980b).

TABLE 2–6   Living Arrangements of Children Under 18 Years Old, by Age and Race and Hispanic Origin: 1980[a] (Numbers in Thousands)

Living Arrangements and Age of Child[b]	White		Black		Hispanic	
	Number	Percent	Number	Percent	Number	Percent
All chidren under 18 years	49,057	100.0	7,815	100.0	4,674	100.0
Living with:						
Two parents	41,915	85.4	3,864	49.4	3,657	78.2
Mother only	6,376	13.0	3,792	48.5	947	20.3
Father only	767	1.6	158	2.0	70	1.5
All children 6–17 years	34,295	100.0	5,562	100.0	3,012	100.0
Living with:						
Two parents	28,767	83.9	2,683	48.2	2,323	77.1
Mother only	4,894	14.3	2,764	49.7	634	21.0
Father only	634	1.8	115	2.1	55	1.8
All children under 6 years	14,762	100.0	2,253	100.0	1,662	100.0
Living with:						
Two parents	13,148	89.1	1,182	52.5	1,334	80.3
Mother only	1,482	10.0	1,028	45.6	313	18.8
Father only	132	0.9	44	1.9	15	0.9

[a] Excludes children under 18 years old who were maintaining their own families or subfamilies or who were living in institutions or with family members other than parents or stepparents.
[b] Statistics for children under 3 years old cannot be computed separately.

SOURCE: Unpublished data from Bureau of Labor Statistics.

TABLE 2-7   Children by Age: 1970 and 1980[a] (Numbers in Thousands)

Age of Child	1970		1980		Change from 1970 to 1980	
	Number	Percent	Number	Percent	Number	Percent
Total U.S. population	204,401	100.0	227,020	100.0	22,619	—
All children under 18 years	65,755	32.2	58,107	25.6	−7,648	−20.5
All children 6–17 years	46,149	22.6	40,688	17.9	−5,461	−20.8
All children under 6 years	19,606	9.6	17,418	7.7	−2,188	−19.8
All children under 3 years	8,389[b]	3.9	8,839	3.9	450[c]	0.0

[a] Excludes children under 18 years old who were maintaining their own families or subfamilies or who were living in institutions or with family members other than parents or stepparents.
[b] Data are from 1975, the first available year data were collected specifying children under 3 years old.
[c] Change from 1975 to 1980; percent of population under 3 years old in 1975 is based on a total U.S. population in 1975 of 212,748,000.

SOURCE: Special Labor Force Reports (1981).

This trend toward smaller families is also associated with changing patterns of labor force participation among women. Whether families are headed by men or women, and whether they are white or black, the average number of children in families is smaller if the mother is in the labor force than if she is not. The number of children ever born to women who are employed or seeking employment outside the home is lower for both whites and blacks in all childbearing age groups (20 to 44 years) (Bureau of the Census, 1980b). Therefore, although causal relationships have not been clearly established, changing patterns of labor force participation and family structure would seem to be linked.

CHANGES IN FAMILY INCOME

The social and economic environment in which children are reared is the most important predictor of their overall well-being. Almost all available data support the conclusion that children's health, education, later employment, and earnings depend to a great extent on the economic status of their families (Calhoun et al., 1980; National Research Council, 1976). Children's economic situations usually reflect their family structure and ethnic background. Children who live in households headed by women or who are black or Hispanic disproportionately live in families whose incomes are below the median and often below the poverty level.

The period since 1970 has been characterized by erratic changes in patterns of family income, resulting in very slow growth in real income. Real median family income increased in the early 1970s, declined during the recessionary period from 1973 to 1975, and then rose in alternate years during the second half of the decade. As a result, median family income in the United States, which reached $21,023 in 1980, was less than 7 percent higher than the 1970 level after adjusting for inflation. Throughout the decade, the average annual increase has been extremely low—0.7 percent, compared to 3.0 percent during the 1960s and 3.3 percent during the 1950s. In addition to the economic problems of recession and high-level inflation during the 1970s, the substantial increase in the number and proportion of female-headed families exerted a downward influence on overall median family income (Bureau of the Census, 1981a). It is important to note, however, that although median family income stagnated during the 1970s, average family size also fell, thus creating a rise in per capita income levels within families.

Regardless of race or family type, children with mothers in the labor force were in families with higher median incomes than children of nonworking mothers. For all two-parent families with children in 1979, the median income was about $21,900 if the mother was in the labor force and $15,900 if she was not (see Table 2-8). In two-parent families a majority of wives were in the labor force if there were only 1, 2, or 3 children present under 18 years of age. In families with four or more children of school age or preschool age, however, the wife was less likely to be working outside the home (Bureau of Labor Statistics, 1980). Although the earnings of wives in black and Hispanic families are not substantially lower than those of their white counterparts, white children in two-parent families benefit from higher median family incomes. This is largely because the average earnings of white husbands are higher.

Even though their earnings are generally lower than their husbands', working wives contribute significantly to family income. Between 1960 and 1978 the average proportion of income earned by the wife in two-parent families rose from one-fifth to one-quarter. That proportion, of course, varied among individual families, depending on work experience, education, and full- or part-time employment. Wives who worked full time all year contributed an average of 39 percent of family income; those who worked part time or who worked full time for 26 weeks or less contributed only 11 percent (Bureau of Labor Statistics, 1980). The

TABLE 2–8   Median Family Income for Children by Age, Type of
Family, Labor Force Status of Mother, and Race and Hispanic
Origin: 1980[a]

	Two-Parent Families			Single-Parent Families Maintained by Women[b]		
	White	Black	Hispanic	White	Black	Hispanic
All children under 18 years	22,900	17,800	16,600	8,400	6,200	5,500
Mother in labor force	24,800	20,800	20,100	11,200	8,200	8,200
Mother not in labor force	20,800	13,500	13,400	4,600	4,700	4,700
All children 6–17 years	25,300	18,300	18,900	10,200	7,200	6,400
Mother in labor force	27,000	21,200	22,600	12,300	8,900	9,400
Mother not in labor force	22,900	13,800	15,200	5,600	5,400	5,300
All children under 6 years[c]	19,800	16,400	14,200	5,200	4,500	4,500
Mother in labor force	21,200	19,800	17,500	8,300	6,300	6,400
Mother not in labor force	18,700	13,100	11,800	3,800	3,500	4,200

[a] Excludes children under 18 years who were maintaining their own families or subfamilies
or who were living in institutions.
[b] Includes only divorced, widowed, or never-married parents.
[c] Statistics for children under 3 years old cannot be computed separately.

SOURCE: Special Labor Force Reports (1980).

monetary advantage of having additional earners in the family has become apparent during this decade, which has been marked by the deep-
est recession since the 1930s and the highest rate of inflation since World
War II. The median income of married-couple families rose more than
for any other family type from 1960 to 1978. Between 1970 and 1978
alone, the median income of these families increased by about 10 percent
in constant dollars (Bureau of Labor Statistics, 1980a).

Children in single-parent families maintained by women were materially better off if their mothers were in the labor force than if they were
not. However, they were not on the average as economically advantaged
as children in two-parent families, regardless of their mothers' labor
force status. In 1980, among children in single-parent families in which
the mother worked, the median family income was less than half that
of all married-couple families and less than $2,000 above the poverty
threshold for a nonfarm family of four ($7,412) (see Table 2-8). It was
higher for white children than it was for black and Hispanic children.
In general the earnings of single mothers are the most important source
of income to their families, providing on the average between 60 and
70 percent of all family monetary resources (Masnick and Bane, 1980).
As we have previously noted, although their rate of labor force partic-

ipation is higher, unemployment is also higher among women in single-parent families than among women living with a spouse. Hence, many of these families are in or near poverty.

The median income in single-parent families in which the mother was not working was only $4,700 in 1980, more than $2,700 below the poverty level (as specified above). The extremely high rates of unemployment among single-parent mothers, especially among blacks and Hispanics; the fact that many of these women work part time; and the fact that many hold low-paying clerical, domestic, or operative positions explain why their median income was the same as or in some cases less than that of all families maintained by unemployed women (see Table 2-8).

In 1980 more than 11 million children, approximately 18 percent of all children in this nation, lived in families with an income below the official poverty level. The poverty rate for children, although significantly lower than in 1960, remained about the same from 1970 to 1979 (about 15 to 16 percent), but has increased since then. Not surprisingly, children in female-headed families are far more likely than those in two-parent families to be poor—more than 50 percent compared to 10 percent in 1980 (Bureau of the Census, 1981a). Black and Hispanic children are significantly more likely to grow up in poverty than their white counterparts. More than 42 percent of all black children under 18 years of age and more than 33 percent of all Hispanic children live in poor families. Although the rate of poverty has declined substantially during the past decade among both white and minority children living in two-parent families, among black and Hispanic children in female-headed families the problems of poverty have become more pronounced. Approximately 66 percent of all black and Hispanic children in single-parent families maintained by women live in poverty, compared to almost 42 percent of white children in this type of family (Bureau of the Census, 1981a). Again, this is largely attributable to the fact that white single mothers are somewhat more likely to be in the labor force than their black or Hispanic counterparts. They are also somewhat more likely to have sources of income other than earnings.

Children constituted about the same proportion of the poor population in 1980 as they did 10 years earlier. Among all families, however, there was a significant increase during these years in the proportion of poor families with children. This occurred despite a simultaneous decline in the proportion of families with children among families generally.[1]

---

[1] It is important to note that during this period, increases in Social Security benefits and the establishment of the Supplemental Security Income program significantly reduced the number of elderly below the poverty level, thus increasing the proportion of younger families with children who were below the poverty level.

Furthermore, in contrast to 1969 when most poor children were likely to live in a two-parent family with an employed head, in 1980 most poor children were likely to live in a single-parent family maintained by a nonworking mother.

Children in two-parent families benefit from higher family income. Regardless of whether they live in one-parent or two-parent families, however, children are materially better off if their mothers are working than if they are not, even though the mother's contribution varies from one household to another. In many middle-class two-parent families, the mother's earnings may do little more than alter savings and spending decisions. In many others her earnings may be essential to maintaining a comfortable though modest standard of living. In female-headed families, women's employment frequently means the difference between poverty and an adequate existence and between independence or dependence on public assistance. For the most part, female-headed families, especially those with children, are able to survive on their own only when the mother has regular employment (Masnick and Bane, 1980).

CHANGES IN THE SETTINGS WHERE CHILDREN SPEND TIME

As family structure and work patterns have changed, so do the settings where children spend time. Traditionally, children below the age of six have spent their days at home, in the care and company of their mothers or other family members; older children have typically returned home at the end of the school day, greeted by their mothers. However, increasing numbers of preschool children are spending some portion of the day outside their own homes in day-care centers, in preschool programs in and outside of schools, or in the homes of other families. School-age children are spending more of their nonschool time in a variety of settings, many of which we know little or nothing about. Many other very young children remain at home with family members or nonrelatives while their mothers are at work, or their parents share their care by working different shifts. In 1978 about 68 percent of 3- to 5-year olds spent some portion of the day in out-of-home care: 54 percent in school-based and other preschool programs, 14 percent in day care centers and family day care homes, and about one-third of the latter group in both types of programs. About 12 percent of children under 3 are cared for in day care centers and family day care homes (Kamerman and Kahn, 1981).

By 1977 more than 300,000 children spent time in 100,000 family day care homes licensed by state agencies (Abt Associates, 1978). In these homes an adult cares for a maximum of six children, often her own and a few others. A variety of sources suggest that these figures severely underestimate the number of children in family day care, since many, if not most, family day-care homes remain unlicensed.

Still other children spend all or part of their day in more formal day-care centers, which must meet state health and safety requirements. These settings typically are larger than family day-care homes, so that the child is spending time in the company of many peers (usually at least 12) as well as several adults. It is estimated that there are about 18,300 licensed day-care centers in the United States, most located in urban or suburban areas (Abt Associates, 1978). In 1978 about 900,000 children, largely aged 3 to 5, were served by these centers, often year-round.

Preprimary school programs—nursery schools and kindergartens—also are growing more popular (see Table 2-9). In 1979 more than 54 percent of all children between the ages of 3 and 5 attended preprimary schools (Bureau of the Census, 1981b). Nursery school enrollment increased by almost 71 percent between 1970 and 1979. School (and preschool) enrollment for children aged 3 to 5 increased by 44 percent during the same years. Although the young children of working mothers are significantly more likely to be enrolled in a preschool program than the children of nonworking mothers, enrollment for all children, including those with nonworking mothers, has in fact risen very substantially. Most nursery school programs are privately sponsored, while the majority of kindergartens are public.

Many characteristics of the child and the family help determine where the child will spend time and how much care will be provided by others. Younger children (those under the age of three) are more likely than three- to five-year-olds to receive care in their own homes or in family

TABLE 2–9   Preschool Enrollment by Age of Child

Age of Child	Percentage Enrolled in School	
	1969	1979
3	9	23
4	23	46
5	69	93[a]

[a] 80 percent in kindergarten, 4 percent in nursery school, 9 percent in first grade.

SOURCE: Bureau of the Census (1981b).

day-care homes than in larger day care centers, regardless of whether their mothers work full or part time (Kamerman and Kahn, 1981). Throughout the preschool years, however, mothers who work 10 to 29 hours a week (part time) are more likely than those who work 30 or more hours a week (full time) to rely on care in their own homes (35.3 percent versus 23.5 percent). In contrast, children of full-time working mothers are more likely to spend time in day-care centers (18.8 percent versus 29.8 percent). Center-based care is also more common for children of employed single mothers.

Further, 1978 data from the Bureau of the Census (1981b) indicate that 3-year-olds are more likely to attend nursery school when their mothers are employed than when they are housewives (30 percent versus 19 percent). Maternal employment also appears related to how much time 3- to 5-year-olds spend in a preschool setting. Children whose mothers work full time are more likely to spend the entire day in nursery school or kindergarten than those whose mothers work only part time.

As a result of these differences, children involved in home-based care spend an average of about nine hours a week in the care of adults other than their mothers. Children participating in preprimary programs average about 18 hours of care, although about one-third of 3- to 5-year-olds attend full-day programs, implying about 30 hours per week in out-of-home group programs.

Both supply studies and household consumer surveys report the primary mode of care. None of these data, however, reveals what may be the most significant aspect of the care arrangements of children of working mothers: the multiplicity, complexity, and diversity of arrangements most parents organize in order to ensure adequate care. Thus, some parents work different shifts or part time in order to share in caring for their child. School-age children spend a substantial portion of the day in school, clearly the major child-care institution outside the family; the majority of preschool-age children (three- to five-year-olds) do so also. In addition, the overwhelming majority of families regularly supplement parental and school care with at least one and usually several other types of care. And these arrangements become still more extensive when there is more than one child in the family. Included among these arrangements may be in-home care by a relative or a nonrelative; out-of-home care by relatives, friends, neighbors, or other paid caretakers; and special arrangements when a usual routine is interrupted. Children under the compulsory school age are especially likely to experience multiple forms of care by multiple caretakers during the course of a normal week if their parents are working. Little information exists on how primary school-age children are cared for when school is closed for vacations and parents work (Bane et al., 1979; Kamerman, 1980). Those enrolled in day-care centers may average the most time in external care, about 28 hours a week (UNCO, 1975), but the numbers of children in such programs are far smaller than the numbers in full-day preprimary programs.

Decisions about where the child should spend time also differ among racial and ethnic groups. White families are much more likely than black or Hispanic families to rely on child care in their own homes provided by nonrelatives (24 percent versus 6 percent and 8 percent). In contrast, 69 percent of Hispanic children receive care from their relatives. Minority families, especially blacks, are more likely to depend on institutional rather than home-based care. As a Congressional Budget Office (1978) report suggests, these relationships are likely the result of the association between race, income, and government subsidy. Government subsidies restricted to licensed child-care arrangements (i.e., day-care centers and some family day-care homes) certainly affect eligible families' decisions about where their children will spend time, as does the cost of various types of external care. Children with full or partial subsidies make up approximately 25 percent of day-care center enrollments; racial minorities account for 28 percent of day-care center enrollments, although they represent only 18 percent of the 3- to 5-year-old population (Bureau of the Census, 1981b).

Racial differences extend beyond child care to school participation. Hispanic children below the age of five are less likely to be enrolled in school than black or white children. Black children between the ages of three and four are the most likely to be enrolled in preprimary school; by the age of five, when kindergarten typically begins, black and white participation is about the same (Bureau of the Census, 1981b). Income differences in the types of schools children attend are also noteworthy. High-income families generally choose private preschools, while families with fewer resources generally rely on publicly funded preprimary education.

There are geographic differences in preprimary school enrollment as well. Three- and four-year-olds living in the central city and the suburbs are much more likely than rural children to attend nursery school (37-41 percent versus 25 percent). The percentages of preschool enrollment are highest in the northeastern United States; enrollment rates for all racial and ethnic groups are lower in other regions.

Available data suggest that the number of children in a family also influences the choice of care. The larger the family size, the lower the cost of care selected. Thus, for all racial groups, combinations of care by family members and nonrelatives increase along with the number of children. When one child in the family reaches the age of 14, that child often assumes responsibility for the care of siblings. For families with children under the age of 6, use of caretakers outside the home drops from about 60 percent to about 30 percent when there is an older sibling (Shortlidge and Brito, 1977). Given the decline in family size, however, the availability of older siblings to care for young children is not as common as 10 to 20 years ago.

Between 1970 and 1978, the sheer number of children attending grades 1 through 8 fell, while the number of high school students rose (see Table 2-10). However, during those years, the percentages of 16- to 17-year-old white males attending school fell slightly (92 percent to 89 percent), while the percentages of black 16- to 17-year-olds of both sexes rose (85 percent to 93 percent for males; 86 percent to 90 percent for females).

More teenagers than ever before are combining school with part-time employment. While in 1940 only 4 percent of 16-year-old boys and 17 percent of 16-year-old girls combined work and school, in 1980, estimates indicate that 30 percent of 9th and 10th graders and 50 percent of 11th and 12th graders work for pay during all or part of the school year. Students are also spending more hours at work. In 1970, 56 percent of 16-year-old male workers and 46 percent of 16-year-old female workers spent 14 hours or more on the job each week.

Finally, the age of college attendance has also shifted over the years; in 1947, 8.1 percent of all college students were between the ages of 14 and 17, while in 1978 only 2.8 percent of college students were under 18.

TABLE 2–10 School Enrollment by Level of School, Race, and Hispanic Origin: 1970 and 1980[a] (Numbers in Thousands)

School Level	White 1970	White 1980	Black 1970	Black 1980	Hispanic 1970	Hispanic 1980	Percent Change 1970–1980 White	Black	Hispanic
Nursery School	893	1,637	178	294	62	146	83.3	65.2	51.4
Kindergarten	2,706	2,595	426	490	263	184	−4.1	15.0	42.9
Elementary School	28,638	22,510	4,868	4,259	1,805	2,363	−21.4	−12.5	30.9
High School	12,723	12,056	1,834	2,200	608	1,048	−5.2	20.0	72.4

[a] Civilian noninstitutional population.

SOURCES: Bureau of the Census (1971, 1981); 1970 Census of Population, Vol. 1, 1C, Persons of Spanish Origin; and unpublished data from the Bureau of the Census Current Population Survey.

IMPLICATIONS FOR THE NEXT DECADE: EMERGING ISSUES FOR POLICY
AND RESEARCH

The dramatic increases in the labor force participation of mothers with
school-age and preschool-age children during the past decade have been
accompanied by changes in family structure. The number and proportion
of single-parent families headed by women has grown rapidly. There
has been a significant decline in the proportion of families with children
and a decline in the numbers of children such families have. Family
income has risen for married-couple families in which the wife-mother
has entered or reentered the labor force. In single-parent families where
the mother is the sole or primary source of support, however, income
has remained the same in constant dollars. Thus, many of these families
have incomes at or near the poverty level and constitute a growing
proportion of the population in poverty. Children of working mothers
spend a greater amount of time each day in the care and company of
individuals other than their mothers. Moreover, each child is likely to
experience a greater range and diversity of care than is generally recognized.

The United States has entered the decade of the 1980s facing severe
economic problems, including inflation, recession, and uncertainty about
the cost and availability of its energy supply. The economic conditions
of the 1970s which permitted the strong and rapid labor force growth
of women is changing. Already there are signs that the rate of growth
may be slowing. Nevertheless, projections suggest that particularly for
women in the 25- to 34-year-old age group, increases can be expected
to continue during the next 15 years, although at a slower pace (Smith,
1979b). It is women in this age group who are also most likely to couple
their employment responsibilities with parenting responsibilities. If recent trends in marital and family characteristics continue, an increasing
number of these women will be single parents for some portion of time
and they will have only one or two children. As Smith (1979b) points
out, women with family responsibilities but without a husband present
in the household are more likely than their married counterparts to be
working or looking for work. Similarly, women with husbands present,
but with fewer or no young children, are also more likely to be in the
labor force.

What seems clear from available data is that women are in the labor
force to stay and that in the future they will increasingly combine work
and family responsibilities. For children, regardless of whether they live
in single-parent or two-parent families, there are likely to be important
consequences. Children, of course, will be affected in different ways,

depending upon a variety of factors, including differences in the age and occupational status of parents and the nature of their employment, their attitudes toward work and their reasons for working, their income, their level of job satisfaction, their work schedules, and their proximity to the workplace. Roles, relationships, and attitudes among family members may also be important, as well as the normative behavior and attitudes of the community, the availability and access to various community-based supports and services, and the policies and practices of employers. Moreover, the consequences of changing patterns of work and family structure for children may vary for those of different ages, sexes, races, and ethnic backgrounds; for those living with one parent and those living with two parents; for only children and those with siblings; for children in families that are poor and those that are affluent; and for children in families that are socially and physically isolated and those with close ties to the community and with relatives and friends nearby.

The issues of how changing patterns of work and related changes in family structure affect children are complex and interrelated. They converge on how children spend their time, where, and with whom. The roles of formal and informal institutions in our society—families, various community institutions, the workplace, and the marketplace—and the interactions between and among them influence the environments in which children live and the experiences they have. Many of these institutions are still based on a traditional notion of family forms, roles, and relationships. Adaptations among institutions, both individually and in combination, to recent social phenomena are just beginning to be identified, analyzed, and understood. Questions inevitably arise about (1) the extent of change by various formal and informal institutions (e.g., how are working parents arranging child care), (2) the direction of causality (e.g., to what extent is the added income of mothers in two-parent families contributing to decisions to send children to private schools or vice-versa), (3) the degree of complementarity or conflict between what goes on in one setting and what goes in others (e.g., how do school schedules adapt to permit participation by working parents), and (4) the extent to which evolving arrangements provide necessary supports for children and their families (e.g., to what extent do substitute care arrangements meet the physical and emotional needs of the child).

The family is widely regarded as the most fundamental institution in our society. Although families are changing in form, they are still the primary systems for bearing and raising children, and no competing institution is in view. How have emerging patterns of work and family structure affected roles and relationships within families? To what extent is the division of labor and responsibility shifting? What are the sources of stress and strength? What variations are found among families living in different social, cultural, and economic circumstances? And with what effects on children?

The community institutions with which children interact in their daily lives are many and varied. They include schools, churches, community social service agencies, recreational facilities, libraries, day-care facilities, and neighborhood groups and associations. The character of communities also varies greatly from one location to another. In particular localities, certain of these institutions may be more or less dominant than others. In addition the past decade has witnessed important social and demographic shifts that have affected the nature of communities and their capacity to meet the needs of their residents. The movement in the early 1960s and 1970s of the middle class to the suburbs of large metropolitan centers left the inner cities with a largely poor black and Hispanic population. Suburban communities became insulated and largely segregated by age, race, and income level. Work and home were physically separated, with adult men leaving the community to women and children during the daytime hours. Inner cities were similarly isolated; the problems of poverty, unemployment, and crime intensified. Although the late 1970s saw some reversal of this exodus to the suburbs, the relevance and effectiveness of many community institutions is nevertheless being questioned. In light of recent social phenomena, how well do these institutions perform their traditional functions (for example, schools in educating children, churches in communicating fundamental moral and religious values, and social service agencies in helping their client populations)? What new demands are being placed on these institutions? What capacities do they have to respond, especially in light of shrinking revenue bases? How does an adjustment in the role of one institution affect the roles of others?

Employers have been confronted with a new work force. The dramatic influx of women, many with children, into the labor market and the increased number of male employees with working wives have placed new demands on employers to provide family-oriented benefits and supports to employees. Simultaneously, rising inflation and declining growth of productivity have caused many employers to reassess their policies and practices. What demands are being placed on employers and how are they responding? What organizational constraints exist in different types and sizes of firms that affect the capacity of employers to provide innovative benefits and services? How do adaptations in the workplace affect working families and their children? How do those adaptations relate to those made by other formal and informal community institutions?

The marketplace has perhaps been the fastest to respond to changing patterns of work and family structure. A variety of conveniences, such as prepared foods, cleaning aids, and disposable diapers, have been introduced to facilitate the tasks of housework and child care. Similarly, new services have emerged, not the least of which is a multimillion dollar per year private day-care industry. What other changes, such as the growth of private education, are being made in the marketplace and how do these changes affect what goes on in other institutions in our society? How well do they meet the needs of working families and their children? At what costs?

The capacity of our society to nurture the next generation productively and effectively is of fundamental concern to researchers, policy makers, service providers, and parents alike. What are the consequences of recent social phenomena and what are the implications of knowing? Clearly, some would argue that society is always changing, institutions adapt, and children and their families get along. Nevertheless, change takes place through a series of planned and unplanned events. In order to develop appropriate policies (both public and private) to support children's normal development and to mediate harmful outcomes, we need first to understand the nature and consequences of changing patterns of work and family life on children. In Part II of this volume, we review the relevant social science research on the effects of changes in the work patterns and work status of parents and related changes in family structure; on how families function, both as a socialization system and as an economic system; on how employers have adapted to the changing family responsibilities of their employees; and on how children themselves have been affected, both in their school performance and in their attitudes about the world in which they live.

REFERENCES AND BIBLIOGRAPHY

Abt Associates (1978) *National Day Care Study: Preliminary Findings and Their Implications*. Prepared for Administration for Children, Youth, and Families, Day Care Division, U.S. Department of Health, Education, and Welfare. Cambridge, Mass.: Abt Associates.

Bane, M. J., Lein, L., O'Donnell, L., Stueve, C.A., and Wells, B. (1979) Child-Care Arrangements of Working Parents. *Monthly Labor Review* 102(9):50–57.

Bureau of the Census (1979) Divorce, child custody, and child support. *Current Population Reports*, Series P-23, No. 84. Washington, D.C.: U.S. Department of Commerce.

Bureau of the Census (1980a) American families and living arrangements. *Current Population Reports*, Series P-23, No. 104. Washington, D.C.: U.S. Department of Commerce.

Bureau of the Census (1980b) Fertility of American women: June 1979. *Current Population Reports*, Series P-23, No. 358. Washington, D.C.: U.S. Department of Commerce.

Bureau of the Census (1980c) Marital status and living arrangements: March 1979. *Current Population Reports*, Series P-20, No. 349. Washington, D.C.: U.S. Department of Commerce.

Bureau of the Census (1981a) Money income and poverty status of families and persons in the United States: 1980. *Current Population Reports*, Series P-60, No. 125. Washington, D.C.: U.S. Department of Commerce.

Bureau of the Census (1981b) School enrollment—social and economic characteristics of students: October 1979. *Current Population Reports*, Series P-20, No. 360. Washington, D.C.: U.S. Department of Commerce.

Bureau of Labor Statistics (1980) *Perspectives on Working Women: A Databook*. Bulletin 2080. Washington, D.C.: U.S. Department of Labor.

Calhoun, J., Grotberg, E., and Rockley, W. R. (1980) *The Status of Children, Youth, and Families*. No. (OHDS) 80-30274. Washington, D.C.: U.S. Department of Health and Human Services.

Congressional Budget Office (1978) *Childcare and Preschool: Options for Federal Support*. Washington, D.C.: U.S. Government Printing Office.

Kamerman, S. (1980) *Parenting in an Unresponsive Society: Managing Work and Family*. New York: The Free Press.

Kamerman, S., and Kahn, A. (1981) *Childcare, Family Benefits, and Working Parents*. New York: Columbia University Press.

Masnick, G., and Bane, M. J. (1980) *The Nation's Families: 1960-1990*. Boston: Auburn House.

National Research Council (1976) *Toward a National Policy for Children and Families*. Report of the Advisory Committee on Child Development. Washington, D.C.: National Academy of Sciences.

O'Neill, J. (1980) Trends in the labor force participation of women. Pp. 28-38 in C. Hayes, ed., *Work, Family, and Community: Summary Proceedings of an Ad Hoc Meeting*. Washington, D.C.: National Academy Press.

Shortlidge, R. L., and Brito, P. (1977) *How Women Arrange for the Care of Their Children While They Work: A Study of Child Care Arrangements, Costs, and Preferences in 1971*. Columbus: Center for Human Resource Research, Ohio State University.

Smith, R., ed. (1979a) *The Subtle Revolution: Women at Work*. Washington, D.C.: The Urban Institute.

Smith, R. (1979b) *Women in the Labor Force in 1990*. Washington, D.C.: The Urban Institute.

Special Labor Force Reports (1981) Working mothers and their children. *Monthly Labor Review* 104(5):49-54.

UNCO, Inc. (1975) *National Child Care Consumer Study*. No. (OHD) 76-31096. Washington, D.C.: U.S. Department of Health, Education, and Welfare.

PART II
A Review of Research

3
Work and Family Through Time and Space

Urie Bronfenbrenner, *Cornell University,* and
Ann C. Crouter, *The Pennsylvania State University*

There are two kinds of activities that appear to be distinctive for *Homo sapiens.* The first is the way we raise our young. To a greater extent than for any other living creatures, the capacity of human offspring to survive and develop depends on an extended period of care and close association in activities with older members of the species. The second unique characteristic is the way we manipulate and transform the environment through the use of our heads and our hands. Over the course of human history the principal context for the first type of activity has been the family; for the second, it has been what in modern times is called the world of work. Moreover, until relatively recently, at least in

The authors express their appreciation to Gerri Jones who provided invaluable bibliographical assistance and typed innumerable successive versions of the manuscript. In our treatment of research on the effects of maternal employment, we are deeply indebted to previous reviews by Maccoby (1958), Stolz (1960), and, especially, Hoffman (1963a, 1974, 1979, 1980). With the proliferation of studies in this area during the past decade, the reviewer's task becomes increasingly difficult. Especially in her most recent assessment, Hoffman simplified our task with her thorough and discerning anaysis of a maze of often disparate findings. We also wish to acknowledge the many references and constructive criticisms that were provided by colleagues and students at Cornell University and elsewhere, particularly Eleanor Maccoby, Jeylan Mortimer, Frank Furstenberg, Robert Rapoport, and Joseph Pleck. Special appreciation is also expressed to the following staff members at the Bureau of Labor Statistics who responded with generosity and consummate care to innumerable requests for unpublished demographic data: Howard Hayghe, Allison Grossman, Elizabeth Waldman, and Ann Young.

our culture, there has been a substantial division between the sexes of primary responsibility for these two spheres, with women specializing in the former and men in the latter. To be sure, there have also been considerable areas of overlap, but the contribution of each sex to activities in the other's traditional realm has typically been overlooked and its importance underestimated.

Over the past three decades a dramatic change has been taking place in modern industrialized societies, including our own—a change both in objective reality and in social attitudes and expectations. The transformation is reflected most visibly in the rapidly increasing participation of mothers in the labor force—especially mothers of young children. For example, over the past 20 years the percentage of working mothers with children under 3 has more than doubled, rising from 16 percent in 1960 to 44 percent in 1981. During the same period, working mothers of school-age children have become the majority, increasing from 43 percent to 66 percent. But the rise in maternal labor force participation is only one manifestation of an evolving pattern of ever-more-powerful reciprocal influences between the world of work on the one hand and the family as a context for human development on the other.

It is the purpose of this chapter to examine the available research bearing on one side of this reciprocal relationship. Specifically, this review addresses a seemingly straightforward question: What is the impact of parental work on the functioning of the family in its child-rearing role? If one takes as a measure of existing knowledge the number of investigations of this question that have been conducted over the past half century, one would expect to have now at hand a substantial body of instructive and unequivocal answers. Unfortunately, the expectation is not realized. It is not that the research has been poorly done or that the results are uninformative. Rather, the issue under investigation has turned out to be exceedingly complex. Thus, the effect of parental work on child-rearing processes and outcomes appears to vary as a function of who the parents are, who the children are, the kinds of parent and child variables under investigation, the circumstances under which the family lives, the nature and conditions of work, the psychological meaning of work and family life to the persons involved and, last but far from least, the historical period in which the investigation was conducted.

A historical perspective has importance both in the social and in the scientific realm. In the former sphere the changes over time have encompassed ideology as well as behavior. Conceptions of the mother's role have altered dramatically, particularly since 1960, and there have been noticeable shifts as well in the scientific models used to study the impact of work on family life. These models have evolved at an accelerating speed toward more complex and comprehensive paradigms encompassing ever-more-extended regions of the environment. And like the image of mother's role, the greatest expansion has taken place during the past two decades. In short, there has been a dramatic development across time and space in both spheres—hence the title of this chapter.

What is perhaps most remarkable about this scientific advance is that until very recently it involved not one evolution but two, each following its own independent and distinctive course. Thus, researchers on the impact of work on family life have treated the job situations of mothers and fathers as separate worlds, having no relation to each other and leading to rather different outcomes. To be sure, when both lines of investigation first began in the 1930s, they focused on the same problem area—the effects of whether or not the parent had a job. But the initial assumptions were at opposite poles. For mothers, it was the fact of being employed that was presumed to be damaging to the child; for fathers, unemployment was seen as the destructive force. Moreover, during its first 20 years, research on maternal employment was almost exclusively preoccupied with detecting effects on the behavior and development of children. Studies of the impact of working on the mother herself emerged only gradually, and the possibility that maternal employment could influence the ways in which fathers behave toward their children has still to be explored systematically. Furthermore, throughout almost a half century of research on the working mother, almost no attention has been paid to the nature of her job. Except for a distinction between working full time and working part time, maternal employment has been conceptualized as a dichotomy; work itself has been treated as an empty set, bereft of any structure or content that might be significant for the mother's role as a parent.

Research on the influence of father's work on family life has followed a strikingly different course. From the earliest studies of paternal unemployment, the principal emphasis has been on the effects on the father himself and on the functioning of the family as a whole. Child outcomes were slow to emerge as primary foci of scientific attention. And even when they did command such attention, they were viewed mainly as indirect outcomes, deriving from the impact of the father's work situation on the mother's child-rearing values and behaviors.

The greatest promise, both for science and for public policy, lies in the planned convergence of these two research trajectories. Perhaps the most effective way to proceed here is to trace the evolution of the two research approaches as a function of historical developments in society and in social science. Although the changes in both domains have been gradual, the year 1960, as we have already noted, is a significant reference point in each trajectory. In the societal realm it marks the emergence of the women's movement as a major force affecting American family life. In the scientific sphere it was a time of crystallization of the substantive and methodological issues that were to set both the directions and limits of subsequent investigation. Finally, in both domains 1960 ushered in a period of even more rapid and sweeping evolutionary change. Hence, our analysis is divided into two parts, the first dealing with research conducted prior to 1960, the second with scientific developments over the past 20 years. Within each of these two periods we examine continuity and change in the questions being posed for investigation, the theoretical and research models being employed, the substantive findings, the conclusions, and the historical and cultural context in which the study was conducted. Then, in a third, concluding section, we set forth the implications of our analysis for future research and public policy.

RESEARCH ON WORK AND FAMILY: PRIOR TO 1960

Given the separation of scientific concerns, investigations conducted during this initial period are conveniently presented under two headings: (1) the effects of maternal employment on children and their mothers, and (2) the effects of the father's occupation on family life.

Research on the Effects of Maternal Employment on Children and Their Mothers

In an analysis of the evolution of research models employed for investigating environmental influences in child development, Bronfenbrenner (1982) points out that the paradigm typically used in the beginning stages of inquiry has certain distinctive features:

(1)   The model may be characterized as child-centered in the sense that no one else's behavior is being examined except the child's.

(2)   The environment is conceptualized in simplistic terms that serve only to identify the child's social location—for example, working class versus middle class, single-parent versus two-parent, family day care versus home care. As Bronfenbrenner (1982:7-8) puts it "The researcher looks only at a *social address*—that is, an environmental label—with no systematic examination of what the environment is like, what people

(3) No specification is made of intervening structures or processes through which the given environment might influence the child's behavior and development. In Lewin's terms (1935) the model is class-theoretical rather than field-theoretical; observed differences in children from one or another setting are explained simply as attributes of a child in the given context.

(4) In the absence of process-oriented theory, the choice of categories for describing the environment tends to be dictated by value-laden social concerns rather than scientific considerations; that is to say, environmental conditions thought to be bad for children are contrasted with those that are regarded as normal, and therefore good.

(5) A similar orientation guides the selection of outcome variables. Problem environments are presumed to produce problem children; hence, the initial emphasis is on indices of malfunction, maladjustment, and problem behavior.

The first 20 years of research on the effects of maternal employment clearly fit the foregoing paradigm. From the mid-1930s, when studies of the topic first appeared, until the mid-1950s, almost all of the published studies focused on the presumed deleterious influence on the child of the mother's working outside the home. This concern mounted with the increased entry of mothers into the labor force during and after World War II. A typical example of professional as well as popular views is cited in a research review by Stolz (1960:751-752):

are living there, what they are doing, or how the activities taking place could affect the child."

The . . . situation has stimulated many articles in magazines and newspapers, elaborating, sometimes with great emotion, on the evils of women working. A well-known sociologist in a book published in 1948 (Bossard, 1948) discusses the employment of mothers in a chapter on "Families Under Stress." He enumerates seven items which he considers obvious costs to children of their mothers working outside the home. These briefly are: (a) mothers are unduly tired, impatient, and irritable; (b) children are lonely when mothers are tired and busy; (c) children feel, and are, neglected; (d) children run riot without supervision; (e) mothers cannot share school experiences with children; (f) mothers cannot do the mending and other services children need; (g) mothers cannot teach children socially approved behavior.

As Stolz points out, these conclusions were presented without factual documentation. The documentation would have been difficult to provide, since the studies conducted during this early period dealt almost

exclusively with the characteristics of children; the psychological state
and behavior of the mother was usually left out of the picture.[1] Given
the investigators' alarmist expectations regarding children of working
mothers, the principal outcome measures selected for these investigations focused on problems of maladjustment (Cummings, 1944; Essig
and Morgan, 1946; Glass, 1949; Hand, 1957; Rouman, 1956) and delinquency (Glueck and Glueck, 1934, 1957; Hodgkiss, 1933). With one
exception, mentioned below (Glueck and Glueck, 1957), maternal employment was conceptualized simply as a dichotomy between mothers
who worked and those who remained at home with the child. There
was no examination of the nature and conditions of work, nor any
exploration of the causal chain through which maternal employment
might affect the child.

The studies published in this early period had two other features in
common: First, most of the investigators reported findings in accord
with their pessimistic prognoses. Second, all of the studies containing
such negative findings were flawed by methodological errors, such as
failure to control for social class, that subsequently called into serious
question the validity of the authors' conclusions. These errors were
documented in a trenchant critique published toward the end of the
period by Maccoby (1958). After dealing with issues of experimental
design, Maccoby evaluated the validity of the research conclusions drawn.
To cite but one example, Glueck and Glueck (1957) reported higher
rates of delinquency among sons of employed mothers, specifically of
mothers who were working only occasionally. Maccoby reanalyzed the
data to demonstrate that the critical factors accounting for the observed
differences were family instability and the kind of supervision that an
employed mother arranged for her children in her absence.

After examining the corpus of research then available, Maccoby
(1958:172) came to the following conclusion:

It is not possible to close this discussion with a box-score which will tell us
whether maternal employment is, in sum, "good" or "bad" for children. It is
clear that there is no single best way of organizing family life. Some mothers
should work while others should not, and the outcome for the children depends
upon many factors other than the employment itself. Some of these factors are:
the age of the children, the nature of the mother's motivation to work, the
mother's skill in child care and that of her substitute, the composition of the
family (especially whether it contains a good substitute caretaker), the stability
of the husband, and the pressure or absence of tension between husband and

---

[1] The few exceptions to this trend are discussed below.

wife. We cannot yet specify how these factors influence the impact upon children of the mother's working. The necessary fact-finding has only just begun.

This assessment, made more than two decades ago, merits our attention for several reasons: First, it specified a set of mediating variables that must be taken into account in all future research on the effects of parental employment on the child. Second, the review anticipated the pattern of findings to emerge in future research: namely, that the effects of maternal employment vary, depending on a series of mediating factors. Finally, it is both a tribute to the cogency of Maccoby's analysis and a reflection on the uneven progress of our science that her caveats and constructive suggestions are almost as valid today as they were 20 years ago. As we discover in reviewing the work conducted in subsequent decades, her recommendations were honored as often in the breach as in the observance.

But the field did move forward. In a review published only two years later, Stolz (1960:773) was able to find three well-designed investigations reporting essentially negative results in four areas of child behavior: "In studies which met these criteria [adequate control of relevant variables] there was no statistical relation found between maternal employment and delinquency (Bandura and Walters, 1959), adolescent adjustment (Nye, 1959), school marks in high school (Nye, 1959) and dependent-independent behavior of five-year-olds (Siegel et al., 1959)."

One must be cautious, however, about interpreting this set of findings as an indication that mothers' employment has no appreciable impact on children once controls are introduced for confounding social background factors. The effects may be more complex. For example, Stolz examined all the studies included in her review for evidence of a differential impact of maternal work status on boys and girls. Although few analyses of this kind had been done, their results suggested that maternal employment might have a negative effect on sons but not on daughters. Thus, Mathews (1934) reported that sons of working mothers expressed less positive attitudes toward home life than their counterparts from families in which the mother did not work; daughters showed the opposite trend. In a similar vein, Hoffman (1959) found that teachers rated sons of employed mothers as more dependent than sons of mothers who did not work outside the home. An insignificant difference in the same direction also appeared in a study by Hand (1957); the author found a higher percentage of maladjusted boys in the working mothers' group, but a lower percentage of maladjusted girls. In subsequent decades, scientific findings of this same trend would constitute persuasive evidence for its validity.

Finally, in her 1960 review Stolz traced the emergence of a new line of inquiry in research on the effects of maternal employment—how it affected the behavior and attitudes of the mothers themselves. The first study of this kind was well ahead of its time both in subject matter and in research method. In 1934 Mathews reported differences in parental behavior and conditions in the home. Her findings were based on questionnaires from 200 children in grades 5 through 9. The mothers of half the children worked full time outside the home; the others were not employed. Each child from the first group was paired with a counterpart from the second; the pairs were matched on sex, grade, school, community, and father's occupation. The statistically significant findings that emerged fell into a pattern: A higher percentage of children with working mothers wore soiled clothes to school, had a sense of hurry around the home, were scolded by a tired mother, and sometimes had to make their own breakfast. Contrary to expectations, their fathers were less active in the home; fewer took responsibility for the care of the children or played games with them. This last set of findings constitutes another pioneering aspect of Mathews' research. To our knowledge, she was the first investigator to explore the possibility that maternal employment might alter the role of the father as a parent.

Stolz (1960:767) points to an important qualification in the interpretation of Mathews' findings: "Mathews' study was made over a quarter century ago, when full-time working hours could be as much as ten or eleven hours a day, when automatic machines were rare in housekeeping, and when fathers lost status (in their own eyes at least) when they participated in family chores." Stolz's comment underscores the possibility that the effects of maternal employment may vary from one historical period to another as the social and economic circumstances change.

A different aspect of paternal reaction to work status is examined in another pioneering study conducted by Berger in 1948. To our knowledge the investigation was the first to explore the linkages between maternal work status, family functioning, and the behavior of the child. Berger's subjects were 22 children who had been referred for psychiatric treatment because of behavior difficulties. They were selected for study because all of the mothers had been employed before marriage and at the time of the study were frustrated because of their desire to return to work. Berger concluded that the children's difficulties represented a reaction to the mothers' frustration in their search for employment. Berger's essentially qualitative interpretations, made without benefit of a control group, are called into question by the results of a more systematic investigation of the same issue. Working with a sample of 379 mothers of preschool children, Sears et al. (1957) compared reactions of three groups: those who had never worked outside the home, those who had been employed previously but were now remaining at home, and those who had gone back to work at least part time since the child was born. Utilizing a variety of measures of tension and role conflict, the investigators were not able to demonstrate any differences among the three groups. Unfortunately, no data were gathered on the reactions of the children.

Hoffman (1959) was the first to demonstrate unequivocally the mediating function maternal attitudes play in influencing the impact of mothers' work status on the child. This investigator divided employed mothers into two groups—those who liked their jobs and those who did not. These groups were compared with a control group of nonemployed mothers matched on husband's occupational level, sex, and ordinal position of the child. Data were obtained through interviews with the mothers, a questionnaire to their school-age children, teachers' ratings, and classmates' opinions. The mothers who liked their work reported significantly stronger feelings of sympathy for their children, less hostility, and less severe discipline than the nonworking mothers. Their children, in turn, expressed more positive attitudes toward the mother and got along better with younger children than with their age mates in school. Compared to their nonemployed counterparts, mothers who disliked their jobs described themselves as asserting less power over their children, but saw their children as being significantly more assertive toward them. The children of these mothers reported more regular participation in household tasks, but exhibited less impulse control, used physical force more often, and responded to frustration in a less adaptive way.

Taken as a whole, the results of well-designed studies conducted prior to 1960 indicate that maternal employment status does not have a uniform effect on children. Evidence of impact did begin to emerge, however, once certain mediating factors were taken into account. One such significant factor was the mother's attitude toward her job. The data also suggest that the consequences of maternal employment may be beneficial to girls, but disruptive to boys. Finally, there are indications that maternal employment influences the parental behavior of both mothers and fathers, but as of 1960 the nature of these effects had yet to be established.

Studies of the Effects of the Father's Occupation on Family Life

We have been able to find only five studies in this area that were conducted prior to 1960. The first four, published between 1936 and

1940 (Angell, 1936; Caven and Ranck, 1938; Komarovsky, 1940; Morgan, 1939), deal with the same topic—the impact on the family of the father's loss of a job during the Great Depression. The four employ a research model and strategy far different from that applied in investigations of working mothers. All are essentially case studies focusing on the reaction of the family as a whole to paternal unemployment. To the extent that children appear in the picture, it is as participants in the father's drama, rather than as persons themselves affected by the experience. As a result, the effects of the father's joblessness on the child's development can only be inferred.

What the studies do provide, however, is rich information on how a critical event in the world of work affected family functioning. In this respect, all four studies present much the same picture. Since the work of Komarovsky (1940) was the most recent and could draw on findings of the earlier investigations, we present it as a representative example of both method and results. The sample was selected from the rolls of the Emergency Relief Administration and consisted of intact families in which the father had been unemployed for at least a year. Each family included one or more children over 10 years of age. During the winter of 1935-36, three interviews were conducted—one with the husband, one with the wife, and one with the child, typically the oldest. There was no control group. The interviews covered patterns of family life both before and after unemployment. The analysis of data was primarily qualitative and was supplemented by crude statistical summaries. The results:

(1)   The husband's unemployment resulted in his loss of status within the family, as manifested by decline of authority, subordination to the wife, and loss of respect from both wife and children. The impact on the husband was mediated, however, by the already existing husband-wife relationship. The poorer this relationship, the greater the negative effects for the husband.

(2)   The decline in paternal authority was particularly marked for adolescent children. The father's relations with a younger child showed a mixed pattern: with some fathers they deteriorated; with others they improved because the father spent more time with the child.

(3)   After the husband lost his job, there was a marked increase in family tensions and disagreements.

(4)   The father, mother, and children all reported changes in the father's psychological state, as manifested by irritability, moodiness, or depression. Whereas the parents attributed these changes to the fact of unemployment, the children did not refer to this causal link.

(5)   Following unemployment, there was a marked decrease in social life outside the family.

Although possible implications of these changes for children's development come readily to mind, we had to wait for almost four decades before they were examined systematically through the analysis of archival data by Elder (1974).

The fifth research study on the effects of father's occupation broke new ground by exploring the influence of the father's job on patterns of child rearing. There may be some scholars who would contend that the scientific study of the impact of work on family functioning began with the investigations of social-class influences on socialization.[2] In these investigations, however, the influence of parental occupation is confounded with other variables such as family income and parent's educational level. The first systematic research to focus explicitly on characteristics of the parent's work situation as a factor affecting child-rearing values and practices appears to have been that of Miller and Swanson published in 1958.

These investigators distinguished two main types of work organization: bureaucratic and entrepreneurial. The former, represented by large-scale businesses, is characterized by relatively more secure conditions of work, manifested by such features as regular hours, stabilized wages, unemployment insurance, and retirement funds. The second, exemplified by small-scale, family-owned businesses, involves greater initiative, competitiveness, risk taking, and insecurity regarding the future. Miller and Swanson hypothesized that, under conditions of comparable income and education, mothers whose husbands worked in one setting would report different child-rearing values and practices from mothers whose husbands worked in the other. In line with these expectations, mothers from bureaucratic backgrounds described styles of upbringing that were more permissive, laid greater stress on the development of interpersonal skills, and emphasized the importance of getting along with others. By contrast, wives of husbands working in entrepreneurial settings were more concerned with individual achievement and striving, were not as

---

[2] As a matter of historical interest, the first researcher to consider the relation of family social status to development was Galton (1874:21-22), who examined the frequency of eminent scientists from families classified into five categories, ranging from "farmers" to "noblemen and private gentlemen." The term "social class" was apparently first applied by Terman (1916), who investigated the correlation between IQ and a measure of the family's social position as judged by the child's classroom teacher. The first study of the impact of social class on socialization practices, however, did not appear until the mid-1930s (Anderson 1936).

indulgent, and accorded less importance to interpersonal relationships in their children's lives. In sum, value orientations in the husband's work situation were manifested in the child-rearing behavior of their wives.[3]

In her review two decades ago, Stolz (1960:775) emphasized the importance of applying Miller and Swanson's thesis to research on maternal employment:

. . . the psychological effect of the wife working outside the home would be different in the entrepreneurial family than it would be in the bureaucratic family. When the economic system emphasizes extreme competition, the marriage relation is enhanced if the husband only works. There is thus no competition between husband and wife and they gain in stability through complementary roles: his active and aggressive, hers passive and accommodative. On the other hand, the bureaucratic situation, as [Miller and Swanson] describe it, takes from the worker the need for striving, for risk taking, and active responsibility for his own future. Under these circumstances, it becomes increasingly possible for women to participate in the economy without as serious a threat to the marital relationship. Miller and Swanson did not follow up this promising lead for comparison of family relationships and child behavior in working mother families living under the two conditions described—but someone ought to do it.

As of 1981, Stolz's perceptive recommendation has still to be implemented.

In considering the major lines of research on work and family life that emerged before 1960, one is struck by a curious fact—during the first 25 years of research in this area, investigators treated the work situations of mothers and fathers, and their effects on the child, as separate worlds. Yet today's student of human development, with the incomparable acuity of hindsight, quickly recognizes that the hypotheses and findings developed in each of these domains have powerful implications for the other. For example, what is the effect on the father's behavior at home of his working hours, or his attitude toward the job? Or, to draw a contemporary implication from research on the effects of paternal unemployment in the late 1930s, what is the impact on parental roles and self-perceptions of the mother's loss of a job, or her entry into the work force? Finally, Miller and Swanson's research indicates that

---

[3] Miller and Swanson's findings were replicated by Caudill and Weinstein (1969) a decade later in a sample of Japanese mothers and their infants. No difference was found, however, in the comparison sample of entrepreneurial and bureaucratic families in the United States. The investigators offer no explanation for the failure to obtain a similar result in American society. One possible reason is the progressive bureaucratization of entrepreneurial settings in the United States over the course of the intervening decade.

the type of organization in which the father works has a significant effect on the mother's child-rearing values and practices. Do the characteristics of the mother's work setting have a similar impact on her parental role or that of her husband? To transport these abstract questions to the more concrete ground of the present analysis, we ask if researchers of the 1960s and the 1970s would profit from the latent lessons of their predecessors' work. We turn next to evidence bearing on this question.

RESEARCH ON WORK AND FAMILY: 1960-1980

The past two decades of investigation in this area show both continuity and contrast with the preceding period. Studies of differences between children of working and nonworking mothers still dominate the scene. Second in frequency are investigations of the effect of work status on the mothers themselves. Research on the impact of fathers' employment on family life continues to be sparse, and the work situations of the two parents are still treated primarily as separate worlds.

But there are also signs of scientific progress. (1) In the area of maternal employment there are many more studies. (2) The research designs are sounder and more complex. (3) The improvement in designs is in part a reflection of more sophisticated theoretical models of the processes through which conditions at work might affect family life. In short, many more of the studies are hypothesis-oriented. (4) The growing focus on process, coupled with the convergence of approaches from different disciplines, has produced a small body of research in which the family is treated as a system embedded in a large social context. These patterns of continuity and change are conveniently examined under five headings, two old and three new.

Research on the Effects of Maternal Employment on Children and Their Mothers

The most frequently supported, if not the most exciting, conclusion documented in research since 1960 confirms a finding that had already begun to emerge in previous decades: *Taken by itself, the fact that a mother works outside the home has no universally predictable effects on the child.* Maternal employment does appear to exert influence, however, under certain conditions defined by the age and sex of the child, the family's position in society, and the nature of the mother's work.

If one wished to select only a single variable to demonstrate the different effects maternal work could have on children, it would probably be the sex of the child. By 1980 there had accumulated an appreciable body of evidence indicating that the mother's working outside the home tends to have a salutary effect on girls, but may exert a negative influence on boys. The findings for girls are not only firmer, but point to the nature of the underlying process involved. The relevant studies have been carefully and comprehensively reviewed by Hoffman (1980). The results indicate that daughters from families in which the mother worked tended to admire their mothers more, had a more positive conception of the female role, and were more likely to be independent (Banducci, 1967; Baruch, 1972; Below, 1969; Douvan, 1963; Peterson, 1958; Smith, 1969).

None of these trends was apparent for boys. Instead, the pattern of findings, especially in recent investigations, suggests that the mother's working outside the home is associated with lower academic achievement for sons in middle-class but not in low-income families (Banducci, 1967; Brown, 1970; Gold and Andres, 1978b, 1978c; Gold et al., 1979). In several of these same studies, daughters of working mothers obtained slightly higher scores than daughters of mothers who remained at home, but the differences were not significant, nor were they qualified by social class. It will be recalled that a similar tendency for maternal employment to have a negative influence on the development of boys was apparent in investigations conducted as far back as the 1930s (Hand, 1957; Hoffman, 1959; Mathews, 1934).

An indication of the more precise nature and early course of this sex difference comes from the preliminary results of a study currently being conducted by the senior author and his colleagues with a sample of 150 two-parent families with young children (Bronfenbrenner et al., 1982). Toward the end of a lengthy open-ended interview, parents were asked independently to give a free description of their three-year-old child. The descriptions were then subjected to a content analysis that yielded, among other measures, an index of the extent to which the child had been portrayed in favorable terms. The results revealed a highly significant, complex, but consistent pattern: The least attractive picture was painted by full-time working mothers of boys. Yet, the most enthusiastic protrayal of daughters was given by mothers in this same full-time employment group. In contrast, the least flattering descriptions of girls came from mothers who did not work outside the home. Finally, the most positive evaluation of all was accorded to boys by mothers who worked only part time.

Next to employment status, the most powerful demographic factor affecting the mother's description of the child was her education. In general, less schooling resulted in a less positive picture. In the case of boys the profile for maternal work status remained unchanged, but for girls there was a turnabout. Among mothers with no education beyond high school, working full time was associated with the least favorable description not only of sons but of daughters as well (although the sons still suffered by comparison). In a separate interview, fathers had also been asked to describe their three-year-old child. The results revealed the same highly differentiated demographic profile, but in somewhat lower relief. No such pattern appeared, however, in descriptions given by parents of themselves and their spouse. It would seem, therefore, that maternal work status may have a distinctive impact on the parents' perceptions of their preschool children, with the number of hours that the mother works being an especially critical factor. To the extent that parents' early perceptions are related to their subsequent treatment of the child, full-time maternal employment may work to the disadvantage of sons but be beneficial for daughters, especially if the mother is well-educated and engaged in a job that she finds personally satisfying. A similarly gratifying outcome may be achieved for boys, but only if the mother works part time rather than full time. Qualitative analysis of the interview protocols suggests that the systematic group differences in parents' descriptions of their children are the product of contrasting patterns of sex-role identification between parents and children, associated with the mother's employment status and satisfaction during the child's early years. It remains to be seen, however, whether these early descriptions have any lasting consequences. Some light will be shed on this issue by the results of a follow-up assessment, currently underway, of the children's behavior and performance now that they are in first grade.

Despite the consistency of findings across several studies, it would be premature to conclude that the mother's working full time outside the home during the preschool years does, in fact, interfere with intellectual development in boys. First, the pattern has been shown only in middle-class families. As one descends the socioeconomic ladder, the trend appears to attenuate and perhaps even to reverse itself. The latter point cannot be clearly determined from available data. In general, among low-income black families, children of employed mothers do better in school than those whose mothers remain at home (Cherry and Eaton, 1977; Kriesberg, 1970; Rieber and Womack, 1967; Woods, 1972), but results from existing studies are not systematically broken down by sex of child or the number of hours that the mother works. Moreover, the findings are either confounded or complicated by family structure, such as one- versus two-parent households, and in one study (Rieber and Womack, 1967) by race as well. This confusion highlights the necessity of maintaining clarity and control with respect to sex, race, family structure, socioeconomic status, and hours of employment when future research is conducted on maternal employment.

That such systematic differentiation can reveal consistent and meaningful patterns is illustrated in a series of studies documenting the presence of strain in the father-son relationship among low-income families in which the mother is employed (Douvan, 1963; Gold and Andres, 1978b; Kappel and Lambert, 1972; McCord et al., 1963; Propper, 1972). This well-documented phenomenon prompted Hoffman (1979) to suggest that in lower-class families the mother's entry into the work force may still be viewed by the family as an indication, real or perceived, of the father's inadequacy. Such an interpretation is consistent with findings from the case studies previously cited of family reactions to paternal unemployment in the Great Depression and receives solid confirmation in Elder's subsequent, more systematic treatment of the same topic (1974).

Returning to the issue of the negative impact of mother's employment on boys from middle-class families, we also find some exceptions to this prevailing pattern. One of the best-designed studies involving adolescents compared children of nonworking mothers with those whose mothers had been employed for the four preceding years (Gold and Andres, 1978a). No significant differences for either sex were found between the two groups on the results of a battery of achievement tests, academic grades, attitudes toward school, or educational or occupational aspirations. As the authors point out, studies reporting the strongest and most reliable effects had been conducted with younger samples. This fact suggests that maternal employment may have significant impact on boys' intellectual development only if the mother works during her son's early years. But this interrelationship has yet to be verified through systematic research. Even more problematic is the absence of any clear understanding of the process involved. As previously indicated, the pattern of findings for girls suggests its own explanation—namely, the employed mother serves as a model to her daughter of initiative and achievement outside the home. No such ready rationale is apparent in the findings for boys. In her review, Hoffman (1980) considers possible explanations for the observed pattern solely within the sphere of differential intrafamilial relationships as a joint function of sex of parent and sex of child. While some of these explanations appear plausible in accounting for the lower achievement of sons of working mothers, they are far less satisfactory in explaining why the reported differences should be most pronounced in middle-class families. We suggest that such phenomena cannot be explained solely within an intrafamilial context, but require examination in a broader theoretical framework that takes into account influences emanating from the external environment. We offer two examples:

In a review of research on environmental influences affecting human development, Bronfenbrenner (1979) documents a general tendency for males to be more susceptible than females to the impact of environmental influences (e.g., Gunnarsson, 1978; Moore, 1975; Weintraub, 1977). The findings on the effect of maternal work on boys' academic achievement are consistent with this trend. But why should the effect be observed in middle-class and not in low-income families? One possibility is the crucial role that maternal employment can play in the household economy. Virtually all of the studies reviewed here that included socioeconomic status as a variable defined it as a function of the father's occupation, or less frequently his education, thus ignoring family income. A reasonable hypothesis is that in lower-income families, the income generated by mother's work may result in a standard of living that offsets any negative consequences for boys that might ordinarily result from her working. In higher-income families, however, mother's income may not make the crucial difference for the family's quality of life and thus may not add enough to compensate for disincentives to academic achievement arising from the mother's involvement in work outside the home.

What might be the nature of these disincentives? One hypothesis is suggested by studies documenting the powerful impact of the peer group in the development of children, especially boys, in American society. In a review of research on this issue, Bronfenbrenner (1970) concludes that in the United States autonomous peer groups tend to undermine processes of adult socialization both at home and at school. The effect is particularly pronounced for males from preadolescence onward. We have been able to find no direct evidence, however, bearing on peer-group influence as a function of maternal work status, social class, and sex of child. The relevant research still remains to be done.

A related alternative explanation focuses on the quality of parental supervision of boys in middle-class and low-income families. Sons of employed middle-class mothers may receive less effective supervision than their peers in families in which mother remains home. The difference may be manifested in such areas as monitoring the boy's homework activities, encouraging friendships that foster social behavior, showing an interest in the child's school activities and progress, or overseeing meals, television watching, bedtime, and other routines. The low-income mother who is not employed may not be able to provide such supervision either, because of greater demands on her time and energy. Such mothers may have a larger family and fewer household labor-saving devices, as well as a different conception of how a male child should act.

Yet another factor mediating the impact of maternal employment status on the development of the child is the mother's attitude toward her life situation. A number of studies indicate that satisfaction with one's role, be it as an employed mother or full-time homemaker, is associated with more effective child-rearing experiences and outcomes, especially for girls (Douvan, 1963; Farel, 1980; Hock et al., 1980; Hoffman, 1961; Kappel and Lambert, 1972; Woods, 1972; Yarrow et al., 1962). Particularly illuminating is Farel's recent research describing school achievement and competence of kindergarten children as a function of the mother's preferred work status. The lowest scores on school performance and social adjustment were obtained by children of mothers remaining at home who believed that their taking a job would benefit the child; next in line were children of employed mothers who regarded their working as bad for the child. Appreciably higher scores were attained by children of employed mothers who felt that a mother with a job was a better mother. Finally, highest scores on five out of six outcome variables were achieved by children whose mothers remained at home and felt that this was best for their children. The statistical interaction was highly significant in all instances.

As the investigator acknowledges, findings of this kind pose a problem in determining the direction of causality. Is the mother's satisfaction with her life situation and her corresponding effectiveness in the parental role the source or the consequence of her occupational status or are the two causally independent? For example, Farel (1980:1185) points out that in her research the mothers of children who performed well may have felt that their child's achievement had "validated their decision to stay home and thus shaped the attitudes to conform to their behavior."

The only way to resolve this dilemma is to obtain data at two points in time. A rare example of the use of this strategy in research on effects of maternal employment appears in a study by Hock et al. (1980). The investigators interviewed mothers in the maternity ward and at three additional times the following year. Mothers who had remained true to their plans not to return to work were compared to those who had originally intended to stay home but then later changed their minds. In accord with the authors' hypothesis, the former group subsequently expressed more positive attitudes about the maternal role, described their infants as being more strongly attached to them, and were less upset by the infant's fussiness. It is not clear, however, whether these results reflect the influence of maternal attitudes or the temperamental and behavioral characteristics of the infants.

Yet another important element missing in studies of this kind is an examination of the objective conditions at home or at work that are the bases for satisfaction or dissatisfaction in each of these settings. Such factors are considered below in the discussion of research on environmental stresses and supports experienced by parents faced with conflicting demands of work and family life.

An additional mediating variable involves the classification of maternal employment into full time versus part time. Of the four studies in which this distinction has been made, three were based on samples in which the children were adolescents (Douvan, 1963; Nye, 1959, 1963). The results indicated that the mother's part-time work may have salutary effects for the teenager, probably by achieving an appropriate balance of parental availability for meeting the adolescent's simultaneous needs for dependence and independence. The fourth study (Kappel and Lambert, 1972), conducted with elementary school pupils, also showed an advantage of part-time employment. This arrangement appears to produce less strain on the father-son relationship than exists in lower-class families when the mother is the full-time breadwinner (see above, p. 54).

Another important variable is the point in the child's life at which the mother enters the work force. Hetherington's (1979:854) research on families experiencing divorce illuminates this point:

If the divorced mother wishes to work and adequate provisions are made for child care and household management, maternal employment may have positive effects on the mother and no adverse effects on the children. However, if the mother begins to work at the time of the divorce or shortly thereafter, the preschool child seems to experience the double loss of both parents, which is reflected in a higher rate of behavior disorders.

But within the family, it is the mother-child relationship that should be the key intervening variable between maternal employment and the behavior and development of children. The available evidence on this score points to generalizations in two areas: (1) A number of studies document the fact that mothers who work make a special effort to compensate for their absence by setting aside time to be with their children and by planning activities for them (Jones et al., 1967; Kliger, 1954; Rapoport and Rapoport, 1971; Yarrow et al., 1962). The tendency is especially pronounced among mothers from middle-class families. (2) Also well established is the finding that working mothers expect their school-age children to take on more responsibilities around the home (Douvan, 1963; Johnson, 1969; Propper, 1972; Roy, 1963; Walker, 1970b). In some situations the imposition of such responsibilities can have a positive effect on the child's development (Elder, 1974; Johnson, 1969; Woods, 1972).

Unfortunately, in other areas of parental activity the evidence is either mixed or nonexistent. Researchers who investigated independence training found that working mothers placed greater emphasis on such activity (Burchinal and Lovell, 1959; Yarrow et al., 1962), except in college-educated families or those with younger children. The critical gap in research is the lack of information about the content of the mother's activities, not only with children, but alone or with other adults. For example, are there differences by maternal work status in the amount of time mothers spend on housework, watching TV, or interacting with other adults, rather than on such one-on-one activities with the child as care giving, conversation, play, educational activity, or discipline?

The above comments and questions apply with equal force to the effect of maternal employment on the child-rearing activities of fathers. Regrettably, the research of the last 20 years has not given us definitive knowledge on this score. The studies published up to 1970 reported that husbands of employed women participated more in housework and child care than those married to women remaining at home (Blood, 1963, 1967; Blood and Hamblin, 1958; Blood and Wolfe, 1960; Hoffman, 1963b; Nolan, 1963; Powell, 1963; Safilios-Rothschild, 1970). Pleck (1981) has recently reviewed the entire corpus of research in this area, including his own and other more recent investigations conducted during the past decade (Nichols, 1976; Pleck, 1977, 1980, 1981; Pleck and Rustad, 1980; Pleck et al., 1978; Robinson, 1977a, 1977b, 1980; Robinson et al., 1977; Sanik, 1977; Vanek, 1974; Walker, 1970a, 1970b; Walker and Gauger, 1973; Walker and Woods, 1976). Pleck's (1981:3-5) careful analysis revealed that, over the entire period, there has been "no appreciable variation in husbands' family participation associated with their wives' employment status." It is true that "the husband of an employed wife performed a higher *proportion* of the couple's family work. . . . This occurred, however, only because employed wives spent less time in family work, not because their husbands spent more." Husbands of wives who are not employed also perform proportionately more of the household tasks and the ratio has been increasing steadily during the past two decades. In other words, over the years wives in general have been spending less and less time in family work, while husbands have been spending more. This trend is independent of the mother's employment status and, hence, appears to reflect a social change in family sex roles taking place over time for all husbands and wives.

Pleck's informative analysis gives rise to two questions especially relevant to this chapter: First, is the wife's progressive decrease in family activities compensated for by a corresponding increase on the part of the husband? Second, can the findings be further differentiated between child care and other types of household work?

Regrettably, the available data do not provide a satisfactory answer to either query. According to Pleck (personal communication), the reported findings on the first issue are contradictory, sometimes even within the same study. And even when child-care activities have been distinguished from other types of family work, the analyses have not been carried far enough to permit a conclusion.

A few studies, fortunately, have begun to focus specifically on fathers' involvement in child rearing. In a recent study by Frodi et al. (1980), 51 Swedish couples were interviewed during the last trimester of pregnancy and again when their infants were 5 months old. The sample consisted of dual-worker couples expecting their first child. The investigators found that fathers were more involved in caring for their infants when work outside the home was important to their wives. Presumably, paternal involvement in child care enabled these wives to maintain a commitment to their jobs. Or, alternatively, the mothers' high commitment to work stimulated the fathers to give more help. The finding supports a major thesis of this review—to achieve a full assessment of the impact of parental employment on children, researchers must examine the work and family roles of both mothers and fathers simultaneously. To cite another example, the most recent study by Gold and Andres (1980) reveals that fathers of 10-year-olds whose mothers work perceive themselves as interacting with their offspring to a significantly greater extent than do fathers of children with nonworking mothers.

Also essential is the investigation of the particular aspects of the mother's work situation that affect the behavior and development of her children. After 40 years of research, the mother's workplace still continues to be treated simply as a social address. Mothers are either present at that address for a certain number of hours per week, or they are not. That is all we know and, it would seem, all we need to know. Yet, in the light of the accumulated evidence, it should by now be obvious that a one-dimensional index of maternal employment—whether measured as a dichotomy, trichotomy, or linear metric in hours—can have only limited scientific or social significance by itself. What is needed is a more differentiated analysis of the work situation that would permit identification of specific job characteristics affecting the lives of workers as parents.

Such an analysis has only recently begun to be undertaken in studies on the effects of maternal employment. Miller et al. (1979:91) interviewed 555 women in order to examine the conditions of work that encourage self-direction, specifically the closeness of supervision, the routinization of the work, and the complexity of tasks. The investigators found that these conditions "are related to effective intellectual functioning and an open, flexible orientation to others, while those that constrain opportunities for self-direction or subject the worker to pressures or uncertainties are related to ineffective functioning, unfavorable self-conceptions, and a rigid social orientation." Unfortunately for the purposes of this review, the researchers have not yet completed their study of the relationship between self-direction and women's parenting values or behaviors with their children, nor have they determined the effects of these maternal work conditions on the children themselves, although such efforts are under way.

Nevertheless, the study by Miller et al. appears to be the first to identify specific job characteristics affecting the psychological development of women. As is seen below, the work represents an extension of a series of investigations previously carried out with samples of males.

Studies of the Effects of the Father's Occupation on Family Life

The first investigator to make a major breakthrough in research on the effect father's job has on family life was Kohn in his now classic work, *Class and Conformity* (1969). Kohn hypothesized that the structure and content of activities in the father's job shaped his value orientations in other aspects of his life, including child rearing. To be sure, Kohn was not the first to propose that what adults did at work could be related to how they brought up their children. Years earlier, Aberle and Naegele (1952) had suggested that middle-class fathers encourage behaviors in their sons that would enable them to hold middle-class occupations. Later, McKinley (1964:129) postulated that "within a particular social class or general occupational stratum, those individuals who enjoy great autonomy in their work will tend to show less hostility in their families and toward their children in the socialization process." Interviews with sons about their fathers revealed that lower-class fathers reportedly disciplined and punished more severely than their counterparts with middle-class occupations.

McKinley argued for a "frustration-aggression" linkage whereby fathers, frustrated by low levels of job satisfaction and work autonomy, act punitively toward their young sons. Kohn followed up on these themes in a series of studies of middle-class and working-class men and their child-rearing values. First, he showed that working-class men, whose jobs typically require compliance with authority, tend to hold values that stress obedience and conformity in their children. By contrast, middle-class fathers prize self-direction and independence, the qualities demanded by their own occupations. Furthermore, these differences in values correspond to differences in reported child-rearing practices. While working-class parents describe punishing children as a consequence of their actions, middle-class parents speak more of reacting to the child's intentions. In addition, working-class parents tend to favor physical punishment, while middle-class parents often use more psychological techniques, such as withdrawal of love, to shape their children's behavior.

Kohn's measure of social class was based on three variables: income, education, and occupation. He proceeded to examine the relative influence of each on the value orientation of his adult male subjects. Income (along with the person's subjective identification of his own class position) turned out to be least important. The key factors were education and occupational position, with the former predominating (Kohn, 1969:191): "Education is the more potent of the two dimensions, being more strongly related to parental values, to self values, to judgments about the extrinsic features of jobs."

The independent contribution of work, however, was subsequently demonstrated by Kohn and Schooler (1973, 1978) in a more fine-grained analysis. That work focused on the dimension of "occupational self-direction"—the extent to which a job requires complex skills, autonomy, and lack of routinization—and its relation to workers' "intellectual flexibility," as measured on a series of standardized tests. Using causal modeling techniques with longitudinal data, Kohn and Schooler demonstrated that the occupational self-direction of a job at one point in time can affect one's intellectual flexibility 10 years later. In fact, the nature of work and one's psychological functioning interact reciprocally, Kohn and Schooler argue, throughout one's working life.

Recently Kohn et al. extended their analysis to parental roles. Using data collected both in the United States and in Poland, Slomczynski et al. (in press) report that in both countries self-direction in work increases self-directed parental values. In this recent analysis the researchers test the generalizability of the relationship between social stratification and values by examining a socialist society. They find that, in general, men in higher occupational positions are more likely to value self-direction for their children, whether in Poland or in the United States.

Mortimer (1974, 1976) documents the full causal sequence for a different psychological domain in research based on Kohn's theoretical model. Mortimer reanalyzed data collected in the 1962-1967 Michigan Student Study to test hypotheses about the process of occupational transmission from fathers to sons. Her analyses revealed a strong tendency for sons to choose their father's occupation. When they did not select the same occupation, they tended to pick jobs involving similar occupational experiences and rewards, as measured by (1) extent of work autonomy, (2) rewards of the occupation, and (3) functions of the work activities. The sample group, it must be remembered, was college educated, and it is not clear whether the same findings would emerge in a less advantaged group.

The special strength of Mortimer's study (1976:253) is the inclusion of parent-child relationships as an intervening link in her model. She found that "the combination of a prestigious parental role model and a close father-son relationship engenders the most effective transmission of vocational values and the clearest impacts on sons' occupational decisions." Thus, warmth in the father-son relationship mediates the extent to which a son is influenced by the father's work in choosing his own vocational direction.

A recent analysis by Mortimer and Kumka (in press) extends the investigation 10 years beyond the subjects' college graduation and examines familial antecendents of occupational attainment. Using least squares regression, the researchers estimated a fully recursive model for two groups of respondents: those of "professional origin" whose fathers were doctors, lawyers, and other professionals, and those of "business origin" whose fathers were managers, salesmen, and other types of businessmen. Mortimer and Kumka (p. 15) summarize their findings as follows:

In the business families, both the father's occupational success and paternal support were found to intensify sons' extrinsic values and further income attainment. In the professional families, these variables instead encourage the development of people-oriented values and the attainment of work with high social content following college.

They conclude by emphasizing the importance of the socialization process and the power of a "close, empathic relationship" between father and son. They pose a series of stimulating questions as yet unaddressed by researchers, including the following (p. 17):

Given that parents with substantively complex work have the more self-directed values . . . do they also structure their children's environments in ways that foster self-direction? Do they provide more independence, give their children less close supervision, or encourage more challenging play activities?

These questions point the way for researchers interested in extending our knowledge about work-family linkages.

A rather different dimension of the job experience involves the extent to which work absorbs one's physical and mental energy. Kanter (1977) refers to this variable as "work absorption." Heath (1977) studied the effects of occupation on the development of men in professional jobs in a longitudinal study and concluded that the need to commit a large amount of time and energy to work often had a "narrowing" effect on those who had little time for nonwork activities, including child rearing. In an earlier article (1976:33), Heath described the impact of work absorption on these men as fathers:

The highly educated professional men, absorbed by their occupations' demands upon their energy and time, expressed great guilt in their interviews about not being more available to their children. The stresses of their occupation also contributed to the other principal paternal inadequacy as judged by both the men and their wives: the men's irritability and impatience with their children.

Heath's research did not go on to examine the impact of parental work absorption on the child, but studies by others suggest that this factor may affect the quantity and quality of time shared by parents and children and, thereby, influence the development of the child. As Douvan and Adelson (1966) point out, the relation between parental involvement and child development is a curvilinear one: too little involvement becomes deprivation, just as too much involvement can stifle the child's development of autonomy. The child's age is an important determinant of the optimal level of parent-child interaction. Thus, parental work absorption may have very different effects on the child at different ages. Even adolescents, well on the way to autonomy from parents, however, indicate that time with parents is still important to them (Bahr, 1978).

Research on Conflict and Resolution in Work and Family Roles

Heath's studies of work absorption are part of a larger body of research emerging in the 1970s that deals explicitly with dissonances between the demands of home and job for both men and women. Most of these investigations focus on the effects of conflicting time schedules. For example, in a study of shift work Mott et al. (1965) found that afternoon workers, away from home from 3 p.m. to 11 p.m., rarely saw their school-age children during the work week. The job of discipline fell to the mother, and the paucity of shared time produced family conflicts over what to do with that little time. Although night-shift workers reported that the 11 p.m. to 7 a.m. shift enabled them to see their children, the arrangement still produced tension between husband and wife. It appears that working other than a normal day shift can alter the pattern of intrafamilial relationships. The Mott investigation did not include an assessment of effects on the children. A subsequent study did so, but unfortunately left the intervening variable of parent-child interaction to be inferred. Landy et al. (1969) examined the impact on daughters of the father's limited absence because he worked a night shift. Their sample included 100 female college students whose fathers had worked nights for varying lengths of time and at different points in the young women's childhood. The outcome measure was the daughter's mathematical skill as measured on a standardized test. Controlling for social class, the investigators found that young women whose fathers had worked nights when they were very young (ages 0-9) had significantly lower scores than those whose fathers either had not worked the night shift at all or had worked nights only when their daughters were older.

Most recently, Bohen and Viveros-Long (1981) exploited an experiment of nature to investigate the impact of flexible work schedules (flexitime) on family life. They were successful in finding two federal agencies engaged in similar work and staffed by similar personnel, but differing in the arrangement of working hours. In one agency the employees worked conventional hours, from 9:00 a.m. to 5:00 p.m.; in the other, workers could choose to arrive within a two-hour range in the morning and adjust their leaving time accordingly. The results of the experiment were somewhat ironic. Measures of family strain and participation in home activities showed a significant difference favoring flexitime primarily for one group of families—those without children. Although fathers with nonemployed wives did report less stress in family management if they were on flexitime, the authors point out that families with children and dual-career couples are under so much pressure that the modest flexitime arrangement under study may not have gone far enough to meet their needs.

Bohen and Viveros-Long (1981:140) also cite a suggestion by Joseph Pleck that a self-selection factor is at work: Those who choose to change their schedules may be the group with the highest level of work-family conflicts in the first place. Flexitime may improve their lot, but not enough to distinguish them from nonflexitime users on measures of work-family interface. Yet another possibility emerges in the light of cross-cultural research pointing to the relatively low priority given to children and family life in American society (Bronfenbrenner, 1970, 1978, 1980; Kamerman, 1980a). It may be that American parents, rather than using flexitime for family activities, engage in adult recreation, socializing, or even moonlighting. Unfortunately, no data were available to permit differentiating among these alternative explanations.

The difficulty of interpretation posed by the results of this study underscores the importance of obtaining information about what families perceive as the problems in their lives arising from the combined obligations of work and parenthood. A pioneering investigation in this regard was conducted by Rapoport and Rapoport (1971). These investigators obtained detailed accounts of the everyday problems, tensions, and experiences of dual-career families in England. It is appropriate that dual-career families were the first targets of inquiry since they provide a particularly revealing example of the contemporary dilemma faced by increasing numbers of parents—the juggling of *two* jobs and *two* work schedules on the one hand, and maintenance of a harmonious family life on the other. The Rapoports used case studies to portray the difficulties encountered in balancing these needs. The result is a series of rich, in-depth portraits.

A qualitative approach to analogous problems is found in the doctoral work of several University of Michigan students in the late 1970s. Golden (1975) used interviews and observations to examine how families with preschool children handled the competing demands of work and family. Hood (1980) interviewed 16 two-worker couples about the transition to becoming a two-worker family when the wife returned to the work force after a period at home with young children. The investigator was concerned with the consequences of that transition for patterns of household work and child care and showed that the fathers in these families gradually became more involved in such activities. Hood and Golden (1979) combined their data to present two portraits of the impact of contrasting work schedules on men's family roles, showing how the "split shift" arrangement, in which mother and father work separate schedules, can result in child-care patterns involving an unusually high degree of paternal participation. Golden's and Hood's studies go beyond the shift-work studies of Mott et al. (1965) and Landy et al. (1969) by examining the impact of job schedules on the functioning of the family as a whole.

Piotrkowski (1979) focused directly on the nature of the work-family interface in a study of 13 working-class and lower middle-class families. Her intent was to develop "grounded theory" (Glaser and Strauss, 1967) by investigating in depth a small group of families. Her study identified three ways in which work spills over into family life via the mood, actions, feelings, and energy level of the worker-parent: "positive carry over," "negative carry over," and "energy deficit." She made a convincing argument that work experience is brought into the family via the worker-parent's emotional state, which partially determines the person's availability to family members, especially children. Piotrkowski's family vignettes capture much of the family process lacking in previous work. For example, we can imagine Heath's absorbed professional men responding with a pattern of "energy deficit" in their families. Once again, however, Piotrkowski's work was based on a small, accidental sample. The issues are raised eloquently, but it is unclear to what extent they occur in the general population.

Finally, Pleck et al. (1978) analyzed the items from the 1977 Quality of Employment Survey (QES) that bear on the extent to which parents perceive "interference" between their job and their family life. The investigators found that the degree to which parents experience such conflict was negatively correlated to family adjustment, job satisfaction, and sense of well-being. Schedule incompatibilities and psychological spillover from work to the family were cited as the two most common sources of work-family interference.

Studies of conflict and resolution between work and family needs represent an important scientific advance in illuminating some of the processes linking these major contexts of modern life. In particular, they focus attention on the critical role of job stress as a factor affecting family functioning and, thereby, the behavior and development of children. Nevertheless, this new research development of the 1970s shares with its scientific predecessors two serious limitations in scope that only now are being recognized and surmounted. In the next two sections we examine these newly explored terrains.

Long-Range Effects of Parental Work on Child Development

Almost all of the investigations we have examined thus far have been cross-sectional in design. As a result, they have overlooked the possibility of sleeper effects in development, which may not become apparent until adolescence or adulthood. Studies in which the subjects were adolescents suggest the existence of such long-range effects (e.g., Banducci, 1967; Douvan, 1963; McCord et al., 1963; Nye, 1952, 1963). But the real test of this phenomenon requires a longitudinal design. Unfortunately there have been few investigations of this kind. The earliest is a research study by Moore (1963), who followed a sample of English children from infancy through elementary school. At the latter point he examined the children's development as a function of the mother's employment history during the preschool years. Children whose mothers worked, particularly when the children were under two years of age, exhibited greater dependence and insecurity. Also, the mothers appeared to be less attached to the children. It is entirely possible, however, that this lack of involvement was as much the cause as the consequence of the mothers' employment status. As Hoffman points out (1974:157), "Since these mothers had sought employment when few mothers of infants worked, they may have been a more psychologically distinct group than one would now find." The same qualification may apply to a retrospective study by Burchinal (1963), which yielded a pattern of significant findings that suggests greater psychological vulnerability for children whose mothers began to work when the child was under three years of age. Consistent with the results of other studies discussed here, in which the age of the child at the time of maternal employment was not controlled, the effect was specific to intellectual performance in boys. No evidence was found of disturbance in social adjustment. Neither boys who were older at the time the mother began working nor girls at any age exhibited this particular outcome.

The specificity of long-range effects of parental employment as a function of the child's age and sex are unequivocally demonstrated in Elder's reanalysis of archival data from longitudinal studies conducted in California with samples of children born in the early and late 1920s (Elder, 1974, 1979; Elder and Rockwell, 1979). Like his predecessors, Elder saw an opportunity to investigate the impact of the Great Depression on family functioning, but he did so within the context of a more powerful research design. The samples of both studies had been selected for other research purposes before the depression occurred. As happens in a mighty storm, some families were directly hit by the economic disaster and others were spared. Those strokes of fortune fell in a virtually random pattern as this factory closed and that one remained in operation, one stock collapsed and another survived. Elder took advantage of this natural experiment to divide his sample into two otherwise comparable groups on the basis of whether the loss of income from the depression exceeded or fell short of 35 percent. Both of those groups were also stratified on the basis of the family's socioeconomic status prior to 1929. The availability of longitudinal data on the children made it possible to assess long-range developmentl outcomes through late childhood, through adolescence, and into adulthood. Finally, because the children in one sample were born eight years earlier than those in the other, a comparison could be made of the effects of the depression on children who were adolescents when their families became economically deprived and those who were still young children at that time.

The two groups presented a dramatic contrast. For those who were teenagers during the depression years, the family's economic deprivation appeared to have a salutary effect on their subsequent development, especially in the middle class. As compared with the nondeprived group matched on predepression socioeconomic status, they did better in school, were more likely to go on to college, had happier marriages, exhibited more successful work careers, and in general achieved greater satisfaction in life, both by their own and by societal standards. Although more pronounced for adolescents from middle-class backgrounds, these favorable outcomes were evident among their lower-class counterparts as well. Through a careful analysis of interview and observation protocols, Elder identified what he regarded as the factor most critical to setting in motion this favorable developmental trajectory: The loss of economic security forced the family to mobilize its own human resources, including its teenagers, who had to take on new roles and responsibilities both within and outside the home, and to work together toward the common goal of getting the family on its feet. This experience provided effective training in initiative, responsibility, and cooperation. In the words of Shakespeare's banished duke, "Sweet are the uses of adversity."

Alas, adversity was not so sweet for male children who were still preschoolers when their families suffered economic loss. The results were almost the opposite of those for the adolescent boys in the earlier investigation. Compared to controls from nondeprived families, these youngsters subsequently did less well in school, showed less stable and successful work histories, and exhibited more emotional and social difficulties, some still apparent in middle adulthood. These negative outcomes were much more marked in families from lower-class backgrounds.

The congruity of Elder's longitudinal findings with those obtained in cross-sectional studies lends credence to the validity of both. In addition, his work demonstrates the necessity for researchers in this area to take into account the age of the child at the time the parents are undergoing a particular kind of employment experience. Even more significantly, his results underscore the importance of not dismissing the possibility of long-range effects in this sphere.

Elder's work is noteworthy in yet another respect. In addition to incorporating the dimension of time and life course in studies of the effects of parental work on human development, he has broadened the range of environmental contexts in which developmental outcomes can be observed. Thus, as children grow older these outcomes become manifest not only in the family but successively in the peer group, school, institution of higher education, and ultimately the world of work, which originally set the space-time trajectory in motion. In this respect Elder anticipates the most recent and far-reaching development in research models for studying the impact of parental employment on family life. The review of work in this broader domain brings our research survey to a close.

Studies of Work and Family in Ecological Perspective

An observation of Cochran and Gunnarsson in their longitudinal study of day care in Sweden (Cochran, 1977; Cochran and Robinson, 1982;

Gunnarsson, 1978) nicely illustrates the necessity of expanding the research model of the environment in studies of the impact of work on family functioning. These investigators report that all of the children in their representative sample of children in day care centers in the city of Göteborg had working mothers, whereas only 24 percent of those cared for in homes had mothers who were employed. Cochran and Robinson used this fact as a basis for arguing the need to untangle the contributions of mother's work status from those of day-care experience in research on the effects of maternal employment on the child. But one can also phrase the issue in another way: To what extent does the availability of quality day care affect the impact of maternal employment on child-rearing processes and outcomes? The same question can be asked regarding the mediating role of the school, informal peer groups, youth programs, health and social services, community organizations, and, last but hardly least, state and national policies that explicitly or implicitly affect the lives of families and children. The importance of the last, both as social influences and appropriate contexts for research, is communicated by the following preliminary findings from an ongoing project by Kamerman and Kahn (personal communication) comparing support systems provided to families in a range of modern industrialized societies:

Mothers of very young children are working outside the home in growing numbers in all industrialized countries. Two-parent, two-wage-earner families (and single-parent, sole-wage-earner families) are increasingly the norm. . . . In response to this development, some countries are expanding child care services as well as cash benefits to protect child and family life. However, the United States lags far behind such European countries as France, Sweden, and the Federal Republic of Germany in the West, and the German Democratic Republic and Hungary in the East in providing either.

It is especially significant for our purposes that many of the supports Kamerman and Kahn describe in their international survey are focused on the world of work. These include, among others, guaranteed maternity and paternity leaves, flexitime, job sharing, and sick leave to parents when children are ill (Kamerman, 1980a). Moreover, these special benefits provided through the workplace supplement more general services made available to all families, such as health care, family allowances, and child care facilities (Kamerman and Kahn, 1978). It is sobering to read, in Kamerman and Kahn's systematic descriptions, paragraph after paragraph beginning, "All countries in the study—except the United States—offer. . . ."

The implications of this state of affairs for the American social and scientific scene is telegraphed by the title of Kamerman's recent book

(1980b): *Parenting in an Unresponsive Society*. The findings reported in this volume are based on a survey of 200 working mothers in single- and two-parent families. Three themes emerging from the analysis have special significance for our concern. The first is the severe stress reported both by single-parent and two-worker families caused by the problem of obtaining satisfactory child care. In contemporary American society, providing for such care often requires elaborate arrangements combining the use of day-care centers, babysitters, and shifting parental responsibilities that require a delicately orchestrated schedule. The strains generated by the task of establishing and maintaining these complex arrangements are reflected in Kamerman's blending of statistical data and case-study vignettes. The second theme emerging from the survey findings is the importance of the father's involvement in household work and child care in two-worker families. Such spousal support, of course, is not available in single-parent households, where all the burdens of work, child rearing, and coordinating child-care arrangements fall on the shoulders of one person—usually the mother. The third major theme emerging from the survey is the key role played by informal support systems in enabling parents to function effectively in the child-rearing role. The participants in these informal structures are readily identifiable (Kamerman, 1980b:108): "Although they frequently mentioned neighbors or friends as providing important help, it is clear from the interviews that the single most important source of help for working mothers is relatives and family. Whether for child care purposes, emergencies, advice, or just encouragement and sympathy, most of these women view 'family' as an essential support system."

Crouter (1982) recently investigated the reciprocal nature of the relationship between work and family lives among 55 employees in a large manufacturing plant. The work setting had an unusual management approach emphasizing decision making and problem solving at all levels of the organization. Employees worked in teams that were highly autonomous. With extensive interviews held both at work and home, Crouter found that most employees perceived spillover from work to personal life *and* from personal life to work. Positive spillover from work to personal life included acquiring skills in communication, decision making, problem solving, and listening that in turn were useful at home and in the community. Another common theme of respondents, however, was the stressful, pressured nature of work in a participative milieu; that stress was brought home. This was particularly true for team advisors, the first-line supervisors in the plant who had unusually time-consuming, demanding jobs. This study also focused on the perceived impact of the family on individuals' work lives. Notably, mothers of children 12 and under were the subgroup reporting by far the highest levels of spillover in this direction—spillover that was primarily negative. These mothers recognized that their parenting responsibilities could make them inadvertently late to work, absent, unable to work overtime, or preoccupied with worrying about a child in unsatisfactory child care. Finally, for the 37 parents in the sample, there was a highly positive relationship between the extent of problematic spillover from work to family and the extent of problematic spillover from the family to work. More research is needed to explore possible causal relationships in this regard.

Neither Kamerman's inquiry nor Crouter's study, however, explored the consequences of these patterns of family stresses and support for the behavior and development of children. As indicated below, we view such investigation as a high priority for the future.

WORK AND FAMILY IN THE 1980s: A PERSPECTIVE FOR SCIENCE
AND SOCIAL POLICY

The implications of our analysis for future directions in research and social policy can be summarized under two headings which restate now all-too-familiar themes:

Recommendations for Future Research on the Effects of Maternal Employment

Of the many possible recommendations that can be made about future research on the impact of maternal employment, we have selected the following 15 as the most important; we begin with those that are more methodologically oriented and proceed to issues of increasing substantive and social-policy concern:

(1)   Studies that are limited to searching for differences in the characteristics of children solely as a function of the mother's employment status have clearly reached the point of diminishing returns. The focus of investigation must shift to the exploration of intervening processes both within and outside the family. This shift, in turn, requires the use of more complex research paradigms for investigating effects of maternal employment. Up to the present time, the overwhelming majority of studies have employed two types of models, each limited to only two points in the causal chain. The first of these models compares children of employed and unemployed mothers; thus, it involves a leap from the very start of the causal process directly to the outcome, leaving everything in between to the imagination. The second examines only the

initial step in the process: the impact of work on the attitudes and actions of the mother. We propose that the paradigm of choice for further research is one that incorporates a minimum of two links: The first assesses the impact of work on family functioning; the second illuminates the extent to which differences in family functioning associated with work status affect the behavior and psychological development of the child.

(2) Whether they are simply descriptive or process oriented, investigations must take into account the influence of mediating factors related to the child's sex, age (both at the time of investigation and during the period of maternal employment), and race; family structure; the socioeconomic position of the family; the circumstances leading the mother to work or stay at home; hours of employment; and the mother's degree of satisfaction or dissatisfaction with her work status. One of these mediating factors—social class—requires special comment. In future studies of the effects of maternal employment, indices of social class should no longer be limited to or equated with occupational status. The concept of social position and its measurement must be broadened and differentiated in order to encompass mediating effects specific to such aspects as each parent's occupation, education, and, especially, contribution to family income. These distinctions appear necessary in view of evidence that each of these factors qualifies the impact of parental work in a different way (Otto, 1975).

(3) Since the mother's decision to enter the labor force may be influenced by preexisting conditions and attitudes relating to work and family life, the direction of influence remains indeterminate in cross-sectional studies. An underused strategy for meeting this problem involves a short-term longitudinal design in which data are collected both before and after the point of employment. As Bronfenbrenner (1979) has pointed out, the exploration of such "ecological transitions" as natural experiments has considerable scientific power, since subjects serve as their own controls and the direct and indirect effects of change can be assessed as they evolve in a variety of domains. Such domains include parental attitudes, patterns of child rearing, and the child's behavior and perceptions in a range of settings both within and outside the home (e.g., day care, peer group, school, or for that matter, the laboratory). In view of the large number of mothers who are now likely to enter the work force, the selection of an appropriate sample should not present great difficulty.

(4) To the extent possible, research on the impact of maternal employment on children's development should investigate the possibility of long-range effects that may not be manifested until later childhood,

adolescence, or adulthood. The most powerful research model for this purpose is, of course, a longitudinal design. But in view of the cost of long-term investigations, both in time and financial resources, the practical strategy of choice may be that of cross-sectional studies of older children and adults, with retrospective information obtained about maternal work patterns at earlier ages. One cohort of special interest is the people who were adolescents during the turbulent 1960s. Not only were the education and occupational training of this group often interrupted and inconsistent, but its members also entered a tight job market during the 1970s. How have these historical events made their mark on this age group in terms of their family life and the socialization and development of their children?

Where long-range longitudinal studies are possible, they should consider not only the changing characteristics of the child, but also the changes taking place in the lives of the child's parents and in the context and content of the experiences to which the child and family are exposed over the life course. Of particular importance in this regard are changing social norms and expectations about the participation of husbands and wives in work and family life. As documented in this review, detrimental effects for the child are more likely to occur when the mother's work status conflicts with her preferences. Thus, any social changes that increase or decrease the proportion of mothers who are placed in dissonant roles may lead to corresponding changes in children's development.

(5) An assessment of the effects of maternal employment on children must take into account the nature of the experience to which the child is exposed while the mother is at work, with specific reference to the content of the activities in which the child is engaged and the significance of the child's companions as role models. Particular attention should be accorded to the characteristics of the child's peer group and the extent to which its values and activities are congruent with those of the family and the school.

(6) A critical class of intervening variables linking maternal employment status to the behavior and development of the child involves the specific nature of the parent-child activities engaged in by working versus nonworking mothers.

(7) Another class of important intervening variables relates to the parental behavior of the father as a function of the mother's work status, including the nature of the activities in which he engages with the child. Research should consider the effects on the mother and child of the father's participation in family life, with the recognition that what may be beneficial for the mother may not be for the child and vice versa.

(8) In examining the effects of maternal employment in two-parent

families, account should also be taken of the father's work schedule and its relation to that of the mother.

(9) Studies of the effects on family and child of the father's job characteristics (e.g., job absorption, content, organization, and complexity of work) should be carried out in relation to the mother's job as well.

(10) Research is needed on the effects of the mother's family situation on her behavior and performance on the job. The family can be an influence on productivity (Voydanoff, 1980) that is all too often overlooked. Investigation should focus on the extent to which conditions of family life, such as unsatisfactory child-care arrangements, are dysfunctional to the employer, as well as the mother.

(11) In light of a series of findings suggesting a negative effect of maternal employment on the intellectual achievement of boys from middle-class families, a special study should be made of this group. In the course of such investigation, attention should be focused not only on the impact of work on interpersonal relationships within the family, but also on the effect on family members of external factors, such as the contribution of maternal employment to family income, and the impact of family work schedules on the exposure of children, particularly boys, to peer-group influences that may impair school performance.

(12) In view of their significance for public policy, special priority should be accorded to studies of the effects of maternal employment status in single-parent families, two-wage-earner families, families in which the mother works part time, and a new and possibly vulnerable minority in American society—mothers who are not employed outside the home.

(13) A new pattern of childbearing is evolving in American society: Increasing numbers of women are postponing having a child until they become well established in a career. As a result, children are brought up by older parents who are farther along in life's trajectory in such key domains as work, marital relations, social life, and community responsibilities. Little is known about the effects of this kind of delayed parenthood on family functioning and the development of children.

(14) Given research findings documenting the destructive long-range effects on young children of the father's loss of a job, similar studies should be undertaken on the developmental impact of maternal employment. Such investigations take on special policy significance in the light of growing rates of unemployment for working mothers with young children and the widening gap between the cost of living and family income, especially for poor families with young children. Many such families are single-parent households in which the mother has to work.

These income changes are shown in Figures 3-1 and 3-2, for the period 1975-1980.[4] The data for 1981 and 1982 are certain to magnify the depicted trends. As the graphs show, family income has not kept up with inflation and the gap has been increasing at an accelerating rate, particularly for female-headed households.

(15) Highest priority should be accorded to research on environmental stresses and supports experienced by working mothers and their families both within and outside the home and job. The importance of identifying specific sources of stress and support in both family and work settings is underscored by research findings regarding the powerful mediating role played by the mother's degree of satisfaction with her employment status. Particular attention should be paid to the impact of family benefits associated with employment. For example, Kamerman and Kingston (see chapter 5) point out that large firms are more likely to have benefits packages for their employees than small firms. That observation is reminiscent of Miller's and Swanson's (1958) distinction between entrepreneurial and bureaucratic work environments. Future research should investigate large versus small work settings, examine their policies with regard to families, and study the positive and negative consequences for families and children of having company-sponsored benefits.

The investigations to be undertaken should include both formal and informal sources of stress and support as well as their interrelation. Particular priority should be given to social experiments designed to alleviate stress and maximize sources of support to the family in its child-rearing role.

---

[4] The 1980 census report on income (Bureau of the Census, 1981:1) documents "the largest decline recorded in the post-World War II period." This precipitate decrease was accompanied by a corresponding increase between 1979 and 1980 of 3.2 million persons below the poverty level, "one of the largest annual increases in the number of poor since 1959, the earliest year for which poverty statistics have been computed." More than a third of the new arrivals (1.2 million) were children. An examination of the more detailed data in appended figures reveals that the poverty rate varied significantly by age, with the highest level, 21 percent, occurring for children under 3, compared to 13 percent for the population as a whole, and 16 percent for those over 65. In other words, more than one-fifth of the nation's three-year-olds were living below the poverty line in March 1980. Given the subsequent rise in cost of living and in unemployment rates, that proportion will, in all likelihood, become appreciably higher in 1981 and 1982. (The poverty index is based on the minimum income sufficient to meet the cost of the Department of Agriculture's economy food plan. The index is adjusted to reflect the different consumption requirements of families, based on size, composition, and other relevant demographic factors.)

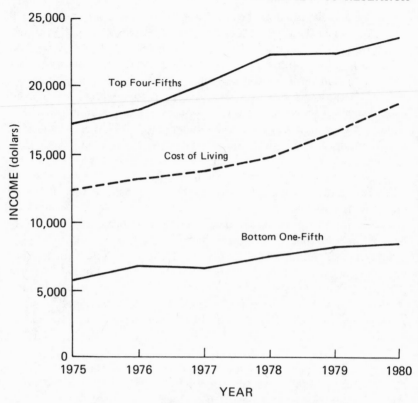

FIGURE 3-1   Change in income (1975-1980) for two-parent families with children under 6: medians for children on bottom fifth and upper four-fifths of the income distribution.

NOTE: Cost of living is computed from the Consumer Price Index, using as a basis the median income in 1975 for all families with children under 6.
SOURCE: "Children of Women in the Labor Force," Bureau of Labor Statistics, 1976-1980, supplemented by BLS staff.

Recommendations for Future Research on the Impact of Work on the Family as a Child-Rearing System

The 15 recommendations presented here take a curiously elliptical form: They substitute for the words "mother" and "maternal," the words "father" and "paternal." The effect of such a substitution is to recognize that all of the forces affecting the roles of mothers as parents and workers have their analogs in the lives of fathers. The significance of this fact for human development is indicated by a growing body of research (e.g., Lamb, 1976) documenting the importance of the father in the socialization and psychological growth of children from early infancy onward. From this perspective, it is important to assess the impact on family and child of such factors as the number of hours the father works or his attitude toward his job and its relation to his role as a parent—variables that have been repeatedly examined in studies of maternal employment.

Our final recommendation has still broader implications for method, theory, and public policy. The convergence and complementarity of research designs and research findings on the developmental impact of maternal and paternal employment underscore the fact that conditions

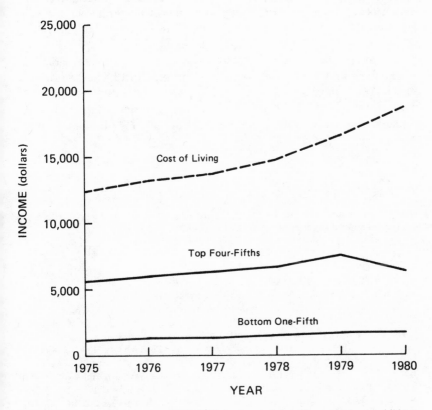

FIGURE 3-2 Change in income (1975-1980) for female-headed households with children under 6: medians for children in bottom fifth and upper four-fifths of the income distribution.

NOTE: Cost of living is computed from the Consumer Price Index, using as a basis the median income in 1975 for all families with children under 6.

SOURCE: "Children of Women in the Labor Force," Bureau of Labor Statistics, 1976–1980, supplemented by BLS staff.

at work have a profound influence on the functioning of the family *as a system*. One cannot understand what is happening in one part of this system without taking into account what is happening in other parts. Moreover, this same overriding principle applies at another, equally necessary level of analysis: The impact of parental work on family functioning and the development of children cannot be understood without taking into account the larger context of which both work and family are a part. The most critical aspect of this larger context has to do with the availability of both formal and informal support systems for the family in such forms as child care, health and social services, necessary financial resources, and assistance and support from relatives, friends, neighbors, and co-workers. It is in this broader area that the richest opportunities lie both for science and social policy.

It is essential, however, that in exploring these broader domains, researchers and policy makers do not fail to accord highest priority to the ultimate impact of research projects and operating programs on families and children. There is the danger that in our recognition of the broader contexts of human development we forget about human beings themselves.

REFERENCES AND BIBLIOGRAPHY

Aberle, D. F., and Naegele, K. D. (1952) Middle-class fathers' occupational role and attitudes toward children. *American Journal of Orthopsychiatry* 22:366-378.

Anderson, H. E. (1936) *The Young Child in the Home*. New York: Appleton Century.

Angell, R. C. (1936) *The Family Encounters the Depression*. New York: Scribner.

Bahr, H. (1978) Change in Family Life in Middletown: 1924-1977. Paper presented at the annual meeting of the American Sociological Association, Chicago.

Banducci, R. (1967) The effect of mother's employment on the achievement, aspirations, and expectations of the child. *Personnel and Guidance Journal* 46:263-267.

Baruch, G. K. (1972) Maternal influences upon college women's attitudes toward women and work. *Developmental Psychology* 6:32-37.

Below, H. I. (1969) Life Styles and Roles of Women as Perceived by High-School Girls. Ph.D. dissertation, Indiana University.

Berger, I. L. (1948) Psychopathologic attitude of frustrated previously employed mothers toward their offspring. *Journal of Nervous and Mental Disorders* 108:241-249.

Blood, R. O., Jr. (1963) The husband-wife relationship. In F. I. Nye and L. W. Hoffman, eds., *The Employed Mother in America*. Chicago: Rand McNally.

Blood, R. O., Jr. (1967) *Love Match and Arranged Marriage*. New York: The Free Press.

Blood, R. O., Jr., and Hamblin, R. L. (1958) The effect of wife's employment on the family power structure. *Social Forces* 36:347-352.

Blood, R. O., Jr. and Wolfe, D. M. (1960) *Husbands and Wives*. New York: The Free Press.

Bohen, H. H., and Viveros-Long, A. (1981) *Balancing Jobs and Family Life: Do Flexible Work Schedules Help?* Philadelphia, Pa.: Temple University Press.

Bronfenbrenner, U. (1970) *Two Worlds of Childhood*. New York: Russell Sage Foundation.

Bronfenbrenner, U. (1978) Who needs parent education? *Teachers College Record* 79:767-787.

Bronfenbrenner, U. (1979) *The Ecology of Human Development*. Cambridge, Mass.: Harvard University Press.

Bronfenbrenner, U. (1980) On making human beings human. *Character* 2:1-7.

Bronfenbrenner, U. (1982) The context of development and the development of context. Pp. 1-64 in R.M. Lerner, ed., *Developmental Psychology: Historical and Philosophical Perspectives*. Hillsdale, N.J.: Erlbaum Associates.

Bronfenbrenner, U., Henderson, C. R., Alvarez, W. F., and Cochran, M. (1982) *The Relation of the Mother's Work Status to Parents' Spontaneous Descriptions of their Children*. Ithaca, N.Y.: Department of Human Development and Family Studies, Cornell University.

Brown, S. W. (1970) A Comparative Study of Maternal Employment and Nonemployment. Ph.D. dissertation, Mississippi State University.

Burchinal, L. G. (1963) Personality characteristics of children. In F. I. Nye and L. W. Hoffman, eds., *The Employed Mother in America*. Chicago: Rand McNally.

Burchinal, L. G., and Lovell, L. (1959) Relation of Employment Status of Mothers to Children's Anxiety, Parental Personality, and PARI Scores. Unpublished manuscript, Agricultural Experiment Station, Iowa State University.

Bureau of the Census (1981) Money income and poverty status of families and persons in the United States: 1980. *Current Population Reports*, Series P-60, No. 127. Washington, D.C.: U.S. Department of Commerce.

Caudill, W., and Weinstein, H. (1969) Maternal care and infant behavior in Japan and America. *Psychiatry* 32:12-43.

Caven, R. S., and Ranck, K. H. (1938) *The Family and the Depression: A Study of 100 Chicago Families*. Chicago: University of Chicago Press.

Cherry, F. F., and Eaton, E. L. (1977) Physical and cognitive development in children of low-income mothers working in the child's early years. *Child Development* 48:158-166.

Cochran, M. M. (1977) A comparison of group day care and family childrearing patterns in Sweden. *Child Development* 48:702-707.

Cochran, M. M., and Robinson, J. (1982) Day care, family circumstances and sex differences in children. Chapter in preparation for *Advances in Day Care and Education*, Vol. 2, forthcoming.

Crouter, A. C. (1982) Participative Work and Family Life: A Case Study of Their Reciprocal Effects. Ph.D. dissertation, Cornell University.

Cummings, J. D. (1944) The incidence of emotional symptoms in school children. *British Journal of Educational Psychology* 14:151-161.

Douvan, E. (1963) Employment and the adolescent. In F. I. Nye and L. W. Hoffman, eds., *The Employed Mother in America*. Chicago: Rand McNally.

Douvan, E., and Adelson, J. (1966) *The Adolescent Experience*. New York: John Wiley and Sons.

Elder, G. H., Jr. (1974) *Children of the Great Depression*. Chicago: University of Chicago Press.

Elder, G. H., Jr. (1979) Historical change in life patterns and personality. Pp. 118-159 in P. Baltes and O. Brim, eds., *Life-Span Development and Behavior*, Vol. 2. New York: Academic Press.

Elder, G. H., Jr., and Rockwell, R. C. (1979) The life-course approach and human development: an ecological perspective. *International Journal of Behavioral Development* 2:1-21.

Essig, M., and Morgan, D. H. (1946) Adjustment of adolescent daughters of employed mothers to family life. *Journal of Educational Psychology* 37:219-233.

Farel, A. N. (1980) Effects of preferred maternal roles, maternal employment, and sociographic status on school adjustment and competence. *Child Development* 50:1179-1186.

Frodi, A. M., Lamb, M. E., Frodi, M., Hwang, C. P., Forsstrom, B., and Corry, T. (1980) Stability and Change in Parental Attitudes Following an Infant's Birth into Traditional and Non-traditional Swedish Families. Unpublished manuscript, University of Michigan.

Galton, F. (1874) *English Men of Sciences: Their Nature and Nurture.* London: MacMillan.

Glaser, B., and Strauss, A. (1967) *The Discovery of Grounded Theory.* Chicago: Aldine.

Glass, N. (1949) Eating, sleeping, and elimination habits in children attending day nurseries and children cared for in the home by mothers. *American Journal of Orthopsychiatry* 19:697-711.

Glueck, S., and Glueck, E. (1934) *Five Hundred Delinquent Women.* New York: Knopf.

Glueck, S., and Glueck, E. (1957) Working mothers and delinquency. *Mental Hygiene* 41:327-352.

Gold, D., and Andres, D. (1978a) Developmental comparisons between adolescent children with employed and nonemployed mothers. *Merrill-Palmer Quarterly* 24:243-254.

Gold, D., and Andres, D. (1978b) Developmental comparisons between 10-year-old children with employed and nonemployed mothers. *Child Development* 49:75-84.

Gold, D., and Andres, D. (1978c) Relations between maternal employment and development of nursery school children. *Canadian Journal of Behavioral Science* 10:116-129.

Gold, D., and Andres, D. (1980) Maternal employment and development of 10-year-old Canadian Francophone children. *Canadian Journal of Behavioral Science* 12:233-240.

Gold, A., Andres, D., and Glorieux J. (1979) The development of Francophone nursery school children with employed and nonemployed mothers. *Canadian Journal of Behavioral Science* 11:169-173.

Golden, S. (1975) Pre-school families and work. Ph.D. dissertation, University of Michigan.

Gunnarsson, L. (1978) Children in Day Care and Family Care in Sweden: A Follow-up. Ph.D. dissertation, University of Michigan.

Hand, H. B. (1957) Working mothers and maladjusted children. *Journal of Educational Sociology* 30:245-246.

Heath, D. B. (1977) Some possible effects of occupation on the maturing of professional men. *Journal of Vocational Behavior* 11:263-281.

Hetherington, E. M. (1979) Divorce: a child's perspective. *American Psychologist* 34:851-858.

Hock, E., Christman, K., and Hock, M. (1980) Factors associated with decisions to return to work in mothers of infants. *Developmental Psychology* 16:535-536.

Hodgkiss, M. (1933) The delinquent girl in Chicago; the influence of broken homes and working mothers. *Smith College Studies of Social Work* 3:259-274.

Hoffman, L. W. (1959) Effects of Maternal Employment on the Child. Paper presented at the National Council on Family Relations, Ames, Iowa.

Hoffman, L. W. (1961) Mothers' enjoyment of work and its effects on the child. *Child Development* 32:187-197.

Hoffman, L. W. (1963a) Effects on children: summary and discussion. In F. I. Nye and L. W. Hoffman, eds., *The Employed Mother in America.* Chicago: Rand McNally.

Hoffman, L. W. (1963b) Parental power relations and the division of household tasks. In F. I. Nye and L. W. Hoffman, eds., *The Employed Mother in America*. Chicago: Rand McNally.

Hoffman, L. W. (1974) Effects of maternal employment on the child—a review of the research. *Developmental Psychology* 10:204-229.

Hoffman, L. W. (1979) Changes in family roles, socialization, and sex differences. *American Psychologist* 32:644-657.

Hoffman, L. W. (1980) The Effects of Maternal Employment on the Academic Attitudes and Performance of School-Aged Children. Unpublished paper prepared for the National Institute of Education.

Hood, J. (1980) Becoming a Two-Job Family. Ph.D. dissertation, University of Michigan.

Hood, J., and Golden, S. (1979) Beating time/making time: the impact of work scheduling on men's family roles. *The Family Coordinator* 28 (October):575-583.

Johnson, C. L. (1969) Leadership Patterns in Working and Non-working Mother Middle-Class Families. Ph.D. dissertation, University of Kansas.

Jones, J. B., Lundsteen, S. W., and Michael, W. B. (1967) The relationship of the professional employment status of mothers to reading achievement of sixth grade children. *California Journal of Educational Research* 43:102-108.

Kamerman, S. B. (1980a) Maternity and parental benefits and leaves: an international review. *Impact on Policies Series*, Monograph No. 1, Fall. New York: Center for the Social Sciences, Columbia University.

Kamerman, S. B. (1980b) *Parenting in an Unresponsive Society*. New York: The Free Press.

Kamerman, S. B., and Kahn, A. J., eds. (1978) *Family Policy: Government and Families in Fourteen Countries*. New York: Columbia University Press.

Kanter, R. M. (1977) *Work and Family in the United States: A Critical Review and Agenda for Research and Policy*. New York: Russell Sage Foundation.

Kappel, B. E., and Lambert, R. D. (1972) Self Worth Among the Children of Working Mothers. Unpublished manuscript, University of Waterloo, Ontario.

Kliger, D. (1954) The Effects of Employment of Married Women on Husband and Wife Roles: A Study in Cultural Change. Ph.D. dissertation, Yale University.

Kohn, M. L. (1969) *Class and Conformity: A Study in Values*. Homewood, Ill.: Dorsey.

Kohn, M. L., and Schooler, C. (1973) Occupational experience and psychological functioning: an assessment of reciprocal effects. *American Sociological Review* 38:97-118.

Kohn, M. L., and Schooler, C. (1978) The reciprocal effects of the substantive complexity of work and intellectual flexibility: a longitudinal assessment. *American Journal of Sociology* 84:24-52.

Komarovsky, M. (1940) *The Unemployed Man and His Family*. New York: Dryden Press.

Kriesberg, L. (1970) *Mothers in Poverty: A Study of Fatherless Families*. Chicago: Aldine.

Lamb, M. E., ed. (1976) *The Role of the Father in Child Development*. New York: John Wiley and Sons.

Landy, F., Rosenberg, B. C., and Sutton-Smith, B. (1969) The effects of limited father absence on cognitive development. *Child Development* 40:941-944.

Lewin, K. (1935) *Dynamic Theory of Personality*. New York: McGraw-Hill.

Maccoby, E. (1958) Effects upon children of their mothers' outside employment. In *Work in the Lives of Married Women*. Proceedings of a conference sponsored by the National Manpower Council. New York: Columbia University Press.

Mathews, S. M. (1934) The effects of mothers' out-of-home employment upon children's ideas and attitudes. *Journal of Applied Psychology* 18:116-136.

McCord, J., McCord, W., and Thurber, E. (1963) Effects of maternal employment on lower-class boys. *Journal of Abnormal and Social Psychology* 67:177-182.

McKinley, D. G. (1964) *Social Class and Family Life.* New York: Free Press of Glencoe.

Miller, D. R., and Swanson, G. E. (1958) *The Changing American Parent: A Study in the Detroit Area.* New York: John Wiley and Sons.

Miller, J., Schooler, C., Kohn, M. L., and Miller, K. A. (1979) Women and work: the psychological effects of occupational conditions. *American Journal of Sociology* 85:66-94.

Moore, T. W. (1975) Exclusive mothering and its alternatives: the outcome to adolescence. *Scandinavian Journal of Psychology* 16:255-272.

Morgan, W. L. (1939) *The Family Meets the Depression.* Minneapolis, Minn.: University of Minnesota Press.

Mortimer, J. T. (1974) Patterns of intergenerational occupational movements: a smallest-space analysis. *American Journal of Sociology* 79:1278-1299.

Mortimer, J. T. (1976) Social class, work, and the family: some implications of the father's career for familial relationships and son's career decisions. *Journal of Marriage and the Family* 38:241-256.

Mortimer, J. T., and Kumka, R. A. (1982) A further examination of the "occupational linkage hypothesis." *Sociological Quarterly.* Forthcoming

Mott P. E., Mann, F. C., McLoghlin, Q., and Warwick, D. P. (1965) *Shift Work: The Social, Psychological, and Physical Consequences.* Ann Arbor: University of Michigan Press.

Nichols, S. (1976) Work and Housework: Family Roles in Productive Activity. Paper presented at the National Council on Family Relations, New York.

Nolan, F. L. (1963) Rural employment and husbands and wives. In F. I. Nye and L. W. Hoffman, eds., *The Employed Mother in America.* Chicago: Rand McNally.

Nye, F. I. (1952) Adolescent-parent adjustment: age, sex, sibling number, broken homes, and employed mothers as variables. *Marriage and Family Living* 14:327-332.

Nye, F. I. (1959) Employment status of mothers and adjustment of adolescent children. *Marriage and Family Living* 21:240-244.

Nye, F. I. (1963) The adjustment of adolescent children. In F. I. Nye and L. W. Hoffman, eds., *The Employed Mother in America.* Chicago: Rand McNally.

Otto, L. B. (1975) Class and status in family research. *Journal of Marriage and the Family* 37:315-332.

Peterson, E. T. (1958) The Impact of Maternal Employment on the Mother-Daughter Relationship and on the Daughter's Role-Orientation. Ph.D. dissertation, University of Michigan.

Piotrkowski, C. S. (1979) *Work and the Family System: A Naturalistic Study of Working-Class and Lower-Middle-Class Families.* New York: The Free Press.

Pleck, J. H. (1977) The work-family role system. *Social Problems* 24:417-427.

Pleck, J. H. (1980) The work-family problem: Overloading the system. In B. Forisha and B. Goldman, eds., *Outsiders on the Inside: Women and Organizations.* Englewood Cliffs, N.J.: Prentice-Hall.

Pleck, J. H. (1981) Wives' Employment, Role Demands, and Adjustment: Final Report. Unpublished manuscript, Center for Research on Women, Wellesley College.

Pleck, J. H., and Rustad, M. (1980) Husbands' and Wives' Time in Family Work and Paid Work in the 1975-76 Study of Time Use. Working Paper No. 63, Wellesley College.

Pleck, J. H., Staines, G., and Lang, L. (1978) Work and Family Life: First Reports on Work-Family Interference and Workers' Formal Childcare Arrangements, From the 1977 Quality of Employment Survey. Unpublished manuscript, Wellesley College.

Powell, K. G. (1963) Personalities of children and child-rearing attitudes of mothers. In F. I. Nye and L. W. Hoffman, eds., *The Employed Mother in America.* Chicago: Rand McNally.

Propper, A. M. (1972) The relationship of maternal employment to adolescent roles, activities, and parental relationships. *Journal of Marriage and the Family* 34:417-421.

Rapoport, R., and Rapoport, R. (1971) *Dual-Career Families*. Baltimore, Md.: Penguin.

Rieber, M., and Womack, M. (1967) The intelligence of preschool children as related to ethnic and demographic variables. *Exceptional Children* 34:609-614.

Robinson, J. (1977a) *How Americans Use Time: A Social-Psychological Analysis*. New York: Praeger.

Robinson, J. (1977b) *Changes in Americans' Use of Time: 1965-1975—A Progress Report*. Cleveland, Ohio: Communciations Research Center, Cleveland State University.

Robinson, J. (1980) Housework technology and household work. In S. F. Berk, ed., *Women and Household Labor*. Beverly Hills, Calif.: Sage Publications.

Robinson, J., Yerby, J., Feiweger, M., and Somerick, N. (1977) Sex-role differences in time use. *Sex Roles* 3:443-458.

Rouman, J. (1956) School children's problems as related to parental factors. *Journal of Education Research* 1:105-112.

Roy, P. (1963) Adolescent roles: rural-urban differentials. In F. I. Nye and L. W. Hoffman, eds., *The Employed Mother in America*. Chicago: Rand McNally.

Safilios-Rothschild, C. (1970) The study of family power structure: a review, 1960-1969. *Journal of Marriage and the Family* 32:539-552.

Sanik, M. (1977) A Twofold Comparison of Time Spent in Household Work in Two-Parent, Two-Child Households: Urban New York State in 1967-68 and 1977. Ph.D. dissertation, Cornell University.

Sears, R. S., Maccoby, E. E., and Levin, H. (1957) *Patterns of Child Rearing*. Evanston, Ill.: Row, Peterson.

Slomczynski, K. M., Miller, J., and Kohn, M. L. (in press) Stratification, work, and values: a Polish-U.S. comparison. *American Sociological Review*.

Smith, H. C. (1969) An Investigation of the Attitudes of Adolescent Girls Toward Combining Marriage, Motherhood, and a Career. Ph.D. dissertation, Columbia University.

Stolz, L. M. (1960) Effects of maternal employment on children: evidence from research. *Child Development* 31:749-783.

Terman, L. M. (1916) *The Measurement of Intelligence*. Boston: Houghton Mifflin.

Vanek, J. (1974) Time spent in housework. *Scientific American* 231(5):116-120.

Voydanoff, P. (1980) *The Implications of Work-Family Relationships for Productivity*. Scarsdale, N.Y.: Work in America Institute, Inc.

Walker, K. E. (1970a) Time spent by husbands in household work. *Family Economics Review* 4:8-11.

Walker, K. E. (1970b) How much help for working mothers? The children's role. *Human Ecology Forum* 1(2):13-15.

Walker, K., and Gauger, W. (1973) Time and its dollar value in household work. *Family Economics Review* Fall:8-13.

Walker, K., and Woods, M. (1976) *Time Use: A Measure of Household Production of Goods and Services*. Washington, D.C.: American Home Economics.

Weintraub, M. (1977) Children's Responses to Maternal Absence: An Experimental Intervention Study. Paper presented at the Society for Research in Child Development meetings, New Orleans.

Woods, M. B. (1972) The unsupervised child of the working mother. *Developmental Psychology* 6:14-25.

Yarrow, M. R., Scott, P., De Leeuw, L., and Heinig, C. (1962) Childrearing in families of working and non-working mothers. *Sociometry* 25:122-140.

4

The Impact of Mother's Work on the Family as an Economic System

Marianne A. Ferber, *University of Illinois,* **and**
Bonnie Birnbaum, *University of Illinois*

Many see the family as a symbol of security and permanence, a stable core in a changing world, the one institution dominated by mutual affection and altruism rather than economic calculation. Like most simple generalizations, this one contains some truths but also some serious misconceptions. As we shall see, the family continues to be a central institution in our society, and the vast majority of people continue to live in families most of their lives. At the same time, a growing proportion move through a succession of different family units, and only a small minority of these families are now composed of the traditional father-breadwinner, mother-homemaker, and children. Similarly, men and women share their lives and raise their children because of emotional, social, and even religious ties, but few would deny that economic factors affect the formation of a family unit, the way its members share responsibilities and rewards, and the probability that it will last.

In recent years the family has undergone important changes that have affected its fundamental nature. The most significant of these changes has been the rapid influx of women into the labor market and the corresponding decrease in the proportion of families with full-time homemakers. The purpose of this paper is to examine existing research concerned with the implications of this trend for the family as an eco-

---

We want to acknowledge a large debt to a book which was published shortly before we began on this chapter, and on which we heavily relied as a source: Ralph E. Smith, ed., (1979a) *The Subtle Revolution: Women at Work.*

nomic system and how different ways of allocating time and responsibilities within the family affect the welfare of its members. In addition to critically reviewing the current state of knowledge, we also suggest directions for further work to be done.

The first section briefly describes the traditional family as an economic unit. The second section examines to what extent the family's existence can be explained by traditional economic theory as an institution that helps its members to achieve maximum well-being. The third section is concerned with recent trends and developments. It documents both the continued dominance of the family and the increasing diversity of family life-styles. The fourth section reviews some useful work analyzing these developments. It focuses on recent changes in the family, with particular emphasis on the growing influx of women into the labor market (one of the prime causes of these changes). This section closes by suggesting directions for new research to expand our knowledge and our ability to develop useful family policies. The final section discusses the availability of data sets that would make possible further empirical research needed to improve our understanding of the interactions of changes in the family and in the economy.

THE TRADITIONAL FAMILY AS AN ECONOMIC UNIT

According to the Bureau of the Census definition, which is generally used by economists, the family is a group of people related by blood or marriage and living in one household. While individual members may own property and retain some of their own earnings, the emphasis is on the family as a unit. Each member is expected to carry out his or her responsibilities, not primarily to barter with other family members but rather to ensure their well-being. By the same token the family is expected to provide for each member's needs to the extent it is able, and quite independently of the individual's contribution. Thus, the very young, the very old, the disabled, the unemployed, and so forth are entitled to share in the same standard of living as the rest of the family.

In precapitalist economies, when the family enterprise was the dominant economic unit, all family members capable of working participated in production. There was always some specialization and division of labor. Adult males generally undertook tasks that required the greatest physical strength and those that necessitated prolonged absences. Mature women often did work involving great endurance. Children and the elderly would do less exacting tasks. But everyone participated in productive activity (Degler, 1980). This was true not only among primitive societies, but in the preindustrial period in the United States as well. The husband would tend the horses and plow the fields; the wife would milk the cows and feed the chickens. Grandma was likely to sew, knit, and participate in the care of infants; grandpa would help repair equipment and furniture; and the children would collect the eggs and churn the butter.

It was only when production moved into factories and work, for the most part, became employment that the situation changed significantly. Adult men more often accepted jobs away from home. While this was also true for many poor women[1] and even children, middle-class wives increasingly became facilitators of consumption rather than producers, and many working-class wives aspired to this role.[2] The heavy burden these working women carried makes this understandable. It was then that the traditional housewife first came into existence.

Women's activities were increasingly confined to the care of children, the nurturing of husband, and the maintenance of the home (Degler,

[1] As Scott and Tilly (1980) point out, young women of the working class were commonly expected to work and to turn over their earnings to the family. It was considerably less common for married women to work, but they generally did when the family was in urgent need of money.

[2] A broader and more reasonable concept of production would include many household activities. Economists have, in recent years, pointed out that combining purchased items with services to provide commodities for direct use is, in fact, a form of production. Sociologists have suggested (Berk and Berk, 1978:32) "the only difference between production and consumption is the 'timetable' on which utility is obtained. On the one hand, it is possible to obtain some satisfactions (and dissatisfactions) immediately through the performance of a particular activity. We normally call this consumption. On the other hand, it is possible to obtain utility some time after the commodities are produced. This is viewed as production."

Common usage, however, ignores these views. We all know that women who are asked whether they work are expected to, and generally do, answer either "yes, I have a job," or "no, I am a housewife." For convenience the word "work" is often used in that sense. The hidden rationale, not altogether unrealistic, implies that work and production refer to activities that determine the socioeconomic status of the family. In earlier days, husband and wife both were productive in this sense, each contributing to output in the family enterprises. But with the Industrial Revolution came the loss of this production function of the family (Kanter, 1977). It is now the earnings of the man (along with whatever unearned income some families may receive) that determines the kind of house the family will live in, the neighborhood where it will be located, the schools the children will go to, and the amount of consumer durables and other goods the family can buy. The activities of the homemaker, no doubt, make a great difference in the neatness within the house and perhaps the yard. The homemaker also helps the children with homework, chooses and maintains the durables, and makes the meals enjoyable occasions as opposed to simply a way of filling the stomach. If she does well, life will be more pleasant for the family, but it is the husband's job (or inherited wealth) that determines whether they are upper class, middle class, or poor. The husband is the breadwinner, and how much of it he wins is more crucial than the way the wife slices and serves it.

1980). These activities were seen as private, nonproductive, domesticated, expressive, and important (Oakley, 1980). The true woman's place was unquestionably as daughter, sister, or most of all wife and mother. Therefore, domesticity was among the virtues most prized (Welter, 1978). There was no longer a farm right outside the house or a shop downstairs where she could work with the children trailing along or while dinner was cooking. At the same time, household size declined because there were fewer boarders, servants, siblings, and parents living with couples (Korbin, 1978). One effect of this was to reduce the number of adults available in households to help take care of youngsters, while at the same time the period of childhood was considerably extended. Thus, the typical traditional family emerged.

According to the stereotype of this family, the responsibility to be the breadwinner rested squarely on the shoulders of the man. If the woman also entered the labor market, it was generally assumed she was either compensating for his inadequacy, working for pin money, or selfishly pursuing a career at the expense of her household responsibilities. If the children worked while they lived at home, they presumably did so in order to be able to spend on extras or perhaps because the parents thought it was good for their moral fiber, but usually only among the poor did they work to raise the family's standard of living.

According to this same stereotype, the responsibility for spending the family's money and for determining and distributing its savings was not as clearly allocated. But here too there were some accepted norms. The wife made most of the purchases, with the exception of the house, the car, and possibly some other durables. This does not mean, however, that she made the decisions on these expenditures. It was generally the husband who decided how much money was to be allocated to various categories of goods and services or even to individual items. For those he used, he was likely to tell her exactly what to buy, as on occasion the children may also have done. In other words, for many types of goods the wife was the purchasing agent rather than the decision maker, even when she did the shopping. She was even less likely to have the main say about major items often purchased jointly by the couple or in determining what type of financial assets to accumulate (Davis, 1976).

While more and more goods and services used by households gradually came to be produced outside the home, a great deal of time and effort was still required to acquire them, maintain them, and use them to produce the kind of standard of living to which American families aspired. It was the wife who had the responsibility for doing this, as well as for providing the many services required to maintain a family. The husband may have helped with her household responsibilities, but not to the extent that it might interfere with his work. And she was not to expect him to do more than he volunteered to do for fear of being considered a demanding wife. Indeed, her great virtue was submissiveness (Skolnick and Skolnick, 1977). She could ask or even require the children to do some chores if these did not interfere with their education or jobs, but preferably only to the extent that these tasks furthered their own development.

As we have seen, the responsibilities of providing for the family were different for each member. But the benefits the family could provide were either conferred on everyone equally or allocated to individuals according to need. It was, however, primarily the head of the household who, in the final analysis, determined the family's life-style, both by being responsible for the income on which it so crucially depended and by making the most important decisions, thus providing the parameters within which the other members of the family had to operate. Hence, there is little basis for the contention by Degler (1980) that although woman was confined to the house, she now had a sphere in which she was superior.

This was the traditional family, once widely accepted as the backbone of American society. Economists, concerned primarily with market transactions, were interested only in the family's relations with the rest of the economy as supplier of resources and consumer of final goods. Except for the pioneering work of Margaret Reid (1934), it was not until the 1960s, when the family was undergoing changes at an accelerating rate, that economic analysis began to be applied to relationships within the family. As we shall see in the next section, the new approach proved to be an interesting combination of sophisticated methodology and assumptions that were often quite unrealistic or outdated. It produced some useful insights, but also many questionable conclusions.

ECONOMIC ANALYSIS OF THE FAMILY[3]

In recent years economists have used economic theory more boldly to explain behavior outside the monetary market sector. . . . As a result, racial discrimination, fertility, politics, crime, education, statistical decision making, adversary situations, labor-force participation, the uses of "leisure" time, and other behavior are better understood. Indeed, economic theory may well be on its way to providing a unified framework for *all* behavior involving scarce resources, nonmarket as well as market, nonmonetary as well as monetary, small group as well as "competitive." (Becker, 1974:299)

---

[3] The material in this section is in significant part based on Ferber and Birnbaum (1977). Sawhill (1977) discussed many of the same issues and made the same points, as did Berk and Berk (1978).

This is a proud claim by the man who did more than any other to break down the barriers that in earlier days constrained economists to a much narrower sphere and whose extensive contributions to the study of the family have earned him an undisputed claim to the title of father of the new home economics.

Gary S. Becker, together with his colleagues and disciples,[4] has developed neoclassical models of the family as a unit that is rational in the sense that it maximizes its well-being. These models explain the family's behavior by using relative prices and income as the main variables.[5] The models are elegant in their simplicity, and a growing volume of sophisticated empirical research shows that they do make a contribution to the understanding of household behavior. However, they ignore many interesting and important aspects of a far more complex reality, and have only limited explanatory power and even less success in predicting changes over time.[6] Furthermore, the underlying assumption that people always behave rationally leads to the baffling implication generally found in this work that all outcomes are in some sense optimal (Blau, 1977). Also, that assumption all too often leads to a tacit endorsement of the status quo.

The cornerstone of this theory of rational household behavior is that rather than acting in response to the dictates of tradition, husband and wife are expected to allocate their time according to relative advantage so they can maximize the amounts of commodities available to the family.[7] At the same time, one finds frequent references to women's household and child-rearing *duties*, while husbands *help* their wives with

---

[4] Becker's seminal work was "A Theory of the Allocation of Time" (1965). Since then a great deal of work has been done to apply economic tools to the nonmarket sectors. Much of the original work was done by scholars trained and/or located at the University of Chicago and Columbia University, often under the auspices of the National Bureau of Economic Research. A substantial portion of the articles published have appeared in the *Journal of Political Economy*, published by the University of Chicago.

[5] While the members of this school of economics would acknowledge no affinity for Karl Marx, it is difficult to avoid the impression that they too attach very great importance to economic variables as the fundamental basis of much of human behavior.

[6] As Clair (Vickery) Brown (1980) points out, for instance, numerous models of labor force participation uniformly underestimated by far the extent of its change. And some of them were mistaken in predicting the direction of the change. As Goode (1974) states, Becker's suggestion that late marriages and difficulty of divorce will be correlated is not substantiated by the facts.

[7] The possibility that the family itself is an inefficient unit, which cannot take advantage of the economies of scale as could a commune, is never considered. Perhaps even more surprising, in view of the fact that Becker was a pioneer in suggesting that employers may forego profit maximization in order to indulge their taste for discrimination, is the failure to consider that spouses may forego maximization for a variety of personal reasons, and that traditions act as constraints on maximizing models.

household work. Some would exclude even the possibility of male help in household work by assuming men's time at home is entirely unproductive (Willis, 1974); this was done presumably to avoid mathematical complications in the model. They appear to be on firmer ground when they assume that women earn less than men in the labor market. But upon closer examination we find they explain these lower earnings largely in terms of lower investments in human capital by women, which in turn are explained by their family responsibilities. Thus, we come full circle: Women spend more time on housework because they earn less in the labor market, and they earn less in the labor market because they spend more time on housework.

Furthermore, the theory that an increase in the relative market efficiency of any member would result in a reallocation of time of all other members toward consumption activities that would permit the former to spend more time in market activities (Becker, 1965) receives little support from time-use studies. On the contrary, we find that the time husbands spend on household work changes remarkably little when the wife enters the labor market, while her leisure time decreases sharply (Robinson, 1977a, 1977b). Nor, as we see later, is there evidence of marked differences in expenditures on services between households with the wife in the labor market and those with a full-time homemaker. Such behavior is not readily explained in terms of rational maximization, but can be understood easily in terms of the traditional view that the household is the woman's responsibility.[8]

The second premise of the new home economics is that the family is an economic unit that allocates production at home and in the market and shares consumption as well as the investments in the physical and human capital of its members (Mincer and Polachek, 1974). However, there are also recurrent references in the new home economics to the fact that assuming a single utility function for the family is not altogether realistic.[9] Such an approach ignores the fact that husband and wife do not necessarily share the same tastes and preferences, and that there tends to be a considerable difference in the extent to which each influences the decision of how to allocate income (Galbraith, 1973:35):

[8] It is interesting to note that in the extensive new home economics literature, which discusses specialization in terms of relative advantage, the possibility of the wife earning more than her husband in the labor market is never mentioned. Admittedly, such cases are unusual in the real world, but they are by no means nonexistent.

[9] Nerlove (1974) was one of the first to question the suggestion originally made by Samuelson (1956) that, under appropriate conditions, it could be assumed that the family would behave as if it were an individual maximizer.

The common reality is that the household involves a simple but highly important division of labor. With the receipt of the income, in the usual case, goes the *basic* authority over its use . . . a natural authority resides with the person who earns the money. This entitles him [sic] to be called the head of the family.

There is, therefore, good reason to believe that maximizing family income does not necessarily mean maximizing the well-being of all individual members. The person who has little say within the family gladly might trade some income for more influence in order to maximize her current well-being. Similarly, because there is diminishing utility involved in spending longer and longer hours on a single type of work, the traditional specialization of husband and wife in market and household work respectively is not likely to be optimal. Most important, however, is the problem that static models tend to ignore inevitable life-cycle changes, including the virtual certainty that one of the spouses will have to carry on alone.

When considering the family consisting of husband, wife, and children, it is important to remember that the children will grow up and that as they do the value of their household work declines precipitously. Meantime, if the wife is a full-time homemaker, her worth in the labor market also declines. This means that the value of her contribution to the family over her lifetime (the value of her work at home plus earnings) is considerably lower than that of the woman who remains in the labor market,[10] even though her contribution may not be less when there are young children in the home.

The reduced earning power of the homemaker becomes even more serious if, for whatever reasons, the marriage is terminated, or if the breadwinner becomes unemployed or incapacitated. The husband, too, is likely to have problems if he has to fend for himself domestically. In addition, he may be expected to pay alimony, child support, or both if his ex-wife is not employed. Thus, complete specialization is a very high-risk proposition for either spouse, especially now that many people can no longer turn to an extended family for support.

It is ironic that just at the time when the traditional family (with its strong proscriptions against divorce and its obligation to take care not only of children but also of the destitute and elderly) was disappearing, economists found ways of portraying the traditional division of labor between husband and wife as the outcome of rational decision making. As we have seen, they do this in part by accepting stereotypes, making

---

[10] For estimates based on opportunity cost (market earnings given up in order to remain at home) for a sample of clerical workers, as well as estimates based on market cost, see Ferber and Birnbaum (1980).

unrealistic assumptions, and at times disregarding the fact that families, unlike their models, are not static.

Apart from these difficulties, questions must be raised about the narrowly economic focus of the new home economics. The application of the tools of economists to areas that previously had been the preserve of the softer social sciences has given rise to the hope that we are moving toward a single structure of hypotheses about social behavior, supported by research in several different fields. Two decades hence we may discover that we have created a rather impressive body of social science literature, which if not unified may at least be confirmatory (Goode, 1974). But this hope will surely not be realized as long as the new approach fails to take note of powerful nonmarket variables whose effects may run counter to those of income variables (Goode, 1974).

When models take into account nonmonetary variables, without pretending to monetize them by attaching a purely hypothetical and imaginary value,[11] a further breakthrough in the direction of greater realism and relevance to policy issues is likely to occur. Such factors as tradition, status, direct satisfaction and dissatisfaction with work, and dependence upon or independence from others, while admittedly not easy to measure, surely would help explain many of the unaccounted-for variations between individuals and changes over time, and most likely would contribute to the resolution of some puzzles that existing theory has done little to resolve.

Unresolved puzzles still abound. For example, according to Becker (1974), the more the man's earnings exceed those of the woman, the greater the incentive for the two to get married. Why is the same not true when the earnings gap is in the opposite direction? The greater a woman's value in the market compared to her contribution in the household, the more likely she is to work for money. Why does she not cut down comparably on her hours of household work?[12] Economic vari-

---

[11] As Goode (1974:347) points out, "The monetary equivalent, so tempting to the economist because of his past training, can create both obstacles and factual errors in the analysis. . . ." A good example of this is when the value of the work of full-time homemakers is assumed to be equal to the wages earned by women in the labor market even though the potential earnings of the former are likely to be lower, if only because they have less labor market experience.

[12] Claire Vickery (1979) suggests this is because purchased and home-produced commodities are not interchangeable, as is generally assumed. Also, as Berk and Berk (1978:462) point out, there is a lack of substitutability among the contributions of all the household members, as shown by evidence that, holding income constant, husbands in high status jobs do a bit more household work. They suggest this shows that the division of household labor is not entirely a function of productive capacity: "*Who* you are matters as much as *what* you are able to contribute."

ables often do reasonably well in explaining variations of behavior between members of the same ethnic, religious, national, or other group, but economists have made little progress in explaining differences between groups. Often the problem is avoided by examining variations only within groups. These are merely a few examples of questions in search of answers, but they should suffice to demonstrate the need for broadening the approach to the study of the family. Only by taking into account the institutional setting and its changing structure can we understand the framework within which and upon which economic variables operate.

Some of the nonmonetary variables can be introduced in quantitative form—for instance, by using attitude scales,[13] as is often done in the other social sciences, or by using dummy variables. Another way to improve upon the current models is to supplement the neoclassical approach with game theory. This could help reduce the tendency to treat the family as a unit and put more emphasis on interpersonal relationships. Some steps in this direction have been taken by a few innovative researchers, such as Manser and Brown (1979, 1980) and Horney and McElroy (1980).

Before considering in greater detail the directions new research has been taking or should take in order to achieve better understanding and greater insight, we first briefly examine existing evidence of recent changes in the roles of men and women and their impact on the family.

RECENT TRENDS IN ECONOMIC AND FAMILY STATUS OF WOMEN AND MEN[14]

The past 20 years have brought dramatic changes in the typical American family. During this period the overall female employment rate rose by more than 50 percent (for married women with children living with their spouses, the rate doubled). Birth rates dropped by 40 percent, and divorce rates doubled (Hofferth and Moore, 1979). Thus, labor force and demographic trends have combined to produce a new modal family—one in which both spouses participate (at least for part of their married life) in the labor force, their expected number of children is

---

[13] Economists generally look askance on the use of such data, but Bowen and Finnegan (1969:237) concede that "While it is always dangerous to attempt to determine why individuals do what they do by asking them, economists probably err more in ignoring interview data of this kind than in overvaluing it."

[14] A good deal of the information on these trends and on their implications is covered in *The Subtle Revolution: Women at Work* (Smith, 1979a). This section of the paper draws heavily upon that material.

relatively small, and there is a good chance they may eventually divorce and marry other partners.

At the same time, and in interaction with these demographic and labor force changes, came shifts in allocation of time within the household (particularly a decrease in home production time for the wife) and a change in attitudes of men and women toward their roles and toward the traditional American family. The purpose of this section is to explore some of these trends in an attempt to provide some insight into the current status of the American family and the directions it might take in the near future.

Labor Force Trends

The growing participation of wives in the labor force during the past decade has occurred to a great extent among mothers. Labor force participation for wives (husband present) with children under 18 increased from 40 percent to 54 percent from 1970 to 1980, while the increase for wives with no children under 18 was only from 42 percent to 48 percent (Bureau of Labor Statistics 1980a; Johnson, 1979.).[15] One of the consequences of the rapid increase in the number of employed mothers of small children has been an increase in the proportion of women voluntarily participating in part-time employment (Barrett, 1979). Between 1965 and 1977 the number of workers on voluntary part-time schedules increased almost three times as fast as the number of full-time workers. Only one-fourth of mothers of preschool children who were employed during 1975 had a job on a full-time basis all year. For mothers of 6- to 17-year olds, the percentage was 40 percent (Hayghe, 1976).

Women's Earnings, Occupations, and Unemployment

Although increasing numbers of women have entered the labor force in recent years, the ratio of the median earnings of full-time, year-round women workers to that of men actually dropped from about 63 percent in the mid-1950s to 59 percent in 1977 (Barrett, 1979; Women's Bureau, 1979). This earnings gap cannot be explained fully by age, education, or prior work experience. It holds true in all regions of the country,

---

[15] This can be explained by the fact that wives with no children under 18 are generally either young wives, some of whom may still be in school, or older wives who have reached retirement age.

and for both blacks and whites.[16] One factor that does play an important role in creating the discrepancy between men's and women's wages is occupational segregation. More than two-thirds of employed women hold jobs in so-called female occupations (Barrett, 1979). Female occupations traditionally tend to be characterized by low pay and limited opportunities for advancement.

In addition, with the recent rapid influx of women into the labor market, occupational crowding in these fields has contributed to the slow growth of wages, particularly in the clerical field. According to Barrett (1979), median earnings of female, full-time clerical workers rose only 4.9 percent in real terms between 1965 and 1975 compared with a 25.4 percent increase for all other female workers over the same 10-year period. There is some evidence that among younger women, there is a trend away from clerical occupations and toward professional and managerial positions.[17] However, a recent survey of 5,000 women aged 21 to 31 (Brito and Jusenius, 1978) indicates that despite these trends, the vast majority of young women who expect to be employed at age 35 would prefer to be in typically female occupations.

Not only do women work in a narrow range of jobs, but they also often earn less than men in the same occupation. This is true even when they work the same number of hours and when relevant characteristics have been held constant. This results partly from differences in job assignments and titles within occupational groupings. For example, within the clerical profession most male clerical workers are post office mail carriers, shipping and receiving clerks, stock clerks, and storekeepers. Women are secretaries, typists, telephone operators, bank tellers, and bookkeepers (Barrett, 1979). Also, Blau (1976b) found that even when men and women are employed in the same detailed occupational category, they tend to be segregated by firm, with women concentrated in the lower-paying establishments.

Another factor which causes actual earnings to be even lower than indicated by the earnings gap is the relatively high proportion of women who are part-time workers (approximately one-quarter of the women

---

[16] The wage gap between nonwhite women and men is considerably less than that for whites; black women earn 23 percent less than black men while white women earn 42 percent less than white men. However, this is because black men earn relatively less than white men, rather than because black women earn more than white women.

[17] According to tabulations provided by the U.S. Department of Labor, Bureau of Labor Statistics, and cited in Barrett (1979), the percentage of young women workers (ages 20 to 34) in clerical occupations decreased from 42 percent in 1968 to 38 percent in 1977. The percentage of young women in professional, technical, and managerial jobs increased from 20 percent to 24 percent in the same time period.

in the labor force in 1976). Part-time employment is heavily concentrated in low-wage occupations. In general, part-time jobs are a subset of the traditional women's jobs. In addition, the wage rates of women part-time workers are usually lower than those of women full-time workers in the same occupations (Smith, 1979b).

Legislation in the 1960s and 1970s has made discrimination on the basis of sex illegal. More recently, affirmative action programs have shifted the emphasis from prohibiting discrimination to redressing past inequities and taking positive action to support future opportunities for women.[18] Thus, progress has been made in redressing the legal and institutional barriers to equality in earnings for women (although enforcement lags behind the letter of the law). As yet, however, changes have been slow in coming—partly due to the slow evolution of women's aspirations and employers' stereotypes as to what is women's work.

In addition to lower wages relative to men and a narrow range of jobs, women also experience greater unemployment. Moreover, there are important trends with respect to the difference in male and female unemployment. First, the differential in unemployment tends to be greater during periods of low unemployment. In part, this can be explained by the fact that many women are eager to work when jobs are plentiful, and drop out of the labor force when they cannot find jobs. Secondly, in addition to cyclical variations, there has tended to be a long-term increase in the differential, at least between the early 1960s and 1980. (This is consistent with the occupational crowding that has characterized female occupations.) The gap closed for some months after that, but the period is too short to draw any firm conclusions about change in the long run.

Because women traditionally have been marginal workers, the seriousness of unemployment for them generally has been minimized. However, most women work because of economic need. Nearly two-thirds of all women in the labor force in 1978 were single, widowed, divorced or separated, or had husbands who earned less than $10,000 in 1977. Even among those who had husbands present who earned more, the earnings of the wife generally made a substantial contribution to the family's income, and the wife's unemployment generally resulted in a reduced standard of living for her family. For example, when the wife

[18] A 1981 U.S. Supreme Court decision in the case of *County of Washington* v. *Guntner* may lead the way for even greater change. The decision discussed the Bennett Amendment to title 7 of the Civil Rights Act of 1964. The Bennett Amendment had prohibited all pay discrimination claims by women, except in situations involving less pay for equal work. This decision leaves open the door to further testing in the courts on the far broader basis of work of comparable worth.

worked full-time year-round in 1978, she contributed 38 percent of her family's income. The wife's contribution is particularly important for low-income families. For families with incomes under $10,000, the wife's contribution was 64 percent; with incomes between $10,000 and $15,000, it was 50 percent (Bureau of Labor Statistics, 1980b). In female-headed households, the woman's contribution was, of course, crucial—as high as 85 percent for the lowest income group.[19]

Trends in the Allocation of Time

Although there have been great changes in the technology and services available to households, data on time spent on home production show little change in the total amount of time housewives spent on housework from the mid-1920s through the mid-1960s (Vanek, 1974). The way time was distributed among various chores showed some change—mainly, there was a decline in more of the routine and repetitive work and an increase in managerial tasks—but there was an amazing constancy in the level of work (approximately 51 to 55 hours per week).

More recent data on time allocation provide conflicting evidence on whether or not significant changes have taken place since the 1960s. Gauger and Walker (1980) conclude that hours of household work have remained relatively stable. In their study, diary data were collected in 1967-68 for a sample of 1,378 families in Syracuse, N.Y. and again in 1977, this time for a sample of 210 families with husband, wife, and two children. These data indicate consistency in household work time over the decade for this subgroup of American families. Table 4-1 summarizes the findings based on the Syracuse sample.

On the other hand, however, comparison of data from two time-use diary studies both conducted by the Survey Research Center at the University of Michigan (one in 1965 and one in 1975) shows that women aged 18 to 65 in urban households where at least one member was in the labor force reported substantially less family care in 1975. This was true for both employed women (a decrease from 27 to 24 hours per week) and housewives (a decrease from 53 to 48 hours per week). Robinson (1980) analyzed the data so that differences in employment status, marital status, family composition, age, and socioeconomic status between the 1965 and 1975 samples were held constant. Once these adjustments had been made, he found that the decrease in housework

---

[19] For female-headed households in 1978 the woman's contribution was 85 percent for families with incomes under $5,000; 84 percent for those with incomes between $5,000 and $10,000; and 80 percent for those between $10,000 and $15,000.

TABLE 4-1 Household Work Time of Husband and Wife in Families with Two Children (Syracuse sample)

	Youngest Child	Employed-Wife Families[a]			Non Employed-Wife Families		
		Husband (Hours[b])	Wife (Hours[b])	N[c]	Husband (Hours[b])	Wife (Hours[b])	N[c]
1967–68	12–17	1.5	5	19	1.5	7	27
	6–11	1.5	5	24	1.5	7	64
	2–5	1.5	6	29	1.5	8	96
	1	1.5	6	10	3	9	53
	Under 1	1.5	8	7	1.5	10	66
1977	12–17	2	6	7	1.5	7	21
	6–11	2	5	4	1.5	7	29
	2–5	3	5	11	2	8	31
	1	3	8	13	3	9	38
	Under 1	3	7	21	3	10	35

[a] Wife employed 15 or more hours per week.
[b] Average hours per day–these figures should be multiplied by 7 days for a work-week figure.
[c] N equals number of families.

SOURCE: William Gauger and Kathryn Walker (1980) chart 2.

was only about 2.5 hours per week for the sample as a whole. This decrease in women's home production was not offset by any increase in men's participation in household chores. When the differences in sample composition were adjusted for, it turned out that men actually contributed 5 percent less time to household work in 1975 than in 1965 (Robinson, 1980). He also found that women's family care was higher in those households where the husbands also spent more time on home production. In a separate analysis comparing households which varied by ownership of different appliances in 1975, he found no evidence that differences in technology could explain the decline in housework. Alternative explanations include a decrease in standards of household production, an increase in efficiency in performing household tasks, or both.

In addition to recent decreases in household time, the 1975 survey shows decreases in market time for both employed married men and women. Although no analysis is available which includes adjustments for differences in sample composition, the unadjusted estimates show a decrease in hours worked for pay per week from 38.4 to 30.1 for married women and from 51.3 to 47.4 for married men (Robinson, 1977a). The decrease in paid work time for men most likely results from earlier retirement, longer vacations, and so forth. On the other hand, the decline in market time for married women most likely reflects the influx of women into part-time jobs. One result of this decline in both market and nonmarket work for married women in the labor force has been a 20 percent increase (since 1965) in the free time available to them (Robinson, 1980).

There is, however, some evidence that the decline in hours of market time of married men and women found in the Michigan survey may be overstated (Vickery, 1979). The Current Population Survey (Bureau of Labor Statistics, 1976), which is based on a national sample of 50,000 households, shows a much smaller decrease in hours on the job. Table 4-2 summarizes the Michigan Survey Research Center and the Current Population Survey (CPS) results for 1965 and 1975. For all groups (except married employed women in 1975) the number of hours in the labor market is higher in the CPS estimates than in the Michigan data. In part, this may be due to differences in definitions (see footnotes to Table 4-2). In addition the relative decline in hours between 1965 and 1975 for both men and women is much smaller in CPS data. The CPS data are based on a much larger sample but have the disadvantage of being reported by one person for the entire household and are not based on diary data. Surveys using both a large sample and diary techniques would

TABLE 4-2   Time Use: Married Men and Women, 1965 and 1975

	Hours in Labor Market		Hours of Family Care		
	Employed Men	Employed Women	Employed Men	Employed Women	House-wives
Michigan Survey Research Center[a]					
1965 urban data	51	38	9.0	28.8	50.0
1975 urban data	47	30	9.7	24.9	44.3
Current Population Survey[b]					
1965	45	35			
1975	43	34			

[a] Michigan Survey Research Center data are taken from Robinson (1977b, Table 4). In this data set, hours in the labor market are defined as all work plus breaks plus commuting.
[b] Current Population Survey data are taken from Bureau of Labor Statistics, (1976, Table 25). In this data set, hours in the labor market are defined as actual number of hours worked during survey week, as reported by one individual in the household for all household members.

be useful in resolving this inconsistency, but would be extremely expensive.

Trends in Marital and Childbearing Patterns

Much has been written in the past decade that indicates increasing concern about the future of the family as the basic unit of American society. What is the basis of this concern? First, Americans are marrying later. Bureau of the Census (1979a) estimates indicate that between 1970 and 1978 there was an increase of about one year in the typical age of first marriage for men and women. It may also be noted that age at first marriage differs little by ethnic groups. It was 22.9 for whites, 22.8 for blacks, and 22.7 for Hispanics in 1975 (Bureau of the Census, 1976a). Another way of looking at the delay in marriage is that 48 percent of the women who were 20 to 24 years old in 1978 had never been married, compared to 28 percent in 1960 and 36 percent in 1970. The proportion of never-married women 25 to 29 years of age also rose from 10.5 percent to 18 percent between 1970 and 1978.

However, although more young women are delaying marriage, the proportion of never-married women among those aged 35 and over has actually been declining—from 7.2 percent in 1960 to 6.1 percent in 1970 to 5.2 percent in 1978 (Bureau of the Census, 1979a). Thus, the proportion of women who will eventually marry (95 percent according to Hofferth and Moore [1979]) is predicted to decrease only slightly.

A second trend that has elicited concern is the much-publicized increase in divorce. Between 1960 and 1978 the divorce rate climbed from 2.2 per 1,000 population to 5.1. It has been estimated (Glick and Norton, 1979) that if the current level of divorce continues, the proportion of marriages ending in divorce may approximate 40 percent. Although blacks have a higher divorce rate than whites, the proportional increase between the two groups since 1960 has been very similar (Bureau of the Census, 1978). But even with the rapid increase in the divorce rate, the fact remains that most married couples are still living together in their first marriages (Bureau of the Census, 1976b).

One indication that, despite changes in marital patterns, marriage itself is still the cornerstone of American life is the high rate of remarriage. Older-cohort experience indicates that approximately four out of five divorced persons will eventually remarry—five-sixths of the men and three-fourths of the women (Bureau of the Census, 1976a). According to the same data, widowed persons, age for age, are less likely than divorced persons to remarry. In 1975 only 50 percent of widowed persons in their early 50s had remarried (65 percent of the men and 40 percent of the women).[20]

For divorced people, close to one-half of the remarriages occur within three years after the divorce, indicating a trend toward shorter intervals between marriages. However, there is some variation by ethnic group, with blacks reporting longer intervals than whites between divorce and remarriage.

A third area that has elicited much attention in recent years is the trend toward a preference for smaller family size. Although there has been some recent evidence of a stabilization in birth expectations, the average number of lifetime births expected by wives 18 to 24 years old has declined from 2.4 per woman in 1971 to 2.1 in 1977. The average number of lifetime births expected by wives 18 to 24 years of age in 1977 did not differ significantly among white, black, or Hispanic wives (Bureau of the Census, 1977b). This is especially interesting because among wives 35 to 39 years old who have nearly completed their child-bearing years, white women have a much lower average number of lifetime births than either black or Hispanic women. The average age of the mother at birth of her last child was 27 in 1970.

Declining birth rates and birth expectations have resulted from an increased preference for smaller family size rather than a trend toward childlessness. The percentage of women aged 18 to 34 reporting that they expect to remain childless is relatively small and varies significantly with the educational level of the woman. As of June 1976, 6.9 percent of wives aged 18 to 34 who had less than a high school education, 8.5 percent who had a high school education, and 14.4 percent who had some college expected to remain childless (Bureau of the Census, 1977a).

Trends Toward Alternative Life-Styles

Although the total number of households has increased by about 25 percent since 1970 (to more than 79 million as of March 1980), the increase among nonfamily households has been much larger than among family households. Nonfamily households (persons living alone or with unrelated persons) increased by 73 percent, while family households grew by only 13 percent (Bureau of the Census, 1980b). However, most households—about 74 percent—are still family households.

From 1970 to 1979 there has also been a shift in the composition of

---

[20] Rates of remarriage are closely related to age. In 1975 the median age at divorce for women 14 to 75 was 27 years, whereas the median age at widowhood was 48 (Bureau of the Census, 1976a).

family households. During this time, the total number of families with children under age 18 increased about 5 percent. However, two-parent families actually decreased by 4 percent, while one-parent families increased by 79 percent (Bureau of the Census, 1980a). Thus, the proportion of one-parent families with children under age 18 living at home increased from 11 percent to 19 percent over the decade. Also, in 1979, 17 percent of families with children under age 18 were maintained by the mother alone and 2 percent by the father alone. This can be compared to 10 percent and 1 percent respectively for 1970.

There are large differences among ethnic groups in family structure. The incidence of one-parent families with children under 18 is much higher (49 percent) among blacks than among whites (15 percent). However, despite this greater incidence, about 68 percent of all one-parent families were maintained by whites in 1979 (Bureau of the Census, 1980a).

An alternative life-style that contrasts sharply with the one-parent family is the extended family. However, only a relatively small group within the population has chosen this form of family arrangement. In 1969 about 89 percent of all families with their own children were nuclear families; fewer than 7 percent consisted of three or more generations (Bureau of the Census, 1972). Moreover, according to recent Census Bureau data, about one-half of U.S. adults actually think that it is a bad idea for older persons to share homes with adult children (Bureau of the Census, 1980c).

WHAT WE KNOW AND WHAT WE NEED TO KNOW ABOUT THE FAMILY
AS AN ECONOMIC UNIT

In the previous section we have examined many of the changes that have been occurring in the family. As we shall see, considerable progress has been made in explaining both the causes and effects of these changes, but a great deal of further work needs to be done before we adequately understand why we arrived where we are today, and where we are likely to go. Nor can we expect to do well in formulating policies to encourage, modify, or inhibit further developments without gaining more profound insight into the relationships between different socioeconomic variables.

In this section we examine some of the most innovative work that has been done in this area, pointing out not only the progress that has been made in explaining causes, effects, and interactions of changes, but also the controversies that continue unresolved and the subjects that remain largely unexplored. In the concluding portion there is particular emphasis on what further research is needed to provide a sound basis for policy formation.

Review of Recent Research: What Have We Learned?

Before beginning our discussion of recent work on the family, a cautionary comment is required. Even where past research results have provided what appear to be conclusive answers, these must not be treated as definitive. For one thing, many relationships are not true for all subgroups. On the contrary, they often are found to differ between urban and rural groups and among various socioeconomic, ethnic, and racial groups. A number of instances of such differences are cited here. Frequently, research has examined either the dominant group only or the population as a whole, in which case the results are primarily applicable to the dominant group. It has also been common to pool smaller groups, which may bring about misleading results. For instance, it is usual to look at nonwhites. If the characteristics of black and Hispanic women are at opposite extremes, they will appear to be more like those of whites than either is separately. The same problem arises when combining non-Christian, or nonurban people.

The absence of better studies may be caused to some degree by a lack of interest on the part of researchers. More likely, it may reflect the fact that it has been difficult to get an adequate sample size for these groups. A very helpful approach, now adopted by a number of data collectors, is to oversample minorities.

A second reason to view existing results with caution is that a finding made at one time may not be applicable at a different time. This is particularly true during a period when everything from economic conditions and institutional arrangements to people's attitudes and beliefs is changing rapidly. Hence, like women's work, the work of researchers is never done, even in those areas in which past controversies appear to have been resolved.

Labor Force Participation As we have seen, there has been a dramatic increase in the labor force participation of married women, although little change in occupational segregation or in the earnings gap between men and women. At the same time, changes have taken place in the nature of the family as an economic and social institution. We have learned a good deal about the complex relationships between the two, but there also remains much to be explained.

A substantial literature, to which both economists and sociologists have contributed, has been accumulated beginning with Mincer's (1960b,

1962) pathbreaking work (Bowen and Finnegan, 1969; Cain, 1966; Oppenheimer, 1970; Sweet, 1968). The contributions of these authors were considerable and should be recognized. They should not, however, continue to be accepted unquestioningly and quoted uncritically.

Mincer's great contribution was to point out that married women do not merely choose between market work and leisure, as is generally true of men, but instead have the third alternative of housework. Hence, their labor supply is likely to be very responsive as wages increase relative to the value of home production. This in large part explains the continuing influx of women into the labor market.

Mincer also discovered what he considered a paradox: He found that cross-sectional data indicate a negative relationship between married women's labor force participation and their husbands' income when everything else, such as wife's education, is held constant. However, over time both these factors have been increasing together. Relying on Friedman's (1957) permanent income hypothesis, he suggests that when a husband's current income is below the level he can plausibly expect to achieve in the long run, the family can achieve its normal level of consumption by a second worker's entering the labor force. This would explain why a wife is just as likely to work even though her young husband has higher real earnings than young men had in earlier years, as long as those earnings are expected to increase over his lifetime.

Not surprisingly, Mincer (1960a) proposed a model that clearly implies that the wife goes to work merely to smooth out family income over time, rather than to accomplish other goals, such as raising the standard of living of the family; safeguarding her own, her children's, and possibly even her husband's future; or perchance even pursuing a career. But it is time to question his assumptions, especially since the clear implication of his theory—that women's labor force participation would be highest during the early years of marriage—is contrary to fact.

Further, the phenomenon that so puzzled Mincer can be explained in simpler and more reasonable ways. It may be relative, not absolute, income that matters. Families may want to have two earners to move from below average to average, or from average to above average, regardless of the mean level of income. Or other conditions may have changed, so that it has become easier or more attractive for women to enter the labor force.

Cain (1966) pointed out the importance of examining not only the labor force participation, but also the extent of this participation, since number of hours worked varies considerably, particularly among women. Unfortunately, even today a really adequate measure taking into account both number of hours per week and number of weeks per year has yet to be developed. Maret-Havens (1977) developed an index based on hours per week and weeks per year as well as number of years worked, but it is complex and has no direct intuitive interpretation (Huber and Spitze, 1982).

The massive work of Bowen and Finnegan (1969) did much to uncover a large number of variables related to women's labor force participation, including the woman's age, number and ages of children, other family income, unemployment rate, industrial and occupational mix, and wage rate. Interesting evidence on this subject has since been added by the guaranteed income experiments in New Jersey, Denver, and Seattle. It was found that married women in low-income families worked considerably less as outside income increased. This trend was true only to a minimal extent for their husbands (Ferber and Hirsch, 1978). Sweet (1968), Oppenheimer (1970), and others pointed to still more factors, such as the increased availability of substitutes for home-produced goods and services, the decline in the number of elderly who are cared for in the family, the higher divorce rate, and increased education. This list seems quite exhaustive. Researchers can, however, be faulted for frequently presenting a simple model of one-way causation, when in reality there are likely to be complex interactions.[21]

Take, for instance, the smaller number of children as an explanation for increased labor force participation. Several studies have found that women's work plans influence their fertility (Clare, 1957; Waite and Stolzenberg, 1976). This confirms the commonsense view that career-oriented women are likely to want fewer children.

Families have become smaller not only because there are fewer children, but also because adults such as parents and other relatives are more likely to live separately. This is considerably more expensive than living in an extended family. It is in part made possible by the additional income women earn, whether it helps them to maintain a separate household if divorced, to save up enough to live separately when they are old, or to help support a parent in a separate establishment.

As pointed out earlier, highly educated women are particularly likely to enter the labor market. Hence, education often is regarded as one more independent factor causing married women to work outside the home. Overlooked is the fact that investment in education is to a considerable extent made in anticipation of entering the labor market. No doubt women acquire education for other reasons, such as improving the mind, becoming a more valuable citizen, meeting a more promising

---

[21] Two sets of authors who do concern themselves with the chicken-egg dilemma are Smith (1979b) and Waite and Stolzenberg (1976).

husband, or becoming a better wife and mother. But in large part, young women acquire their education in order to get better paying and otherwise more rewarding jobs.

Last, we turn to the view that the disproportionate expansion of women's occupations was a fortuitous economic development, making it possible for more women to find jobs. The emphasis is on an upward shift in demand for women workers, but the view ignores a possible shift in the supply (particularly in Oppenheimer, 1970). Yet, elementary economics tells us that (all other things being equal) an increase in demand will result not only in an increase in quantity, but also in an increase in relative price. Women's earnings have not, however, increased relative to those of men. On the contrary, earnings in occupations dominated by women or those experiencing a great influx of women have tended to lag behind (Ferber and Lowry, 1976a). Furthermore, for some decades women's unemployment rate has increased proportionately more than men's. A plausible explanation of these facts is an upward shift in the supply of women, rather than women responding to an upward shift in demand.

One factor contributing to the upward shift in supply was the increase in young working-age women due to the baby boom following World War II. A factor causing married women to enter the labor force may well be the decline in the real earnings of their husbands that is associated with the rapid rate of inflation. While real wages for women have also declined, the wife's contribution nonetheless adds to the family's real income.

Thus, we find that the simple view of economic changes as the cause to which women simply react is not entirely accurate. Changes in attitudes very likely play a role.[22] This is not to suggest that attitudes are shaped in a vacuum or that economic factors of the sort discussed above do not influence them. We would, however, suggest that broader socioeconomic factors also need to be taken into account. The two world wars showed that women could do many jobs from which they had previously been excluded, and the civil rights movement brought emphasis on equal opportunity for all. With growing concern about the population explosion and with the availability of new birth control technologies, a high birthrate became less desirable and more avoidable. Increasing reliance of the elderly on Social Security and pension plans reduced economic returns parents would expect from their children. More recently, an increase in prices more rapid than the increase in

[22] See, for example, Bowen and Finnegan (1969), who recognize that attitudes have changed but argue that this mainly has been the consequence of economic factors.

money income has added to the impetus toward two-earner families. Thus, one would expect increasing acceptance of roles for women other than as full-time mothers and housewives.

Many studies and surveys have documented the extent to which the views of men and women—not only those who are in the labor market, but even housewives—have changed (see, for instance, Ferber, 1982; Oppenheimer, 1970; and Waite, 1982). The tendency of people to go along with accepted standards, which for a long time inhibited the entry of women into the labor market, is beginning to work in the opposite direction. Says Smith (1979b:17): "As women who do not work outside the home become a minority, keeping up with the Joneses will increasingly require Ms. Smith to enter the labor force." Thus, women's increasing labor force participation creates a momentum of its own.

Women's Earnings, Occupations, and Unemployment Having discussed the large change in the labor force participation rate of women, we turn our attention to the absence of major changes in the occupational distribution of women or in the ratio of women's to men's earnings. Continued occupational segregation, considerably greater than in some other countries (Ferber and Lowry, 1977), has been widely noted and discussed (Beller, 1980; Blau and Hendricks, 1979; Polachek, 1976; Zellner, 1975). Many factors have been cited as causing this situation, and there is no reason to assume that they are mutually exclusive. Differences in early childhood training and sex-typicality of parents' occupations (Hofferth, 1980) are among these; so are occupational counseling of boys and girls and training in high school. For instance, Hofferth (1980) finds that being in traditionally female occupational programs, especially vocational programs such as homemaking in high school, is detrimental to the later economic well-being of noncollege women. Last, differences in admissions of young men and women to educational and training programs and discrimination by employers in assigning male and female applicants to various entry positions (Cabral et al., 1982) all have no doubt made their contribution.

One set of factors deserves to be singled out, however, because it shows the interdependence of woman's role in the labor market and in the family. First, potential labor force discontinuity influences occupational choice because there are considerable differences in the extent to which skills deteriorate when a person takes time out (Polachek, 1976). Second, the person who has family responsibilities will be rather reluctant to take a job that has long and inflexible hours or demands a lot of time in travel; rather, such individuals may seek part-time work or a job that permits coordination with children's school schedules. For these reasons, occupational segregation is likely to continue as long as it is primarily women who have the household responsibilities and as long as job-sharing and flexitime arrangements are not widespread. Furthermore, the same considerations that induce women to crowd into female occupations also make it more difficult for them to move up the ladder within any given occupation, causing another kind of segregation in which women have the low-level jobs while men reach the top.

Both these types of segregation, at times referred to as horizontal (men and women in different occupations) and vertical (men and women in the same occupation, but at different levels), contribute significantly to the male-female earnings gap,[23] although they by no means explain all of it. Again, a wide variety of factors has made a contribution, from less work experience and shorter hours for women, to a greater tendency for women to permit the spouse's job to determine location,[24] to outright discrimination. Corcoran and Duncan (1978) found that of the wage gap between white men and white and black women respectively, 2 percent and 11 percent were explained by differences in education, 28 percent and 14 percent by differences in work history, 10 percent and 8 percent by years of training on current job, and 2 percent and −2 percent (the difference here is in the opposite direction) by indicators of labor force attachment, for a total of 42 and 31 percent respectively. The author did not, however, take into account differences in occupational distribution.

Along with low earnings, another problem women encounter is an unemployment rate that for some time increased relative to that for men. There is no evidence this was caused by women's occupational distribution (Barrett and Morgenstern, 1974). Nor is there a convincing case that the problem was primarily caused by women's tendency to be new entrants or reentrants, as is often suggested (Bancroft, 1966; Hoyle, 1967; Niemi, 1975), because this is likely to be more than compensated for by women who remain out of or drop out of the labor force as discouraged workers. Also, higher labor force participation rates are as likely to be caused by those who stay as by new entrants (Blau, 1976a). Last, Bergmann (1973) shows persuasively that women's higher turnover rate would contribute only to their unemployment rate under very un-

[23] Estimates vary from those who claim that most of the earnings gap could be accounted for by differences in occupational distribution, if there were a sufficiently detailed breakdown of categories (Sanborn, 1964; Whitman, 1973), to others who suggest that it accounts for only about 5 percent of the earnings gap (Polachek, 1975). Ferber and Lowry (1976a) concluded that the truth lies in between.

[24] Ferber and Kordick (1978) found that this is true even of very highly educated women and that it does have a negative effect on their earnings.

usual circumstances. Most likely, the same crowding effect mentioned earlier—of more and more women moving into a limited number of occupations, particularly during periods when the overall unemployment rate is relatively moderate—caused the increasing unemployment gap between men and women.[25] In any case the gap rather suddenly closed in 1980 when male unemployment increased far more rapidly, pointing toward a possible change in the relationship from then on.

With respect to the low earnings and high unemployment rate of women, more progress has been made in finding causes than solutions. More work needs to be done to reduce barriers to the entry of women into nontraditional jobs, from improving the effectiveness of current affirmative action legislation or finding more successful approaches and improving equal opportunities for women in government training programs, to encouraging more employer flexibility with respect to job sharing, part-time work, flexitime, and even career patterns, particularly in jobs outside the usual female ghettos.

Allocation of Time   Although women's earnings have not increased as much as men's, they are, nonetheless, considerably higher in general than the value of the time spent on homemaking. In a recent study Ferber and Birnbaum (1980) estimated the total lifetime contribution (the value of housework plus earnings) to her family of a clerical worker who is a high school graduate with two children to be (in 1977 dollars) $176,000 higher if she is employed than if she is a full-time homemaker. The difference for a college graduate is $157,000.[26] For an occupation not noted for high pay, these results make the homemaker option look like a poor choice for the family, especially for the wife and children who may one day have to live largely, or entirely, on her income.

There are many reasons why such a large proportion of couples none-

---

[25] For a more detailed exposition of this view, see Ferber and Lowry (1976b). It should be noted that in recent months, this trend appears to have been reversed.

[26] A number of representative profiles of married women (husbands present) with a specified number of children were selected. Take-home pay was estimated, based on regressions derived for female clerical workers at the University of Illinois, Urbana-Champaign, as reported in Ferber and Birnbaum (1981). The number of hours each would spend on housework was estimated, using Robinson (1977a), and home time was valued at the wage rate of household workers with the same level of education as the homemaker. The total lifetime earnings and the value of home time were added for each of the profiles to obtain their total lifetime contribution.

In our estimates the difference is less for the college graduates because the additional four years in school reduce the maximum number of years they can spend in the labor market, because in clerical occupations there is little reward for college education, and because college graduates cut down less on child care when they are employed (reported

theless opt for the wife to undertake the homemaker role when the children are born. Tradition and the belief that there is no close substitute for a mother's care in a child's early years no doubt play a role. Young couples are likely to be unrealistically optimistic about the nature and durability of their relationship and to discount the probability of the need for the wife to become the breadwinner. They are also often unaware of the extent to which the cost of dropping out of the labor market goes beyond the loss of present earnings because the woman would have to reenter the labor market not only at a lower wage than the one she received earlier, but even farther below the wage she would be earning if she had accumulated more experience. Studies by Hanoch (1976) and Heckman (1979) suggest that estimating wages of women not in the labor market on the basis of those who are overstates their wages by more than 20 percent (Smith, 1980).

In many instances a crucial factor is that the woman tends to be severely overcommitted if she continues full-time employment during the years when there are young children in the home. Through time-use data collected in the mid-1960s (Robinson 1977a, 1977b), it was calculated that women with young children who worked for pay 35 hours

---

in Ferber and Birnbaum, 1980). Incidentally, these estimates do not attempt to measure relative efficiency of each hour spent in home production by the employed wives as compared to full-time homemakers. Research needs to be done on that subject.

The data shown in the text are based on the assumption that high school graduates are in the 25 percent tax bracket and college graduates in the 30 percent bracket. Other job-related expenses, however, were not taken into account. It is interesting to speculate about the extent to which these reduce the gap between women who are in the labor market and those who are not.

The most obvious job-related expenses are for commuting and child care. If we assume that the working woman spends, say, $600 per year on transportation, this would add expenditures of $28,000 for the high school graduate and $25,000 for the college graduate. If each had two children and spent $20 per week 50 weeks a year for child care per child from birth to age 4, and $6 per week for after-school care 50 weeks per year per child from age 5 to 10 (and the full-time homemaker does not use comparable services), this would add expenditures of $11,600. (The amounts are only educated guesses, but appear to be in a reasonable range in 1977 dollars. The figures for child care may seem low. It must be remembered that much of it is subsidized and that many children are cared for by relatives for little or nothing. Furthermore, there are tax credits available for child-care expenses.) Using these data for job-related expenses reduces the difference in the estimated lifetime contribution of the employed wife compared to the full-time homemaker to $136,000 for the high school graduate, and $119,000 for the college graduate.

It should also be noted that women who enter the labor market while receiving Aid to Families with Dependent Children funds and possibly food stamps and Medicaid might find their income from these sources reduced to such an extent that it would amount to a 100 percent tax rate. Obviously, their situation would be entirely different from the one used in our example.

a week also spent an average of about 35 hours on housework, including child care. When the average amount of time spent commuting (4 hours) and fulfilling personal needs (9 hours personal care, 8 hours eating, 56 hours sleeping) were added, such women had only about 21 hours of discretionary time per week. This helps explain why so many women leave the labor market or work part time. Having left the labor force, they find that potential earnings decline, making reentry less attractive over time. It also explains why those women who continue to work have little energy during these years for tackling demanding jobs and climbing the career ladder.[27]

The husband, on the other hand, only spent about 12 hours a week on housework, whether or not his wife was in the labor market.[28] According to one report, fathers added only five minutes of time to child care for every hour mothers reduced their time when they went to work (Robinson, 1977a).

Recent analyses based on diary data collected in the 1975-76 Study of Time Use found that there was a nonsignificant increase of about 15 minutes per week in husbands' family work when their wives were employed (Pleck and Rustad, 1980). These trivial changes are not consistent with the assumption of rational decision making inherent in the new home economics unless one assumes that husbands value leisure far more than wives. Family income over the life cycle, measured in dollar terms, could be increased significantly for many families if the husband undertook enough of the houshold work to make it possible for the wife not to drop out of the labor force during the child-rearing years. Traditional attitudes are, no doubt, an important barrier to this solution.

Numerous surveys, even those made in very recent years, show the extent to which women's role in the household still is regarded as pri-

---

[27] Recent findings by Pleck and Rustad (1980) that the work overload for employed mothers has been considerably reduced applies to those who work only part time. Furthermore, as the authors point out, child care is defined narrowly in this study, and included only when it is the primary activity.

[28] Interestingly, Robinson (1977b) reported at least a small increase between 1965 and 1975, but in a later publication found that when he adjusted for differences in sample composition there was actually a 5 percent decline (Robinson, 1980). Hoffman (1977), however, claims that when family size and age of children are controlled, husbands of working wives do more housework. Also, a recent study (Pleck et al., 1978) finds an increase in husband's family work associated with wife's employment. The increase occurs primarily among parents, and is largely child-care time. However, this study did not use time-diary data, but rather respondents' summary estimates of their time use. Pleck and Rustad (1980) point out that this type of estimate is generally inflated and, in fact, estimates of time spent in family work for both husbands of employed and nonemployed wives are much higher than those obtained with diary data.

mary. For instance, in 1977, 52 percent of a sample of young married women and 63 percent of their husbands, agreed with the statement that the "wife should only work if it does not interfere with household responsibilities" (Ferber, 1982).[29] In the same sample 60 percent and 82 percent respectively agreed with the statement that "if there are young children, the wife should not work unless there is serious financial need." Such opinions are, no doubt, associated with the view that the services of the wife and mother, if not entirely irreplaceable, are at any rate far more valuable than the wages of a housekeeper or the cost of a day-care center would indicate.[30]

As long as we are unable to measure the psychic satisfaction to the husband of having his food prepared, his house cleaned, and his children cared for by his own wife, and her satisfaction or dissatisfaction in performing these services, it is possible to argue that such traditional couples may, in fact, maximize their well-being. But it is also possible that they are simply following traditional patterns, which became established in earlier days under quite different conditions. We shall return to the question of whether research provides evidence that full-time homemaking is the optimal arrangement for the family, and particularly for the children. But in the meantime, we turn from the issue of expenditure of time to the issue of expenditure of money. As we shall see, here too questions arise about optimization for the family and even more so for individual members.

Expenditure Patterns and Savings   While it is relatively easy to predict the direction, if not the extent, of the impact of the wife's work outside the home on the amount of time she spends on housework, the effect on many types of expenditures is a far more complex issue. It is not surprising, therefore, that contradictory hypotheses have been proposed, with a variety of different explanations.

One view, based on the permanent-income hypothesis (which holds that consumption expenditures are determined by expected lifetime income, and further assumes that a wife's earnings are necessarily regarded as temporary), suggests that a family with a working wife will save more

---

[29] Also, Mason et al., (1970) found that even women who advocate equal rights in the labor market tend to have traditional ideas about basic division of labor between men and women in the household (though this was less true for black than white women). Similarly, Thornton and Freedman (1982), who report major changes in women's general sex-role attitudes since the early sixties, point out that this was not the case for specific aspects of women's roles, such as sharing of housework.

[30] This may also help to explain why women who enter the labor market hire surprisingly little household help (Strober and Weinberg, 1980).

than a one-earner family with the same income and spend more on consumer durables, considered a form of savings (Mincer, 1960a, 1960b). Another view, which leads to the same conclusion, is that the wife's earnings are regarded as an extra and are spent on such extras as consumer durables (Drucker, 1976). Somewhat different assumptions produce different results. If the wife's earnings are not regarded as temporary and if level of income is all that matters, expenditures on consumer durables should be the same as for a one-earner family, whether or not they are regarded as savings. Obviously, each of these hypotheses also has different implications for consumer expenditures on other goods and services.

An alternative set of considerations influencing expenditures on consumer durables, which may have more appeal to people not versed in the niceties of economic theory but which is equally inconclusive, relies on the obvious fact that an employed wife will be under pressure to spend less time on housework. One view is that she will therefore want to buy more household appliances, which are considered labor saving. The other view holds that these appliances generally are used to produce a higher standard of living and actually use more of a woman's time (Galbraith, 1973).[31]

Not surprisingly, in view of all these conflicting considerations, empirical evidence indicates little or no differences in expenditures on consumer durables between families with and without an employed wife (Strober, 1977; Strober and Weinberg, 1980). Some differences in expenditure patterns and savings nonetheless may be predicted with confidence. Expenditures on job-related items, such as commuting, child care, clothing, Social Security, and taxes are greater for the family with an employed wife, while savings are somewhat smaller, given the same income. But, we also know that income is higher than if the wife were not in the labor force. As mentioned previously, wives who are employed full time contribute more than one-third of a family's income. Therefore, both consumption and savings are greater because of her earnings. It is estimated that without wives' contribution to income, their families would spend 50 percent less on clothing, transportation, and retirement (Vickery 1979); and while there is evidence that families with working wives save less than others with the same income (Strober, 1979; Vickery, 1979), they are likely to save more than they would without the wife's earnings.

It must not be overlooked, however, that when two families have the

---

[31] It is also possible that women who are full-time homemakers are more inclined to accumulate durables because they have more pride in ownership.

same money income, the one with a full-time homemaker is considerably better off because she has more time to produce goods and services at home and avoids the job-related expenses on which the employed wife spends about 15 percent of her earnings (Vickery, 1979). Lazear and Michael (1980) estimate that after taking into account taxes, extra purchases related to working, and the loss of the woman's time in the home, the two-earner family needs about 30 percent more income than the one-earner family to maintain an equivalent standard of living. Also, to the extent that the family adopts expenditure patterns dependent on two incomes, they lose the flexibility the one-earner family has of having an additional worker entering the labor market to tide them over in an emergency. On the other hand, the contribution the full-time homemaker can make by economizing on food and clothing, two areas on which she has traditionally concentrated, has greatly decreased, since the proportion of family income spent on these items has declined from 45 percent in 1950 to 25 percent in 1972 (Vickery, 1979). This may help to explain why homemakers, as well as employed wives, are beginning to spend somewhat less time on housework (Robinson, 1977b).

Thus, the primary impact on expenditures and savings patterns of the wife's work status is via the effect on family earnings and not via changes related to her different life-style and economizing on home time. This is particularly surprising because the employed wife appears to exercise more influence on expenditure decisions (Ferber, 1982), and one might expect her to use that influence to buy goods and services that would reduce time needed for housework. This is an area where a great deal of additional work needs to be done to help us gain better insights.

Marital and Childbearing Patterns   So far, we have dealt with women who are, or expect to become, wives and mothers, and we have discussed the effects of their family status on their labor force participation, occupations, and earnings, as well as the allocation of time and expenditures of their families. Next, we examine the extent to which a woman's labor market status influences her position within the family and then turn to the question of how it affects the well-being of her family.

As we have seen, the increasing labor force participation of women is not associated with a significant decline in the proportion of women who marry at some time during their lives. But the greater economic independence of women has no doubt contributed to pushing the age of first marriage upward. For example, there is evidence that seems to indicate that women delay marriage when they have numerous prospects for well-paying jobs. Preston and Richards (1975) found that the proportion of single women at ages 22 to 24 was likely to be higher in localities where jobs were plentiful and their earnings relative to men's were good. Schoen and Urton (1979), investigating marriage patterns in twentieth-century Sweden, also found support for this hypothesis.

The change in attitudes toward premarital sex and the greater economic independence of women, which is associated with more education, no doubt also have contributed to pushing the age of first marriage upward. However, cohabitation does not appear to be a substitute for marriage, but rather appears to precede it or follow its termination.[32] Nor do young women today choose between employment on the one hand and marriage on the other; they often try to accommodate their paid work to their household responsibilities. Leaving the labor market or school at time of marriage is increasingly unusual.[33] Thus, there is no reason to expect a substantial increase in the proportion of women who will never marry.

To the extent that an either/or choice for women is still common, it is between labor force participation and children. As we have seen, the proportion of mothers with preschool children who are in the labor force is now as high as 45 percent. But that is considerably lower than the 62 percent participation rate of mothers with school-age children. The latter also are more likely to work full time. These data clearly indicate that young children continue to be an impediment to a woman working outside the home, although it also has been found that the presence of older children has the opposite effect (Lehrer and Nerlove, 1980; Mahoney, 1961). It is therefore not surprising that women's work plans influence their intended childbearing. Those with a strong career orientation have fewer children and may postpone childbirth until they are established in the labor market. That women Ph.D.s, a particularly career-oriented group, had on the average only 1.6 children in the late seventies,[34] when the average for the total population was 2.1, and tended to have them considerably later than less-educated women, tends to confirm this.

---

[32] For many couples, informal living together appears to be a prelude to marriage. Less attention has been paid to cohabitation among the elderly, but it is not at all uncommon. Most likely it is spurred by Social Security rules, which would often severely reduce incomes if two recipients married.

[33] One bit of evidence for the latter is the rapid increase in the proportion of women Ph.D.s who are married. Ferber and Kordick (1978) found that about half of women who received a degree between 1958 and 1963, but almost three-fourths of those who received it between 1967 and 1971, were married.

[34] Based on a national sample of Ph.D.s (Ferber and Huber, 1979). An alternative hypothesis, proposed by Myrdal and Klein (1956), is that alert women are both more likely to work and to practice birth control.

Interestingly, so far there is little evidence of a major trend toward couples opting to be childless, or child-free as some prefer to call it, and there is considerable disagreement about whether the decline in the birthrate will go much further. Some even argue, on the evidence of the recent slight increase in the birthrate, that the trend will be reversed. It appears far more likely that this tiny baby boom is merely a phenomenon of the young women who have postponed marriage and childbearing (Freedman and Coombs, 1966) and now are having their first, and possibly only, child. In fact, a convincing case can be made that the decline will continue in the long run as young women continue to find the costs of child rearing increasingly unattractive and alternative uses of their time and energy increasingly inviting (Huber, 1980).

Radical change also has taken place in family stability. While most people continue to live in families most of the time, the chances of children living in the same family until they establish independent households, and of marrying only once in a lifetime,[35] have been rapidly decreasing. This is widely regarded both as a symptom and cause of society's malaise. For it is widely believed, apparently even by social scientists, that two people who live together "forever after" are most likely to be happy and that children raised by such a couple are most likely to grow up well adjusted and successful. These ideas often are complemented by the view that the higher labor force participation of women is one of the primary causes of the increasing rate of marital dissolution.

A strong case can be made for the great dependence of the breadwinner husband and the homemaker wife on each other as a deterrent to divorce, but there are serious problems with this prescription for marital stability. First, empirical evidence on whether wives' employment has a negative effect on marriage is mixed.[36] One recent study

[35] It is even less likely that they will live with only one partner all their lives. But we are not dealing with that issue here, since two legally unrelated people do not constitute a family.

[36] Hoffman and Holmes (1976), as well as Nye (1963), found no such evidence, while Sawhill et al. (1975), did. It must also be remembered that even if it is found that employed women are more likely to get divorced, it may be that a woman with an unsatisfactory marriage may go to work in anticipation of a possible breakup. It is interesting to note that two studies found divorce (or separation) to be more likely when the wife's earnings exceed those of her husband than when the opposite is true (Cherlin, 1977; Moore et al., 1978). The former also has widely been regarded as deviant (Blood and Wolfe, 1960) and is probably unacceptable to many husbands and possibly wives as well. One solution is for the wife to avoid earning so much. Alternatively, we might hope that in time a husband who has a very successful wife will be proud of her regardless of his accomplishments, as is almost invariably true today of the wife's attitude toward her husband.

(Booth, 1977) concludes that it is not the fact of a wife's working but changes in her work status that cause problems. He found that both husband and wife showed more symptoms of stress and marital discord when the wife had recently entered or left the labor force than when the wife had not recently changed status. In another study Huber and Spitze (1980) found that both husband and wife are more inclined to think of divorce as the wife's labor market experience increases, but they point out that they have no information on actual divorce. Second, it is questionable whether economic interdependence holding two people together who otherwise might prefer to live separately is desirable either for them or for their children. Third, and by no means least important, the wife who is a full-time homemaker is far more dependent on the husband than vice versa because not only his money income but also his social status is likely to be relatively unaffected by the termination of the marriage. He may be directed by the court to pay alimony, child support, or both, but the amounts involved tend to be small and are frequently not paid.[37] This also helps to explain why women, often doubly handicapped in the labor market because of less work experience and the need to take care of children, descend into poverty after a divorce.[38] This descent is all the more likely because 80 percent of such women today (as opposed to 44 percent in 1940) establish their own households (Cutright, 1974). Their problems are made more serious by the frequent difficulties such women have in establishing an independent credit rating. This is in large part caused by their failure to maintain a separate credit history while they were married. Remarriage is the one frequent route out of poverty (Hill and Hoffman, 1977),[39] and most divorced women do remarry.

The disparity in the extent of dependence on the ongoing marriage adds to a husband's bargaining power. An angry "if I do not like it, I do not have to put up with this" or an impatient "if you do not like it, you can go" has a lot more credibility coming from him. It may well give the husband the upper hand in cases in which there is a real contest

---

[37] Mean child support in 1975 was $2,430, but this figure reflects the impact of large payments received by a relatively small number of women. About one-fourth of all mothers with no husband present received child support, and only four percent of the four-and-a-half-million divorced or separated women received alimony (Bureau of the Census, 1979b). Also Ross and Sawhill (1975:47) cite a study for a metropolitan county in Wisconsin showing that within one year of divorce, 42 percent of fathers had made no court-ordered child support payments and that after 10 years the proportion rose to 79 percent.

[38] Their plight is eloquently described by Bergmann (1980).

[39] The proportion of nonwhite female-headed households living in poverty is particularly high. See, for instance, Johnson (1978).

or may even result in the wife routinely subordinating her preferences to his. Consonant with such a hypothesis, studies show that husbands whose wives do not work outside the home have a more dominant role in decision making than those whose wives are in the labor market (Ferber, 1982).

The increasing proportion of women who work outside the home, however, may have a favorable indirect effect on the status of the full-time housewife. If women are becoming increasingly aware that they have options, husbands who want them to stay home may have to offer better terms for doing so. This may help to account for the surprising fact that the number of hours of housework for the full-time housewife, which had not declined through most of this century (Vanek, 1974), has recently gone down substantially (Robinson, 1977b) and that housewives own as wide a variety of household appliances as working wives (Robinson, 1980; Strober and Weinberg, 1980).[40] The improvement in the housewife's position would tend to mitigate the general trend toward a downgrading of her role, best illustrated by the declining importance attached by both men and women to having a full-time homemaker in the family (Ferber, 1982; Hoffman, 1977).

The Changing Status of Women and the Family So far, to the extent that economic variables are involved that can be and to a considerable extent have been measured, we have concentrated primarily on changes in women's lives and their effects on the family. We would, however, be seriously remiss if we ignored important implications for the well-being of women, men, and children that go beyond narrowly economic concerns. Considerable work has been done on the impact of women's labor force participation both on their own and their husbands' satisfaction with various aspects of life and on the development of their children. Unfortunately, much of it has disregarded the likelihood that the impact will be quite different depending on the context of different personalities, family situations, and social environments. It is not surprising, therefore, that so often the results are inconclusive or contradictory.

One example is the varied findings with respect to the employed woman's own satisfaction with her marriage. Some studies have discovered negative effects (Blood and Wolfe, 1960; Michel, 1967), some show no relationship (Blood, 1963; Pleck, et al., 1978; Powell, 1963), while others show a positive one (Burke and Weir, 1976; Feld, 1963; Ferree, 1976). Wright (1978) reviewed six large national surveys conducted by

---

[40] When income and assets are held constant.

the University of Michigan and the National Opinion Research Center between 1971 and 1976. He found no consistent or significant differences in patterns of life satisfaction between full-time homemakers and employed wives.[41] One study emphasized that employed mothers experience more anxiety and guilt but also have better self-concepts and enjoy their children more (Rallings and Nye, 1979). Other studies, however, found that less-educated homemakers were considerably more satisfied than more highly educated ones (Nye, 1963) and that more educated, employed wives were more satisfied than less educated ones (Burke and Weir, 1976; Hoffman and Nye, 1974; Johnson, 1978). These findings are likely to be related to the more attractive opportunities of the more highly educated in the job market, as well as their less traditional attitudes. Women who work part time are generally the most satisfied (Johnson, 1978). There is also evidence that family income and family size interact with work status in determining the wife's satisfaction (Blood, 1963; Feld, 1963; Feldman and Feldman, 1973; Ferree, 1976; Gover, 1963; Nye and Hoffman, 1963).

Whatever the exact findings of these numerous studies, they are likely to be biased against discovering a positive effect of labor force participation on marital satisfaction. If, as is entirely probable, women who have higher ambitions and more demanding standards or are dissatisfied with their marriage enter the labor market, a negative (or less positive) correlation is likely to be found, even if employment increases their satisfaction. What we would need to know is whether women in and out of the labor force would be more or less satisfied if their work status were different.

In virtually all other respects the effects on the woman's outlook and attitude of working outside the home appear consistently positive. Women in the labor market are more likely to exceed their life expectancy as calculated by actuarial tables (Palmore and Stone, 1973). They tend to experience better physical and mental health and greater satisfaction with life in general (Burke and Weir, 1976; Feld, 1963) and have higher self-esteem (Birnbaum, 1971; Feldman and Feldman, 1973; Ohlbaum, 1971). In a national sample, 76 percent of working women said they would go on working even if they did not need to (Dubnoff et al., 1978). While there is likely to be a problem of positive bias, since healthier,

[41] The many studies on this topic were conducted over a rather long period of time, which raises the question of whether the different findings might be caused by changes that took place during the approximately two decades covered. A careful examination leads us to reject this explanation. Negative effects of employment are found both in 1960 and 1967, no effects in 1963 and 1978, and positive effects in 1963 and 1976.

more self-confident women are likely to enter the labor force, evidence
is at least consistent with the possibility that working outside the home
has a favorable effect on a woman's own well-being. As we shall see,
this is not necessarily the case for her spouse.

A number of studies found that husbands of employed wives, especially those in the lower class, reported less marital satisfaction, greater
job pressures, and less physical and mental well-being (Axelson, 1970;
Burke and Weir, 1976; Feld, 1963; Gianopulos and Mitchell, 1957;
Rallings and Nye, 1979). However, this appears to have been less true
when the wife was employed by choice (Orden and Bradburn, 1969) or
worked part time (Johnson, 1978) and has not been found at all in at
least one recent study (Feldman and Feldman, 1973). How can we
explain these mainly negative correlations between a husband's satisfaction and his wife's employment and his general tendency to be less
accepting of market work for his wife, even though both spouses share
in the benefits of the additional income and the wife carries the main
burden of the additional work?

One answer is a possible negative bias because wives of unsuccessful
husbands are more likely to enter the labor market. Beyond that, a
widely accepted explanation is that the husband perceives the shift to
the two-earner family as a loss of status and power for himself and views
any increase in household responsibilities as demeaning. He sees recent
changes as eroding his secure position and threatening his masculine
identity. The wife, on the other hand, believes she is expanding her
sphere and increasing her influence and security. These perceptions are
not all illusory. As previously mentioned, women are likely to play a
larger role in family decision making when they earn income and to gain
bargaining power when they are no longer entirely dependent on the
continuation of their marriage for their livelihood.

At the same time, the husband does stand to gain from a more equal
sharing of household tasks, not only because of the higher income when
the wife enters the labor market, but also because of the possibility of
having a happier and more successful wife, of learning better how to
fend for himself in case the need should arise, and of getting to know
his children better. It may be that when men come to accept a more
egalitarian ideology, they will enjoy a partnership marriage more than
they ever did the old paternalistic one. But there is little evidence that
this day has arrived yet for most of them.

The most emotionally charged issue is the question of the effect of
the employed mother on her children. While in principle, maternal and
paternal employment and the time both parents spend with their children
should be considered, we concentrate on the mother's role since this

whole chapter focuses on the rapid increase in the labor force participation of married women.

Early research focused almost exclusively on possible negative effects
of maternal employment, often under very unfavorable conditions. When
there is an investigation of the immediate impact on her children of the
mother entering the labor market right after a divorce, for example, it
is likely to reveal dire results, especially if the divorce plunged a previously middle-class family into poverty. But these results are not necessarily representative. Follow-up studies to determine the longer-range
impact have been very rare, and there is little evidence that parental
divorce contributes to later-life difficulties of the children (Kulka and
Weingarten, 1979). It now has been found that many of the problems
that were attributable to divorce and employment of mothers are in
large part attributable to the low income level of such households (Johnson, 1980; Ross and Sawhill, 1975).

Recent, more even-handed research has discovered that, even in the
short run, much depends on the quality as well as the quantity of time
mothers spend with children, on the quality of the substitutes provided,
on social attitudes toward the family's life-style, and on the age and sex
of the children.[42] Bronfenbrenner and Crouter (see Chapter 3 in this
volume) find that the most frequently supported conclusion in this type
of research since 1960 is that "Taken by itself, the fact that a mother
works outside the home has no universally predictable effects on the
child."

Some specific results, however, have been reported. Research on the
relationship between mother's employment and the development of her
children shows no evidence of adverse effects of quality day care even
for infants and preschoolers (Belsky and Sternberg, 1978; Etaugh, 1978;
Rubenstein and Howes, 1979). And some studies show evidence of
favorable results, especially on social adjustment (Gold and Andres,
1978; Gold et al., 1979). These findings may be explained in part by
the tendency of working mothers to cut back far more on housework
than on child care,[43] so that with smaller families, they spend nearly as
much time in one-on-one interaction with young children (Goldberg,
1977).

The impact on school-age and older children of mothers who are
successful in their paid work generally appears to be favorable, perhaps
because the mother herself is more satisfied, is likely to have more

---

[42] Many of these points are made by Clarke-Stewart (1977).

[43] This has been found to be particularly true of well-educated women. See, for instance,
Leibowitz (1975) and Robinson (1977a).

structured rules and more consistent behavior in her relationship with her children (Hoffman, 1974), is less possessive (Holmstrom, 1972), and gives growing children more independence. Daughters, especially, hold employed mothers in higher esteem than those not employed (Hoffman, 1979). Both sons and daughters of employed mothers are more likely to favor equality for women (Rallings and Nye, 1979). Last but not least, a woman who is in the labor market greatly reduces the economic impact on children of a possible divorce, because labor market experience is one of the best forms of insurance against dire poverty.

However, as Bronfenbrenner and Crouter report (Chapter 3 in this volume), there may be a negative influence of maternal employment on sons' academic achievement, at least for middle-class families. Nevertheless, the authors suggest that the evidence is not sufficient to conclude that the mother's working outside the home necessarily causes this problem. While a good deal has been learned about the short-term impact of maternal employment on children, far less work has been done about long-term consequences on them as adolescents and adults. One interesting study (Duncan and Duncan, 1969) did investigate these, finding that the children of working mothers achieved higher occupational status. It would be most useful to discover how children's educational, career, and marital patterns are influenced.

Whatever the findings of researchers, many women may choose to spend at least some time as full-time homemakers and mothers or feel bitter if they find it necessary to be employed. It may be that the woman who chooses her work status freely according to her own inclinations will be a better wife and mother and a more fulfilled person, whatever her choice is. However, the young woman who chooses to be a full-time homemaker for a long time should be cautioned that this option may pose substantial economic risks.

Research and Policy Formation: What We Need to Learn

Before discussing what additional research would be particularly useful for policy formation, we turn briefly to the proper role of the researcher in shaping policy goals. Proponents of the positivist view hold that the function of social scientists is not to concern themselves with what should be, but to describe what is; not to try to tell people where they should go, but only to tell them how to get there. However, totally value-free research is rarely, if ever, possible, and experts inevitably exert influence by the topics and approaches they choose for their investigations and by the way they present their results. Research can focus on ways to facilitate or to impede a particular course of action; assumptions may be chosen that make the conclusions more or less favorable; indifferent results may be presented as not particularly good or not particularly bad. We suggest that the best procedure is for researchers to state clearly their own values, so that their work may be judged accordingly. In other words, we advocate a sort of truth-in-packaging approach.

Following our own advice, we acknowledge a preference for individually chosen arrangements among mates, rather than traditionally assigned roles. However, children should still have lesser and different responsibilities and rights than adults. We also acknowledge the responsibility of society, which for practical purposes means the government, to provide a decent minimum standard of living for everyone, especially children. At the same time, we concede the government's right to attempt to reduce the need for such support, to the extent that this can be done without infringing on crucial individual liberties and the right to privacy.

With these values in mind, we turn to a discussion of some of the most important issues influenced, directly or indirectly, by government policies. Researchers can make a great contribution not only by finding better ways to achieve agreed-upon goals, but also by making sure that decision-makers are aware of the unintended, as well as the intended effects various policies are likely to have.

Labor Force Participation   As we have seen, low earnings of women are among the chief causes of poverty in this country, mainly because of their impact on female-headed families. It is also clear that extensive labor market experience is the best insurance a woman can have for herself and her children against poverty and welfare dependence in case her husband is unwilling or unable to support them. Therefore, research on how best to reduce remaining barriers to labor force entry will be most useful. We already know that women are very responsive to the level of take-home pay in decisions on whether to enter the labor market.[44] Government efforts are already underway to reduce tax penalties for two-earner couples. And policies which reward them may in due course be considered as a means not only of helping families but also of reducing the cost of welfare programs. Some such possibilities are discussed below:

(1)   Under present income tax rules the wife's earnings are effectively taxed beginning in the highest tax bracket applied to her husband's

---

[44] Several recent studies (Hausman, 1981; Leuthold, 1978, 1979) particularly focus on the effect taxes have in this respect.

income.[45] Thus, her disposable wage rate is generally reduced and the family not only loses some of the benefits of income splitting enjoyed by one-earner couples but is also likely to pay higher taxes than two single workers would. This so-called tax penalty for married couples increases as the percent of income earned by the lesser-earning spouse and the combined income go up (Gordon, 1979). One step toward ameliorating this bias might be to give the couple the option of filing individual returns, as if they were not married.[46]

(2) A married woman who takes a job pays Social Security taxes, beginning with the first dollar she earns, but frequently receives no additional benefits beyond those she would get as a wife. A variety of solutions have been suggested, from requiring payments by the home-maker to exempting the working woman from payments up to the level beyond which she would receive additional Social Security benefits. Given the economic problems the Social Security system currently faces and the heavy burden Social Security taxes place on the poorest wage earners, more research needs to be done on ways to remove the inequity for two-earner couples without adding to the other difficulties. Particular emphasis also must be placed on finding ways to make women's old age no less secure than men's.

(3) A more generous allowance for job-related expenses, particu-larly child care, and/or subsidized child care are ideas worthy of further study; the effects of such policies in other countries also warrant inves-tigation. Shifting a burden from parents to nonparents is not unprece-dented in a country long dedicated to public or publicly subsidized education for older children. That policy also reduces the expenses of parents.

(4) More work needs to be done on the single-parent family, in which one adult carries the full burden of household responsibilities alone, so that this situation can be taken into account in calculating the

---

[45] The IRS allowed a maximum deduction of $1,500 to the lower-earning spouse in 1982 and will allow $3,000 in 1983. It also allows a sliding-scale credit for child-care expenses up to 30 percent for families with income under $10,000, for a total of no more than $2,400 for one child and $4,800 for more than one.

[46] It also has been suggested that the value of home production could be taxed in order to bring the tax burden of the one-earner family up to that of the family with two earners. In principle this idea has much merit. It need not be a means of increasing the overall tax burden, for rates could then be reduced correspondingly. In practice, however, there are serious obstacles. The outcry by one-earner families would surely be great and probably influential. They would particularly emphasize the plight of those who could no longer afford a full-time homemaker and ignore the fact that such families presently do not carry their fair share of the burden of public expenses. A second problem is the difficulty of measuring the value of nonmarket output for each family.

level of needed support, whether from the government or from the absent parent.

It is clear that the parent who contributes only money should carry a larger share of the financial burden, even if the earnings of father and mother are equal. In fact, it is still the mother who is the single parent in the overwhelming majority of cases. She also is likely to earn less, particularly if she was not in the labor market full time during her marriage. Better estimates of the value of household time could make a contribution to the determination of the appropriate amount of alimony and child support. Also important is the search for better ways to enforce the payments.

An April 1979 survey of child support, alimony, and property settlements by the Commerce and Health and Human Services departments (see Bureau of the Census, 1980c), showed that 28 percent of the 7.1 million mothers of children with no father present were living below the poverty line. Only about 50 percent of these 7.1 million mothers were supposed to receive child support in 1978. Of these women, 49 percent received the full amount that they were due, 23 percent received less than the full amount, and 28 percent received no payment at all. Among women who were supposed to receive child support, the poverty rate was 17 percent. However, even if they had been able to collect the full amount owed, the number who were poor would not have decreased significantly (U.S. Department of Commerce, 1980). Thus, although better enforcement of child support would be of help, it is clear that it would solve only a small part of the problem.

Most important therefore is further research on the means of increasing women's earning capacity, so that they and their children would not be so heavily dependent on either government or ex-husbands. Ross and Sawhill (1975) report that in the mid-1970s welfare benefits for a family of four approximated the amount earned by working full time year-round at minimum wage. When, in addition, the value of food stamps, subsidized medical care, and so forth is considered, women (especially those with large families) would have to be able to earn substantially more before it would pay for them to enter the labor market.

Since some women will still choose to remain at home while their children are young, programs directed toward helping displaced homemakers need to be considered. Thus it would be helpful to have studies that indicate the kind of training and assistance that would be useful to them. However, in the long run, policies aimed toward prevention of loss of earning power rather than cure after having lost it appear more promising.

(5) It would be useful to learn more about the effects of existing legislation intended to open up typically male occupations to women,[47] give women more-equal upward mobility, and presumably increase their earnings. Some have hoped to upgrade the status of typically female occupations by encouraging more men to enter them. We need to learn more about the impact on women in such cases, for there is the risk that men will move in at the top (as principals of grade schools, directors of libraries, etc.), thus offsetting or perhaps more than offsetting possible benefits to women. Since occupational segregation will in any case decrease slowly, more work also should be done on the possibility of requiring equal pay for comparable work, an issue currently being litigated.

(6) One of the avenues to labor market participation often used by immigrant groups in the past, which might also be helpful to women, is opening small individual businesses. While the outlook for this type of endeavor is not rosy today, it could be improved if the Small Business Administration provided more help and if women were guaranteed equal access to credit. More research on the use of skills generally possessed by long-time homemakers and on the use of women's networks also should be helpful in this area.

(7) The possibility of increasing the availability of part-time work in a greater variety of occupations, and on more favorable terms, should be investigated, as should other ways for making work schedules less rigid, such as flexitime and job sharing. Some Western European countries have made great progress in these respects, and we should try to learn from their experiences (see Kamerman and Kingston, Chapter 5 in this volume). It would be useful to study the impact of more flexible work arrangements, not only on women but also on men and on employers.

(8) Several recent studies have found that volunteer work, long recognized for its value to the community, is also a means for the volunteer to maintain or acquire marketable skills (Mueller, 1975; Schram, 1979). Finding out how such doubly useful activities could be encouraged would be worthwhile. One possibility would be to treat their money value as a tax deduction, in the same way that financial contributions to charitable organizations are now. Such a policy change would remove the present advantage of contributing money rather than time. The main obstacle to remedying this is the difficulty in determining the dollar value of time.

---

[47] An interesting alternative approach, used in Sweden, is to give bonuses to businesses who employ a specified minimum proportion of both men and women.

This is one more reason for increasing our knowledge of the value of nonmarket work.

Earnings Entering the labor force is the first step toward making a woman potentially self-supporting and capable of lifting her family above the poverty level. But many of the typically female occupations have earnings so low as to be inadequate, or barely adequate, even for these minimal purposes. And many offer little or no prospect for career advancement. Therefore, women are caught in a vicious cycle: They drop out and stay out of the labor market because their rewards are so low, and their rewards are low in part because they do not spend more time in the labor market. One way to get out of this is for women to enter a broader range of fields, improving the prospects not only for those who do, but also for the smaller number who remain in traditional occupations. More research needs to be done on how women can be encouraged to enter typically male occupations. One need not believe that women should or can be equally represented in all fields, but only that present occupational segregation is greater than warranted. Improved job counseling from junior high school on could encourage young women to get more and different kinds of education and training that would help prepare them to enter the professions and skilled trades in which they have been severely underrepesented.

All the policies that would encourage women to spend more time in the labor market would be helpful not only in giving them more work experience but also in giving them greater incentive to enter occupations in which experience is more highly rewarded. Similarly, decreasing occupational segregation, which would increase women's earnings, would also give them more incentive to remain in the labor market.

Unemployment One of the most important variables in explaining the rate of increase in women's labor force participation is the unemployment rate. Before World War II, women often tried to find jobs when their husbands were unemployed, so there was an influx into the labor market when the unemployment rate was high. This tendency has been dwarfed in recent times by women actively looking for jobs when the unemployment rate is low (Ferber and Lowry, 1976b).

Holding the unemployment rate down also helps women in another way. When employers are confronted by a tight labor market and have difficulty finding the kind of workers they want, they are more likely to forget whatever prejudices they (or their workers or customers) may have and hire the workers they can get. The experience during World War II, the last period of really low unemployment in this country, provides convincing evidence on this point. During these years, the elderly, the nonwhite, the female, and the disabled all experienced access to positions from which they had, up to that time, been excluded.

Last, but not least, resistance to the entry of new workers is minimized when established workers do not have to fear for their jobs. For all these reasons, one of the greatest contributions to improving the position of women and of other disadvantaged groups is low unemployment.

Marital and Childbearing Patterns The decision whether, when, and whom to marry, and whether to have children, are matters that should be left within the private sphere. But as indicated earlier, government policies nonetheless impinge on these decisions directly or indirectly, purposefully or inadvertently. There have been laws regarding marriage and divorce, as well as birth control and abortion, and neither the tax structure nor welfare programs have been neutral with regard to different life-styles. To some extent this is inevitable. Policies aimed at fulfilling one goal, such as protecting the right of children to a decent opportunity for developing their potential, conflict with other goals, such as the parents' right to make decisions for their children or equity between families with and without children. Therefore, compromises are inevitable. Careful research before introducing new policies or relatively small-scale experiments before introducing a full-blown program should be helpful in learning more about their costs and benefits, and both should be spelled out clearly.

(1) In order to enable people to choose their marital status and living arrangements freely, the government should avoid setting up undue obstacles to, or imposing penalties on, marriage, divorce, the cohabitation of unmarried individuals, or extended families.[48]

(2) Benefits to be received from the government should not be contingent on marital status. Thus for instance, provisions against payment of aid to dependent children when the mother is married need to be questioned. Similarly, Social Security rules providing that a widow who remarries loses some of her benefits should be reconsidered.

(3) In order to make childbearing voluntary, information on and availability of birth control should be encouraged. This is desirable not only because individuals should be free to choose in these matters, but also because there is reason to believe that desired children are least likely to be neglected, abused, or both. Incidentally, such children are

---

[48] It is a little-known fact that local ordinances frequently limit their definition of family to more or less its nuclear form.

also least likely to become public responsibilities. Furthermore, voluntary childbirth also maximizes the opportunity for parents to be able to choose their work plans.

Many of the policies suggested to avoid discouraging labor force participation and to encourage higher earnings for women also have an impact on marital and childbearing status, although it is not always clear in which direction. Reducing the penalties on two-earner families or the advantages for one-earner families reduces the incentive for a couple to remain single when both partners plan to work. But it also reduces the incentive for one-earner couples to marry. A woman with better earnings prospects may be considered a more promising partner by some men, but threatening by others. Similarly, when parents have higher earnings, the higher value of their time makes children more expensive, but their larger income enables them to afford more children. Only continued research will enable us to determine what the outcomes, on balance, are likely to be.

(4) As discussed earlier, much research has been done recently on the effect of employed mothers on their children. It has uncovered little evidence of harmful results. On the contrary there is reason to believe that, on balance, benefits outweigh any possible harm. However, surprisingly little work has so far been done on the impact of the characteristics of fathers and other caretakers, other than studies of organized day-care programs (Hofferth and Moore, 1979). This omission needs to be remedied in order to provide a sounder basis for policies on child care for working couples.

STRENGTHS AND WEAKNESSES OF EXISTING DATA SETS

Compared to earlier times, there has been a tremendous increase in the information available on a multitude of socioeconomic variables. Inundated as we are today by voluminous and reasonably reliable data collected by various government agencies as well as an increasing number of private institutions, it may seem surprising that social scientists still decry their inadequacy. Some explanation of this paradox might be useful at this point.

An analogy with the natural sciences may be constructive. Researchers in these fields were able to make some progress by observing the subjects of their study with the naked eye, but no one is surprised to find that they were able to make far more progress when they expanded their vision outward by use of the telescope and inward by such devices as the x ray, spectroscope, and microscope. Nor is anyone puzzled, let alone outraged, by the fact that they continue to devote additional resources to learn ever more of the remaining secrets of nature.

Similarly, social scientists were able to acquire some understanding of humankind and of society by personal observation and by reading about the observations of others. The best among them managed to gain a surprising amount of insight when such limited evidence was combined with vigorous deduction. More recently, the collection of data has made possible greater progress through careful empirical work and the testing of hypotheses. It has been partly a process of learning the right questions to ask. But social scientists have not been as fortunate as natural scientists. The type of information needed by them is not only difficult, expensive, and time-consuming to collect, but there is also a growing public resistance to further collection of data. Such data collection is widely considered an intrusion on the subject's privacy. This is only one reason, as we are all painfully aware, that the social sciences lag far behind the natural sciences in the knowledge explosion.

Information needed for studying the family as an economic unit is mainly derived from surveys. In addition to the obvious need for data that are reliable, there are a number of other requirements:

(1)   While for some purposes samples of special populations are most desirable, for other purposes it is necessary to have data representative of the total population. Furthermore, the sample must be large enough to support the statistical techniques used in modern research. As we shall see, many of the otherwise interesting data sets are less useful because they do not meet these criteria.

(2)   Information on individuals, rather than mere averages for groups, is often necessary. Assume, for example, that we are concerned with labor force participation of married women and that we find women in the labor market are more highly educated and also have husbands with higher earnings. Only appropriate data for individuals would enable us to determine that, holding husbands' earnings constant, more highly educated women are more likely to be in the labor force, while, holding education constant, we would find that those whose husbands have higher earnings are less likely to be in the labor force.

(3)   Data are needed not just for a single point in time but for an extended period. We find, for instance, that at any given time fewer women than men are in the labor force. In the absence of longitudinal data it is not possible to determine whether most women enter the labor force but many drop out for a time, or whether many women work throughout their adult lives but a minority never work outside the home. There are also instances when relationships are found to be quite dif-

ferent for longitudinal rather than cross-sectional data. As we have seen, this is true when husbands' earnings and wives' labor force participation are examined.

(4)   It is often inadequate to have only economic data. In order to be able to disentangle the complex issue of cause and effect, it may be very helpful, or even indispensable, to have available information on relevant social and psychological variables as well. As we have seen, in recent years women increasingly have fewer children and are increasingly more likely to be in the labor force. Only they can tell us whether they chose to have fewer children because they planned to work, decided to work because they had small families, or decided both to work and have smaller families for some other reason. Or again we know that married women who are in the labor market are very likely to have husbands who approve of working wives. This could be so because women are likely to follow their husband's preferences, because what the wife does influences the husband's preference, because like-minded people are more inclined to marry each other, or a combination of each.[49] Longitudinal data on attitudes as well as behavior help to resolve such puzzles.

(5)   Last but not least, data on nonmarket activities, particularly the use of time for household work and leisure, are important both for their own sake and because of their relevance to behavior in the market sector. Again, an example will be useful to clarify this point. Women are more likely to work part time than men and to work shorter hours whether they work part time or full time. This often is interpreted to show that women are not very job-oriented, not willing to make sacrifices on behalf of their jobs as men do. But we also know that for every hour married women spend on a paid job, their household work is reduced by only a fraction of that time. This raises the possibility that they have to be very career-oriented and willing to make sacrifices in order for them to spend as much time in the labor market as they do.

Given such exacting requirements, it is not surprising that few data sets come close to satisfying them. Table 4-3 lists all of the large data sets and a selection of others that contain many of the variables widely used by students of the economic behavior of individuals as members of family units. The information provided gives some indication of the extent to which each satisfies the requirements specified above.

Inspection of the table makes it obvious that the most serious limi-

---

[49] Some evidence that longitudinal data can help to resolve questions of cause and effect was uncovered using data from the Consumer Panel of Young Married Couples and is reported in Ferber (1982).

TABLE 4-3 Selected Information on Some Data Sources

	Size	Representative of Total Population	Individuals	Longitudinal	Attitudes	Employment Status	Ethnicity
Americans View Their Mental Health, Survey Research Center, Ann Arbor, Mich.	4,760	X	X		X	X	
Business and Family Life of Self-Employed Women, Radcliffe Data Resource and Research Center, Cambridge, Mass.	230		X		X	X	X
Consumer Panel of Young Married Couples, Survey Research Laboratory, University of Illinois, Urbana	720[a]		X	X	X	X	
Current Population Surveys, Bureau of the Census, Suitland, Md.	180,000[b]	X					
European Men and Women, European Omnibus Survey, Directorate-General for Information of the European Commission	8,791	X	X		X		
Experiences of Unemployed Insurance Recipients During the First Year After Exhausting Benefits, Mathematica Policy Research, Princeton, N.J.	10,861			X	X		X
Family and Individual Coping Following Job Loss, Boston College, Chestnut Hill, Mass.	160	X	X			X	
Family Health in an Era of Stress, Roper Center, University of Connecticut, Storrs	1,254[a]	X	X		X	X	X
General Social Surveys, National Opinion Research Center, Chicago, Ill.	1,500[b]	X	X		X	X	
Growth of American Families, Survey Research Center, Ann Arbor, Mich.	1,304		X		X	X	
Job Mobility and Job Loss, Wellesley Center for Research on Women, Wellesley, Mass.	325		X		X	X	X
National Longitudinal Surveys, Center for Human Resources Research, Ohio State University, Columbus	20,000	X	X	X	X	X	
National Study of Social Services to Children and their Families, Administration for Children, Youth, and Families, Washington, D.C.	9,597	X			X	X	X
National Survey of Family Growth, National Technical Information Service, National Center for Health Statistics	9,797 (1973) 8,611 (1976)	X					X
National Survey of Working Women, Radcliffe Data Resource and Research Center, Cambridge, Mass.	111,496				X		X

New Jersey Income Maintenance Experiment, Institute for Research on Poverty Data Center, University of Wisconsin, Madison — 1,35?

Panel Study of Income Dynamics, Survey Research Center, Ann Arbor, Mich. — 6,007[a] / 18,975 — X X X X X

Quality of American Life, Survey Research Center, Ann Arbor, Mich. — 9,356 — X X X X X

Quality of Employment Survey, Survey Research Center, Ann Arbor, Mich. — 4,564 — X X X X X

Seattle and Denver Income Maintenance Experiments, Research Center, SRI International, Menlo Park, Calif. — 4,800[a] — X X

Study of the American Family and Money, Roper Center, University of Connecticut, Storrs — 1,247[a] / 2,194 — X X X X X

Survey of Child Care Needs of Lower-Paid Personnel, Radcliffe Data Resource and Research Center, Cambridge, Mass. — 371 — X

Survey of Income and Education, Bureau of the Census, Suitland, Md. — 150,000[a] — X X X

Survey of Income and Program Participation, Bureau of the Census, Suitland, Md. — 9,600[c] — X X X X

Survey of Modern Living, Survey Research Center, Ann Arbor, Mich. — 2,264 — X X X X X

Survivor Families with Children, Department of Health and Human Resources, Washington, D.C. — 5,752 — X X X X

Terman Gifted Group, Stanford University, Stanford, Calif. — 476 — X X X X X

Time Use in Economic and Social Accounts, Survey Research Center, Ann Arbor, Mich. — 2,406 — X X X X X X

Two-Career Families in Corporate World, Career and Family Center, New York, N.Y. — [d] — X X X

Women in Clerical Work, Department of Sociology, Boston University, Boston, Mass. — 196 — X X X X X

Continuous Work History Sample, Social Security Administration, Washington, D.C. — [e] — X X X X

[a] Families.
[b] Per year.
[c] Households.
[d] Information not available.
[e] One percent of earners covered by Social Security.

tation is the small number of longitudinal data sets. There are only seven, four of which are chosen from special populations. And one of the remaining three is relatively small. This no doubt explains the very extensive use in current research of the remaining two, the National Longitudinal Surveys and the Panel Study of Income Dynamics. Since both are ongoing operations, they are likely to continue to provide invaluable sources for researchers. Even they, however, have deficiencies, although they are minor compared to their contributions.

The National Longitudinal Surveys consist of four cohorts of about 5,000 individuals each: men who were 45 to 59 years of age at the inception of the study, women between 30 and 44, young men between 14 and 24, and young women between 14 and 24. Since they were first selected in 1966, 1967, 1966, and 1968, respectively, the cohorts have been periodically interviewed. More recently, two years of data on young men and women aged 14 to 21 have been added. A wealth of information relating directly or indirectly to their labor market experiences has been accumulated. There are some shortcomings. In a number of cases, more than one individual from a household happened to be included in the samples, and surveyors have matched relatives from the four samples to yield samples of siblings, spouses, parents, and offspring. Ideally, however, one might wish that all individuals from a family would be included. This would mean subjects could not be restricted to the particular age specifications. But having people of all ages would in any case be an advantage as long as the number in particular age groups would not have to be reduced severely.

Second, it is regrettable that in some surveys no data on nonmarket work have been collected and that earnings histories are incomplete. Third, information on job characteristics, such as promotions, job autonomy, and decision making capacities, generally is not available. Fourth, labor market experience is not measured as precisely as one would wish, for respondents are asked to report only the number of years in which they worked at least six months. Last but not least, occupation and education of respondent's mother is not assessed at all for some samples (Bielby et al., 1977).

The Panel Study of Income Dynamics is a longitudinal survey begun in 1968 which originally included 5,000 families. In the first 12 years of the study, data on some 20,000 men, women, and children were collected. Detailed information on income sources and labor supply was obtained. In addition the study has included questions dealing with child care, achievement motivation, family planning, medical care, neighborhood characteristics, and spare-time activities (Rainwater and Rein, 1980).

One important drawback of the data is that surveyors frequently interviewed the so-called head of the household, rather than obtaining first-hand information from all adults.[50] It is regrettable also that some of the interesting questions asked on the National Longitudinal Surveys about job and marital satisfaction were not included here and that in the first six years of the survey the coding for occupation and industry was not as detailed as in later years.

To remedy these deficiencies, each of the already massive studies would have to be expanded and would require even more funds than are needed to keep their present operation going. However, such expansion would further increase the usefulness of these already valuable data sets. One more way to enhance their usefulness would be to permit data users who need information not presently available to piggy-back additional questions onto those already asked.[51] This need not add to the cost of the present panels of subjects; researchers could be requested to pay for the additional expense of getting new information. There would, however, be the problem of adding to the length of the interviews or questionnaires, which might cause more people to drop out of the panels.

Panel mortality is a serious problem, as is the great costliness of maintaining them. For this reason it has been suggested recurrently that the best way to improve the availability of data needed in social science research would be for the government to expand its data collection operations. In this day of outcry against high government spending and concern about government intrusions on privacy, such a move is not very likely. Social sciences could contribute to changing this situation by doing all they can to safeguard against abuses of information collected and by continuing to demonstrate that more and better data enable them to make more and better contributions as scholars and policy makers.

REFERENCES AND BIBLIOGRAPHY

Axelson, L. (1970) The working wife: differences in perception among Negro and white males. *Journal of Marriage and the Family* 32(3):457-464.
Bancroft, G. (1966) Lessons from the pattern of unemployment in the last five years. Pp. 191-226 in R. A. Gordon and M. S. Gordon, eds., *Prosperity and Unemployment*. New York: John Wiley and Sons.

[50] A good illustration of why this is important is Berk's and Shih's (1980) finding that both wives and husbands each report the other's contribution to be lower than the other person reports his or her own.

[51] This type of opportunity has been provided to researchers who have used the Consumer Panel of Young Married Couples. Unfortunately, the costs would be very high.

Barrett, N. (1979) Women in the job market: occupations, earnings, and career opportunities. Pp. 31-62 in R. E. Smith, ed., *The Subtle Revolution: Women at Work*. Washington, D.C.: The Urban Institute.

Barrett, N., and Morgenstern, R. (1974) Why do blacks and women have high unemployment rates? *Journal of Human Resources* 9(4):452-464.

Becker, G. S. (1965) A theory of the allocation of time. *Economic Journal* 75:493-517.

Becker, G. S. (1974) A theory of marriage. Pp. 299-344 in T. W. Schultz, ed., *Economics of the Family*. A conference report of the National Bureau of Economic Research. Chicago: University of Chicago Press.

Beller, A. H. (1980) Occupational Segregation by Sex: Determinants and Changes. Paper presented at the Population Association of America meeting, Denver, Colo.

Belsky, J., and Sternberg, L. D. (1978) The effects of day care: a critical review. *Child Development* 9(3):920-949.

Bergmann, B. R. (1973) Labor Turnover, Segmentation and Rates of Unemployment: A Simulation-Theoretic Approach. Unpublished manuscript, Department of Economics, University of Maryland.

Bergmann, B. R. (1980) Women's Work Participation and the Economic Support of Children. Unpublished manuscript, Department of Economics, University of Maryland.

Berk, R. A., and Berk, S. F. (1978) A simultaneous equation model for the division of household labor. *Sociological Methods and Research* 6(4):431-468.

Berk, S. F., and Shih, A. (1980) Contributions to household labor: comparing wives' and husbands' reports. Pp. 191-228 in S. F. Berk, ed., *Women and Household Labor*. Beverly Hills, Calif.: Sage Publications.

Bielby, W. T., Hawley, C. B., and Bills, D. (1977) Research Uses of the National Longitudinal Survey. Paper prepared for the Social Science Research Council Conference on the National Longitudinal (Parnes) Survey. Washington, D.C. October 14-16.

Birnbaum, J. A. (1971) Life Patterns, Personality Style and Self Esteem in Gifted Family Oriented and Career Committed Women. Ph.D. dissertation, University of Michigan.

Blau, F. D. (1976a) Longitudinal patterns of labor force participation. Pp. 27-55 in H. S. Parnes et al., eds., *Dual Careers: A Longitudinal Analysis of the Labor Market Experience of Women*, Vol. 4. Columbus, Ohio: Ohio State University.

Blau, F. D. (1976b) *Equal Pay in the Office*. Lexington, Mass.: Lexington Books.

Blau, F. D. (1977) Review of C. B. Lloyd, ed., Sex discrimination and division of labor. *Industrial and Labor Relations Review* 30(2):254-255.

Blau, F. D., and Hendricks, W. E. (1979) Occupational segregation by sex: trends and prospects. *Journal of Human Resources* 14(2):197-210.

Blood, R. O., Jr. (1963) The husband-wife relationship. Pp. 282-305 in I. Nye and L. W. Hoffman, eds., *The Employed Mother in America*. Chicago: Rand McNally.

Blood, R. O., Jr., and Wolfe, D. M. (1960) *Husbands and Wives: The Dynamics of Married Living*. New York: The Free Press.

Booth, A. (1977) Wife's employment and husband's stress: a replication and refutation. *Journal of Marriage and the Family* 39(4):645-650.

Bowen, W. G., and Finnegan, T. A. (1969) *The Economics of Labor Force Participation*. Princeton, N.J.: Princeton University Press.

Brito, P., and Jusenius, C. (1978) Occupational expectations for age 35. *Years for Decision*, Vol. 4. R&D Monograph No. 24. Washington, D.C.: U.S. Department of Labor.

Brown, C. (Vickery) (1980) Toward An Institutional Theory of Household Decision-Making. Unpublished working paper, Institution for Industrial Relations, University of California, Berkeley.

Bureau of Labor Statistics (1976) *Employment and Earnings* 22:7. Washington, D.C.: U.S. Department of Labor.
Bureau of Labor Statistics (1980a) *News* (December). Washington, D.C.: U.S. Department of Labor.
Bureau of Labor Statistics (1980b) *Perspectives on Working Women: A Data Bank.* Washington, D.C.: U.S. Department of Labor.
Bureau of the Census (1972) Family composition. *1970 Census of Population, Subject Reports,* No. PC(2)4A. Washington, D.C.: U.S. Department of Commerce.
Bureau of the Census (1976a) Number, timing, and duration of marriages and divorces in the U.S.: June 1975. *Current Population Reports,* Series P-20, No. 297. Washington, D.C.: U.S. Department of Commerce.
Bureau of the Census (1976b) Marriage, divorce, widowhood and remarriage by family characteristics: June, 1975. *Current Population Reports,* Series P-20, No. 312. Washington, D.C.: U.S. Department of Commerce.
Bureau of the Census (1977a) Fertility of American women: June 1976. *Current Population Reports,* Series P-20, No. 308. Washington, D.C.: U.S. Department of Commerce.
Bureau of the Census (1977b) Fertility of American women: June 1977, (advance report). *Current Population Reports,* Series P-20, No. 316. Washington, D.C.: U.S. Department of Commerce.
Bureau of the Census (1978) Marital status and living arrangements: March 1977. *Current Population Reports,* Series P-20, No. 323. Washington, D.C.: U.S. Department of Commerce.
Bureau of the Census (1979a) Marital status and living arrangements: March 1978. *Current Population Reports,* Series P-20, No. 328. Washington, D.C.: U.S. Department of Commerce.
Bureau of the Census (1979b) Divorce, child custody, and child support. *Current Population Reports,* Series P-23, No. 84. Washington, D.C.: U.S. Department of Commerce.
Bureau of the Census (1980a) Household and family characteristics: March 1979. *Current Population Reports,* Series P-20, No. 352. Washington, D.C.: U.S. Department of Commerce.
Bureau of the Census (1980b) Households and families, by type: March 1980, (advance report). *Current Population Reports,* Series P-20, No. 357. Washington, D.C.: U.S. Department of Commerce.
Bureau of the Census (1980c) American families and living arrangements. *Current Population Reports,* Series P-23, No. 104. Washington, D.C.: U.S. Department of Commerce.
Burke, R. J., and Weir, T. (1976) Relationship of wives' employment status to husband, wife and pair satisfaction and performance. *Journal of Marriage and the Family* 38(2):278-287.
Cabral, R., Ferber, M. A., and Green, C. (1982) Men and women in fiduciary institutions: a study of sex differences in career development. *Review of Economics and Statistics* 63(4):573-580.
Cain, G. G. (1966) *Married Women in the Labor Force: An Economic Analysis.* Chicago: University of Chicago Press.
Cherlin, A. (1977) The effect of children on marital dissolution. *Demography* 14(3):265-272.
Clare, J. (1957) The Relationship of Non-Familial Activities to Fertility Behavior. Ph.D. dissertation, University of Michigan, Ann Arbor.
Clarke-Stewart, A. (1977) *Child Care in the Family: A Review of Research and Some Propositions for Policy.* New York: Academic Press.

Corcoran, M., and Duncan, G. J. (1978) A summary of part I findings. Pp. 3-46 in G. J. Duncan and J. N. Morgan, eds., *Five Thousand American Families—Patterns of Economic Progress*, Vol. 6. Ann Arbor, Mich.: Institute for Social Research.

Cutright, P. (1974) Components of change in the number of female household heads aged 15-44: United States 1940-1970. *Journal of Marriage and the Family* 36(4):714-721.

Davis, H. L. (1976) Decision making within the household. Pp. 73-98 in R. Ferber, ed., *Selected Aspects of Consumer Behavior: A Summary from the Perspective of Different Disciplines*. Prepared for the National Science Foundation Directorate for Research Applications, Research Applied to National Needs. Washington, D.C.: National Science Foundation.

Degler, C. N. (1980) *At Odds, Women and the Family in America from the Revolution to the Present*. New York: Oxford University Press.

Department of Commerce (1980) *News* (November 1). Washington, D.C.: U.S. Department of Commerce.

Drucker, P. (1976) Why consumers aren't behaving. *The Wall Street Journal* (December 1):18.

Dubnoff, S. J., Veraff, J., and Kulka, R. A. (1978) Adjustment to Work, 1957-1976. Paper presented at the meeting of the American Psychological Association, Toronto, Ontario.

Duncan, B., and Duncan, O. B. (1969) Family stability and occupational success. *Social Problems* 16(3):273-285.

Etaugh, C. (1978) Effects of Nonmaternal Care on Children: Research Evidence and Popular Views. Paper presented at the meeting of the American Psychological Association, Toronto, Ontario.

Feld, S. (1963) Feelings of adjustment. Pp. 331-352 in I. Nye and L. W. Hoffman, eds., *The Employed Mother in America*. Chicago: Rand McNally.

Feldman, H., and Feldman, M. (1973) *The Relationship Between the Family and Occupational Functioning in a Sample of Rural Women*. Ithaca, N.Y.: Cornell University Press.

Ferber, M. A. (1982) Labor market participation of young married women: causes and effects. *Journal of Marriage and Family* 44(2):457-468.

Ferber, M. A., and Birnbaum, B. G. (1977) The new home economics: retrospect and prospects. *Journal of Consumer Research* 4(1):19-28.

Ferber, M. A., and Birnbaum, B. G. (1980) Housework: priceless or valueless? *Review of Income and Wealth* 26(4):387-400.

Ferber, M. A., and Birnbaum, B. G. (1981) Labor force participation patterns and earnings of clerical workers. *Journal of Human Resources* 16(3):416-426.

Ferber, M. A., and Huber, J. A. (1979) Husbands, wives, and careers. *Journal of Marriage and Family* 41(2):315-325.

Ferber, M. A., and Kordick, B. (1978) Sex differentials in the earnings of Ph.D.s. *Industrial and Labor Relations Review* 31(2):227-238.

Ferber, M. A., and Lowry, H. M. (1976a) The sex differential in earnings: a reappraisal. *Industrial and Labor Relations Review* 29(3):377-387.

Ferber, M. A., and Lowry, H. M. (1976b) Women—the new reserve army of the unemployed. *Signs: Journal of Women in Culture and Society* 1(32):213-232.

Ferber, M. A., and Lowry, H. M. (1977) Woman's place: national differences in the occupational mosaic. *Journal of Marketing* 41(3):23-30.

Ferber, R., and Hirsch, W. Z. (1978) Social experimentation and economic policy: a survey. *Journal of Economic Literature* 16(4):1379-1414.

Ferree, M. M. (1976) Working class jobs: housework and paid work as sources of satisfaction. *Social Problems* 23(4):431-441.

Freedman, R., and Coombs, L. (1966) Childspacing and family economic position. *American Sociological Review* 31(5):631-648.

Friedman, M. (1957) *A Theory of the Consumption Function.* National Bureau of Economic Research, New York. Princeton, N.J.: Princeton University Press.

Galbraith, J. K. (1973) *Economics and the Public Purpose.* Boston: Houghton Mifflin.

Gauger, W. H., and Walker, K. E. (1980) *The Dollar Value of Household Work.* Information Bulletin 60, New York State College of Ecology. Ithaca, N.Y.: Cornell University Press.

Gianopulos, A., and Mitchell, H. W. (1957) Marital disagreement in working wife marriages as a function of husband's attitude toward wife's employment. *Journal of Marriage and the Family* 19(4):373-378.

Glick, P. C., and Norton, A. J. (1979) Marrying, divorcing, and living together in the U.S. today. *Population Bulletin* 32(5):3-39.

Gold, D., and Andres, D. (1978) Relations between maternal employment and development of nursery school children. *Canadian Journal of Behavioral Science* 10(2):116-129.

Gold, D., Andres, D., and Glorieux, J. (1979) The development of Francophone nursery school children with employed and nonemployed mothers. *Canadian Journal of Behavioural Science* 11(2):169-173.

Goldberg, R. J. (1977) Maternal Time Use and Preschool Performance. Paper presented at the meeting of the Society for Research in Child Development, New Orleans, La.

Goode, W. J. (1974) Comment on Becker's "A theory of marriage." Pp. 345-351 in T. W. Schultz, ed., *Economics of the Family.* A conference report of the National Bureau of Economic Research. Chicago: University of Chicago Press.

Gordon, N. M. (1979) Institutional responses: the federal income tax system. Pp. 201-221 in R. E. Smith, ed., *The Subtle Revolution: Women at Work.* Washington, D.C.: The Urban Institute.

Gover, D. A. (1963) Socioeconomic differential in the relationship between marital adjustment and wife's employment status. *Marriage and Family Living* 25(4):452-456.

Hanoch, G. (1976) A Multivariate Model of Labor Supply: Methodology for Estimation. Rand Corporation Paper R-1980, Santa Monica, California.

Hausman, J. (1981) Labor supply. Pp. 29-72 in H. Aaron and J. Pechman, eds., *How Taxes Affect Economic Behavior.* Washington, D.C.: The Brookings Institution.

Hayghe, H. (1976) *Marital and Family Characteristics of the Labor Force.* Special Labor Force Report No. 183. Bureau of Labor Statistics. Washington, D.C.: U.S. Department of Labor.

Hechman, J. (1979) Sample selection bias as a specification error. *Econometrica* 47(1):153-161.

Hill, D., and Hoffman, S. (1977) Husbands and wives. Pp. 29-69 in G. J. Duncan and J. N. Morgan, eds., *Five Thousand American Families—Patterns of Economic Progress,* Vol. 5. Ann Arbor, Mich.: Institute for Social Research.

Hofferth, S. (1980) Some long-run labor market effects of vocational education on young women. *Education, Sex, Equity and Occupational Stereotyping: Conference Report.* Washington, D.C.: National Commission for Employment Policy.

Hofferth, S., and Moore, K. (1979) Women's employment and marriage. Pp. 99-124 in R. E. Smith, ed., *The Subtle Revolution: Women at Work,* Washington, D.C.: The Urban Institute.

Hoffman, L. W. (1974) Effects of maternal employment on the child—a review of the research. *Developmental Psychology* 10(2):204-228.

Hoffman, L. W. (1977) Changes in family roles, socialization, and sex differences. *American Psychologist* 32(8):644-657.

Hoffman, L. W. (1979) Maternal employment: 1979. *American Psychologist* 34(10):859-865.

Hoffman, L. W., and Nye, F. I., eds. (1974) *Working Mothers.* San Francisco, Calif.: Jossey-Bass.

Hoffman, S., and Holmes, J. (1976) Husbands, wives, and divorce. Pp. 23-76 in G. J. Duncan and J. N. Morgan, eds., *Five Thousand Families*, Vol. 4. Ann Arbor, Mich.: Institute for Social Research.

Holmstrom, L. L. (1972) *The Two-Career Family.* Cambridge, Mass.: Schenkman.

Horney, M. J., and McElroy, M. B. (1980) A Nash-Bargained Linear Expenditure System: The Demand for Leisure and Goods. Report 8041, Center for Mathematical Studies in Business and Economics, Duke University.

Hoyle, K. C. (1967) Why the unemployed look for work. *Monthly Labor Review* 90(2):32-38.

Huber, J. A. (1980) Will U.S. fertility continue to decline? *Sociological Quarterly* 21(4):481-492.

Huber, J. A., and Spitze, G. (1980) Considering divorce: an expansion of Becker's theory of marital instability. *American Journal of Sociology* 86(1):77-89.

Huber, J. A., and Spitze, G. (1981) Wives' employment, household behaviors and sex-role attitudes. *Social Forces* 60(1):150-169.

Johnson, B. L. (1978) Women who head families, 1970-77: their numbers rose, income lagged. *Monthly Labor Review* 101(2):32-37.

Johnson, B. L. (1979) *Marital and Family Characteristics of Workers, 1970-78.* Special Labor Force Report No. 219, Bureau of Labor Statistics. Washington, D.C.: U.S. Department of Labor.

Johnson, B. L. (1980) Single-parent families. *Family Economics Review* (Summer/Fall):22-27.

Kanter, R. M. (1977) *Work and Family in the United States: A Critical Review and Agenda for Research and Policy.* Social Science Frontiers. New York: Russell Sage Foundation.

Korbin, F. E. (1978) The fall in household size and the rise of the primary individual in the United States. Pp. 69-82 in M. Gordon, ed., *The American Family in Social-Historical Perspective.* New York: St. Martin's Press.

Kulka, R., and Weingarten, H. (1979) The Long-Term Effects of Parental Divorce in Childhood on Adult Adjustment: A Twenty Year Perspective. Paper presented at the annual meetings of the American Sociological Association, Boston.

Lazear, E., and Michael, R. (1980) Real income equivalences among one-earner and two-earner families. *American Economic Review* 70(2):203-208.

Lehrer, E., and Nerlove, M. (1980) Women's life-cycle time allocation: An econometric analysis. Pp. 149-168 in S. F. Berk, ed., *Women and Household Labor.* Beverly Hills, Calif.: Sage Publications.

Leibowitz, A. (1975) Women's work in the home. Pp. 223-243 in C. B. Lloyd, ed., *Sex, Discrimination and the Division of Labor.* New York: Columbia University Press.

Leuthold, J. H. (1978) The effect of taxation on the probability of labor force participation by married women. *Public Finance* 33(3):280-294.

Leuthold, J. H. (1979) Taxes and the two-earner family: impact on the work decision. *Public Finance Quarterly* 7(2):147-161.

Mahoney, T. A. (1961) Factors determining the labor force participation of married women. *Industrial and Labor Relations Review* 14(4):563-577.

Manser, M., and Brown, M. (1979) Bargaining analyses of household decisions. In C. B. Lloyd, E. S. Andrews, and C. L. Gilroy, eds., *Women in the Labor Market.* New York: Columbia University Press.

Manser, M., and Brown, M. (1980) Marriage and household decision-making: a bargaining analysis. *International Economic Review* 21(1):31-44.

Maret-Havens, E. (1977) Developing an index to measure female labor force attachment. *Monthly Labor Review* 100(5):35-38.

Mason, K. O., Czajka, J. L., and Arber, S. (1970) Change in U.S. women's sex-role attitudes 1964-74. *American Sociological Review* 41(4):573-594.

Michel, A. (1967) Comparative data concerning the interaction in French and American families. *Journal of Marriage and the Family* 29(2):337-344.

Mincer, J. (1960a) Employment and consumption. *Review of Economics and Statistics* 42(1):20-26.

Mincer, J. (1960b) Labor supply, family income and consumption. *American Economic Review* 50(2):574-583.

Mincer, J. (1962) Labor force participation of married women: a study of labor supply. Pp. 63-97 in H. G. Lewis, ed., *Aspects of Labor Economics.* Princeton, N.J.: Princeton University Press.

Mincer, J., and Polachek, S. (1974) Family investments in human capital: earnings of women. *Journal of Political Economy* 82(2):S76-S108.

Moore, K. A., and Hofferth, S. L. (1979) Women and their children. In R. Smith, ed., *The Subtle Revolution: Women at Work.* Washington, D.C.: The Urban Institute.

Moore, K. A., Waite, L. J., Hofferth, S. L., and Caldwell, S. B. (1978) *The Consequences of Age at First Childbirth: Marriage, Separation and Divorce.* Paper 1146-03. Washington, D.C.: The Urban Institute.

Mueller, M. (1975) Economic determinants of volunteer work by women. *Signs* 2:325-338.

Myrdal, A., and Klein, V. (1956) *Women's Two Roles: Home and Work.* London: Routledge and Kegan Paul.

Nerlove, M. (1974) Toward a new theory of population and economic growth. Pp. 527-545 in T. W. Schultz, ed., *Economics of the Family.* A conference report of the National Bureau of Economic Research. Chicago: University of Chicago Press.

Niemi, B. (1975) Geographic immobility and unemployment. Pp. 61-89 in C. B. Lloyd, ed., *Sex, Discrimination, and the Division of Labor* New York: Columbia University Press.

Nye, F. I. (1963) Personal satisfactions. Pp. 320-330 in F. I. Nye and L. W. Hoffman, eds., *The Employed Mother in America.* Chicago: Rand McNally.

Nye, F. I., and Hoffman, L. W., eds. (1963) *The Employed Mother in America.* Chicago: Rand McNally.

Oakley, A. (1980) Prologue: reflections on the study of household labor. Pp. 7-14 in S. F. Berk, ed., *Women and Household Labor.* Beverly Hills, Calif.: Sage Publications.

Ohlbaum, J. S. (1971) Self-Concepts, Value Characteristics and Self- Actualization of Professional and Non-professional Women. Ph.D. dissertation, U.S. International University, San Diego.

Oppenheimer, V. K. (1970) *The Female Labor Force in the United States: Demographic and Economic Factors Governing Its Growth and Changing Composition.* Berkeley, Calif.: University of California.

Orden, S. R., and Bradburn, N. M. (1969) Working wives and marriage happiness. *American Journal of Sociology* 74(4):392-407.

Palmore, E. B., and Stone, V. (1973) Prediction of longevity: a follow-up of the aged in Chapel Hill. *The Gerontologist* 13(1):88-90.

Pleck, J. H., Lang, L., and Rustad, M. (1978) Men's Family Work Involvement and Satisfaction. Unpublished manuscript, Center for Research on Women, Wellesley College.

Pleck, J. H., and Rustad, M. (1980) Husbands' and Wives' Time in Family Work and Paid Work in the 1975-76 Study of Time Use. Unpublished manuscript, Center for Research on Women, Wellesley College.

Pleck, J. H., Shepard, L. J., and O'Connor, P. (1978) Wives' Employment Status and Marital Adjustment: Yet Another Look. Institute for Social Research, University of Michigan, Ann Arbor.

Polachek, S. W. (1975) Occupational biases in measuring male-female discrimination. *Journal of Human Resources* 10(2):205-229.

Polachek, S. W. (1976) Occupational Segregation Among Women: A Human Capital Approach. Report No. ASPER/PUR-75 1909A. U.S. Department of Labor.

Powell, K. S. (1963) Family variables. Pp. 231-240 in F.I. Nye and L. W. Hoffman, eds., *The Employed Mother in America*. Chicago: Rand McNally.

Preston, S., and Richards, A. (1975) The influence of women's work opportunities on marriage rates. *Demography* 12:209-222.

Rainwater, L., and Rein, M. (1980) Tracking family experience in the seventies. *Contemporary Sociology* 9(6):779-785.

Rallings, E. M., and Nye, F. I. (1979) Wife-mother employment, family and society. Pp. 203-226 in W. R. Burr, R. Hill, F. I. Nye, and I. L. Reiss, eds., *Contemporary Theories About the Family*. London: The Free Press.

Reid, M. G. (1934) *Economics of Household Production*. New York: John Wiley.

Robinson, J. (1977a) *How Americans Use Time. A Social-Psychological Analysis of Everyday Behavior*. New York: Praeger Publishers.

Robinson, J. (1977b) *Changes in America's Use of Time: 1965-1975*. Cleveland, Ohio: Cleveland State University, Communications Research Center.

Robinson, J. (1980) Housework technology and household work. Pp. 53-68 in S. F. Berk, ed., *Household Labor*. Sage Yearbooks in Women's Policy Studies, Vol. 5. Beverly Hills, Calif.: Sage Publications.

Ross, H. L., and Sawhill, I. V. (1975) *Time of Transition. The Growth of Families Headed by Women*. Washington, D.C.: The Urban Institute.

Rubenstein, J. L., and Howes, C. (1979) Caregiving and infant behavior in day care and in homes. *Developmental Psychology* 15(1):1-24.

Samuelson, P. A. (1956) Social indifference curves. *Quarterly Journal of Economics* 70(1):1-22.

Sanborn, H. (1964) Pay differences between men and women. *Industrial and Labor Relations Review* 17(4):534-550.

Sawhill, I. V. (1977) Economic perspectives on the family. *Daedalus* 106(2):115-125.

Sawhill, I. V., Peabody, G. E., Jones, C. A., and Caldwell, S. B. (1975) Income Transfers and Family Structure.Washington Paper 979-03. Washington, D.C.: The Urban Institute.

Schoen, R., and Urton, W. (1979) A theoretical perspective on cohort marriage and divorce in twentieth century Sweden. *Journal of Marriage and the Family* 41(2):409-415.

Schram, V. (1979) Determinants of Volunteer Work Participation by Married Women. Ph.D. dissertation, University of Illinois, Urbana.

Scott, J. W., and Tilly, L. A. (1980) Women's work and the family in nineteenth century Europe. Pp. 91-124 in A. H. Amsden, ed., *The Economics of Women and Work*. New York: St. Martins Press.

Skolnick, A. S., and Skolnick, J. H. (1977) *Family in Transition*. Boston: Little, Brown.

Smith, J. P. (1980) *Female Labor Supply: Theory and Estimation*, Princeton, N.J.: Princeton University Press.

Smith, R. E., ed. (1979a) *The Subtle Revolution: Women at Work*. Washington, D.C.: The Urban Institute.

Smith, R. E. (1979b) The movement of women into the labor force. Pp. 1-19 in R. E. Smith, ed., *The Subtle Revolution: Women at Work*. Washington, D.C.: The Urban Institute.

Strober, M. H. (1977) Wives' labor force behavior and family consumption patterns. *American Economic Review* 67(1):410-417.

Strober, M. H. (1979) Should Separate Family Budgets be Constructured for Husband-Wife-Earner (HWE) and Husband-Only-Earner (HOE) Families at Various Income Levels? Paper prepared for Bureau of Labor Statistics Expert Panel, U.S. Department of Labor, Washington, D.C.

Strober, M. H., and Weinberg, C. B. (1980) Strategies used by working and nonworking wives to reduce time pressures. *Journal of Consumer Research* 6(4):338-348.

Sweet, J. A. (1968) *Family Composition and the Labor Force Activity of Married Women in the U. S.* Ann Arbor, Mich.: University of Michigan.

Thornton, A., and Freedman, D. (1982) Consistency of Sex Role Attitudes of Women, 1962-1977. Institute for Social Research working paper to be published in *American Sociological Review*.

Vanek, J. (1974) Time spent in housework. *Scientific American* 231(5):116-120.

Vickery, C. (Brown) (1979) Women's economic contribution to the family. Pp. 159-200 in R. E. Smith, ed., *The Subtle Revolution: Women at Work*. Washington, D.C.: The Urban Institute.

Waite, L. J. (1982) Projecting female labor force participation from sex-role attributes. *Social Science Research*.

Waite, L. J., and Stolzenberg, R. M. (1976) Intended childbearing and labor force participation of young women: insights from non-recursive models. *American Sociological Review* 41(2):235-252.

Welter, B. (1978) The cult of true womanhood: 1820-1860. Pp. 313-333 in M. Gordon, ed., *The American Family in Social-Historical Perspective*. New York: St. Martin's Press.

Whitman, M. V. (1973) Hearings Before the Joint Economic Committee, 93rd Congress, Part 1, p. 21. U.S. Congress, Washington, D.C.

Willis, R. J. (1974) Economic theory of fertility behavior. Pp. 25-75 in T. W. Schultz, ed., *Economics of the Family*. A conference report of the National Bureau of Economic Research. Chicago: University of Chicago Press.

Women's Bureau (1979) *The Earnings Gap Between Women and Men*. Washington, D.C.: U.S. Department of Labor.

Wright, J. D. (1978) Are working women really more satisfied? Evidence from several national surveys. *Journal of Marriage and the Family* 40(2):301-313.

Zellner, H. (1975) The determinants of occupational segregation. Pp. 125-145 in C. B. Lloyd, ed., *Sex, Discrimination, and the Division of Labor*. New York: Columbia University Press.

5
Employer Responses to the Family Responsibilities of Employees

**Sheila B. Kamerman, *Columbia University,*
and Paul W. Kingston, *University of Virginia***

In 1980 about 94 million of the approximately 107-million-person labor force were civilians employed in nonagricultural industries (Bureau of Labor Statistics, 1982). Of these, about 65 million, or about 70 percent of the total labor force, worked for private industries. Most of these employees were married, or parents of minor children, or both. Inextricably and fundamentally, the family lives of these workers are conditioned by the organization of work and the policies and practices of the nearly four million companies at which they are employed.

Our concern here is to provide a selective overview of what is known about the ways in which these diverse employers are meeting or attempting to meet the needs of employees with family responsibilities.

(1)   Which employers have instituted which kinds of policies for which workers, and how are different types of workers affected?

(2)   What factors influence the prevailing patterns of family-related policies, as well as the emergence of new policies?

(3)   What is known about the consequences of employers' policies for families with children and for the children themselves?

(4)   What are the consequences of these policies for employers, for other community services, for the larger society?

(5)   How is all of this known and with what degree of confidence?

(6)   What issues and questions emerge?

Sheila B. Kamerman's work on this paper was supported by the Carnegie Corporation.

Obviously the scope of our concern is broad, but, as the reader will see, the state of knowledge is limited. Moreover, although the questions we address are basic to understanding what employers provide, our conclusions necessarily raise still more general issues.

We note a key restriction of this analysis at the outset: About 40 million people in the labor force are not considered here. Among the omitted are those in the military; in agriculture; the self-employed; federal, state, and local employees; and the 7.4 million who were unemployed at the time of the 1980 survey.

Given the magnitude of the task that we are addressing, we have elected to focus on what is provided employees working in the private for-profit sector only. Constituting two-thirds of the work force, this private sector is where most of the changes are taking place in response to shifts in the work force and in the society at large.

We have further narrowed our focus to highlight employee benefits and services—the practices often described as fringe benefits—as well as policies and recent initiatives in the scheduling of work. We therefore discuss both those policies and practices that have emerged from recent concerns for work redesign and the quality of work life and those that have evolved over time from some implicit assumptions about employer-employee relationships and compensation and allocation of wages. We emphasize throughout, however, an inclusive view of what should be considered in analyzing the family-related policies of employers. We examine both those policies that have been consciously designed to accommodate the family lives of employees, as well as those that have major family effects, despite other-than-family purposes in their development.

Our presentation involves two assumptions:

(1) In advanced industrialized societies, when men and women are in the labor force at the same time, they are likely to be parents. Certain adjustments and adaptations are needed at the workplace and elsewhere in the society if they are to fulfill home and work tasks adequately and rear their children well. If such responses are not forthcoming, adults may have difficulty in one, the other, or both domains; employers may experience problems at the workplace; and children may suffer, as may ultimately society.

(2) We must know what employers now provide, for whom, how, and with what consequences if we are concerned about the nature and extent of the changes now occurring in the society and the responses needed. Only with this knowledge is it possible to address adequately the more basic question of whether employers should, in fact, be responsible for adapting to this changed labor force; and if so, what, how

much, how, and for whom they should provide. However, our intent is not to prescribe what employers should or should not provide for their employees. Rather, we believe that an informed discussion first requires knowing what employers do now provide, and for whom. We hope to contribute to that preliminary discussion.

EMPLOYER RESPONSES: A FRAMEWORK FOR STUDY

Any effort to assess systematically (1) what employers are doing for employees with family responsibilities and (2) what is known about why, how, and for whom this is being done, and with what consequences, is predicated on two related assumptions: There is some consensus about what these responses are and there is a reasonably defined body of information about them. Neither of these assumptions is valid. Nor, moreover, is there much indication that many business activities that could be defined as significant for family life were deliberately developed out of employer awareness of employee's family circumstances.

Our first task, therefore, is to indicate the kinds of employer provisions which we think play a critical role in the personal and familial lives of employees. We are convinced that all deserve attention, although their scope is far broader than what we can address here.

Underlying any discussion of employer responses to the family responsibilities of employees is the recognition that jobs—the availability of jobs and job security—are primary and the foundation of all else. Nothing that one employer does or can do has meaning for those who are unemployed or those who live in constant fear of losing their jobs. Although obviously of major importance, this prime concern is clearly beyond the scope of this paper.[1]

The adequacy of wages is also a central concern for families.[2] The

---

[1] Individual employers can ease the problems of the unemployed or those in fear of losing their jobs. In a more fundamental sense, however, this is an issue for public policy, not for the policies and practices of individual employers.

That labor market policies focused specifically on achieving full employment exist in other mixed economies, such as Sweden and to a lesser extent the Federal Republic of Germany, should seem to indicate that such a goal is feasible, at least in part, although not yet accepted in the United States. Job security, however, is increasingly being addressed in this country, although not nearly to the extent that it has been an accepted goal of labor-management relations in Europe.

[2] See, for example, Avizahar (1977). From another perspective, wage policy in Australia (Australian Department of Social Security, 1979:7) and the initial establishment of a minimum wage in 1907 were predicated on the assumptions that (1) "Wages policy . . . [was] the primary means of assuring minimal adequacy of family income," and (2) an adequate minimum wage should cover a male worker, his nonworking spouse, and two independent children.

concept of a family wage has been explored, discussed, and even attempted, although unsuccessfully. The alternative of a statutory family benefit designed to supplement wages in the labor market is at the heart of the concept of a child or family allowance. Indeed, the problems that exist because wages are based on the market determination of the value of an individual's labor, with no relationship to individual or family needs, were important considerations in the French development of a family allowance system.[3] This general concern, however, is also beyond the scope of this paper.

A third component of employer provision relates to conditions of work. Although issues of occupational health and safety are clearly salient, especially the relation of certain substances to infertility or genetic damage, we have omitted this subject from the core of this paper. Nor do we address the still-in-the-future issue of off-site work or the current efforts to restructure or redefine work, to modify labor-management decision-making processes, or to share work in the sense of sharing unemployment. All of these are interesting and viewed by some as important and relevant. Given the limitations of a paper, however, we have chosen to focus on what we believe are the most significant among current employer responses.

We concentrate on two aspects of what employers can and do provide their employees: (1) what we would describe as the corporate social welfare system—the benefits (cash and in-kind) and the services provided employees by their employers; and (2) the scheduling and hours of work or what is increasingly described as alternative work schedules or patterns.

Work schedules have received much attention in recent years. Various innovations in work scheduling are popularly viewed as the most promising new developments at the workplace to accommodate the family needs of a changing labor force, particularly since it includes a growing number of women who are married, have children, or both.

We begin first, however, with a discussion of the contemporary corporate social welfare system, the evolutionary product of earlier paternalistic practices. In aggregate the diverse practices of this system provide a concrete picture of the nature and scope of employer responsibility to family life. However, since employee benefits have been largely viewed as providing protection for the individual worker, rather than as playing

---

[3] Family or child allowances, provided by the government as an income supplement to offset some of the economic costs of rearing children and delivered through the income-transfer or tax system, exist in 67 countries today. Among all the industrialized countries, only the United States fails to provide this important family benefit. For some discussion of family allowances in France, see Questiaux and Fournier (1978).

a significant role in meeting the family responsibilities of employees, our reasons for focusing on these policies should be outlined.

Neither published research nor other general discussion suggests that systematic attention has yet been paid to the family-benefits component or the family consequences of employee benefits. Neither employers when providing benefits, nor employees when claiming them, nor unions when negotiating them, seem to view these benefits as important for family as well as individual well-being. Although certain benefits—life insurance, for example—are clearly viewed in a family context, most discussion of employee benefits is directed at employer-employee concerns for protecting the individual worker. Yet we are convinced that failure to consider these benefits would be a major error in any serious assessment of how employers are meeting the family needs of employees. Indeed, we argue that apart from actual jobs, job security, and wages, employee benefits—the corporate social security system—constitute the single most important category of employer provision affecting families.

We base our argument on four considerations:

(1) Wages and salaries are supplemented significantly through these benefits—by about 24 percent, according to the Bureau of Labor Statistics (BLS) survey for 1977 (1980a); more than one-third, according to the 1978 and 1979 Chamber of Commerce surveys (1980).[4] Moreover, the nonwage elements of the benefits package (e.g., employer contributions to pensions, life insurance, and health insurance) are not taxable to recipients, thus providing an even greater increment to employee earnings.[5] Furthermore, benefits generally constitute an increasingly large proportion of total employee compensation: two and one-third times as large in 1977 as in 1966. To put it somewhat differently, benefits

[4] According to the national income accounts, employee benefits as wage supplements constituted only 18 percent of direct compensation. (National income accounts are statistical data, such as national output and income and their components. The most comprehensive measure of national output, for example, is the gross national product. In the United States these data are published at regular intervals by the Department of Commerce.) Since wages paid for time not worked, such as holidays, vacations, rest time, and coffee breaks, and employer-funded or subsidized services constituted about half the benefits package described in the other surveys and are not included in the national accounts tabulations, exact comparisons are not possible. For comparison, federal employees receive a benefits package equal to about 15 percent more than that provided employees in the private sector. This difference, however, is almost entirely attributable to more liberal retirement benefits and sick leave for federal employees. When total compensation (wages and benefits) is compared, the difference is reduced to nine percent.

[5] Wages paid for time not worked (paid leave for vacations, holidays, and personal time) are, of course, taxable.

increased 171 percent between 1969 and 1979, while wages and salaries grew 107 percent (Chamber of Commerce, 1980).

(2) Many of these benefits carry with them coverage for dependents, ensuring protection against loss of earnings and thus family income under specified circumstances, as well as coverage for medical and sometimes dental and vision expenditures. The significance of these benefits for family as well as individual economic well-being is obvious and measurable.[6]

(3) The right to job-protected, released time is an important part of employee benefits. The significance of vacations, holidays, maternity leaves, and personal leaves for noneconomic well-being—for health and a variety of quality-of-life dimensions—should be clear, although perhaps difficult to measure. However, we would stress that it is the protection of wages at such times that makes these leaves possible for most employees.[7] The value of these paid leaves for family life, including both spousal and parental relations, would seem extremely important; thus far, however, no studies have been directed at any aspect of this issue.

(4) Despite the impressive growth in coverage by these plans and the increase in benefits levels, a significant portion of the labor force still faces substantial barriers in obtaining these basic protections through place of employment. Those who are or become unemployed obviously face even more severe problems.

We supplement discussion of these benefits with a brief review of what is known about developments in employer-sponsored services for employees.

EMPLOYEE BENEFITS AND SERVICES: THE CORPORATE SOCIAL WELFARE SYSTEM

An employee benefits plan is defined as (Kolodrubetz, 1972:10): "Any type of plan sponsored or initiated unilaterally or jointly by employers

---

[6] The projected Department of Health and Human Services Survey of Income and Program Participation (SIPP), the first national longitudinal household survey, was to have included extensive data on in-kind (noncash) employee benefits. However, because of budget cuts for 1982, this survey has been either postponed or eliminated. A preliminary report of the characteristics of the recipients of employer-provided benefits (pension plans and group health insurance plans) is included in the Bureau of the Census (1981a, 1981b) reports.

[7] Statutory unpaid maternity, parental, and/or child-care leaves in several European countries, which are often available as supplements to paid leaves, provide a dramatic

or employees and providing benefits that stem from the employment relationship and are not underwritten or paid *directly* by government (Federal, State, Local)."[8] In general, these plans provide (1) income maintenance (protection against loss of earnings) when regular earnings are cut off because of death, accident, sickness, disability, retirement, or unemployment; (2) released time with income maintenance for specified purposes such as vacations, holidays, and personal needs; (3) payment of medical expenses associated with illness, injury, and/or other types of health and medical care; and (4) payment of expenses for certain specified nonmedical services, such as legal services, education, and counseling. Some companies may also provide services directly.[9]

Richard Titmuss (1969) describes such benefits and services provided by employers to their employees as "occupational welfare," an important contribution to the well-being of those fortunate enough to be in the labor force.[10] He points out how these, as well as benefits provided certain categories of taxpayers ("fiscal welfare" in his terms), could be compared with the visible, more traditional, and often more stigmatized form of "social welfare"—the benefits and services provided directly by government, often to those in particular need. The pattern of benefits now made available to employees represents the product of an evolving capitalist system, conditioned by particular American circumstances.

Looking Backward

Under the labels "welfare capitalism," "employee welfare," "industrial paternalism," and "industrial welfare," many have described the beneficence of employers in more or less positive terms. Regardless, it is clear that the concern of employers for their individual employees and their familial circumstances is not a new development. Indeed, one could trace its origins back to the relationships on the feudal manor, where

---

illustration of the contrast in value. By far, most eligible employees use the available paid leave; and by far, most eligible employees do not take advantage of the unpaid leave because they cannot financially afford to. See, for example, Kamerman (1980b).

[8] We include in our discussion as well what are termed "employee welfare plans."

[9] The first private pension plan was instituted by the American Express Company in 1875. By 1929, 400 such plans were identified in a private survey. The 1921 Internal Revenue Act did grant favorable tax treatment to employer contributions to pension and welfare plans, but this had little immediate effect on these developments. By 1974 there were more than 52,000 retirement plans and 139,000 health and welfare plans in the United States (Bureau of Labor Statistics, 1976a,b).

[10] This collection was first published in London in 1958. The essay was delivered originally as a lecture in 1956.

serfs owed total fealty to their lords in return for protection as well as economic support.

Of more direct relevance, however, is the emergence of welfare capitalism in the United States in the late nineteenth century, paralleling the development of early welfare statism in Germany with the beginnings of social insurance, as well as the growth in the United States and elsewhere of a strong movement of voluntary social welfare agencies, such as the charity organization societies and the settlement houses (see Brandes, 1976; Hareven and Langenback, 1978; Wallace, 1978).[11] Several developments contributed to the growth of welfarism as an institutional response to nineteenth-century industrialization: the rapid growth of a labor force that was viewed by some as intractable and even dangerous to the established order; the desire to socialize entering workers into very different life and work styles and thus to exercise social control through a variety of devices; the surge of immigration to the United States; and a concern, by some, for instituting a more benevolent and humanitarian component into the harshness of a radically changing world. Thus, responding to similar types of concerns and moving in somewhat similar directions, these three movements began: public statutory provision, private voluntary agencies, and industrial welfare. Statutory provision was particularly pronounced in Europe, while private voluntary agencies and industrial welfare were widespread in both Europe and the United States.

The welfare capitalism of the late nineteenth and early twentieth centuries is the direct antecedent of the industrial social welfare developments of today. Concerned specifically with the amelioration of what employers viewed as their major problems—high employee turnover, labor militancy, and the threat of government interference—some employers identified, too, a more lofty goal (Brandes, 1976:33): "The propagation of an improved American working man: thrifty, clean, temperate, intelligent, and, especially, industrious and loyal."

The disruption in family life as women and children left home to enter the labor force is often identified as contributing significantly to both a growing discontent among workers and a growing social disorganization in the society. Indeed, some employers are described as consciously designing their welfare program as much to shore up a weakening family

---

[11] Brandes (1976:6) defines welfare capitalism as "any service provided for the comfort or improvement of employees which was neither a necessity of the industry nor required by law." For a somewhat different perspective on the historical evolution of the relationship of work, family, and community, see Janowitz (1978).

structure (viewed as the cause of many other problems) as to ameliorate a series of workplace problems. The strategies used by employers to achieve these goals are familiar: housing, medical care, schools,[12] recreation services, religious facilities, advice and counseling services, food and other goods, pension plans, and profit sharing.

Company welfarism emerged during the years when industrializing societies were searching for ways to respond to the rapid rate of change occurring at work, at home, and in the society at large. The movement peaked during the 1920s, a decade of prosperity, leveling out during the latter half of the decade. Some ascribe the apparent slowdown in developments to growing employee resentment of employer paternalism. Other factors may have included the growth in technology, lessening the importance of labor in many large industries; the expansion of voluntary agency and public community services, thus reducing the need for company provision; and the growing availability of automobiles, which expanded access to alternative services and reduced the need for company houses, company stores, and company towns.

Yet most importantly, the demise of business welfarism occurred because of the depression. Employers could provide a variety of extras only when profits were high; the pressure to provide these benefits existed only when the labor market was tight and the competition for workers high. Neither was the case in the 1930s. Furthermore, legislation and policies of the New Deal dealt a direct and final blow to such practices. The Wagner Act[13] and other legislation made company unions illegal, and the act and the National Labor Relations Board created under it actually encouraged the growth of trade or labor unions. Thus, one adversary that business had hoped to constrain through the development of company beneficence had won a significant victory. Once this struggle against the unions was lost, there was little reason for continuing welfare programs in the unionized, core sectors of the economy. Finally, the economic and social havoc of the 1930s demonstrated the inability of private efforts, both profit (business) and nonprofit (voluntary social agencies), to meet the needs of a significant portion of the population faced with overwhelming financial and social problems. Only government, the federal government in particular, had the power, the wherewithal, the authority, and the mission to provide large-scale relief. In the United States the move toward government as the basic provider of essential benefits and services began with the New Deal. By the end

---

[12] These included infant schools through the primary grades, but also all forms of adult education.

[13] The popular name of the National Labor Relations Act.

of the Great Depression, primacy in this field of welfare benefits had moved from the private sector to the public sector. The growth in the role of government and in the nature, scope, range, and extent of its social provision, especially during the last 20 years, is an accepted, integral, and dramatic part of this story.[14]

Nevertheless, despite the demise of company welfare in this paternalistic form and the concomitant trend toward government provision, the role of private industry did not disappear in toto. It merely surfaced again in somewhat modified form after World War II and focused on a narrower range of provision than earlier. Before World War II, employee benefits plans were practically nonexistent, especially for production workers. The phenomenal upsurge in their growth since then occurred largely as a result of four factors: (1) wage controls during World War II and in the immediate postwar period that permitted benefits plans while denying wage increases; (2) the National Labor Relations Board's interpretation of the 1947 Labor Management Relations Act, permitting pensions to be included as a collective bargaining issue; (3) the 1949 report of the Steel Industry Fact Finding Board, which maintained that industry had both a social and an economic obligation to provide workers with social insurance and pensions; and (4) the wage freeze during the Korean War, continuing the earlier pattern set during World War II of permitting benefits plans.

Prevailing Provisions: Benefits

Now, once again, there is growing interest in the potential for industry to broaden the scope, range, scale, and goals of its social policies and programs, in part because of a growing disaffection with government and the conviction that there are limitations to what government can and, according to some, should do. This discussion of industry's potential to assume a larger role must be informed by a clear sense of what industry is actually doing—who is covered in what ways.

However, because of recent changes in government data-collection procedures, it is difficult to analyze comprehensively industry's present role.[15] The last national survey of expenditures for employee compensation was in 1977; the program has been discontinued because of budget

[14] For an excellent overview of these developments, see Advisory Commission on Intergovernmental Relations (1980).

[15] Following passage of the Welfare and Pension Plans Disclosure Act of 1959, data became available for the first time on almost the entire universe of employee benefits plans—those negotiated under collective bargaining agreements as well as all others, including a representative sample of small plans. All private organizations having at least

constraints. All current and future Bureau of Labor Statistics reports of benefits plans will be limited to data from a sample of large and medium-size firms in the private sector, selected to provide comparability in determining federal employee compensation packages.[16] Although other surveys are carried out by governmental and nongovernmental organizations, none is as comprehensive as previous BLS efforts.[17]

To report on current practices then, we must necessarily draw on several data sources that are not fully comparable. In summarizing below available data on coverage related to such key benefits as pensions, health and medical plans, and paid leaves, we generally rely on the single best source of information and only briefly allude to other sources. We also note the scope of some recent initiatives in the provision of employee benefits. Even though all of the data together do not comprise a comprehensive view, it should be readily apparent that the corporate welfare system is highly unequal in the provision of benefits and that the likelihood of workers receiving benefits varies by their place in the occupational-industrial structure.

Pensions When the Social Security Act was passed in 1935, one objective was to provide a minimum floor of income for the retired elderly. About 95 percent of the labor force today is covered by Social Security (89 percent) or some other public retirement program (6 percent). The same proportion is benefiting among the currently retired aged 65 or older. However, then and now the minimum floor of retirement income is expected to be supplemented by other sources of retirement income, such as private pensions and personal savings. Dependence on Social

---

26 participants in their plan were required to file with the U.S. Department of Labor detailed descriptions of their plans, including all amendments. For more broadly defined welfare plans, filing was required only for larger firms. In general, similar filings were required under the Employment Retirement Income Security Act of 1974 (ERISA), which replaced the 1959 legislation. Until the mid-1970s the Bureau of Labor Statistics (BLS) published digests of major provisions of selected leading health, insurance, and pension plans, that is, those viewed as setting the trends in plan development. In addition BLS published reports based on its biennial surveys of expenditures for employee compensation. These included data on costs, establishment policies, and the prevalence of collectively bargained plans.

[16] For a summary of this Level of Benefit Survey, see Bureau of Labor Statistics (1980b). For a more extensive description, see Bureau of Labor Statistics (1981b).

[17] For example, the U.S. Chamber of Commerce's now annual Survey of Employee Benefits and the Bureau of National Affairs' surveys are based largely on self-selected samples. The Conference Board's *Profile of Employee Benefits* (Meyer, 1974, 1981), although by far the most comprehensive, is based on samples heavily weighted toward large and medium-size companies.

Security alone, without coverage by an employer-provided pension, is increasingly likely to mean poverty or a very low income for retirees. Indeed, according to a report from the President's Commission on Pension Policy (1980:7), "one of the results of the near universal coverage of social security and of the lack of coverage of employer pensions is the creation of a two-class retirement income system." Employees themselves view entitlement to a pension as the second most important benefit they receive at work, after health and medical insurance; they also rank it second in their list of benefits they most desire to see improved (Quinn and Staines, 1979).[18]

In 1979, 43 percent of all private wage and salaried workers aged 14 and older were covered by a pension or other retirement plan on their current job[19] (see Table 5-1). These rates were slightly higher than those for 1972, the last time a comparable survey was carried out.

Almost 80 percent of the noncovered workers were employed by companies in which pensions were not available to any employee and therefore are unlikely ever to have coverage on their current job unless their employers institute new plans. The others worked for companies providing pensions to some employees, but not to the particular worker surveyed.

As might be expected, those workers who are well situated in the occupational-industrial structure are apt to have coverage. For example, more than 80 percent of union workers in companies with 500 or more employees had pension plans (but only 12 percent of the employed labor force were in this group). Coverage was highest in high-wage industries, such as communications and public utilities (82 percent) and lowest in

---

[18] The results reported here and elsewhere in this paper are based on the 1977 cross-section sample. (Surveys conducted in 1969 and 1972 are useful for trend analysis. Also available is a 1973-1977 panel study.) The 1977 survey has 1,515 respondents; it is a nationally representative sample of all employed adults, aged 16 or older, currently working for 20 hours or more per week. The 1977 survey includes the core material of the preceding surveys—earnings and fringe benefits, work task and job content, working hours, and attitudes toward various aspects of work. In addition it includes new items related to the employment of the spouse and the impact of employment upon family life.

[19] These data are based on the results of a May 1979 Survey of Pension Plan Coverage, carried out as a supplement to the Current Population Survey. The sample of 19,999 individuals represents an estimated 72 million private workers who make up 75 percent of the employed labor force. (Inclusion of those aged 14 to 16, in contrast to other BLS surveys that include only those 16 and older, does not significantly affect the results.)

The best preliminary report of the results of this survey can be found in Rogers (1980). In response to some critics, Rogers points out that if analysis is confined to those employees meeting ERISA standards for participation, 61 percent of the private labor force are covered. ERISA standards, however, characterize only 57 percent of the labor force.

TABLE 5–1   Extent of Pension Coverage by Selected Characteristics of Workers in Private Industry in 1979

Characteristics	Percentage with Pension Coverage
Total	
All private wage and salary workers	43
aged 14 and older	
Sex	
Male	50
Female	31
Race	
White	56
Nonwhite	46
Age	
Under 25	19
25–29	45
30–44	52
45–54	58
55–64	56
65 and older	18
Extent of employment	
Full time	51
Part time	9
Earnings of full-time workers	
Under $15,000/year	
Men	41
Women	35
Over $15,000/year	
Men	74
Women	68
Selected Industries	
Manufacturing	63
Trade	
wholesale	47
retail	21
Service	
nonprofessional	15
professional	37
Transportation, communication, utilities	64
Construction	37
Finance, insurance, real estate	48
Firm size/union coverage	
Union	
under 100 employees	65
100–499 employees	72
500 or more employees	82
Nonunion	
under 100 employees	13
10–499 employees	42
500 or more employees	63

SOURCE: Rogers (1980). Earnings data are from Beller (1980).

retail trade and service industries (30 to 39 percent). Concomitantly, the unemployed and workers who were disproportionately concentrated in the peripheral sectors of the economy—young adults, racial minorities, women, those with low incomes—generally lacked coverage. Only 19 percent of workers under age 25 (27 percent of the private labor force) were covered. That percentage is substantially lower than the rate (52 percent) for those in the prime working years. Coverage for white workers was 56 percent, as compared to 46 percent for nonwhites.

Women were covered to a significantly lesser extent than men: 31 percent compared to 50 percent. (A similar discrepancy existed between male and female private, full-time workers.) Fewer than one-tenth of all part-time workers were covered, further exacerbating the problem for women, since women in private industry are three times more likely than their male counterparts to work part time. Some combination of industry, firm size, and union membership seems to put women at a disadvantage with regard to pension coverage.

Pension coverage is notably correlated with earnings, too: 10 percent of workers earning less than $5,000 a year were covered, while 70 to 80 percent of those earning more than $15,000 per year were covered.

The value of a pension to workers and their families is significantly affected by vested status. (Vested workers have a nonforfeitable right to a future benefit based on earned credits even though they stop participation in the plan prior to retirement age.) In 1979 just less than half (48 percent) of private workers covered by a retirement plan had vested rights. However, since many older workers have no pension coverage, only a third of all private workers aged 55 and older were vested. Women workers were less likely to be vested than men (51 percent versus 41 percent). That discrepancy largely appears to reflect the fact that women have fewer years of service under their plans.

To summarize: Only half the private labor force is currently covered by a private retirement or pension plan.[20] More than half of the nonwhite members of the labor force and more than two-thirds of the women still do not have this type of protection. Moreover, many who have coverage, especially among women, are likely to be entitled to low benefits. There has been little change in this picture since 1972, despite the enormous growth in the numbers and proportion of women in the labor force. There are only limited data available on the family characteristics of

---

[20] The negative consequences of the absence of coverage by private pension plans is discussed in the President's Commission on Pension Policy (1980). One major recommendation involves mandating such coverage. Some preliminary data are available from the 1980 household survey reported in Bureau of the Census (1981a).

these employees and on the extent to which employees have coverage for their dependents.[21]

Health and Medical Benefits In 75 countries other than the United States, including all but one other advanced industrialized country, health insurance or health services are provided primarily as a statutory benefit. In the United States it is plainly the most important benefit provided through the *corporate* social security system. Eighty-four percent of those responding to the 1977 Quality of Employment Survey (Quinn and Staines, 1979) listed health and medical insurance as the single most important fringe benefit they receive, far more than listed any other benefit. And almost half the respondents listed this benefit as the one they most wanted improved. The overwhelming majority of people, especially the young and middle-aged who have health insurance, obtain such protection through their employers. Thus, any increase in the number of employed generates an increase in the number of people with such coverage, while an increase in the unemployment rate usually carries with it a decrease in coverage.

The proportion of full-time civilian workers with some type of employer-sponsored group health insurance grew from 50 percent in 1950 to about 75 percent in 1979. Approximately the same findings were obtained in a similar survey conducted in 1972.[22] Coverage was lower for those in private employment (73 percent) than for full-time government employees (83 percent), lower for women (67 percent) than for men (76 percent), and lower for younger workers (62 percent) than for those aged 25 to 60. Only about 15 percent of part-time employees were

[21] The 1977 Quality of Employment Survey (Quinn and Staines, 1979) does include data on the family characteristics of respondents. In a subsequent section, we separately analyze by family type the distribution of various benefits, as shown by the above survey.

[22] For a historical overview, see Kolodrubetz (1974a,b). For the best and most recent analysis of health insurance coverage based on household survey data, see U.S. Department of Labor (1981a). For an earlier analysis that attempts to integrate both program and consumer data, see U.S. Congress, Congressional Budget Office (1979) *Profile of Health Care Coverage: The Haves and Have-Nots.* That report points out the problems in obtaining valid and reliable data, underscoring especially the gap between program and survey data. For example, Rogers (1980) points out that close to 20 percent of those interviewed in the 1979 pension survey did not know the approximate number of employees in the firms where they worked.

The results of the National Health Care Expenditures Survey (1977-1979) should provide the most comprehensive information about health insurance coverage for the noninstitutionalized civilian population. However, these results are only available selectively thus far. See, for example, U.S. Department of Health and Human Services (1980).

covered by health insurance through their jobs. A significant proportion of those employees who had no health insurance benefits at work were, however, covered as dependents of employees who were covered. Almost 75 percent of the unemployed had coverage, 33 percent of these through public programs. Coverage generally depended on such factors as the industry of employment, length of time in a particular job, and length of unemployment. Coverage was especially likely to be high for those working in major industries such as mining, manufacturing, and transportation, and low for those employed in agriculture, forestry, construction, entertainment, and services.

The employed who lacked coverage accounted for more than 33 percent of those without health insurance. Still more important, 33 percent of the uncovered full-time wage earners were heads of families; 80 percent of these families had no coverage at all. Indeed, the lack of health insurance for this small portion of the employed has greater ramifications than for any other group. The uncovered employed had eight times as many dependents as the uncovered unemployed.

Young adults, aged 19 to 24, in or out of the labor force, were twice as likely to be without health insurance as any other age group. However, 70 percent were in families in which three-quarters of the heads had coverage. Although more than half of the uncovered were not in the labor force, more than half of these were in families headed by someone with health care coverage. That figure underscores the importance of family-benefit type coverage.

Clearly, health insurance provided as an employee benefit is essential for individuals and families if they are ineligible for Medicaid benefits. The lack of coverage for employees who are parents, especially for young unmarried women, can have severe and deleterious consequences for children. A major problem remains, therefore, for those employees and their families who do not receive such benefits through their jobs.

Employment status affects the extent, the kind, and the adequacy of health care coverage. Reliable data on the number of people with adequate coverage are unavailable. It is estimated that about 15 percent of those with private health insurance, usually provided through their jobs, are not covered for major medical or catastrophic illness expenditures. This estimate may be an undercount, because the most detailed information has been obtained up to now from employer reports to the U.S. Department of Labor, and single establishments with fewer than 25 employees are not required to report unless they are part of a multiestablishment plan. Although recent data are not yet available, the results of a 1972 survey (Kolodrubetz, 1974b) show that only 50 percent of the workers in establishments with fewer than 25 employees had major medical coverage, while 90 percent of those in businesses with 100 or more employees did.

Finally, coverage for routine physician visits, pediatric care, prescriptions, and so forth is still more limited. While there are no reliable data for dental or eye care coverage, in the 1970s these were considered the new and popular benefits in companies viewed as having Cadillac employee benefits plans.[23]

In effect, comprehensive health and medical care insurance is provided only to a small group of workers employed in a select group of industries and companies. As we move away from this elite core, health and medical coverage becomes less adequate both in range and extensiveness. A significant number of employees with family responsibilities still have no, or very limited, coverage of even the most basic services.

Maternity Benefits and Leaves   Because employee benefits relating to pregnancy and maternity so directly affect family lives, they deserve separate attention. Indeed, through judicial and legislative controversy these policies and practices have brought to a head the issue of corporate responsibility in accommodating the family needs of employees.

Unlike 75 countries, including all other advanced industrialized societies, the United States has no statutory provision that guarantees a woman the right to a leave from employment for a specified period, protects her job while she is on leave, and provides a cash benefit equal to all or a significant portion of her wage while she is not working because of pregnancy and childbirth (Kamerman, 1980). Although most countries provide these benefits through national health insurance, 16 countries have such benefits despite the absence of health insurance. Various policy instruments other than health insurance have been used to provide maternity benefits. They include unemployment insurance (Canada and Austria), a special maternity benefit (Israel), parent insurance (Sweden), employment benefit (Britain), and a benefit combining health insurance and mandated employer provision (Federal Republic of Germany). Among the western European countries, three-months paid maternity leave is the minimum. The Federal Republic of Germany provides seven and one-half months and Sweden, nine months. The modal pattern is increasingly moving toward six months.

To the extent that paid maternity leaves exist in the United States, they do so as part of the employee benefits system. The Pregnancy Discrimination Act of 1978 requires that pregnant employees be treated

---

[23] About one-sixth of the private labor force is estimated to have dental coverage.

the same as employees with any temporary disability. This presumably means that women employed in firms providing short-term sickness or disability insurance have paid maternity leaves. However, the fact that the new law prohibits discrimination based on pregnancy is no guarantee that women employees are actually eligible for pregnancy-maternity benefits or, indeed, that eligible employees are granted the benefits to which they are entitled. How this legislation has affected pregnant working women is not yet clear. Among other matters, there is still controversy on what is considered compliance with the law. Unfortunately, there is no available data source which can provide an up-to-date view of the scope and nature of childbirth-related benefits.[24]

Perhaps the most representative picture drawn by employees of the availability of benefits is provided by the Quality of Employment Survey (Quinn and Staines, 1979). Three-quarters of the women working at least 20 hours per week in 1977 stated that they were eligible for maternity leave with full reemployment rights. This level of eligibility represents a substantial growth since 1969 when 59 percent were eligible. Yet maternity leave with pay is still far from common. In 1977, 29 percent had this benefit, about double the proportion who had it seven years before. The seventies were a period, then, in which companies were willing to make some limited commitments to women employees but not to protect them against loss of income. For most, the birth of a child did not necessarily mean a choice between that child and a job, but the overwhelming majority still had to forego all earnings while on leave. The financial consequences could be severe for a single mother or a woman married to a man earning a low wage. And the child would, of course, also be affected.

Like many other employee benefits, eligibility for both maternity leave with reemployment rights and maternity leave with pay varies by the nature of the company (see Table 5-2). Women employees of firms with 500 or more employees were clearly most apt (89 percent) to have a guaranteed job if they took maternity leave and, indeed, the likelihood of such a guarantee increased directly with firm size. At the very smallest firm, with fewer than 10 employees (the work site of 14 percent of the women who responded to the Quality of Employment Survey), only 39 percent claimed to have this guarantee. Of still greater importance, while about 4 out of 10 employees at the largest firms could take maternity

---

[24] A national survey focused on this question was in the field at the time this paper was written (S. B. Kamerman and A. J. Kahn, codirectors, Survey of Maternity Benefits and Leaves in Private Industry).

TABLE 5–2   Maternity Policies by Establishment Size

Number of Employees at Work Site	Percentage Eligible for Maternity Leave with Reemployment Rights (%) (N)		Percentage Eligible for Maternity Leave with Pay (%) (N)	
1–9 employees	39	22	10	6
10–49 employees	71	98	18	25
50–499 employees	80	96	37	44
500 or more employees	89	84	47	42
Total	74	300	29	117

NOTE: Percentages computed on a base of those definitely claiming coverage or not; all responding "don't know" excluded.
SOURCE: 1977 Quality of Employment Survey. Special analyses prepared by the authors in connection with their Survey of Maternity Benefits and Leaves in Private Industry.

leave with pay, fewer than 1 in 10 of the women in the smallest firms had this benefit.

Maternity benefits were particularly low in the wholesale and retail trade and nonprofessional service industries. But with the slight exception of the financial-insurance industry, no major industrial groups stood out as particulary progressive. However, the laggard status of the trade and service industries appears to reflect in large part the generally small size of the firms within these industries. And as we have noted, female employees of small firms were much less likely to be granted maternity benefits than those in the larger firms, regardless of the industry. Indeed, among smaller firms with fewer than 50 employees, there was relatively little variation by major industrial category.

It is striking that so many women employees—about 16 percent—did not know whether they were entitled to maternity leave of any sort. For a point of comparison, almost all respondents knew whether or not they had medical insurance. Thus, assuming the positive claims for coverage are accurate, actual eligibility may have been somewhat more widespread than reported here. Of course, maternity benefits are not important to all women employees in the same way health insurance is likely to be—hence, the lower level of awareness. It is notable, though, that the proportion of "don't know's" was generally higher among the employees of smaller firms. Since employees of smaller firms are not relatively unaware of their other benefits, this pattern of response may suggest that many smaller companies simply do not have clearly formulated maternity policies. Informal ad hoc arrangements may be particularly prevalent within smaller firms, and women employees may therefore be uncertain of what is available to them.

Undoubtedly, many different policies with widely varying ramifications for female employees are here grouped together under the rubrics of "maternity leave with reemployment rights" and "maternity leave with pay." Yet, we can provide a limited sense of the details of these plans from the sketchy findings of a Conference Board study (Meyer, 1978).[25] Like other Conference Board surveys, this study is heavily weighted toward the practices of larger corporations and accordingly cannot be used for projections about all sectors of the economy.[26] Moreover, the Pregnancy Discrimination Act of 1978 should have a significant impact on the extensiveness of these benefits. We can, therefore, only note similarities and variations in the maternity policies just prior to enactment of this legislation of companies in what may be loosely called the large corporate sector.

The Equal Employment Opportunity Commission's sex discrimination guidelines (1972) mandate that "the commencement and duration" of maternity leave as well as the "availability of extensions" must be in accord with the "same terms and conditions" that apply to leaves due to other temporary disabilities. These guidelines clearly had effects on corporate policies relating to maternity leave. In 1964 about three-quarters of the manufacturing firms in a Conference Board survey specified the point at which pregnant employees could no longer work—usually three to six months after conception. The 1978 study, by contrast, indicates that almost all companies have eliminated a fixed time limit on pregnant women's right to continue working, as long as they are healthy and able to do their work.[27] Most companies also do not set restrictions on when in the pregnancy the maternity leave may start. Furthermore, these larger corporations appear remarkably willing to grant maternity leaves to new employees. Less than half report a service requirement and about another quarter require three months or less employment. However, corporations were less consistent in allowing sick pay for absence days resulting from pregnancy: about two-thirds made these payments.

[25] Few details on the sample are available. This study is based on responses from 309 companies that Conference Board staff describe as "mostly large and medium-large." They informally allude to a response rate of "about half." Sixty-nine percent of the responding companies are in manufacturing and banking.

[26] As an indicator of the inherent bias of this survey, it may be noted that 97 percent of the companies in the Conference Board survey reported granting unpaid maternity leave. Only 75 percent of the female workers in the Quality of Employment Survey reported being eligible for such leave.

[27] Some three-quarters of the companies do require certification from pregnant women's physicians that it is safe to continue working.

There is hardly a corporate consensus on what the length of leave should be. Of the companies reporting a maximum leave, somewhat less than half grant four to six months off; approximately a quarter offer extremely limited leaves of three months or less; and about an equal number grant more than six months, although rarely more than a year. (Extensions are generally granted on a physician's certification of continued disability.) These maximums usually apply to the length of the entire leave (which may be started during pregnancy), but some only limit the time of leave after delivery.

Although the right to a leave from work, with full job protection, at the time of childbirth may offer some help to women, few can afford to take more than a very brief leave unless they and their families are protected against loss of income. Unfortunately, the payment of disability pay during maternity leave seems to be far from prevailing practice. Some 40 percent of the companies in the Conference Board study reported that they paid mothers on maternity leave, about half through an uninsured sick-pay plan and another half through a short-term disability insurance plan or a combination of the two. Generally, the insured plans limit benefit payments to six weeks. The uninsured plans do not set special limits, but pay benefits for as long as a doctor certifies disability within the parameters applicable to other benefits. Particularly crucial is length of service: the median allowable period of benefit payments for a one-year employee is two weeks; for a five-year employee, it is nine weeks. We assume that the Pregnancy Discrimination Act has led to a significant increase in the number of women covered by such benefits as well as the benefit duration. Thus far, however, there are no data supporting this.

In short, what this review of maternity benefits indicates is that most employed pregnant women received little or no accommodation from their employers in the 1970s. The practice of granting at least some unpaid maternity leave has become fairly general practice, but even within the corporate sector this leave is usually limited to a half year or less. The more important benefit, a leave with pay, was available to fewer than one-third of employed women in 1978 and this advantaged minority could count on only about six weeks of benefits. For the five states providing temporary disability insurance coverage, thus including maternity coverage, benefit levels also tend to be low and of brief duration[28] (see Table 5-3). Maternity policies have undoubtedly been liberalized

---

[28] The five states are California, Hawaii, New Jersey, New York, and Rhode Island, as well as Puerto Rico.

TABLE 5–3 State Nonoccupational Disability Laws (1981)

	Employers Covered	Permissible Plans	Employee-Employer Contributions	Benefit Duration[a] and Benefit Levels[b]	Maternity
CALIFORNIA[a] Unemployment Compensation Disability Benefits (UCD). Employment Development Department Sacramento, CA 95814	Employers of one or more employees.	(1) State plan or (2) Private voluntary plan may be insured or self-insured, but needs majority consent of employees to be set up. Plan must meet all state plan requirements and exceed at least one of the requirements.	Employee contributions consist of 0.6 of first $14,900 ($17,000, 1/1/82). No employer contributions.	Benefits are based on schedule using quarterly earnings figures. Maximum $154 ($175, 1/1/82).	Covered the same as any other disability.
HAWAII[a] Temporary Disability Insurance Law (TDI). Department of Labor and Industrial Relations, P.O. Box 3769, Honolulu, HI 96812	Employers of one or more employees.	(1) No state plan (2) Private plan may be insured or self-insured and must equal or exceed statutory requirements. No employee consent necessary.	Employees must contribute the lesser of 1/2 of 1% of statewide average weekly wage or 1/2 the cost subject to a maximum of $1.21 weekly. Employers must pay the balance of costs incurred.	Benefits consist of 55% of average weekly wage rounded to next higher dollar, maximum $134, minimum $14 or average weekly wage, if less.	Covered the same as any other disability.

TABLE 5-3 (Continued)

	Employers Covered	Permissible Plans	Employee-Employer Contributions	Benefit Duration[a] and Benefit Levels[b]	Maternity
NEW JERSEY[c] Temporary Disability Benefits (TDI). Department of Labor and Industry, P.O. Box 2765, Trenton, NJ 08625	Employers with minimum annual payroll of $1,000, with one or more employees.	(1) State plan or (2) Private plan may be insured or self-insured and must equal or exceed state plan requirements. If plan is contributory, majority consent of employees is necessary.	For both employers and employees, the contribution level is 1/2 of 1% of first $6,000 annual earnings.	Benefits consist of 66% of average weekly earnings to next higher $1, maximum $117, minimum $10.	Covered the same as any other disability.
NEW YORK[c] Disability Benefits Law (DBL). Workers' Compensation Board, 2 World Trade Center, New York, NY 10047	Employers of one or more employees (4 or more domestics) on each of 30 working days in calendar year.	(1) State plan or (2) Private plan may be insured or self-insured and must equal or exceed state plan requirements. No employee consent necessary.	Employee contributions are 1/2 of 1% of first $60 weekly earnings. Employers must pay the balance of costs for standard plans.	Benefits are 50% of average weekly earnings, maximum $95, minimum $20 or employee's average weekly wage, if less.	Covered the same as any other disability.

167

	Coverage	Plan	Financing	Benefits	Treatment
PUERTO RICO Disability Benefits Act (DBA). Bureau of Employment Security, Hato Rey, PR 00917	Any employer who during any day of the current or preceding calendar year, has, or had in employment, one or more employees.	(1) State plan or (2) Private plan may be insured or self-insured and must equal or exceed state plan requirements. Majority employee consent needed to set up plan if contributory.	Both employers and employees pay 1/2 of 1% of the first $9,000 in wages.	Benefits set at 60% of weekly earnings, maximum $105, minimum $7 (on base annual income of $150). Death benefit—$3,000 accident, death, and disability benefit up to $3,000.	Covered the same as any other disability.
RHODE ISLAND[c] Temporary Disability Insurance Benefits (TDI). Department of Employment Security, 24 Mason Street, Providence, RI 02903	Employers of one or more employees	(1) State plan only. (2) No private plans allowed.	Employees contribute 1.2% of a taxable wage base equal to 70 percent of the average annual wage for all workers covered under TDI ($7,800 in 1981).	Benefits set at up to a maximum of 60% of average wage of all employees receiving TDI benefits.	Covered the same as any other disability.

[a] Benefits begin on 8th day with a 26-week maximum duration for all states except California.
[b] Benefits are tax-free.
[c] Recipients of unemployment benefits can intermit or obtain additional protection if they become disabled while unemployed.

in the last decade or so, but employer accommodation to childbearing is still very far from being a worker's right.

In discussing *maternity* benefits, we do not mean to slight the accommodations which may be made for fathers who want to take on child-care responsibilities, nor the importance of such policies. It is a measure of prevailing sex-role norms and corporate policy that only a few advocates mention paternity leaves. The only data that exist on their availability as an employee benefit are in a survey of the leading corporations in the country (Catalyst Career and Family Center, 1981). Twenty-five percent of the respondents to that survey said they permit fathers some unpaid leave at the time their wife gives birth. In contrast, in Sweden both parents are equally entitled to a parental paid leave after childbirth, while in Norway and Finland, fathers may take a portion of their wife's maternity leave.

All of what we have discussed applies to natural parents only. Although a recent report (Hewett Associates, 1980) indicates that 14 companies provided adoption benefits in 1980 (and 18 in 1981), not only is this coverage available just to a minute portion of the labor force, but the benefit relates only to adoption costs, not to a paid leave at that time.

Vacations The tradition in American business, in sharp contrast to European practice, is a short vacation. Among the member countries of the European Economic Community, for example, the standard minimum annual vacation is four weeks (European Economic Community, 1979). Several countries provide longer vacations. In 1978 in West Germany only 10 percent of the labor force had less than a 4-week vacation, 41 percent had 4-5 weeks, and 49 percent had more than 5 weeks. All workers in Sweden now have 5 weeks of paid vacation as do all in France. Holidays are, of course, additional. Moreover, vacations in the United States are provided voluntarily by employers on an individual firm or industry basis, rather than mandated as in Europe.

A recent estimate indicates that the average American worker has two weeks of vacation plus additional holidays. In large and medium-size firms, a paid vacation is now standard practice for full-time workers, yet only workers with considerable service are eligible even for two weeks of vacation time. According to a 1979 Bureau of Labor Statistics study (1980c),[29] in plans providing paid vacation at qualifying periods

---

[29] This study is based on a 1979 national survey of 1,253 establishments. Depending on the industry, the minimum employment size of the sampled establishments was 50, 100, or 250.

of service, almost three-quarters of the workers with less than a year of service have a week or less of vacation. Even after a year of service most production workers still have only a week of vacation, although most white-collar workers have two weeks. Only after 10 years of service does the three-week vacation become the rule for all classes of workers.

Since this sample excludes small firms, the practices reported in this survey should not obscure the fact that a paid vacation is still far from a universal benefit. According to the 1977 Quality of Employment Survey (Quinn and Staines, 1979), a fifth of all employees working at least 20 hours per week do not have a paid vacation. As with other benefits, workers in small firms generally have less coverage. About 30 percent of the workers employed at sites with fewer than 50 workers do not have paid vacations; by contrast, paid vacations are available to virtually all workers employed at firms with more than 500 workers. Also, as we discuss later, part-time workers often have no paid vacation time.

Even when employees have paid vacations, however, we have no data on the patterns of vacation taken among workers in two-paycheck families. Can employees choose their vacation time to fit personal and family needs? What, in fact, are the preferences for vacations among dual-worker families? Is it to vacation together, although briefly, with children when school is closed, or to stagger vacations and extend the time spent with children, just as some couples choose shift work for similar purposes?

Counter to the view that American workers are generally unwilling to trade income for leisure, there is some evidence that substantial numbers of workers desire more time off the job, particularly vacation time, even at the cost of added income. More than 40 percent of the workers in a 1978 nationally representative survey (Best, 1980) indicated that they would give up some *current* income for added vacation time, although the amount they were willing to forego was generally slight. (Vacation was clearly preferred to reductions in the work day; the former may be viewed as true leisure time, while reduced work days may simply create greater possibilities for nonmarket housework.) Interestingly, women workers, workers in dual-earner families, and workers with young children were particularly apt to choose added vacation time. Best (1980:142) offers a compelling view of why they indicate this preference for vacation: "Such persons are pushed and battered in an almost ceaseless treadmill of job and family duties, and it is not surprising that they are willing to make significant monetary and non-monetary tradeoffs to escape for some extended period to a different pace of life."

Families and Benefits As we have emphasized, in America such employee benefits as pensions, health insurance, and paid time off essentially complement or substitute for public provision. How a family fares within the private benefits system critically affects its way of life. In the preceding sections, however, we have noted (often with imperfect data) only how coverage for a specific benefit varies by individual worker characteristics, not how different kinds of families are covered *as a family*. Pension coverage of a family, for example, depends on the number of workers in the family and the retirement benefits accrued by each. A family's health insurance may also depend on how many members work and the extent to which coverage is extended to a worker's dependents. Moreover, its overall welfare depends on its extent of coverage on all key benefits.

Unfortunately, though, there are little data, across the range of key benefits, on the *family coverage* which workers acquire through their involvement in this system. Based on findings from the 1977 Quality of Employment Survey (Quinn and Staines, 1979), we can indicate only the household composition of workers eligible for a package of important benefits. This package consists of medical insurance, sick leave with pay, and a retirement program. (Note that coverage on medical insurance does not necessarily extend to the workers' dependents and that both contributory and noncontributory plans are considered together.) The findings are presented in Table 5-4, which also indicates coverage for the individual benefits within the package, as well as for life insurance.

As is clear, less than half of all employed workers report having a benefits package consisting of health insurance, paid sick leave, and a retirement program. Married males living with their wives (with or without children) have the highest eligibility rate for this package, but even they are almost as likely not to have coverage as to have it. In addition to their other hardships, the large majority of women raising children alone lack coverage for these basic benefits. Only slightly more than a third have these three benefits, a smaller percentage than for workers in all other household types. Of course, their low level of coverage represents a particularly acute problem because they bear the prime, if not sole, responsibility for their children.

We may note briefly that life insurance, especially critical to those with dependents, is not extended to about a third of all workers. Again, females raising children alone appear particularly vulnerable.

Although such worker-reported data must be viewed with some caution, it is plain that many families are not entitled to even a set of basic provisions in the employee benefits system.[30] However, the actual extent to which there are gaps in family coverage within this system cannot be measured now. We need data, with the family as the unit of analysis, on the kinds of coverage extended to workers' dependents and the benefits earned by all family members.

We now turn to a brief consideration of corporate relocation policies—the concern of relatively few families—and a new and still largely untried development in the design of benefits programs—cafeteria or flexible benefits plans.

Relocation   Although corporate relocation policies affect far fewer families than the previously discussed benefits, we include a brief discussion because they appear so critical to the family lives of transferred workers, generally middle- and upper-level managers.

With only initial doubts about the value of the approach, American corporations have aggressively followed the policy of transferring executives from location to location in order to meet the perceived managerial needs of the company. For transferred executives, the move from one community to another obviously entails considerable costs—the direct costs of moving a household as well as the varied psychic costs that the executives and their families may bear because of the disruption in their lives.

In recognition of the substantial direct costs, large corporations generally have instituted relocation policies that reimburse the transferred executive for many of the expenses of the move (Collie and DiDomenico, 1980; Runzheimer and Company, 1980.) Since the mid-sixties, large corporations typically have picked up such costs as shipping of household goods, trips for house hunting, and temporary living expenses at the new location. Also, with the emergence of a highly inflated housing market and difficult financing conditions, corporations have instituted a variety of policies to ease the sale and purchase of a home.

Indeed, by emphasizing economic assistance, corporations seem to meet the main concerns of most executives about transfers. According to a 1980 survey, among companies experiencing problems with employees' reluctance to accept transfers, the major reasons are high mortgage interest rates and higher costs of housing and living in particular regions (Collie and DiDomenico, 1980).

Increasingly, however, executives' concerns for their family's welfare

---

[30] See Footnote 22 for a comment about worker-reported versus employer-reported benefits.

TABLE 5-4 Benefits Coverage by Household Composition: Findings from the 1977 Quality of Employment Survey

Benefits[a]	Single Male Living Alone or All Children 18+	Single Female Living Alone or All Children 18+	Single Male, at Least 1 Child Under 18	Single Female, at Least 1 Child Under 18	Married Male Lives with Wife, No Child or All 18+	Married Female Lives with Husband, No Child or All 18+	Married Male with Wife, at Least 1 Child Under 18	Married Female Lives with Husband, at Least 1 Child Under 18	Total All Employed Workers
Benefits[b] package	46%[b] (41)	43% (45)	few cases	37% (16)	53% (111)	46% (50)	53% (215)	44% (62)	48% (602)
Medical insurance	82% (77)	70% (76)	few cases	67% (30)	83% (181)	77% (85)	84% (351)	73% (106)	79% (1015)
Paid sick leave	62% (57)	64% (67)	few cases	57% (26)	67% (144)	56% (61)	69% (284)	59% (85)	64% (816)
Retirement program	67% (62)	58% (63)	few cases	67% (29)	76% (164)	64% (72)	73% (304)	65% (93)	68% (874)
Life insurance	65% (60)	57% (62)	few cases	57% (25)	73% (157)	67% (72)	70% (289)	58% (83)	66% (833)

[a] Consists of medical insurance, paid sick leave, and a retirement program.
[b] Percentages were computed on a base of all employed workers providing a definite answer; all responding "don't know" were excluded. "Total of all employed workers" includes respondents not placed in a household composition category.

SOURCE: Table prepared from a special analysis of the data done for this paper.

have introduced new considerations into the design of relocation policies. Many companies report greater difficulty in convincing executives to move. This resistance is often attributed to a quality-of-life concern. Many executives appear to favor stability in their own and their family lives over the promise of career advancement. Even more, this growing concern may reflect the increasing numbers of two-career families among the executive ranks. A 1979 survey (Runzheimer, 1980) indicates that almost a fifth of the executives who refused a transfer did so because of the career concerns of a working spouse.

While human-resource professionals have raised the need for corporations to respond to both the psychic concerns of family members and the career interests of spouses, the actual implementation of such responsive policies has not been common.[31] A few companies offer workshops and counseling for executives and their families about the practical and emotional implications of making a move, but such policies are still at the progressive vanguard. A 1979 survey of 600 corporations indicates that 30 percent offer some assistance to working spouses in finding a new job, double the number in the preceding year. However, this assistance generally seems minimal, involving informal aid or referrals to an employment agency. Few companies appear to have revised nepotism policies to accommodate the transfers of a couple employed by the same firm.

Moreover, although many corporations report that acceptance of transfer is less critical to career advancement than it used to be, they show few signs of cutting back on their policy of transferring many executives. Such a cutback may have a more beneficial effect on the family lives of executives than any number of counseling sessions.

As a final point, we should emphasize that industry's relocation policies are essentially the concern of a few—those in middle- and high-level management. Transfers of lower-level employees are rare. Thus, it may be a relevant issue for the limited number of professional-managerial dual-career families rather than for the much larger number of families with dual workers in lower-status jobs.[32]

Flexible Benefits (Cafeteria) Plans   At the cutting edge of benefits plans under discussion today are the so-called flexible plans. Many observers,

---

[31] See Levenson and Hollmann (1980) for a statement detailing the need for such policies and possible corporate response.

[32] Catalyst, the nonprofit organization concerned with problems of labor force reentry for women and career development for women executives, has focused on the problems of dual-career families in its current national survey.

including staff at the U.S. Chamber of Commerce, view these plans as the wave of the future, given the current trends in labor force composition. Although specific benefits vary among companies, almost all now design their benefits systems as if every employee were part of a one-worker family with spouse and children at home. Thus, a male worker may be given health insurance for himself and his dependents even though his wife has equally good coverage from her employer for herself and her dependents. It is a system, then, which has not caught up with the reality of many two-earner families. The employee benefits system also appears predicated on the assumption that employees have similar needs and that these needs are largely the same through all stages of the life cycle. Yet plainly some workers would attach greater value to, say, a paid maternity leave than retirement benefits and would be willing to forego some of the latter for more generous maternity benefits. By the same token, others would surely prefer to forego maternity and other benefits for higher retirement payments. Indeed, in one company which offered a flexible plan, single mothers selected more vacation time, health and life insurance coverage, and lower pension coverage than the standard package provided.[33]

In response to such considerations, there has been considerable discussion about the value of instituting flexible benefits systems—or, as they are aptly called, cafeteria systems. As this approach is usually portrayed, employees are allowed to choose from a range of options the benefits package that best suits their individual and family needs. Sometimes a basic core may be required, with the choice limited to supplementary benefits. As needs change, workers may adjust their package accordingly.

Nevertheless, advocates for such flexible systems far outnumber actual users. To date, only a handful of companies have instituted a cafeteria system, although many more are exploring the possibility. As the number of companies providing flexible benefits grows, there could be an interesting opportunity to learn more about which employees choose what kinds of benefits, why, and with what consequences.

TRW is the company that first developed the concept of a flexible benefits package. American Can is among the few companies in addition to TRW that has such a plan in operation. American Can's experience with its flexible benefits program may illustrate some of the difficulties and gains companies face in instituting such a program. The company

---

[33] Information provided in personal communication with the human resources personnel at American Can.

provides noncontributory basic or core benefits for health insurance, disability benefits, group term life, pension benefits, and vacations. The cost difference between the core benefits and the benefits provided under the previous benefits plan determines an employee's allotment of flexible credit dollars, which may be used to purchase other benefits. In addition, employees may purchase additional benefits through payroll deductions (unsigned, 1980).

The initial implementation of this program entailed considerable administrative cost and effort. For one thing, since the legal and tax implications were not clear, the company consulted the Internal Revenue Service and the Securities and Exchange Commission so that the plan would be in accord with applicable tax and securities law requirements. Without any existing guide to follow, the company also had to break new ground in deciding what kind of benefits should be in the plan and which benefits should be flexible. (Adverse selection of benefits is a potential problem because claims on particular types of insurance may be prohibitively frequent unless risk is dispersed across a sufficiently large, diverse group.) Further, the company set up an extensive program to explain the options, including the tax ramifications of using flexible credits instead of payroll deductions to pay for optional benefits (American Can, 1980).

Surveys of employees indicate overwhelming approval of the program. The fact that 92 percent of the employees changed their benefits coverage from the prior standard package to the flexible one certainly suggests their willingness to tailor benefits to their individual needs. It also suggests that the existing plan was not as responsive as it might have been.

Since the program does not, and was not intended to, create any direct savings, the considerable administrative tasks involved with setting it up may persuade other companies not to follow American Can's lead. Indeed, the complexities involved with a cafeteria system and the extensiveness of employee data needed simply may be beyond the capacity of virtually all but the largest corporations. There is at least one compensation, however: American Can officials believe that the program offers an effective way to retain good employees and attract new ones. Also, since the plan allows the company to alter option costs and plan design, the company may help control the escalation of benefit costs. Nonetheless, American industry lacks easily adoptable models suitable for diverse corporate settings. The creation of such model programs requires the cooperation of federal regulatory and taxing agencies, insurance companies, and industries themselves. Recent tax legislation may facilitate further experimentation. More than a dozen companies have moved to establish such plans in the past year and far more are considering such a move.

Prevailing Provisions: Services

Thus far we have discussed the benefits voluntarily provided by some employers to some employees. We turn now to a brief examination of another part of what we have termed the corporate social welfare system—the services part of the benefits-services package. Although the line between benefits and services is not precise, we use benefits to mean cash or cash equivalents (money or voucher), while services are defined as the collective provision of personal help (or support for the supply of such help) rather than direct support of consumption.

These personal services are comparable to the personal social services funded and/or delivered by government or voluntary agencies, just as the benefits described above can be compared to statutory benefit provision in the United States and elsewhere. Despite the absence of any systematic data on extent, coverage, and expenditure, there is some indication that the 1970s witnessed a substantial growth in the provision of personal services at or through the workplace. The range of services now includes legal assistance, information, and referral; counseling; diverse educational programs; and even a few child-care programs (Kahn and Kamerman, 1982; Ozawa, 1980).

U.S. companies currently are estimated to spend $10 billion a year for the education and training of close to 13 million people. Some estimates go as high as $100 billion a year and 16 million people. Some of this money goes for on-site training, but an estimated $500 million goes for tuition aid, and most for off-the-job education (Watkins, 1980).

The literature on these personal services is anecdotal or descriptive and program-specific. There has been no systematic study of the quality or quantity of services provided, of employees' attitudes toward them, or of the effects of such services.[34] The interest and enthusiasm with which these programs have been greeted seems astonishing, given the suspicion and resentment expressed by workers in earlier years regarding similar types of services. A few people have raised questions of pater-

---

[34] Masi (1982) made an initial attempt at reviewing what is available. For some program descriptions, see Akabas et al. (1979). See also Roger Ricklefs, "In House Council. Firms Offer Employees a New Benefit: Help in Personal Problems," *Wall Street Journal*, August 13, 1979 and Barbara Lovenheins, "More Care Given Employees' Psyches," *The New York Times*, April 1, 1979.

nalism, confidentiality, possible value conflicts, and so forth (e.g., Babalinsky, 1980; O'Toole, 1980). Others have warned of the potential for generating dependency, in words like those used to describe the dependency allegedly engendered by the use of government benefits (Samuelson, 1980). The picture is at best fragmentary and incomplete.

Child-Care Services   Recently there has been an upsurge of interest in this country in child-care services provided by employers at the workplace for the children of employees (e.g., Perry, 1980; Department of Labor, 1981b). One obvious way to provide care for children whose parent (or parents) is employed, so the discussion goes, is to bring the children to work. While the parents work, the children can be cared for in some group arrangement. With this proximity, parents have the opportunity to see their children at certain times during the day, regularly check on their progress, and be readily available for any emergency. It is an arrangement that seemingly can reduce the typical disjunction between work and family life. Other possible advantages for families include the typically lower costs of group care as opposed to individual family arrangements, as well as the convenience of not having to commute to another location in order to drop off and pick up children.

Certain disadvantages of work-site child care, documented in earlier U.S. experience and in many European countries (which are increasingly eliminating such services), have largely been ignored in public discussions. These disadvantages include the concerns parents have with disrupting a child-care arrangement if they wish to change jobs, the problems of transporting children long distances during peak commuter hours, the lack of neighborhood friends when a child's relationships are limited to the children of other employees, and parental preferences for neighborhood-based care (Kamerman and Kahn, 1981).[35] Moreover, there are a variety of other options whereby employers can subsidize child-care services for employees. Indeed, these options are now receiving increasing attention. Employers are considering providing a voucher or a full or partial reimbursement to employees for the costs of child care, subsidizing a number of slots in various community-based facilities near employees' residences, sharing with other firms in the support of community-based services, and developing an information and referral service for existing services in addition to providing some subsidies. Thus far few such initiatives have been carried out.

Only 2 percent of the 1977 Quality of Employment Survey (Quinn

---

[35] Typically, in Europe child-care services for children aged three (and increasingly two) and older are provided through public preschool programs.

and Staines, 1979) respondents said that child-care services were available at their jobs. A comprehensive 1978 survey of employer-sponsored day care clearly documents its rarity. It found only 9 day-care centers sponsored by industry, 7 sponsored by labor unions with funds from employers of the members, 14 sponsored by government agencies, and 75 sponsored by hospitals. In addition, there were 200 centers sponsored by the military. The extremely limited involvement of private industry is particularly notable; in fact the number of industry-sponsored centers has actually declined since 1970.[36] By 1981, 10 more industry-sponsored centers had begun operation (U.S. Department of Labor, 1981b).

Apart from other reasons, the cost considerations of employers have undercut prospects for wider adoption of such services. Perry's (1980) survey indicates that employers typically bear start-up costs (an average of $125,000 in 1978), as well as pay subsidies for the ongoing operation (an average of $57,000, a little more than half of the average annual operating budget). Center directors report that the introduction of the facility has led to decreases in job turnover, lower absenteeism, easier recruitment, and favorable publicity for their companies. However, such reports hardly represent a cost-benefit analysis suggesting an economic incentive to employers. In fact, employers who dropped their on-site facilities typically cited the direct costs as their reason.[37]

On the other hand the typically low costs charged employees would seem to create a widespread demand. (The average weekly charge was about $24.) However, out of a list of 18 job benefits included in the Quality of Employment Survey (Quinn and Staines, 1979), on-site child care was the least likely to be designated the most important benefit. And of the workers desiring additional fringe benefits, fewer than 10 percent cited on-site child care as the one additional benefit most desired. At present there does not appear to be any great push on the employees' side for on-site child care.

There is certainly no evidence documenting that workplace child care actually offers a better way to meet work and family responsibilities

---

[36] These figures were obtained through state licensing agencies. However, data from the Quality of Employment Survey (Quinn and Staines, 1979:59) indicate a wider availability of these facilities. In 1977 about 2 percent of the respondents (all of whom were in the work force and employed for at least 20 hours per week) indicated that they had at their jobs "a place for employees' children to be taken care of while parents are working."

[37] Promotional brochures, such as Stride Rite Corporation's *Stride Rite Children's Center: How We Do It*, are intended to stimulate interest but essentially rely on appeals and corporate responsibility, and only vaguely allude to economic benefits.

than other child-care arrangements, in particular the alternatives mentioned earlier. Perhaps an additional incentive to employers would (1) increase their experimentation in supporting such services and (2) reveal more clearly the real preferences of employees, as well as whether such provisions attenuate work and family strain. The 1981 federal tax legislation (the Economic Recovery Tax Act) establishing a new dependent-care assistance benefit and permitting employers a wide range of options in sponsoring child-care services for employees as a tax-free benefit may provide just such an opportunity.

THE SCHEDULING AND HOURS OF WORK: EXISTING PATTERNS AND
NEW DEVELOPMENTS

In Rosabeth Kanter's words (1977:31), "family events and routines are built around work rhythms (at least more generally than the reverse)." The predominant rhythm of contemporary American work life is provided by the 5-day, 40-hour work week, a pattern firmly institutionalized at least since the end of World War II.[38] And yet it is a rhythm plainly out of synchronization with the family lives of many workers, particularly at certain points in the life cycle. This pattern of work scheduling became the rule at a time when family responsibilities generally were divided along traditional lines—that is, the man served as breadwinner and the woman was expected to assume all family and home responsibilities—in particular, child care. However, such scheduling obviously places enormous strains on the many contemporary families that differ from the traditional model, especially families with both parents or the only parent in the labor force. Indeed, a third of all workers in the national Quality of Employment Survey (Quinn and Staines, 1979) reported a problem with inconvenient or excessive hours of work. They reported that work schedules interfered with family life and that they had too little control over their hours of work. Coupled with the typical year-round commitment to work, this work scheduling also constricts each individual employee's opportunities to enjoy the personal satisfactions of a varied life (Best, 1980).

---

[38] More than 80 percent of private wage and salary workers work full time (35 or more hours per week). Close to 80 percent of these work a 5-day week and 64 percent a 5-day, 40-hour week. Nineteen percent of private-sector employees work part time, slightly more than the percentage of part-time employees in the general labor force (about 17 percent). The major trend today is toward compression of weekly hours into fewer days, with the 5-day week overwhelmingly dominant even for those working 41 to 48 hours per week. The only other trend worth noting is the slight move toward a shorter week (4 to 4.5 days) especially for full-time employees working 35 to 39 hours per week (Hedges, 1980).

Initiatives to enhance the flexibility of work scheduling and make it more compatible with the diverse family lives of workers often have been small-scale and halting. But in Stanley Nollen's words (1980:6), "a new show is being cast." Here we report the existing evidence on the scope and impact of some of the leading developments: flexitime; permanent part-time work; and a variant of it, job sharing. As will be apparent, the lack of much systematic analysis of these developments underscores their relative novelty.

Flexitime

Essentially, flexitime is work scheduling that permits employees some discretion in determining arrival and departure times. Although the total number of hours in the work week (or month, sometimes) generally remains fixed at the standard full-time level, employees are not locked into a nine-to-five routine.

Although most employees—and to a lesser extent, employers—like the general idea of flexitime, they may not always be talking about the same thing. In actual practice this label refers to a variety of scheduling innovations, incorporating quite different levels of flexibility (Golembiewski and Proehl, 1978). Most plans allow daily variation in starting and stopping time, but they differ in their requirements for advanced notice of change. Also, to ensure necessary communication among workers, most require that all employees be present during a specified core period. Each program makes its own determination concerning "core period," "band width" (number of hours between the earliest starting time and the latest finishing time), and "flexible hours" (number of hours within which choices about starting and stopping may be made). Such variables can change from plan to plan (see Figure 5-1, which illustrates these variations.). Furthermore, some plans allow workers to carry forward a surplus or deficit of hours as long as they work a full week, and a few even allow this banking of hours across weeks. Yet, for all the diversity of these plans, the common element is that they give the worker some control over working time which had previously been held by management.

About 7.6 million workers, or 12 percent of all those in full-time, nonfarm wage and salary jobs in May 1980, were on flexitime or other schedules that permitted them to vary the time their workdays began and ended. Another 2.7 million part-time employees also were allowed to work other than fixed schedules. About 13 percent of working parents were on flexitime. The option was more common for fathers than mothers (14 versus 10 percent), but about the same for parents of school-

AM											PM
7	8	9	10	11	12	1	2	3	4	5	6

Flexible Time	Core Time	Lunch	Core Time	Flexible Time

- - - - - -Core period- - - - - -   Single 5-hour core pe-
                                       riod, 11-hour band
                    Band   width, 6 flexible hours.
———————— Width ————————

AM											PM
7	8	9	10	11	12	1	2	3	4	5	6	7

Flexible Time	Core Time	Flexible Time	Core Time	Flexible Time

        Core   Core   Double core period (2
      - -Period- -   - -Period- -   hours each),
                            Band   12-hour band width, 8
——————————— Width ——————————— flexible hours.

FIGURE 5-1   Examples of flexitime schedules. Employees determine their own hours during flexible time; they must be present during the core period. Band width indicates the number of hours between the earliest starting time and the latest finishing time.

age and preschool-age children (U.S. Department of Labor, 1981c). As Golembiewski and Proehl (1978) valuably observe, moreover, there are also indeterminate numbers of workers on de facto flexitime: managers, many professionals, and the self-employed, as well as many office workers whose bosses wink at informal arrangements rather than force an issue with an employee or go to the trouble of instituting a formal program (Nollen, 1979a).[39]

Flexitime first appeared at a German plant in 1967 and was introduced in the United States by Control Data Corporation in 1972. (Incidentally, the German managers appeared to be primarily motivated by a narrow concern to reduce traffic congestion rather than to accommodate the workers' family responsibilities.) Given the very brief experience with flexitime, it is perhaps surprising that its use has spread as quickly as it has. Between 1974 and 1979 according to Nollen (1979a), the level of usage doubled, and it is continuing to increase.

[39] Flexitime generally continues to be more widely used in Europe. While current estimates in the Federal Republic of Germany are 10 to 15 percent of all employees, 40 percent of all employees are covered in Switzerland.

Flexitime has been adopted in a wide range of work settings. Nollen and Martin's (1978a) nationwide projections indicate only modest variations in adoption rates based on industry type, sector, and firm size.[40] Organizations with flexitime programs seem more apt to be offices (especially banking and insurance companies) than factories, and service producers rather than goods producers. Yet, to counter any misperceptions, these authors (1978a:13) emphasize, "flexitime is not rigidly incompatible with mass-production technology—it is only less common than in other technologies." In other words the technical barriers to its adoption do not appear insurmountable, although not all work settings are as readily adaptable.

The willingness of some employers to make the necessary adoptions is undoubtedly spurred by a widespread perception that flexitime has the direct economic benefit of enhancing productivity as well as the indirect benefit of improving employee morale—all for a relatively slight expenditure of managerial energy and direct costs. Many of the existing studies rely on rather soft data, such as unvalidated managerial and employee reports on productivity impacts in postimplementation, cross-sectional studies. Still, Golembiewski and Proehl's (1978) review of the empirical literature indicates that in a number of different types of settings flexitime quite consistently appears to reduce tardiness, absenteeism, sick leave, and overtime.[41] Nollen's (1979b) review of the literature also documents a widespread economic gain to employers; about half of all firms experienced direct financial gain, and few had net losses.[42] Also, in the general absence of any negative impacts on organizational behavior, the consistent finding of employee appreciation for flexitime creates an added impetus for its adoption. It is worth reiterating that the studies on which these conclusions are based were generally unsophisticated in design, but the overwhelming weight of the evidence suggests the economic value of a wider adoption.

Flexitime is also appealing to a wide constituency because it is supposed to improve family life. Any number of proponents (Bohen and Viveros-Long, 1981) have advocated flexitime as a way to help workers mesh their work and home lives.[43] Potential benefits are easily imag-

[40] These conclusions must be viewed with considerable caution because of the small size of their sample as well as its unrepresentative industrial distribution and likely response bias.

[41] Golembiewski and Proehl's review (1978:838) encompasses 16 studies that meet their standard of making a "serious effort to gather a range of data about F-T effects . . . and are reported in sufficient detail to permit relatively confident interpretations."

[42] This review is based on 8 surveys and 30 case studies.

[43] Their comprehensive review (Chapter 2), detailing how various proponents foresee the benefits for families in quite different terms, highlights an important point.

inable. Some parents can coordinate their work schedules more closely with available child-care arrangements or the school day. Others might come home at an earlier time to enjoy some recreational activity with family members or to prepare a family meal. Yet, perhaps because the benefits are assumed so readily, there is hardly any systematic analysis of how flexitime actually affects family life.

In a series of related papers, Richard Winett and his associates (Winett and Neale, 1980) provide the only rigorous evidence documenting a beneficial impact. Their analysis is based on the innovative use of time logs and highly focused questionnaire items in two small-scale, quasi-experimental studies. Each study involved a modest longitudinal component (five and nine months); the participants were office workers in two large federal agencies. In both agencies the workers on flexitime spent more time in the evening with their families than they had prior to its adoption. However, the fact that even the more flexible of the plans allowed a band width of only two hours greater than the standard day inherently limited any increase in family time. The time allotted to family activities among those working on flexitime in this agency increased from a mean of about three hours to four-and-a-quarter hours. In addition the participants on flexitime reported less difficulty in a number of specific aspects of family life, including spending time with their spouse during the week; seeing friends during the week; pursuing education, recreation, and hobbies; and having relaxed evenings.

However, Bohen and Viveros-Long's (1981) study of flexitime among other federal employees is notably less supportive of its benefits for family life.[44] Their study employed a comparative ex post facto design. The family experiences of employees in two matched federal agencies—one on standard time, one on flexitime—were compared in a cross-sectional analysis. In brief, they found no differences in time spent on home chores and child rearing, no difference in the equity in the division of family responsibilities between parents, and only very minor differences in scores on an index of stress.

Clearly, the literature on the family effects of flexitime is extremely limited and hardly conclusive. The extent to which flexitime affects various aspects of the family lives of different kinds of workers in diverse settings is simply unknown. Our lack of knowledge is particularly pronounced with regard to the impact of flexitime on the social-psychological aspects of family life. Nevertheless, Stanley Nollen's (1980:11) cautionary note seems well worth heeding:

---

[44] In discussing the implications of their study, they believe their findings suggest that (1981:144) "families with the most work-family conflicts need more help than flexitime."

Realistically, flexitime is a fairly minor alteration of the work environment and not that potent in the face of ingrained family practices. Unless both parents have liberal flexitime programs and are ready to alter family roles as well as work hours, the kids will still be mother's responsibility and child care will still be needed.

Researchers, policy makers, and most importantly families themselves therefore should not expect flexitime to be a panacea for the conflicts between work and home life. Any gains in quality of family life will likely be modest, although no less worth promoting for that reason.

Permanent Part-Time Work

Although permanent part-time work is now frequently advocated as a way to help individuals reconcile work and family responsibilities, there is of course little that is novel or rare about part-time work per se. Currently, about 18 percent of all nonagricultural employees and 19 percent of all private employees work part time.[45] By comparison, about 14 percent of the nonagricultural labor force worked on a part-time basis in 1950 and 21 percent in 1971. Part-time workers, however, generally have remained concentrated in low-pay, low-status occupations: sales, clerical, service, and to a lesser extent laborer positions. They also have remained disproportionately female: A third of all women employees work part time, as compared to a seventh of men employees. A substantial portion of part-time work is involuntary, including one-third of the part-time employment of single mothers and 20 percent of wives.[46]

One may infer readily that many workers, particularly women, have turned to part-time jobs in order to accommodate their family responsibilities. Women with children under the age of 15 constitute 27 percent

[45] Following the conventions of the Bureau of Labor Statistics, we define part-time workers as having jobs entailing fewer than 35 hours per week. About half of all part-time employees work 15 to 29 hours; a quarter work 30 to 34 hours; and another quarter work fewer than 15 hours.

[46] See Deuterman and Brown (1978) and Nollen et al. (1978) for documentation and further detail. The rate of part-time employment varies enormously among industrialized countries, but there is no clear explanation of this. Regardless, women are always more likely than men to work part time. The differences among countries deserve analysis. They might be related to availability of child-care services, but also to the function of the female labor force.

The Bureau of Labor Statistics distinguishes between voluntary part-time work (i.e., the worker prefers to work less than 35 hours per week) and involuntary (i.e., the worker has to settle for a part-time job in the absence of a full-time position). With some fluctuation, in recent years about 80 percent of all part-time workers have been voluntary. For some discussion of involuntary part-time work, see Terry (1981).

of all voluntary part-time workers, almost twice their proportion in the total labor force. On the other hand, given the prevailing distribution of child-care responsibilities within families, married men are particularly apt not to work part time voluntarily. Married men represent about half of all workers, but only a quarter of the voluntary part-time work force. Moreover, 1977 Bureau of Labor Statistics survey data (Nollen et al., 1978:139) explicitly indicate that almost half of all female part-timers cited "taking care of a home" as their reason for part-time work.[47] Very few men in part-time jobs cited this reason. In short, part-time work has primarily been a woman's option as families attempt to mesh job and family lives.

What is new, though perhaps not readily definable, is an expanded concept of *permanent* part-time work. As Cohen and Gadon (1978:67) write, it "connotes some kind of career-relatedness with potential for upward mobility that has not in the past usually been associated with part-time work." The idea is that part-time workers need not be shunted into irregular, undesirable jobs, but instead should have access to permanent positions that offer the range of responsibilities and rewards available to full-time workers. An option for a career-type part-time job would likely appeal to a wide range of people: the young mother who interrupts her career to have children, but wants to receive some income and to maintain her job-market competitiveness; the older male worker who wants to taper off rather than abruptly end a career; and the housewife with grown children who wants some out-of-the-home involvement and added income, but is not interested in a full-time commitment. Indeed, a few surveys suggest that a considerable number of current full-time workers in career-type positions would prefer part-time status. For example, in a large survey of Wisconsin state employees, 6 percent indicated that they would cut back on hours if they had the option. Similarly, a survey of employees in the California Department of Motor Vehicles showed that 29 percent would be interested in part-time work at some time in their career (Nollen et al., 1978).

Nevertheless, there is little evidence that many employers have notably responded to any such demand. The standard of a career-type position is obviously vague, but at minimum it would seem to entail some permanency. Assuming that year-long employment suggests some permanency, it is relevant to note that in recent years only slightly more

---

[47] Other reasons were going to school, 27 percent; unemployment, 13 percent; illness or disability, 5 percent; retirement, 1 percent; and other, 6 percent. Among the male part-timers, the most common reasons were going to school, 50 percent, and unemployment, 21 percent.

than a third of all part-time workers have worked year-long (48 or more weeks). Thus, about a tenth of the labor force is composed of permanent part-time workers—approximately the same percentage that has existed for more than a decade. Morever, as previously suggested, part-time workers generally remain excluded from managerial and professional ranks. Such positions, of course, offer the best career-type prospects. About 3 percent of all managers and 11 percent of professional, technical, and kindred workers work part time on a voluntary basis. (Most in the latter category hold jobs without administrative responsibilities.) The percentage of managers in part-time positions has remained essentially unchanged since the 1960s, while the percentage of professionals and technical and kindred workers has grown slightly since that time (Deuterman and Brown, 1978). An overwhelming number of permanent part-time workers, then, still must attempt to build their careers in relatively low-status jobs in low-paid sectors of the economy, particularly retail trade and other service-sector jobs.[48]

Besides the poor pay, which even permanent part-timers generally receive, part-time jobs frequently do not have the benefits package that most people would consider an essential feature of a career-type job. Having made this generalization, we must note that relevant sources of data are all limited and do not permit any exact specification of the benefits available to part-time workers.[49] Nevertheless, two surveys (Meyer, 1978; Nollen and Martin, 1978b) of mostly large private enterprises suggest that permanent part-time workers are only about half as likely as their full-time counterparts to receive such key benefits as health insurance, sick pay, and life insurance (see Table 5-5). They fare slightly better in pension benefits and are most likely to be eligible for a paid vacation.[50] We should stress that these surveys undoubtedly overstate the level of benefits typically available to permanent part-time

[48] A regression-based analysis indicates that about two-thirds of the wage gap between part-time and full-time workers is accounted for by the high concentration of part-timers in occupational-industrial categories in which all workers are poorly paid (Owen, 1978).

[49] The Quality of Employment Survey (Quinn and Staines, 1979) is not a suitable data set to explore this issue because only those currently employed for remuneration 20 hours or more per week were eligible for inclusion in the sample. Since the average number of hours worked per week among part-timers is 18, the QES cannot offer a representative sample of this group.

[50] The Conference Board study (Meyer, 1978) is based on responses from 309 companies. The respondents appear to have been disproportionately drawn from the ranks of large and medium-large companies. The American Management Association (Nollen and Martin, 1978) study is based on a subsample (N = 481) of 805 responses to a survey of 2,889 organizations. Two populations were sampled: some 2,000 organizations that

TABLE 5–5   Percentage of Employers Extending Benefits Coverage
to Part-Time Workers in 1978

Benefits	Conference Board Survey	American Management Association Survey
Health insurance	42	54
Sick pay	38	58
Life insurance	38	53
Pension plan	60	63
Paid vacation	68	80

NOTE: Percentages are here computed on a base of companies that offer each benefit to full-time employees. This entailed recomputing published AMA data.
SOURCE: Mitchell Meyer (1978), *Women and Employee Benefits* (The Conference Board) and Stanley Nollen and Virginia Martin (1978b), *Alternative Work Schedules, Part 2* (AMACOM).

workers. Each survey disproportionately includes large firms and the sampling frames appear biased toward relatively progressive firms. Since many part-time workers are employed in small service-sector companies in which the benefits for all employees are relatively poor, these surveys cannot be used for nationwide projections that include all sectors of the economy.[51]

Even if movement toward permanent part-time work appears extremely limited, the available research indicates that employers may have some economic incentive to expand its use. One comprehensive review of the related literature suggests the following:

(1)   In a majority of work settings, part-time workers have proven more productive than full-timers and produced work of higher quality.

---

were customers of the AMA and an undocumented list of 798 "suspected users of one or more alternative work schedules." This sample also overrepresents larger firms, and the sampling frames seem to introduce an explicit bias toward progressive firms. Plainly, there are considerable discrepancies between the surveys, pointing to both the large sampling errors associated with small samples and the fact that the samples were drawn from somewhat different populations.

[51] A notably bleaker picture emerges from a large-scale 1972 Bureau of Labor Statistics survey of employees (as opposed to companies) conducted in four metropolitan areas, although the data are more out of date (Daski, 1974). For example, by averaging the figures for the four regions, surveyors found coverage of part-time office workers to be as follows: hospitalization, 16 percent; sick leave, 7 percent; and retirement benefits, 15 percent. Full-time workers were at least several times more apt to receive these benefits than their part-time counterparts. A 1979 household survey found a similar pattern for health insurance coverage (15 percent) (U.S. Department of Labor, 1981a).

(2) Part-time workers usually have lower turnover than their full-time counterparts and have lower absenteeism rates, although not consistently.

(3) Additional personnel-administration costs for part-timers are usually minor or nonexistent.[52]

(4) And although at times the management of work may be somewhat complicated by a part-time work force, actual supervisory costs, as well as equipment and facilities costs, generally do not seem to increase (Nollen et al., 1977).

This review encompasses studies of diverse kinds of workers—clerical personnel, production workers, teachers, nurses, social workers, and laborers. The findings generally are corroborated by two survey-based analyses of firms employing part-time workers (Nollen and Martin, 1978a,b).[53] Not all of the typical benefits accrue to all users of part-time workers, nor are the benefits generally dramatic in effect. Further, many of the case studies from which these conclusions are derived are limited in scope and rigor. Still, in aggregate they certainly undercut any wholesale dismissal on economic grounds of the potential value of part-time workers.

However, the use of part-timers does not generally seem affected by employers' calculation of relative costs. Studies by Nollen et al. (1977, 1978) indicate that the main motivation to use part-timers involves some specific scheduling difficulty. (Concomitantly, part-timers are primarily sought for work situations in which there is a cyclical demand for a product or service and job tasks are relatively discrete.) Employers not using part-time workers seem apt to express some diffuse hesitancy about them, not some strong opposition on economic grounds.

Employer worries about an expanding part-time work force appear to coalesce only around the issue of fringe benefits. Their concern stems from the following: Social Security and unemployment compensation may cost proportionately more for part-timers; health insurance is not readily prorated (although most other benefits are); and Employee Retirement Income Security Act of 1974 (ERISA) regulations relating to pensions create proportionately higher administrative (not contributory)

---

[52] If full fringe benefits were paid part-timers, costs could conceivably rise. But in general, actual fringe-benefits costs are lower because not all benefits are usually paid to part-timers.

[53] Responses from 68 companies—mostly in manufacturing and finance-insurance—are analyzed in Nollen et al. (1977); the study is explicitly exploratory and is not based on a representative sample of firms.

costs.[54] However, with fairly minor changes in policy, firms can institute fringe benefits packages for part-timers that are both considerably more equitable than existing packages and proportionately no more costly.[55] We would note that in one recent survey, working mothers listed part-time work with full benefits as the work alternative that would most relieve their work-family tensions (General Mills, 1981).

By way of summary we should emphasize that our discussion has necessarily focused on the *potential* value of permanent part-time work to employers and employees, because there appears to be little actual development of this employment policy. Certainly, there are very limited data about its scope and even less on its impact on workers and their family lives. The available evidence indicates a positive incentive for employers to use part-time employees in a variety of positions, but this evidence has proven insufficient to spur any notable growth.

Of course, it should be recognized that permanent part-time work is unlikely to provide a solution for single-parent working families, which need the income from a full-time job. The extent to which a policy could attract two-parent working families willing to trade some income for more time at home remains to be seen.

Job Sharing

A variety of initiatives that may be gathered together under the rubric of job sharing represent some of the more innovative attempts to accommodate the frequent desire for part-time careers. As Gretl Meier

---

[54] ERISA stipulates that all otherwise qualified employees working 1,000 hours or more a year must be treated alike in a firm's pension plan. Because employer contributions are proportional to an employee's earnings, contributory costs are not higher for part-timers, but the cost of record-keeping is the same for part-timers and full-timers and thus proportionately higher for the former.

[55] The federal government offers one model to its part-time employees. Annual and sick leaves are prorated by both hours and years worked; retirement and life insurance are based on earnings. For health insurance the government pays 60 percent for both full-time and part-time workers. Part-time workers who are covered through a spouse (or otherwise) do not have any incentive to participate; thus, the government saves the entire cost of health insurance for these workers. Companies could also turn to the much-discussed but little-implemented cafeteria system of providing employee benefits. The total value of employee benefits could be prorated for part-time employees, who could then make choices to fit their personal and family needs. Before cafeteria plans can be generally offered to part-time employees, though, life and health insurance companies must overcome their reluctance to include part-time workers in group plans. See Lazar (1975) for a detailed description of a benefits package designed to be equitable for part-time workers.

(1978:2) observes, both terminology and practice are still evolving, but to distinguish the new job sharing from other employment practices, it may be defined as "an arrangement whereby two employees hold a position together, whether they are as a team jointly responsible for the whole or separately for each half."[56] Shared jobs, then, involve the restructuring of positions generally designated as full time for one person—for example, two teachers are jointly responsible for a 5th grade class, one in the mornings, one in the afternoons; or two clerks together hold a position in a county medical office, with alternate days of work and some informal division of tasks so that they can concentrate on those that best fit their particular skills and interests.

For many workers seeking a part-time commitment to work, the fact that the job sharer holds part of a full-time position is likely to be appealing. As noted above, most existing part-time jobs are low-status, low-paying jobs with very limited career prospects. By contrast, shared jobs, being sufficiently important to have previously warranted a full-time worker, frequently could offer a level of responsibility and pay that surpasses the typical part-time job. (The full-time salary is split between the job sharers.) The job sharer can thus have a part-time *career*, although perhaps one with relatively limited prospects for advancement.

Although it is easy to imagine a widespread desire for such arrangements, particularly among parents who want time with their children as well as some involvement in a career, very few workers actually share a job. Most discussions are necessarily anecdotal, but Meier's (1978) exploratory, unsystematic survey at least suggests where the initial developments have been concentrated.[57] Teachers have apparently taken the lead in job sharing. Significant numbers of job sharers have a variety of nonmanagerial, white-collar office jobs, and still others work in the so-called helping professions (counseling, social work, and psychology). There is little evidence of job sharing among either high-income workers (management and the elite professions) or blue-collar workers.

---

[56] Other terms used to describe this arrangement are splitting, pairing, twinning, and tandem employment. It is important to distinguish these arrangements from work sharing. Some analysts, borrowing from the depression-induced idea and European practice, have suggested a reduction of work time for all employees (or all in particular categories) as an alternative to layoffs. See, for example, Levitan and Belous (1977). Work sharing is thus an inclusive, involuntary response to the prospect of unemployment, not an attempt to enhance the range of options available to individual workers. See also Haulot (1979).

[57] Meier (1978:35) surveyed 238 job sharers. Questionnaires were sent to "previously identified job sharers and then to those located through inquiries to organizations which had earlier requested information from New Ways to Work, to women's groups, and other community centers, and to various state, county and city personnel officers." As she is well aware, it is clearly impossible to draw valid estimates from this survey.

These limited initiatives have primarily occurred in public and voluntary, not-for-profit organizations. Private industry has clearly lagged in trying out job-sharing arrangements, and the relatively few instances seem to have been initiated by employees on an ad hoc basis. As might be expected from the nature of the occupations involved in job sharing (and women's relative inclination to trade off income for more leisure), the overwhelming number of job sharers are women. Indeed, Meier (1978) found that more than three-quarters of the job sharers in her survey worked on a team of two females, and more than half had young children. All-male teams appear to be rare.

While there are no systematic studies showing the effects of job sharing on family life, the pioneers of job sharing generally tend to view it favorably, especially because they have "the opportunity to balance work life with non-work time" (Meier, 1978:58). But of course the wider acceptance of job sharing depends on its appeal to employers. There is some very limited evidence (Olmsted, 1977) suggesting an increase in productivity with the introduction of job sharing. This conclusion is based on two small-scale studies among social workers and city workers, as well as some anecdotal reports. However, still very much unknown is under what circumstances the productivity of the job sharers would be sufficient to justify economically any additional managerial burden or costs for employee benefits.

Compressed Work Week

In the early 1970s there was some limited movement toward a compressed work week—usually a 4-day, 40-hour week. Yet, the idea never really caught on, and a recent survey indicates that its use is now declining (Nollen and Martin, 1978c). We do not discuss it here as a family-related innovation because, in general, it would not appear to have positive consequences for family life. Workers on the four-day week would have an extra day at home, but this time off would be out of synchronization with the activities of other family members (e.g., children in school), and on work days they would have reduced time to share in family activities.

Shift Work

About 10 million nonagricultural wage and salary workers who usually work full time (about 16 percent of the labor force) work evenings, nights, or other shifts that differ from typical daytime schedules (Hedges and Sekscenski, 1979). (An undetermined number work rotating shifts.)

This proportion has remained stable since 1973. About half this group works the evening shift (4 p.m. to midnight); the remainder are divided about equally between those working the night shift (midnight to 8 a.m.) and those working a miscellaneous shift (a long day or a rotating shift). The largest number of late-shift jobs are in factories and the service occupations (e.g., health work and retail sales). Although males, young single adults, and minorities are relatively more likely than other groups to work late shifts, of interest here is the fact that married men and women represent about three-fifths of all full-time workers on the evening shifts and two-thirds of those on the night shift (the same as on the day shift).

Those who work late shifts usually do so by choice; they may be paid premium pay for choosing what is generally viewed as a difficult schedule. Working a late shift is reported to have negative effects on workers and their families, including the disruption of family, marital, and parental roles and responsibilities (e.g., Maurice, 1975).

Why then discuss late-shift work in the context of a search for a more adaptive work schedule, unless it is to stress its adverse consequences?

It seems that some adults now deliberately choose shift work in order to manage work and family life more easily. In one study of full-time working mothers with preschool-age children, most of the women who worked evening or night shifts (or whose husbands did) stated explicitly that the choice was deliberate and carefully thought out, as a way to provide "good care at no cost" (Kamerman, 1980a:49). Some viewed the pattern as temporary, until children were in school or older. Furthermore, data from the 1979 Panel Study of Income Dynamics indicate that a surprisingly large proportion of parents reported that the husband, wife, or both care for the child by splitting shifts or working at home (Morgan, 1980). (In assessing how parents provide child care, the survey specified husband-wife split shifts as a possible care option.) Indeed, except for school and family day care, splitting shifts was the most common child-care arrangement, especially for parents in their 30s and early 40s and for parents with two or more children. Similarly, in a recent reanalysis of data from the 1977 Quality of Employment Survey, Staines and Pleck (1982) found that about 28 percent of the two-earner couples surveyed who did not have formal child-care arrangements for young children (aged 0-5) worked on different shifts.

Whether parents work split shifts because no satisfactory alternative arrangements for child care are available, choose such schedules out of a desire to care for their children themselves, or for other reasons is unclear. If the choice is made because no alternative form of care is available, a set of fundamental issues about child-care policy emerges.

If, on the other hand, parents value this arrangement but are constrained by the rigidity of conventional work schedules, some of the alternative work schedules discussed earlier might alleviate strain. Regardless, we should know more about who is choosing shift work, whether the pattern is increasing for those with children, why, and what the consequences may be.

ISSUES AND IMPLICATIONS

Our review of the benefits and services incorporated in the private or corporate welfare system should make it clear that the system is not at all uniform in what it provides workers. Thus, although private pension plans represent the most common way for workers to augment Social Security benefits, about half of the private labor force is not covered by one. Similarly, while the overwhelming majority of employed workers rely on their employers for health insurance (on a contributory or non-contributory basis), some have much more extensive coverage than others, and some have no coverage at all. For the most part the well paid and the highly skilled are eligible for the most generous benefits, and levels of coverage vary significantly among sectors of the economy.

Particularly notable is the difference between the coverage extended to those workers employed in the large corporate core sector of the economy and those employed in small businesses. Large firms have taken the lead in instituting virtually all benefits, and coverage remains far greater at such firms than at small firms. It must be remembered, however, that only 22 percent of the labor force works at firms with 500 or more employees. In contrast, some 27 percent are employed at firms with fewer than 20 employees and another 27 percent at firms with 20 to 99 employees. Although large corporations have a central role in the economy, it would be highly misleading to focus solely on their compensation policies.

Our analysis here complements more general perspectives that emphasize the divergence between large and small business sectors, a difference portrayed in such terms as "dual economy" and "core and periphery" (Averitt, 1968; Doeringer and Piore, 1971). The companies in the primary or core sector are large, generally well capitalized, stable, often unionized, and disproportionately concentrated in manufacturing and finance. They are able to offer relatively good employment conditions, including wages, job security, and benefits. By contrast, small businesses are often undercapitalized and organizationally unstable, generally nonunionized, and largely engaged in services and trade. Workers in this sector pay an income penalty, as compared to those with similar experience and education (Beck et al., 1978; Stolzenberg, 1978). This penalty apparently extends to benefits coverage as well. We are not arguing that the economy—and by extension, the private welfare system—is rigidly bifurcated into large and small business sectors or large and small employers, but benefits coverage strongly tends to be much less extensive in small firms. Any attempts to reform the corporate welfare system must recognize that smaller companies generally have less ability than larger ones to extend benefits coverage and are often subject to different kinds of market and employee pressures.

The ramifications of this nonuniform system on income inequality should not be overlooked. At a time when the poverty debate is increasingly stressing the need to consider the monetary value of in-kind transfers such as food stamps, Medicaid, and housing allowances, it seems equally important to examine the value of in-kind benefits that employers provide employees when assessing income for the nonpoor and formulating a poverty standard.

The unskilled, racial minorities, and women—in general, the poorly paid—are concentrated in sectors of the economy that offer poor benefits. Thus, if employee benefits are counted as part of an employee's wage, income differentials between men and women, whites and blacks, the skilled and unskilled, and high-salaried and low-salaried workers are likely greater than commonly thought. Moreover, if the value of benefits is taken into account, the notch problem may be exacerbated for those moving from reliance on Aid to Families with Dependent Children (AFDC) with the attendant publicly provided benefits, to jobs likely to carry no benefits or inadequate ones. In short, those least in need are best provided for. And the working poor are likely to have the least protection—neither the public benefits available to the very poor nor the private benefits provided those with the better jobs.

Indeed, consideration of employee benefits and services introduces a significant dimension of stratification—those who are adequately protected by the corporate welfare system versus those with minimal or no protection. This will remain a significant dimension as long as key benefits continue to be provided by private employers as a type of compensation (within minimal governmental guidelines). The provision of benefits is inevitably, though differentially, subject to market forces. Thus, this result is virtually guaranteed.

Evolution of the System

There are those who would say that any exploration of how industry is responding to labor force changes is really an examination of what can be expected of market forces in response to social change. Looking at what employers are doing is only a first cut at the larger question. We would argue that employee benefits and services are not a pure market response but rather a mixed response comprising a public subsidy for private initiative. The supply of corporate welfare is subsidized as constituting a portion of the cost of labor and, therefore, not paid for out of the employer's taxable income. The demand for benefits is also subsidized in that they are not included as taxable income to the beneficiary. Indeed, there are two separate issues: (1) the balance between how much the employer is willing to pay out and how much the employee is willing to accept, and (2) the particular combination of cash and in-kind benefits. Of course, the employer is concerned only about the cost of the total package—both cash and in-kind. Nevertheless, what makes these benefits attractive to both the employer and the employee is that the benefits to each outweigh their respective costs, some of which are borne by the government. In effect the growth in the corporate welfare system is already a response to public policy initiatives. If this policy is viewed as acceptable, what is the argument for stopping here and what for doing something more or something different?

Yet, if in a broad sense market forces conditioned by tax policies largely shape the private component of our mixed welfare system, it is still difficult to specify a theory explaining the evolution of this private component. That is, in concrete terms how have specific economic, political, and social considerations affected the emergence and development of employee benefits and services? How have various government actions (including legal mandates, tax policies, and public provision of benefits) conditioned the practices of private employers? These issues are difficult even to approach because the private welfare system generally has not been viewed in the holistic persective we have urged throughout this paper.

At best we have limited assessments of such specific initiatives as the gradual extension of pension and health insurance coverage and the mandatory inclusion of maternity in disability plans. The first two cases seem both a response to government incentives and an illustration of the ability of unions to take a lead in favorable economic conditions. (They set a pattern that nonunionized employers were compelled to emulate, at least in part.) The third case, maternity coverage, indicates the significance of intermittent government intervention, even in the face of considerable industry opposition.

Clearly, in other areas industry itself has been the prime initiator in introducing new benefits. (Management, by all accounts, also has taken the lead in introducing flexitime, a scheduling innovation with possible benefits for family life.) A sense of good business, not necessarily restricted to short-run profit calculation, seemingly has prompted companies, particularly the large corporations, to take this role. Many have at times viewed employee benefits and services as a way to attract and hold good workers, take advantage of tax laws regarding compensation, undercut unionization drives, or build a progressive corporate image. Generally, however, it seems that a tight labor market favors the expansion of benefits, and company profitability sets the limits.

The evolution of the corporate welfare system, then, is affected by a number of pressures. But it is not now possible to say under what circumstances particular forces are activated and with what consequences. We can say confidently, however, that neither companies nor unions have yet assessed benefits policies in terms of their impact on family life. Nor has either side viewed employers as inherently bearing much responsibility for the families of employees. To the employer, benefits are viewed largely as costs; to workers, they are a bargaining issue, simply part of a wage settlement. The proper or desirable role of employers vis-a-vis employees' families is not normatively (or legally) prescribed.

Nonetheless, it seems safe to predict that the present system will be challenged in several ways. While unions have not treated family benefits as a high priority, some union officials and observers of organized labor view a new focus on such benefits as likely over the next decade. Unions recognize that in order to halt their decline in membership they must become more successful in recruiting women workers. Accordingly, they are likely to have greater interest in understanding more about benefits programs, with an explicit concern for families, as well as in developing a new agenda for worker demands.

Whether the government will take any significant initiatives in mandating change is surely at issue. For awhile it appeared that implementing the Equal Employment Opportunity Commission (EEOC) guidelines, the Pregnancy Discrimination Act of 1978 provisions, and related court decisions might have an impact on a wide range of maternity and parent-related employee policies. The EEOC guidelines require employers to grant employees who are medically able to return to work following pregnancy the same right to take a child-care leave as is given for any other type of personal leave. There is continued discussion of the significance of equal employment opportunity laws as a way for women, organized and unorganized, to redress a variety of gender-based discriminatory employment practices (e.g., Leshin, 1978, 1979). One of the more contentious areas in recent years, and one that has not yet been studied systematically, is the possible impact of these laws on employee benefits.

At present the business community slowly appears to be realizing the inevitable connections between corporate policy and family life. A recent spate of conferences on this issue involving business executives and academics may reflect heightened corporate sensitivity and even serve to stimulate further business interest. Undoubtedly, though, any such sensitivity will be critically affected by the prevailing economic conditions.

There is no reason to believe that market forces alone will lead to a system that is attuned to family needs and offers adequate benefits and services to all employees. If one takes the position that industry should do more for families, it therefore seems necessary to consider the possible roles of government-mandated change and government-initiated tax incentives. We believe that it is impossible to mandate a uniform private benefits system because (among other reasons) not all companies can afford relatively generous coverage. Small companies would be especially hard pressed. Nevertheless, the fact that government mandates relating to maternity benefits and leaves have been effective illustrates the value of selective government regulation. Our purpose here is not to propose specific reforms but only to suggest that there are several possible levers of change and that a variety of approaches seems desirable.

Yet, consideration of how much and precisely how government should be involved in changing the employee benefits-services system rests on a more basic question: What should be the relationship between benefits provided by government and those provided by the employers? What are the consequences of each provision for each system? What are the costs and who bears them? And for benefits—who would receive them? Should the roles be supplementary, complementary, substitutive? Can government regulatory policy bridge the distinction between public and private provision so that it does not matter who does what? For example, government itself could provide statutory maternity benefits and leaves, require that employers provide them, or issue regulations making it very difficult for businesses not providing them to remain in operation. In each case there may be some employees who fall through the cracks.

In assessing the best mix of public and private efforts, it is essential to address the following concerns: What is the responsibility of the institution in which work takes place for the personal and familial consequences of work conditions and work arrangements? How can employers more fully and responsibly take into account their inevitable impact on the personal and familial lives of their employees without intruding inappropriately into their lives? What are the consequences for the families and children of employees when employers extend their activities in this way or fail to do so? These questions represent the core of a major social and public policy issue for the 1980s; they are also part of an important research agenda.

Our review of what is known about existing practices should contribute to the development of such an agenda, which should include attention to such questions as:

(1)   What benefits and services are available to employees with different familial characteristics?

(2)   How and why are employee benefits and services instituted and with what costs and benefits to employers?

(3)   How are benefits and services used by employees and with what consequences?

(4)   How do employee benefits and services relate to existing public and private provision?

A RESEARCH AGENDA

The research agenda we propose here is necessarily broad in scope because there has been little systematic attention paid to how employers have adapted in ways that are responsive to the family needs of their employees. A number of analyses deal with specific adaptations in isolation, such as flexitime, but even then the connection between the adaptation and family life is often only a tangential concern or is assumed to be implicit. Indeed, as we have contended, the domain for study has not been adequately conceptualized.

Before calling for specific research efforts, though, we would like to make some preliminary general observations. Most current research on employer responses to employees' family responsibilities has focused on the problems caused for family life by a fixed 8-hour work day and a 40-hour work week. The solution generally is viewed as some adjustment in work scheduling. Thus, research is directed toward identifying and experimenting with different patterns, and to a much lesser extent, assessing their consequences for family and work life. (As previously noted, there is little evidence yet of family effects.) Certainly, the time constraints imposed by fixed work schedules represent a real problem for employees, and alternative schedules may ease this problem for some. Our thesis, however, is that issues relating to scheduling are only one part—and a relatively small part at that—of the ways in which employer policies and practices affect the families of employees. Indeed, we have emphasized how employee benefits (and much less so, employer-provided services) have major but inadequately recognized roles. We do not mean to suggest that there has been little discussion of employee benefits. Yet the discussion to date has focused on individual entitlements and their impact on a particular category of problem or need: income in retirement, coverage for health and medical care, and so forth. There has been little discussion of the role these benefits play in meeting employees' family responsibilities generally (regardless of the motives of employers in providing them). Also critically lacking is a holistic perspective on how these privately provided benefits and services represent a parallel or complementary social welfare system that is available to particular segments of the work force.[58] Only a rudimentary understanding exists at present of how this system interacts or meshes with government-provided or government-funded benefits and services, as well as what the consequences are of having two parallel systems paid for in different ways.

Accordingly, without minimizing the need for continued study of the role and consequences of alternative work patterns (and we subsequently suggest specifics), it is in the area of employer-provided benefits and services that we would primarily urge new work. Such new endeavors could be especially important for a systematic analysis of the interrelationships among government, work, community, family, and children.

In the following sections, then, we list promising lines of inquiry that relate to our general perspective on the importance of employee benefits and services. As will be apparent, the range of issues involved necessitates diverse kinds of data and methodological approaches. We then suggest some important research issues related to the scheduling of work.

The Distribution of Benefits

Our review of data on the distribution of benefits in the private sector reveals several critical gaps:

(1) A good deal is known about what a core group of large companies in selected industries provides, but very little is known about what is provided in most small and even medium-sized companies. Women, minorities, and young adults are likely to be employed in the firms that

---

[58] Two articles do suggest this perspective, however: Glazer (1975) and Chaikin (1980).

appear to provide the least coverage. Systematic and reliable data on employee benefits for firms of all sizes, including those with fewer than 25 employees, are essential if we are to begin to draw any policy-relevant conclusions. (Data elicited from workers in nationally representative surveys may be used to get some sense of policies at smaller firms, but the accuracy and detail of such data may not be sufficient.)

Regular, ongoing surveys of employee benefits in companies of all sizes are essential if we are to gain even the most basic picture of what job-related entitlements employees have. (A stratified national sample of companies may be the best approach.) The discontinuation after 1977 of the biennial Bureau of Labor Statistics (BLS) Survey of Employee Compensation because of congressionally imposed budgetary constraints seems particularly short-sighted given the critical need for such data. The list of 25 benefits covered by the BLS Level of Benefits Survey planned for 1983 suggests the categories of benefits on which data are needed. (Only 11 will be analyzed by the bureau.[59]) Unfortunately, the sample selected for this study is not appropriate for providing a national picture of all employers. Supplementary special surveys may need to be designed and implemented to obtain a picture of the employer with fewer than 25 employees.

(2) More comprehensive data on the coverage offered part-time workers are also needed. It is important to obtain this information because some workers, especially women with children at home, turn to part-time employment as a way to meet both family and work responsibilities.

(3) Perhaps most critically needed in this area are data on the extent of benefits coverage that the *families* of workers have. As we have noted, such data are entirely lacking for the range of key benefits. In a significant though indeterminate number of cases a family's coverage reflects the contributions of several workers. The extent of the benefits gaps within our mixed social welfare system should be assessed in this light. Data relating to family coverage also are necessary for estimates of the extent of benefits waste and hence of unnecessary cost.

---

[59] The 11 items are as follows: work schedules, paid lunch and rest periods, paid vacations, paid holidays, paid personal leaves, paid sick leaves, accident and sickness (short-term disability) insurance, long-term disability insurance, health insurance, pension plan, and life insurance. The other items on which data will be collected but on which no analyses are planned include the following: medical appointments, income continuation (severance and supplementary unemployment insurance), profit-sharing and savings plans, other types of paid leave, and such miscellaneous benefits as child-care services, educational services, relocation allowances, and recreation facilities discounts.

Information of this kind could be elicited in special addenda to such national surveys as the Survey of Income Program Participation (SIPP) and the Michigan Panel Study of Income Dynamics (PSID). (At this writing, unfortunately, SIPP has been either eliminated or deferred, and support for the PSID has been substantially reduced as well.)

Services

There are very limited data on services sponsored or provided by employers. Nor has any effort been made to study how these services have been integrated with existing community provisions such as child care, counseling, and recreation. Do employees want them, use them, prefer them to community resources?

On the basis of program descriptions, we know that some employers provide employee-assistance services (counseling) at the workplace; others purchase such services from an off-site provider; while still others, particularly small businesses, have opted for joining together to share collectively in subsidizing services in the community (e.g., Akabas et al., 1980; Masi, 1982). Some unions, especially those with low-skilled workers as members, have taken still a different tack, urging closer linkages with existing public resources. However, since all these efforts are relatively novel, nationally representative surveys of firms about these matters will likely be unrewarding. Instead, we suggest an ongoing monitoring effort, based on material in the personnel administration literature (including consulting firms' newsletters) as well as on contacts with so-called informed observers. Certain particularly promising initiatives then may be selected for more intensive case-study analyses.

The Nature and Effects of Employee Benefits and Services

Historically, there has been great debate about whether government-provided benefits encourage dependency on the part of recipients. However, there has been little parallel discussion of whether employer-provided benefits foster dependency of employees. How and in what ways do the corporate and the statutory welfare systems differ? Is the difference largely in the way they are viewed by the society? Or the way they are perceived by beneficiaries? What are the consequences for workers and their families of receiving these employee benefits versus not receiving them? Of having government-provided benefits versus employer-provided benefits? How can these consequences and effects—economic and noneconomic—be identified, assessed, and compared?

The Mesh with Government and Community Services

We have argued that the employee benefits and services system both parallels and complements public welfare provisions. Yet little is known about how the public and private systems mesh in actual practice.

Particular attention should be directed to assessing the extent of the notch problem for those moving from AFDC to jobs likely to carry few, if any, benefits. Subsequently, social experiments might be tried. Waivers could be provided that would enable AFDC recipients to continue receiving Medicaid if the jobs they obtain do not provide basic hospital and surgical benefits. An alternative model could entail government subsidies along with employer and employee contributions to support health insurance funds for small employers on a collective basis, so that economies of scale could be realized and no single employer would have to bear disproportionate costs. Developing some way to ensure availability of key benefits such as health insurance, maternity leaves, and paid vacations may be critical if movement off public assistance is to be facilitated.

More generally, a detailed, comprehensive accounting is needed of both the gaps that now exist within the mixed welfare system and the waste entailed by unnecessary duplicate coverage. Survey data relating to private-employment practices are a necessary complement to government-program data in this task. The need for this kind of accounting has been recognized in the debates surrounding the various proposals for national health insurance, but similar reasoning is required across the range of key benefits. Such accounting is a necessary preliminary to models proposing more efficient, generous, or equitable mixes of private and public efforts.

Furthermore, information is needed on how workers and their families participate in this mixed system. No data are available as yet on how employee benefits and services packages are used by workers and how they relate to existing community services. Case studies of individual companies of different sizes in different industries and in different communities could provide a rich source of information and new insights into how this system works. How do employees learn about what is available?

Providing benefits and services to employees carries monetary costs, some of which are borne by the employer, some by the employee, some passed along to the consumer, and some borne by the government or the taxpayer. What are the net costs of these benefits to business, how are they allocated, and who bears them? Where does the burden fall among employer, employee, and society, and with what consequences?

What Do Families Want?

We have noted that by and large the private benefits system is based on the unrealistic premise that families have a single breadwinner and that family needs are relatively stable throughout the life cycle. In turn there has been an implicit assumption in our discussion that most families have certain needs, but only limited knowledge or understanding exists of how desires for benefits are actually structured and how these desires vary through life.

Flexible benefits plans offer possibilities for valuable natural experiments relating to employee preferences. What do employees with family responsibilities want in the way of job-related benefits and services? What do they think about possible risks? What kinds of protection do they view as essential? Do they want such protection to be provided through work, or would they prefer higher wages and the freedom to purchase what they want privately? (And would they, in fact, do so?) If the number of companies providing flexible benefits plans increases, there could be a rich opportunity for studying what employees actually select in contrast to what employees responding to survey questions say they would do.

To expand the number of participants in this experiment, however, it would be helpful if easily adaptable model cafeteria systems could be established. Such models should provide specific guidelines for diverse kinds of companies.

Benefits and Services: The Ramifications for Children and Family Life

What we have discussed up to now represents a necessary foundation on which studies of some of the effects of parental work on children and family life can be instituted. Our sparse knowledge about adult-parent entitlements limits any systematic study of this critical topic. Nevertheless, case studies of companies could at least begin to explore the consequences for family life and parent and family life-styles, behavior, and attitudes. And those studying children and families could begin to focus more on the work life and workplace of parents and what is provided, or not provided, by employers.

Among the questions to be asked are the following: Do more generous leave policies (maternity, paternity, vacation, and personal) affect parent-child and spouse-spouse relationships? And if so, in what ways are attitudes and actual behavior affected? Does the absence of certain benefits have identifiable negative consequences for families with children (e.g., the failure to obtain needed medical care and the inability to share in a child's important school activity)? Are there certain benefits that are more or less important to particular types of families (e.g., one-parent or low-income families)? What are the consequences of these benefits, or their absence, for child development? Such knowledge would permit more deliberate public policy decisions about the need for such benefits.

A similar line of questioning could be valuably addressed to the consequences of on-site day care, with explicit comparisons to other types of employer-sponsored child-care arrangements.

We know very little about how families socialize youth into adult work roles. As this process is studied, one question is the role played by the parent's workplace in shaping parental values and attitudes. Do employees in firms with extensive benefits have a more positive attitude toward work than other employees? If there is a difference, does it have any consequence for children and youth as they view jobs?

The Ramifications of Work Scheduling

Although the advantages of flexitime for family life have been widely touted, there has been remarkably little rigorous analysis of its impact. To build on the limited initial efforts, researchers should consider a wider range of outcome measures, including both behavioral indicators of time management and social psychological attitudes relating to work and family roles. Moreover, these effects should be assessed in a variety of settings so that both variations in flexitime arrangements and other work-related conditions may be considered. It is also critical to specify how these effects vary by the family characteristics (structure, number, and age of children; work schedules of other family members in the labor force) of workers.

Similar research should be addressed to the experiences of part-time workers; systematic analysis in this area appears to be entirely lacking. We strongly urge researchers to consider differences in the nature of the part-time work, with particular attention to the relatively few career-type part-time positions. In addition to work and family variables suggested above, it also may be valuable to consider the work histories of those with part-time jobs.

We certainly do not mean to suggest that this agenda exhausts all valuable research topics relating to our general concerns. Yet its very scope, as well as the need to pursue some topics almost from scratch, indicates that there is a formidable task ahead.

REFERENCES AND BIBLIOGRAPHY

Advisory Commission on Intergovernmental Relations (1980) The federal role in the federal system: the dynamics of growth. *A Crisis of Confidence and Competence.* 10 vols. Washington, D.C.: U.S. Government Printing Office.

Akabas, S. H., Kurzman, P. A., and Kolben, N. S., eds. (1979) *Labor and Industrial Settings: Sites for Social Work Practice.* New York: Council on Social Work Educators.

Akabas, S. H., Kurzman, P. A., and Kolben, N. S. (1980) Labor and industrial settings. In *Private Sector Initiatives to Promote Mental Health.* Unpublished digest of the proceedings of the General Mills American Family Forum, Washington, D.C.

American Can Corp. (1980) News about American Can's flexible benefits program. In *Your Way,* a publication of American Can Corp.

Australian Department of Social Security (1979) Changing family patterns and Social Security protection: the Australian scene. *International Social Security Review* 32(1): 3-20.

Averitt, R. (1968) *The Dual Economy: The Dynamics of American Industry Structure.* New York: Horton.

Avizahar, M. (1977) The family wage. *Journal of Social Policy* 6(1):47-54.

Babalinsky, R. (1980) People vs. profits: social work in industry. *Social Work* 25(6): 471-475.

Beck, E. M., Horan, P., and Tolbert, C., III (1978) Stratification in a dual economy: a sectoral model of earnings determination. *American Sociological Review* 43:704-720.

Beller, D. (1980) *Patterns of Workers Coverage by Private Pension Plans.* Labor Management Services Administration, Pension and Welfare Benefit Programs. Washington, D.C.: U.S. Department of Labor.

Best, F. (1980) *Flexible Life Scheduling.* New York: Praeger.

Bohen, H., and Viveros-Long, A. (1981) *Balancing Jobs and Family Life: Do Flexible Work Schedules Help?* Philadelphia, Pa.: Temple University Press.

Brandes, S. D. (1976) *American Welfare Capitalism 1880-1940.* Chicago: University of Chicago Press.

Bureau of Labor Statistics (1976a) Employee expenditures for employee compensation. Pp. 175-183 in *Handbook of Methods for Surveys and Studies.* Bulletin 1910. Washington, D.C.: U.S. Department of Labor.

Bureau of Labor Statistics (1976b) Employee benefit plans. Pp. 192-194 in *Handbook of Methods for Surveys and Studies.* Bulletin 1910. Washington, D.C.: U.S. Department of Labor.

Bureau of Labor Statistics (1980a) *Employee Compensation in the Private Non-Farm Economy, 1977.* Summary. Washington, D.C.: U.S. Department of Labor.

Bureau of Labor Statistics (1980b) Labor month in review. *Monthly Labor Review* 103(7):2.

Bureau of Labor Statistics (1980c) *Employee Benefits in Industry: A Pilot Survey.* Report 615. Washington, D.C.: U.S. Department of Labor.

Bureau of Labor Statistics (1981a) Employment data from the household survey. *Monthly Labor Review* 104(11):63-67.

Bureau of Labor Statistics (1981b) *Employee Benefits in Industry, 1980.* Bulletin 2107. Washington, D.C.: U.S. Department of Labor.

Bureau of Labor Statistics (1982) *Monthly Labor Review* 105(1):63.

Bureau of the Census (1981a) Characteristics of households and persons receiving noncash benefits: 1979. *Current Population Reports.* Series P-23, No. 110. Washington, D.C.: U.S. Department of Commerce.

Bureau of the Census (1981b) Characteristics of households receiving noncash benefits:

1980. *Current Population Reports*, Series P-60, No. 128. Washington, D.C.: U.S. Department of Commerce.

Catalyst Career and Family Center (1981) *Corporations and Two-Career Families: Directions for the Future*. New York: Catalyst Career and Family Center.

Chaikin, S. C. (1980) Divided labor movement. *The Journal of the Institute for Socioeconomic Studies* 5(3):1-17.

Chamber of Commerce of the United States (1980) *Employee Benefits 1979*. Washington, D.C.: Chamber of Commerce of the United States.

Chamber of Commerce of the United States (1979) *Employee Benefits 1978*. Washington, D.C.: Chamber of Commerce of the United States.

Cohen, A., and Gadon, H. (1978) *Alternative Work Schedules: Integrating Individual and Organizational Needs*. Reading, Mass.: Addison-Wesley.

Collie, H. C., and DiDomenico, P. (1980) Relocation trends—moving into the 80's. *Personnel Administrator* 25(September):19.

Daski, R. (1974) Area wage survey focuses on part-timers. *Monthly Labor Review* 97(4): 60-62.

Department of Health and Human Services (1980) *Who are the Uninsured?* Data Preview 1. Washington, D.C.: U.S. Department of Health and Human Services.

Department of Labor (1981a) *Group Health Insurance Coverage of Private Full-Time Wage and Salary Workers, 1979*. Washington, D.C.: U.S. Department of Labor.

Department of Labor (1981b) *Employers and Child Care: Establishing Services at the Work Place*. Washington, D.C.: U.S. Department of Labor.

Department of Labor (1981c) *10 Million Americans Work Flexible Schedules, 2 Million Work Full-Time in 3 to 4-1/2 Days*. February 24 Office of Information News Release. Washington, D.C.: U.S. Department of Labor.

Deuterman, W., and Brown, S. (1978) Voluntary part-time workers: a growing part of the labor force. *Monthly Labor Review* 101(6):3-10.

Doeringer, P., and Piore, M. (1971) *Internal Labor Markets and Manpower Analysis*. Lexington, Mass.: Heath.

Equal Employment Opportunity Commission (1972) *Guidelines on Discrimination Because of Sex*. Washington, D.C.: Equal Employment Opportunity Commission.

European Economic Community (1979) *Report on the Development of the Social Situation in the European Community in 1978*. Brussels and Luxembourg: European Economic Community.

General Mills (1981) *The General Mills American Family Report 1980-81, Families: Strengths and Strains at Work*. Minneapolis, Minn.: General Mills.

Glazer, N. (1975) Reform work, not welfare. *The Public Interest* 40 (Summer):3-10.

Golembiewski, R. T., and Proehl, C. W., Jr. (1978) A survey of the empirical literature on flexible workhours: character and consequences of a major innovation. *Management Review* 3(October):837-853.

Hareven, T. K., and Langenback, R. (1978) *Amoskeag: Life and Work in an American Factory City*. New York: Pantheon.

Haulot, A. (1979) The staggering of annual holidays with pay. *International Labor Review* 118(2):191-204.

Hedges, J. N. (1980) The workweek in 1979: fewer but longer workdays. *Monthly Labor Review* 103(8):31-33.

Hedges, J. N., and Sekscenski, E. S. (1979) Workers on late shifts in a changing economy. *Monthly Labor Review* 102(9):14-22.

Hewett Associates (1980) *Adoption Benefits*. Unpublished draft report.

Janowitz, M. (1978) *The Last Half Century.* Chicago: University of Chicago Press.

Kahn, A. J., and Kamerman, S. B. (1982) *Helping America's Families.* Philadelphia, Pa.: Temple University Press.

Kamerman, S. B. (1980a) *Parenting in an Unresponsive Society: Managing Work and Family Life.* New York: The Free Press.

Kamerman, S. B. (1980b) *Maternity and Parental Benefits and Leaves: An International Review.* New York: Columbia University Center for the Social Sciences.

Kamerman, S. B., and Kahn A. J. (1981) *Child Care, Family Benefits and Working Parents.* New York: Columbia University Press.

Kanter, R. M. (1977) *Work and Family in the United States: A Critical Review and Agenda for Research and Policy.* New York: Russell Sage Foundation.

Kolodrubetz, W. W. (1972) Two decades of employee benefit plans, 1950-1970: a review. *Social Security Bulletin* 35(4):11-22.

Kolodrubetz, W. W. (1974a) Two decades of employee benefit plans. *Social Security Bulletin* 37(4):

Kolodrubetz, W. W. (1974b) Group health insurance coverage of full time employees, 1972. *Social Security Bulletin* 37(4):17-35

Lazar, E. (1975) *Constructing an Employee Benefit Package for Part-time Workers.* New York: Catalyst Career and Family Center.

Leshin, G. (1978) *Equal Opportunity and Affirmative Action in Labor Management Relations.* Los Angeles: UCLA Institute of Industrial Relations.

Leshin, G. (1979) *EEO Law: Impact on Fringe Benefits.* Los Angeles: UCLA Institute of Industrial Relations.

Levenson, M. K., and Hollmann, R. W. (1980) Personal support services in corporate relocation programs. *Personnel Administrator* 25 (September): 45-51.

Levitan, S., and Belous, R. (1977) *Shorter Hours, Shorter Weeks: Spreading the Work to Reduce Unemployment.* Baltimore, Md.: The Johns Hopkins University Press.

Masi, D. A. (1982) *Human Services in Industry.* Lexington, Mass.: Lexington Books.

Maurice, M. (1975) *Shiftwork.* Geneva: International Labour Office.

Meier, G. (1978) *Job Sharing: A New Pattern for Quality of Work Life.* Kalamazoo, Mich.: Upton Institute.

Meyer, M. (1978) *Women and Employee Benefits.* New York: The Conference Board.

Meyer, M. (1981) *Profile of Employee Benefits: 1981.* New York: The Conference Board.

Meyer, M., and Fox, H. (1974) *Profile of Employee Benefits.* New York: The Conference Board.

Morgan, J. N. (1980) Child care when parents are employed. Pp. 441-556 in M. S. Hill, D. H. Hill, and J. N. Morgan, eds., *Five Thousand American Families: Patterns of Economic Progress,* vol. 4. Ann Arbor, Mich.: Institute for Social Research.

Nollen, S. (1979a) *New Patterns of Work.* Scarsdale, N.Y.: Work in America Institute

Nollen, S. (1979b) Does flexitime improve productivity. *Harvard Business Review* (September-October):12-22.

Nollen, S. (1980) What is happening to flexitime, flexitour, gliding time, the variable day? and permanent part-time employment? and the four day week? *Across the Board* 17 (April):6-21.

Nollen, S., Eddy, B., and Martin, V.C. (1977) *Permanent Part-Time Employment: An Interpretive Review.* No. PB268391. Springfield, Va.: National Technical Information Service.

Nollen, S., Eddy, B., and Martin, V.C. (1978) *Permanent Part-Time Employment: The Manager's Perspective.* New York: Praeger.

Nollen, S., and Martin, V. C. (1978a) *Alternative Work Schedules Part 1: Flexitime*. New York: AMACOM.

Nollen, S., and Martin, V.C. (1978b) *Alternative Work Schedules Part 2: Permanent Part-time Work*. New York: AMACOM.

Nollen, S., and Martin, V.C. (1978c) *Alternative Work Schedules: Part 3*. New York: AMACOM.

Olmsted, B. (1977) Job sharing—a new way to work. *Personnel Journal* 54 (February): 78-81.

O'Toole, P. (1980) The menace of the corporate shrink. *Savvy* 1 (10) (October): 49-52.

Owen, J. (1978) Why part-time workers tend to be in low-wage jobs. *Monthly Labor Review* 101(6):11-14.

Ozawa, M. H. (1980) Development of social services in industry: why and how? *Social Work* 25(6):464-470.

Perry, K. S. (1980) *Child Care Centers Sponsored by Employers and Labor Unions in the United States*. Washington, D.C.: U.S. Department of Labor.

President's Commission on Pension Policy (1980) *President's Commission on Pension Policy, An Interim Report*. Washington, D.C.: U.S. Government Printing Office.

Questiaux, N., and Fournier, J. (1978) France. Pp. 117-182 in S. B. Kamerman and A. J. Kahn, eds., *Family Policy: Government and Families in Fourteen Countries*. New York: Columbia University Press.

Quinn, R. P., and Staines, G. L. (1979) *The 1977 Quality of Employment Survey: Descriptive Statistics, with Comparison Data From the 1969-70 and 1972-73 Surveys*. Ann Arbor, Mich.: Institute for Social Research.

Rogers, G. T. (1980) *Pension Coverage and Vesting Among Private Wage and Salary Workers, 1979: Preliminary Estimates from the 1979 Survey of Pension Plan Coverage*. Working Paper Series. Washington, D.C.: U.S. Department of Health and Human Services.

Runzheimer and Company (1979) *A Study of Employer Relocation Policies Among Major U.S. Corporations—1979*. White Plains, N.Y.: Merrill Lynch Relocation Management.

Samuelson, R. (1980) A rebel with cause. *National Journal* 12(17):690.

Staines, G. L., and Pleck, J. H. (1982) Work Schedules Impact on the Family. Unpublished draft of research monograph, Rutgers University.

Stolzenberg, R. (1978) Bringing the boss back in: employer size, employee schooling, and socioeconomic achievement. *American Sociological Review* 43(December):813-828.

Terry, S. L. (1981) Involuntary part-time work: new information from the CPS. *Monthly Labor Review* 104(2):70-74.

Titmuss, R. (1969) The social division of welfare. Pp. 34-55 in R. Titmuss ed., *Essays on the Welfare State*. Boston: Beacon Press.

Unsigned (1980) Successful pilot project leads to program for all salaried employees. *Employee Benefit Plan Review Research Reports* (February).

U.S. Congress, Congressional Budget Office (1979) *Profile of Health Care Coverage: The Haves and Have-Nots*. Washington, D.C.: U.S. Government Printing Office.

Wallace, A. F. C. (1978) *Rockdale*. New York: Alfred A. Knopf.

Watkins, B. T. (1980) Post-compulsory education by U.S. companies may be a $10 billion business. *The Chronicle of Higher Education* September 22:7.

Winett, R. A., and Neale, M. S. (1980) Results in experimental study of flexitime and family life. *Monthly Labor Review* 103(11):29-32.

6
Small Employers, Work, and Community

Carolyn Shaw Bell, *Wellesley College*

INTRODUCTION

Increased attention has been focused lately on how work relates to home and community life. That is largely because of the most significant labor force development in two generations: the emergence of a new typical family, one with two adult workers. Today, many more people are involved in the worlds of both work and family than they were in the recent past.[1] Thirty years ago fewer than 70 percent of people 18 years old and older received income; today 92 percent of this adult population

---

[1] Both economists and managers have recently begun to adopt a framework for analyzing the labor market or for developing personnel policies that specifically recognize workers' links to home and community. Two quotations give the flavor of such recognition. Many others could be cited, but only from recent work. Fusfeld, for instance, comments (1980:786):

> First, the labor market is reviewed as a social process. Michael Piore sees the productive work of the individual not simply as one aspect of supply and demand in the market, but as part of the entire social context within which the individual functions: family, peer groups, community. The individual selects an occupation, works, earns, stays or migrates, within a context of a variety of formal and informal social institutions. Attitudes, motivations, and actions are determined by those institutions within which individual activities are embedded. One of those institutions is the labor market itself, and the individual responds to the push and pull of market forces, but that is only one set of forces influencing behavior. Furthermore, the social context is continually changing as the individual matures, rears a family, is integrated into the larger community, and moves toward old age.

209

does (Bureau of the Census, 1961, 1974, 1980). Although the change partly reflects the higher incidence of transfer payments,[2] an overwhelming rise in employment has significantly increased the number of people with wages and salaries or earnings from paid work. As a result, family income typically consists of the pooled earnings and other income received by family members. The family breadwinner, identified as a husband and a father, is in the distinct minority; concomitantly, the division of labor between paid and unpaid family members has shifted.

Quite visibly, new strains and challenges have emerged as people try to manage their responsibilities to family, as well as those to community and work. Almost of necessity a variety of arrangements have developed that ease some problems. But clearly, many people have difficulty finding a suitable way to handle their often conflicting pressures.

Analyzing these changing relationships is complicated not only because employment has grown so rapidly but also because it is misleading to talk of typical practices in the work world. Employers differ substantially in legal form of organization, in conditions of work, in numbers and types of jobs, in proximity to workers' homes and community activities, in participation in local affairs, and of course in compensation. In particular the size of the employing organization significantly affects the ways in which both employer and employee define and cope with the relationships among work, home, and community. The small, local service establishment and the large, multiplant manufacturing corporations are very different kinds of operations.

To be sure, large corporations dominate the economy, accounting for a large proportion of total assets and value added. In the extractive

---

For management studies, Schein exemplifies the new approach (1978:10-11):

> Any human resource planning and development system must attempt to match the needs of the organization with those of the individual. If such a system is to work, much more effort must be devoted to understand fully the needs and characteristics of the individual. These needs derive not only from the individual's working life, but also from the interaction within the total "life space" of issues of work, family and self-development. One of the weaknesses of traditional employee and management development systems has been the tendency to assume that employees can be conceived of as leaving family and self at home when they come to work and that, therefore, the organization need worry only about creating opportunities for *work-oriented* development activities. As the study of adult development progresses, it is becoming more and more clear that work, family and self-concerns interact strongly within people throughout their lives. This interaction simply cannot any longer be ignored.

[2] Some 51 million persons received transfers, both public and private, in 1978 (Bureau of the Census, 1980).

industries, manufacturing, and the rapidly expanding service sector that represents most economic growth, a few firms account for most of the output. In 1977 the 6,000 firms employing more than 500 people accounted for 0.1 percent of all companies but almost half of total sales and total employment (Bureau of the Census, 1981). However, any analysis based on the behavior of the large corporations provides little useful information about millions of workers employed in millions of smaller units, many of them outside private business altogether. In 1977 some 2.8 million firms employing fewer than 50 people provided one-third of total business sales and employment. This point serves as the impetus for this paper. Too often discussions of American workers (and management) focus exclusively on business, and within the business sector on large corporations. Such an approach implies that corporate practices are generally representative or are the only ones worth considering.

Some analysts opposing this focus have created a growing but somewhat disparate literature on the "dual economy" with its "core/periphery" to differentiate large and small businesses (e.g., Averitt, 1968; Beck et al., 1978; Bluestone et al., 1973; Edwards et al., 1975; Galbraith, 1958, 1967). Firm size influences market power and to some extent the conditions of employment, particularly job stability and opportunities for advancement. All firms cannot, of course, be unambiguously sorted into any two-sector model, but the literature does call for systematic attention to small businesses, which have frequently been neglected in analysis of the relationships among work, family, and community. This attention is warranted also because of a kind of small business mystique and ideology that have been present throughout American history.

As Stuart Bruchey, the economic historian, says in his introduction to a collection of essays on small business in American life (1980:1), "Small business not only belonged to every sector of the economy, it also reached out to affect the degree of social mobility, urban power structures, the legal systems and the formation of important values shared by Americans (to say nothing of its effects on labor relations, technological innovation and big business itself). In a word, small business has formed an integral part of American life." While small firms no longer dominate, they account for a significant share of both output and employment. The number of jobs provided by small firms varies by kind of business; 1 out of 6 workers in manufacturing was hired by a firm with fewer than 100 employees, but over half of all retail workers were employed by such small companies.

It is also the case that millions of workers are not employed by business, either small or large. But if data on what goes on in small firms is scarce, information about employment in nonprofit or government agencies or about the working conditions of those who are self-employed is practically nonexistent. In what follows, the reader should remember that of about 95 million people currently employed, only about 60 million work for private business. This chapter ignores the work, family, and community responsibilities of the other 35 million; instead, it focuses on small business to reduce an overemphasis on the policies and practices of the large corporation. Those who work for small firms may serve in the following discussion as examples of the millions of Americans who do not work for giant corporations. How do they fare?

The paper discusses small firms as:

- providing significant sources of employment
- providing a distinctive type of employment, both in terms of economic rewards and work relationships
- standing in a distinctive relationship to family and community life
- serving as potential agents for change to help employees better accommodate their nonwork responsibilities, given the particular constraints which these firms face

The discussion of these distinctive impacts of small businesses quickly reveals a substantial lack of information: Good data about the work-family-community nexus are generally sparse, but they are especially lacking for smaller companies. Identifying the significant gaps will provide the context for a research agenda.

WHERE PEOPLE WORK

Defining a small business is always arbitrary. One may use production, sales volume, or number of employees as the scale and still must select the correct magnitude to measure large and small. No single definition exists; the Small Business Administration uses a variety of measures. Maximum size standards for Standard Industrial Classification (SIC) industries use annual sales volume and occasionally other characteristics as well. The maximum number of employees is a criterion, but only for a few SIC classifications. Thus, a small typewriter manufacturer is one with fewer than 1,000 employees and a small storage battery manufacturer has fewer than 500 employees; but a small hospital contains no more than 150 beds, excluding cribs and bassinets, and a small department store is one with less than $7.5 million volume, while a small shoe store has less than $2.5 million annual sales. Of course, any size standard

TABLE 6–1   Number of Employees and Percent of Total
Employment, Business Establishments by Employment
Size-Class, 1977

		Employment Size-Class of Establishment			
	Total	1–49	50–99	100–249	250+
Number	64,975,580	27,789,763	7,630,090	8,876,798	20,678,929
Percentage	100	43	12	14	31

SOURCE: Bureau of the Census (1979c).

set by dollar sales requires constant revision with continued inflation
(Small Business Administration, 1980).

Nonetheless, allowing for definitional ambiguity, just in sheer numbers ours is an economy of small businesses. Table 6-1 uses the business
establishment as the reporting unit; a single firm or company may have
more than one establishment or place of doing business. It indicates for
1977 the percentage of total business employment in small workplaces,
defining small with four different categories. Forty-three percent of all
employees have fewer than 50 co-workers, and more than half (55 percent) have fewer than 100 co-workers. In fact, more than three-quarters
(3,300,000 +) of the establishments in the United States have fewer than
10 employees. These data on employment by large and small work
places, defined by number of employees, show that small establishments
provide a somewhat greater share of total employment than do large
ones.

Table 6-2 uses the firm or company as the reporting unit; it also
excludes the agricultural, transportation, and finance workers counted
in Table 6-1. But even so, small companies account for millions of jobs.
Companies with fewer than 100 workers employed 40 percent of those
working in private enterprise; firms with between 100 and 250 workers
employed almost 10 percent. A company with 100 workers is not small
compared to a firm with 20 but neither is it a giant corporation.

Obviously some policy, explicit or implicit, that affects workers' home
and community life exists in all employing organizations. What has not
been explored is how actual practice within each establishment reflects
centrally determined policy or the decisions taken by managers at the
establishment level. Employees at some small establishments (e.g., fast
food chains) may have levels of compensation and other conditions of
work that are identical to those of thousands of employees in other parts
of the same large firm or agency. For them, the small size of their
establishment is mostly inconsequential. However, managers at estab-

TABLE 6–2   Number of Employees and Percent of Total
Employment, Companies by Employment Size-Class, 1977

| | Total | Employment Size-Class | | | |
		1–49	50–99	100–249	250+
All industries					
Number	49,775,765	16,317,947	3,655,212	3,790,138	26,012,468
Percentage	100	3	7	8	52
Mineral industries					
Number	645,975	140,364	50,710	56,015	398,876
Percentage	100	22	8	9	61
Construction industries					
Number	3,887,221	2,320,866	358,563	338,761	869,031
Percentage	100	60	9	9	22
Manufacturing					
Number	21,952,260	2,332,008	1,217,247	1,627,676	16,775,329
Percentage	100	11	6	7	76
Wholesale trade					
Number	3,571,992	2,173,778	435,585	373,437	504,408
Percentage	100	61	12	10	14
Retail trade					
Number	13,560,387	6,254,184	1,053,964	758,682	5,498,557
Percentage	100	46	8	6	40
Selected service					
Number	6,157,930	3,096,747	539,143	635,557	1,175,584
Percentage	100	50	9	10	19

SOURCE: Bureau of the Census (1981).

lishments of other large firms may be granted considerable discretion in setting practices in accord with local labor market conditions and prevailing customs relating to employer-employee relationships. Employees of these establishments in effect work for a small company. In short, as it affects employees' lives the workplace may be either establishment or firm.

For some purposes it may be useful to define a small employer as one without an officially designated personnel officer, let alone the job of vice-president for human relations. A small employer has not divided managerial duties into such specialized activities nor, perhaps, explicitly recognized them.

Future Developments

Small business should be an immediate focus of concern in analyzing the connections between work and family life because of its importance iñ creating employment. Although future developments are not easy to predict, a variety of data suggest that small employers, not giant corporations, have created most of the new jobs in the past 20 years.

Between 1960 and 1980 the total labor force grew from 74 to 104 million people; some 32 million jobs have been added. They reflect a rise in the amount of part-time work and moonlighting, as well as a shift in the composition of the labor force with the substantial growth of new entrants.[3] The growth of teenage employment represents not only a population increase but also a shift in social attitudes allowing part-time paid employment, meshed with school activities, for children in middle- and upper-income families (Freeman and Wise, 1980), especially for teenage girls.[4] Employment among married women has been discussed exhaustively elsewhere, but it should be noted that most of these new entrants want full-time rather than part-time jobs.[5]

The phenomenon of occupational segregation leads to the strong supposition that small employers created a disproportionate share of new jobs for teenagers and women.[6] In the private sector, small business accounts for a large share of clerical and office jobs as well as jobs in retailing, food service, seasonal and recreational activities, and a variety of other services. Women and teenagers are highly concentrated in these industries, which provide many entry-level jobs and were the areas of rapid expansion during the past decade or so.[7] Thus, for example, despite the giant food chains or multimillion-dollar department store enterprises, small specialty stores account for millions of jobs: In 1977 more than two-thirds of all retail employees worked with fewer than 50 people (Bureau of the Census, 1980).

[3] Between 1967 and 1978 the number of persons on voluntary part-time schedules (i.e., not working shorter hours because of lack of employment or inability to find full-time work) rose from 8 million to 12 million (Department of Labor, 1979). Also see Deutermann and Brown (1978).

[4] Between 1958 and 1978 the number of young people (16 to 19) in the labor force more than doubled: As a percentage of the relevant age group, the number of males with employment experience increased by 10 percent; the number of females with employment experience increased by 60 percent (Department of Labor, 1979).

[5] In 1978, of some 37 million employed women (over 18), only 22 percent were voluntarily working part time.

[6] Most studies of occupational segregation show little change in the concentration of women in jobs they have mainly held since early in the century. See Blau and Hendricks (1979).

[7] One exception, clerical and nonproduction workers in manufacturing, should be noted. It may not be realized that the decline in the proportion of manufacturing jobs over the past few years has been concentrated among production workers. The volume of clerical and office work, technical and semiskilled white-collar jobs, has grown even within the manufacturing sector, which of course is dominated by large firms.

In the government sector the number of small offices or agencies (in terms of number of employees) has risen as a fraction of the total because of the proliferation of local government agencies.[8] Again, the business of such offices consists largely of paper work or simple clerical jobs readily filled by the new entrants to the labor force. As for the nonprofit sector (tabulated for the first time by industry in the 1977 census), no hard data exist to show its growth, but casual observation suggests that the volume of activity among social service, artistic, and educational endeavors has risen sharply. In 1977, average employment in such establishments was fewer than 20 people, and some 2.5 million people held such jobs (Bureau of the Census, 1981).

Aside from the analysis of labor force growth and occupational segregation, explicit data on job creation for the private sector also point to a disproportionate role played by small enterprises. Several studies use three size classes: fewer than 100 employees, 100 to 999, and more than 1,000. A comparison of census data from 1958 to 1972 shows that medium-size firms experienced the smallest increase in labor force, with employment rising by 57 percent for larger firms and 48 percent among small enterprises (Zayas, 1979). In a 10-city survey of firms' future plans, 38 percent of small businesses expected to increase employment as compared to 27 percent of the 2 larger classes. Furthermore, nine percent of the large employers but only five percent of the small ones expected a decrease in employment (U.S. Congress, 1979).

The Birch data, a file of some 5 million establishments, have most frequently been cited on the job-generating activity of small businesses. According to these research findings, small firms with fewer than 20 employees generated more than two-thirds of the 7 million or so jobs created between 1969 and 1976. More than half the total represented small independent firms rather than establishments or branches of corporate giants (Birch, 1979).

Next to nothing is known about why this phenomenon exists; however, there is no reason to expect it to disappear in the immediate future. Opportunity for employment obviously is a vital concern to families of workers or potential workers. Consequently, the role of the small employer in generating new jobs needs further investigation.

---

[8] Between 1970 and 1977, when state and local government employment rose by 2 million, both the number of government units and the average employment per government increased. For states, the ratio of full-time-equivalent employment to 10,000 population increased from 113 to 134 or by one-fifth; at the local level, the ratio rose to 17 percent, from 306 to 355. The change did *not* reflect the rise in school employment: The ratio for education moved from 210 to 237, or by 13 percent only (Bureau of the Census, 1979b).

WORKING AT SMALL FIRMS

Overview of Data

To calculate the proportion of the work force employed at small establishments tells nothing about the nature of work at such places or its impact on community and family life. But the necessary data on the nature and impact of that work do not exist. Any discussion of small business as a workplace, then, will inevitably lack empirical content.

Data to explore family-work-community relationships have never been collected; data that might reveal such relationships cannot be extracted from existing files. For a wide range of data the employer is the reporting unit, and facts about their workers consist of payroll entries. For the individual worker, information can be obtained about hours, type of work, wage rate, and weekly and monthly earnings. Information about all workers and about other characteristics of the employer also exists. But such data about workers collected from their employers may not correspond with data about the same workers from other sources.[9]

For another wide range of data, the household is the reporting unit. The U.S. Census of Population (the decennial census) records a wealth of detail about individuals as family members and workers, reported either by individuals themselves or another member of the household. Periodically, the Census Bureau's *Current Population Survey* of a sample of the entire population reports information about individuals as workers, as people with school activities and family responsibilities, income, education, a particular residence, location, and so on (Bureau of the Census, 1978). Yet neither survey includes the question "How many other people are employed where you work?" Moreover, the individual's employer and occupation are self-defined.

The Surveys of Income and Expenditure (Bureau of Labor Statistics) also provide data on household or family income by source, occupation of head, and number of earners; some information about the activity of households can therefore be garnered. Again, however, there is no information on the characteristics of the employer for which any household member works.

The upshot is that there is considerable information about people as

---

[9] One study at the Bureau of Labor Statistics obtained information from respondents to the household survey that enabled a check with employers to confirm some items. Discrepancies turned up that did not appear to warrant rejecting households as sources of information, but did make the error term harder to calculate (Hedges and Meller, 1979).

workers, but no link exists or can be constructed between the data sets that focus on workers as payroll entries and those that focus on workers as members of households.

Nothing at the employer level reveals marital or family status or community activity on the part of the worker; nothing at the household level reveals any characteristics of the employee's workplace or firm. One result is that wage information about a worker collected from an employer tells nothing about that person's total income, let alone total family income.

Tabulations of individual workers can be classified and cross-classified by occupation, age, hours and time spent at work, marital status, education, and total family income as well as individual earnings. But they cannot be so classified by size of employer or even legal form of employing organization. Nevertheless, the number of employed workers—classified by size and type of organization, location, occupation, average pay, hours worked, and fringe benefits—can be tabulated from employers' reports. But these data tell nothing about the marital status or education of the workers.

It follows that data by size of employing unit on workers as people with family and community activities do not exist. To compound the problem, as previously noted no agreed-upon definition of large and small employers exists. Different researchers establish their own working definitions.

Analyzing the work-family-community connection at small firms, therefore, requires using incomplete sources and informed conjecture. However, since the Quality of Employment Survey (QES) does include some information on the size of a worker's place of employment, it may be useful for exploring some of the issues raised in the subsequent discussion (Quinn and Staines, 1979). The fact that the QES includes information on establishment size and not on firm size, however, limits its value.

COMPENSATION AND FRINGE BENEFITS

Because the term fringe benefit is so ambiguous, any discussion of compensation differences needs careful definition. Since this chapter considers only workers in paid employment,[10] it is clear that wages, salaries,

---

[10] Many of the issues discussed also exist for volunteers, who may work side by side with paid employees. The school teacher has a volunteer aide, the librarian a one-day-a-week helper, the social worker consults the psychiatrist who donates time, and so on. For some unknown number of volunteers the initial decision to seek work and the work pattern that results require the same kinds of adjustment to family and community activities as

commissions, tips, or whatever form of remuneration exists will be paid in money. (The timing and mechanism of such payments will differ, and having one's paycheck cashed or deposited in one's bank account may provide real benefits. Probably more people who work for small employers than for large ones receive pay envelopes containing currency.)

Most paid employees also receive compensation in the form of insurance premiums paid by employers. Some are required by law: payroll taxes to protect workers against loss of income from unemployment, injury at work, or disability. The incidence of social security taxes, ostensibly shared by employer and employee, is generally thought to fall totally on workers; these "contributions" provide entitlement to future pensions for workers and their survivors. Not required by law, at least not yet, are employers' payments for supplementary pension schemes or for insuring against loss of income because of medical or hospital expenses. All these, plus directors' fees and a few other minor items, are calculated as wage and salary supplements in the national income accounts: In 1977 they amounted to $173 billion. With money wages and salaries of $984 billion, fringe benefits account for 15 percent of total compensation.[11]

Higher estimates, like those prepared by the U.S. Chamber of Commerce or other business associations, calculate other costs to employers rather than simply these supplements to wages and salaries, resulting in a much larger ratio of fringe benefits to wages. Other forms of nonwage compensation include: paid holidays and vacations beyond those required by law, uniforms or equipment provided, subsidized (or full-cost) housing or food service, recreational and health facilities, contributions to childrens' educational expenses, and the like. New forms of services provided at the workplace, including child care, personal counseling, career development, or financial planning, may also be regarded as fringe benefits, although a more useful term would be nonwage compensation.

To what extent workers are eligible for and actually benefit from such forms of compensation is unknown. All quantitative data about fringe benefits come from sample surveys, most of which omit small employers and, of course, also omit details about the family circumstances of workers.

---

for paid workers. Volunteer work also helps to link all three spheres since many community activities use the time donated by family members with resources donated by employers.

[11] Other calculations of fringe benefits come from surveys by the Social Security Administraton and by the Wages and Hours Division of the U.S. Department of Labor. The latter reports only those situations in which collective bargaining exists, situations affecting a small minority of all workers.

The discrepancy between household and employer as data sources causes particular trouble in this area because many forms of nonwage compensation apply not only to the worker but to the family as well. Thus, medical insurance can be purchased for individual or family membership; a pension scheme may include provisions for the worker-beneficiary's surviving family members; recreational facilities may be available to workers' children; and so on. With the rise of the multiearner family, obviously many individuals can benefit in their role as worker and also in their roles as spouse or parent or child of a worker. The net compensation of any individual or the additional nonwage real income provided to a family thus bears no relation to the money expenditures or other cost or payroll calculations made by employers.

Despite the lack of data, however, clear evidence exists that small and large employers differ significantly in their provision of fringe benefits beyond those required by law (Skolnick, 1976; Yohalem, 1977). Two possibilities exist: Small employers do not offer the benefit at all (e.g., no health insurance or pension plan), or they require higher contributions from the employee than do large employers, many of whom pay the entire cost. Furthermore, decisions about the particular schemes of nonwage compensation, eligibility conditions, and the amounts involved will generally not be a subject of employee-employer negotiation in small organizations.

Although workers in small enterprises are less likely to receive such nonwage compensation or more likely to receive it in smaller amounts than if they worked for large employers, their relative position is changing rapidly, again due to the rise of the multiearner family and also to inflation. The latter generates two opposing forces. On the one hand, as the value of money declines, workers receiving real benefits (health services, housing) gain in relative income. But the decline in value also applies to future pensions, and workers whose compensation has been split between current money wages and contributions to private pension benefits lose in relative wealth or income.

From a policy standpoint it is significant that the President's Commission on Pensions has recommended universal pension coverage for all workers to supplement the Social Security system. Like various plans for national health insurance, this would remove a major difference between large and small employers in fringe benefits provided, although, of course, not in the variety of benefits or their total amount. The extent to which a further uniformity in the private benefits system can or should be mandated, however, is far from a settled issue.

Some initiatives have been taken by government and by small businesses themselves to demonstrate alternative approaches to benefits-services provision. The Simplified Employee Pension (SEP) is the federal government's effort to make it easier for small businesses to provide retirement plans for their workers. Created as part of the revenue act of 1978, SEPs represent a cross between a pension plan and an Individual Retirement Account (IRA). SEPs are designed to encourage small businesses to provide pension programs, but many small businesses are still not aware of the program. Others have not instituted such programs because the law forbids discriminating among employees-beneficiaries and therefore owners of small companies cannot single out themselves and a few top employees for special treatment. Nevertheless, some employers do want to provide for their workers and could find the SEP a feasible way to do this.

Some small businesses have initiated their own shared enterprise in providing services for employees. In one medium-sized city a group got together to sponsor a counseling service. In a suburban community a group of small- and medium-sized businesses formed a coalition to sponsor a local child-care program that would serve the children of their employees as well as the children of other residents in the community. Several youth job-training experiments have involved the participation of small businesses.

WORK PRACTICES AND RELATIONSHIPS

In perhaps less measurable ways, large and small employers also seem to differ in how they set policies and in their actual employment conditions. In part this difference may reflect the relative influence of the owner-manager and of workers' organizations. In the private sector, labor unions represent only one out of five workers and occur chiefly in large corporations. Employee associations in the government sector also exist chiefly in large agencies (and their membership has been declining as a portion of total government employment) (Bureau of the Census, 1979a). Although collective bargaining contracts vary widely and do not always deal with conditions of employment beyond wages and hours of work, they at least require formal specifications of the terms of employment. And whether or not any worker's organization exists, larger firms will more likely have rules specifying the obligations and responsibilities of both employee and employer, all buttressed by bureaucratic organization. A considerable literature on organization suggests that this is the almost inevitable concomitant of organizational size.

By contrast, in smaller firms the decision-making process is likely to be less formal, with many aspects of employer-employee relationships handled in personal, nonuniform ways. Conceivably, this kind of relationship sometimes permits a flexibility that could benefit workers with distinctive circumstances (e.g., particular scheduling difficulties caused by family responsibilities). By the same token, however, any accommodations to individual circumstances can be revoked at the discretion of the employer. Indeed, the employer would generally seem to have the greater power to exploit the employee-employer relationship. For employees then, the gains which may be provided by the flexibility of a small organization may be offset by the loss of guaranteed rights.

However, compared to executives at large units, the owner-managers of small firms seem more likely to live in the same community with workers, to be subject to similar sources of information and pressure, and to know employees as individuals. Such personal ties may induce a broad (though perhaps paternalistic) concern for the welfare of employees, including their family lives. How the conflicting pressures of business and personal ties are resolved in actual practice in different enterprises remains at issue, but several considerations suggest that interpersonal relations and informal arrangements may play a critical role at smaller firms.

Hiring practices offer the first example. Job search for workers consists of two major routes: referrals by family and friends and direct application to employers (Corcoran et al., 1980; Department of Labor, 1976a).[12] Data from the federal-state employment service as well as the census show a difference by size of firm: Large employers and agencies use more formal hiring practices, recruit actively, and of course may be subject to specific regulations or contract agreements about new hiring. Smaller employers depend relatively heavily on referrals by family, friends, and those already employed; personal recommendations count more than credentials or test results. This emphasis on referrals obviously binds work and family life in a distinctive way, even if the social-psychological and economic ramifications are not well understood.

Another example consists of the rather loose retirement practices that appear common at smaller firms. These may point to a general willingness to be flexible on personnel matters. In the absence of formal codified rules or policy typical of the small employer, mandatory retirement at age 65 seems to have been frequently ignored. Presumably, the worker in the small enterprise still has greater control over the date of retirement than the employee of the giant firm (Reno, 1976; and unpublished

---

[12] "About half of all workers heard about their current job through a friend or relative and about half knew someone who worked for their current employer before they began work" (Corcoran et al., 1980:34).

research of the Administration on Aging). Phased retirement might also be more prevalent in small businesses, which schedule part-time or part-year work on an ad hoc basis without having to set up a complex framework of regulations or policy. But whether those who work for large and small employers differ in their own retirement plans is not known.[13]

This very informality, however, may complicate efforts to discern the policies of smaller firms. Part-time work, flexitime, or even job sharing, for example, could exist at smaller firms without ever being recognized by such technical terms.[14] Learning about such unstructured employment practices at smaller firms probably requires case studies rather than large-scale surveys. Certainly, aggregate data also seem inappropriate for analyzing the impact of small businesses on community life.

INFLUENCES ON COMMUNITY LIFE

Under the rubric of corporate social responsibility, most discussion of how business has contributed or should contribute to community affairs refers to the activities of large corporations. In part this reflects an accurate appraisal of the considerable societal power of the giant firm and in part the lack of information about other firms.

Only recently have analysts begun to redress this imbalance and consider the involvement of smaller firms in the kinds of activities that are often deemed socially responsive. In general, however, these studies are limited in scope and lack both conceptual clarity and methodological rigor in defining what is socially responsive. For instance, some research suggests that the extent of socially responsive behavior increases with firm size, but the degree of difference between large and small firms seems to vary greatly depending on what activity is being considered. Moreover, in this research, involvement is crudely measured by presenting managers with a list of socially responsive activities and asking them to check which their organizations are currently practicing. Lists include such disparate items as contributions to the arts, education, and

---

[13] The retirement decision is complex and involves job satisfaction, availability of alternative employment, pension benefits, and discrimination, as well as employer and employee attitudes. Research is now going on to investigate the change in mandatory retirement age as it affects both employer and job holder.

[14] The National Council for Alternative Work Patterns, Inc., lists organizations known to offer flexitime, a compressed work week, job sharing, permanent part-time work, or any combination thereof. The majority of entries consists of large employers (more than 100 employees); of course, many instances of work flexibility must exist unknown to this directory. See also Winett and Neale (1980) and Kamerman and Kingston (Chapter 5 in this volume).

ecology; hiring and training programs for minorities and the handicapped; procedures for handling consumer complaints, product defects, and truth in advertising; and fair prices (see, for example, Gomolka, 1975; Eilbirt and Parket, 1979).

In another example of inconclusive research, banks were studied and attempts were made to measure the intensity of involvement with relatively hard behavioral data on four separate activities. Organizational size was significantly (and negatively) correlated with commitment to employ female officers, but there was no correlation between size and three other responsive activities—employment of minorities, loans for low-income housing, and loans to minority enterprises (Kedia et al. 1978). Another study, based on in-depth interviews of executives in one city, suggests that smaller firms, including local companies and local branches of national companies, were substantially involved in a wide range of responsive activities, often on an ad hoc, informal basis.

Even if the present studies are inconclusive, they do point to the possible effect of firm size on certain kinds of social involvement, as well as the need to differentiate among responsive activities and to consider the impact of informal practices in subsequent research. Nonetheless, in analyzing the connections between small business and community life, it seems important to consider impacts—often subtle and small-scale—that are not included on the usual lists of responsive activities. Clearly, small firms lack the resources of larger businesses to contribute financially, but other activities, particularly of personal involvement, have significant consequences for a community. In some areas, small employers can work directly with schools to set up training programs, or provide facilities for neighborhood socializing and communication, or cooperate in a safety campaign. All such projects help both community and enterprise. Small enterprises may loom large in a community if they provide the only source of employment for teenagers and mothers who want some part-time work close to home. Probably the type of community involvement of small businesses depends on the employer's personal sense of community rather than any public relations motive. But whether small businesses have these or any other distinctive involvements in community life can now only be a matter of impressionistically-based conjecture. What is needed is a series of community studies concerned with this point.

A RESEARCH AGENDA

This discussion is brief and frequently speculative because it lacks data for more detailed analysis of small business, especially its impact on community and family life. But small business should not be studied in isolation; the sector must be analyzed within the context of the entire economy so that both its distinctive characteristics and its similarities with larger businesses become clear. Any efforts to understand, much less change, business practices as they relate to home and community life must recognize the full diversity of the private sector. For a satisfactory understanding to emerge, however, researchers must redress the disproportionate focus on large corporations and include small firms in their analysis of business practices.

Specific issues for research follow:

(1) Firm size (and perhaps for some purposes, establishment size) should be considered as a potentially critical variable in analyzing coverage on key forms of nonwage compensation. However, to provide a complete picture, the proposed 1983 Bureau of Labor Statistics Level of Benefits Survey should be augmented so that a representative sampling of the very smallest firms are included in the analysis. In addition, national surveys of workers should routinely include items on firm size. In the analysis of both employer-based and employee-based data sets, researchers should consider how interactions between industry type and firm size affect the distribution of wage and nonwage compensation.

These recommendations do not fully resolve the problem (discussed earlier) of having employer-based data that are not linked to data on the families of employees. However, it seems prohibitively expensive to require employers to furnish data on the families of their employees or to modify existing data sets so that employer-based data can be linked with employee-based data. Even if employer-based data are relatively reliable, reasonable estimates of the family coverage of workers at various size firms can probably be derived from nationally representative samples of workers.

(2) A systematic effort at identifying which companies have instituted SEPs, why, and with what consequences might provide some insights into the impact of a new government policy specifically designed to redress some of the inequities experienced by those working for small businesses. Is such a policy an effective way to proceed, and for what kinds of employees? Which employees are likely not to benefit? If this policy is effective, does it suggest some value in seeking out ways for small businesses to provide more in the way of health insurance benefits?

Some effort at identifying interesting and innovative experiments in the sponsorship of direct provision of services for employees (what exists, what works, for whom, with what consequences) could affect government and social services agency policies as well as the policies and practices of employers operating small businesses.

(3) The discussion of work practices and relationships at small firms,

as well as of their impact on community life, suggests the need for a research methodology sensitive to informal activities and often subtle impacts. For example, mail or telephone surveys may lead to significant underestimates of the amount of flexitime schedule use in business. Many small businesses with informal flexibility in work scheduling for some employees do not have a formally designated policy or even a consistent de facto practice. Accordingly, as a preliminary, relatively low-cost initiative in this area, a small number of community case studies would be valuable. These case studies could include firms of all sizes in diverse industries and employ in-depth interviews and site visits.

In addition to a focus on firm activities, these case studies could also consider the effects of work on family life, including the lives of children. In what ways do the characteristics of the workplace or firm, including differences associated with size, affect family relationships, and the behavior and attitudes of its members? Very little is known about these matters.

REFERENCES AND BIBLIOGRAPHY

Anderson, B. E., and Sawhill, I. V. (1980) *Youth Employment and Public Policy*. Englewood Cliffs, N.J.: Prentice-Hall.

Averitt, R. (1968) *The Dual Economy: The Dynamics of American Industry Structure*. New York: Horton.

Beck, E. M., Horan, P., and Tolbert, C., III (1978) Stratification in a dual economy: a sectoral model of earnings determination. *American Sociological Review* 43:704-720.

Birch, D. L. (1979) *The Job Generation Process*. Program on Neighborhood and Regional Change. Cambridge, Mass.: MIT Press.

Blau, F. D., and Hendricks, W. E. (1979) Occupational segregation by sex: trends and prospects. *Journal of Human Resources* 14(Spring):197-210.

Bluestone, B., Murphy, W., and Stevenson, M. (1973) *Low Wages and the Working Poor*. Ann Arbor, Mich.: Institute of Labor and Industrial Relations, University of Michigan.

Bruchey, S., ed. (1980) *Small Business in American Life*. New York: Columbia University Press.

Bureau of the Census (1961) Income of families and persons in the United States: 1959. *Current Population Reports*, Series P-60, No. 35. Washington, D.C.: U.S. Department of Commerce.

Bureau of the Census (1974) Money income of families and persons in the United States: 1972. *Current Population Reports*, Series P-60, No. 90. Washington, D.C.: U.S. Department of Commerce.

Bureau of the Census (1978) *The Current Population Survey: Design and Methodology*. Technical Paper No. 40. Washington, D.C.: U.S. Department of Commerce.

Bureau of the Census (1979a) 1977 Census of Governments, vol. 3. *Employment*. Washington, D.C.: U.S. Department of Commerce.

Bureau of the Census (1979b) 1977 Census of Governments, vol. 4. *Historical Statistics on Governmental Finances and Employment*. Washington, D.C.: U.S. Department of Commerce.

Bureau of the Census (1979c) *County Business Patterns, 1977.* Washington, D.C.: U.S. Department of Commerce.

Bureau of the Census (1980) Money income of families and persons in the United States: 1978. *Current Population Reports,* Series P-60, No. 123. Washington, D.C.: U.S. Department of Commerce.

Bureau of the Census (1981) *General Report On Industrial Organization* (1977 Enterprise Statistics:ES77-1). Washington, D.C.: U.S. Department of Commerce.

Corcoran, M., Datcher, L., and Duncan, G. J. (1980) Most workers find jobs through word of mouth. *Monthly Labor Review* 103(8):33-34.

Department of Labor (1976a) *Employment and Earnings.* Tables A-15 and A-16. Washington, D.C.: U.S. Department of Labor.

Department of Labor (1976b) *Recruitment, Job Search and the United States Employment Service.* R&D Monograph 43. Washington, D.C.: U.S. Department of Labor.

Department of Labor (1979) *Employment and Training Report of the President.* Washington, D.C.: U.S. Department of Labor.

Deutermann, W. V., Jr., and Brown, S. C. (1978) Voluntary workers: a growing part of the labor force. *Monthly Labor Review* 101(6):3-14.

Edwards, R., Reich, M., and Gordon, D., eds. (1975) *Labor Market Segmentation.* Lexington, Mass.: Heath.

Eilbirt, H., and Parket, I. R. (1979) The current status of corporate social responsibility. *Business Horizons* Library (August):5-14.

Freeman, R. B., and Wise, D. A. (1980) *Youth Unemployment.* Cambridge, Mass.: National Bureau of Economic Research.

Fusfeld, D. R. (1980) Reviewing Michael Piore's "Birds of passage: migrant labor and industrial societies." *Journal of Economic Issues* 14(September):785-789.

Galbraith, J. K. (1958) *The Affluent Society.* Boston: Houghton Mifflin.

Galbraith, J. K. (1967) *The New Industrial State.* Boston: Houghton Mifflin.

Gomolka, E. (1975) An analysis of social responsibility activities undertaken by small business companies. Pp. 336-338 in *Proceedings of the Academy of Management.* Mississippi State, Miss.: Academy of Management.

Hedges, J. N., and Meller E. F. (1979) Weekly and hourly earnings of U.S. workers, 1967-78. *Monthly Labor Review* 102(8):31-41.

Kedia, B. L., Kuntz, E. C., and Stevens, D. B. (1978) Correlates of some socially responsive behaviors of banks in Texas: a multidimensional approach. Pp. 246-250 in *Proceedings of the Academy of Management.* Mississippi State; Miss.: Academy of Management.

Quinn, R., and Staines, G. (1979) *The 1977 Quality of Employment Survey.* Ann Arbor, Mich.: Institute for Social Research.

Reeder, J. (1978) Corporate social involvement at the local level. Pp. 256-259 in *Proceedings of the Academy of Management.* Mississippi State, Miss.: Academy of Management.

Reno, V. (1976) Incidence of compulsory retirement. Pp. 123-136 in *Reaching Retirement Age.* Washington, D.C.: Social Security Administration.

Schein, E. (1978) *Career Dynamics.* Reading, Pa.: Addison-Wesley.

Skolnick, A. M. (1976) Private pension plans, 1950-1974. *Social Security Bulletin* 39(June):3-17.

Small Business Administration (1980) Small business size standards. *SBA Rates and Regulations.* Part 121, Section 121, 3-1(b). Washington, D.C.: Small Business Administration.

U.S. Congress (1979) *Central City Business.* Joint Economic Committee, Subcommittee on Fiscal and Intergovernmental Policy. Washington, D.C.: U.S. Government Printing Office.

Winett, R. A., and Neale, M. S. (1980) Results of experimental study of flexitime and family life. *Monthly Labor Review* 301(November):29-32.

Yohalem, M. R. (1977) Employee-benefit plans, 1975. *Social Security Bulletin* 40 (November):19-28.

Zayas, E. R. (1979) The Role of Small Business in the Creation of New Jobs. Paper submitted to the U.S. House of Representatives, Committee on Small Business, Subcommittee on Antitrust, Consumers, and Employment. 95th Congress, 2nd Session. Washington, D.C.

7

The Influence of Parents' Work on Children's School Achievement

Barbara Heyns, *Center for Applied Social Science Research, New York University*

INTRODUCTION

An essay that promises to review the relationships between work, family, and the achievement of children could encompass a range of topics nearly as broad in scope as the social sciences. This review is necessarily more limited and selective. It has three main purposes: (1) to develop a conceptual and methodological critique of research on work and family life; (2) to review relevant empirical research on work conditions and family life as they influence the educational performance of children; and (3) to identify fruitful directions for further research.

The review begins with an overview of paternal work status followed by a lengthy assessment of maternal employment. Ideally, one would wish to examine how the work roles of both parents and the resultant division of labor within the family affect family life and children. However, little research examines family work patterns or attempts to link specific characteristics of these patterns to outcomes for children; most studies focus on either maternal or paternal employment. Moreover, the empirical literature is largely cross-sectional. It compares and contrasts families with diverse employment conditions at one point in time, rather than asking how families adapt to, or directly influence, changes in work patterns over time.

Concern about changes in work and family life tends to be fueled by trends in maternal employment and changes in the size, stability, and composition of families. Such trends imply historical and structural changes

229

of considerable magnitude; however, cross-sectional research cannot examine or explain the causes of such change. Moreover, the conceptual tools developed in cross-sectional research to describe and assess the linkages between work and the outcomes for children may be inadequate for a broader understanding of social change.

This essay is not intended to be a comprehensive treatment of the literature on the socialization of children or on changes in family life, work, and child rearing. The issues addressed touch research areas addressed by a number of disciplines. The studies included are those with empirical data, those that offer promising new perspectives, and those that illuminate flaws or inadequacies in the conceptual and methodological tools employed. I exclude studies of infants and preschool children except where the analysis is specifically directed to later school achievement; correspondingly, I ignore most recent work on maternal deprivation (Skard, 1965) and on child rearing in the early years (Kamerman, 1980). Many of the studies of the relationship between family work status and children's achievement are premised on conceptions of social class or family socioeconomic status that may be outdated. These studies ignore changes in maternal employment or family life over time. Intrafamilial processes that could shed light on these relationships are not examined and frequently not discussed.

The literature on maternal employment is reviewed more extensively and more critically than research in other areas, both because it is most relevant to changes in the work status of parents and because its focus is often specifically on the achievement of children. Even though these studies were often pioneering efforts at conceptualizing and using variables that other studies simply ignored, intensive scrutiny is still warranted.

Finally, I do not include a systematic review of recent work in family history (Hareven, 1975; Laslett, 1978; Tilly and Scott, 1978) that reinterprets the relationships between work and family life. Nor do I look in depth at the literature on cohorts across the life cycle, although there have been dramatic changes in patterns of family formation and work commitments over time (Sweet, 1979a, 1979b; Taeuber and Sweet, 1976; Uhlenberg, 1974). I suspect these approaches may provide more information than cross-sectional studies on how macrostructural change affects both work and family life. But thus far they have not addressed the achievement of children.

The organization of the review is straightforward. In the next section, I describe the dependent variable—children's achievement—and the interpretations given to it. Then I discuss research on paternal work status and children. The lengthiest section, on how maternal employment affects school achievement, examines three areas: (1) the effects in minority and low-income families, (2) the measurement of the time mothers commit to work, and (3) the characteristics of mothers' jobs that influence their families. Then I review the methodological difficulties that plague research in this field. Finally, and with trepidation considering the complexities involved, I discuss the most promising directions for new research.

ACHIEVEMENT MEASURES AS DEPENDENT VARIABLES

The focus of this section is on studies that deal with school achievement. A large number of distinct measures of achievement can be classified under this heading; in fact, among the studies reviewed there were scarcely two that used identical measures. Despite the diversity of specific measures, most analysts share a general idea of what is meant by school achievement and a common conception of how one gathers data. As an outcome measure for children, achievement is assumed to be a consequential matter; it is quite likely that no other dependent variable is used as often or discussed as much.

The bulk of the studies reviewed here used a test of cognitive achievement or ability as the key measure; a few early studies used grades, teacher's assessments, or self-reported performance. Measures of lifetime success, such as the educational attainment, occupational prestige, or income of a child, have rarely been studied in conjunction with maternal employment.

For the purposes of this paper, I use the general term achievement to apply to any test administered in schools. When the form or battery used by the researchers is well known, I report the specific test. Since the research results do not differ by subject matter, I do not distinguish between the outcomes in math or reading, for example.

Test scores, at least in their conventional forms, are relatively conservative measures of academic achievement. They have been shown to be highly reliable and, hence, relatively unchanging over time. Dramatic changes in performance on tests have rarely been documented. Cognitive tests tend to be more highly related to measured intelligence and social background than to what is taught or learned in schools. Despite these properties, test scores are clearly relevant to the life chances of children; no other outcome measure predicts total amount of schooling or general adult success so well.

The tactic adopted in this paper is similar to that taken by the majority of authors reviewed: analyze and report the measures of achievement available, note the specific test or data source, and interpret the results in general terms. Although a large number of specific measures of achievement exist, most authors are concerned with general theoretical issues. The common assumption is that all test scores tap an underlying construct called achievement, rather than a specific skill. When the research incorporates other concepts or measures, such as attitudes toward school, aspirations, or levels of attainment, the outcome measures are reported.

PATERNAL WORK STATUS AND THE ACHIEVEMENT OF CHILDREN

Apart from influencing social class, how does a father's work status affect the achievement of offspring? To what extent does paternal work, or the lack of it, influence the employment of wives, the patterns of child rearing, and the outcomes for children? While social theorists have pondered these questions for centuries, rigorous empirical studies designed to answer them are rare. As Bronfenbrenner and Crouter (in this volume) tell us, work and family issues are separated by distinctive research traditions and disciplinary boundaries. Most analysts have accepted what Kanter (1977:Chapter 7) called "the myth of separate worlds." In this view, work is quite distinct from family life. It occurs in a different place, at a different period of time, and it requires unique skills.

Many Americans tend to deny that there are direct connections between work and family. Aberle and Naegele (1952) asked a sample of middle-class parents how their occupational lives affected their behavior in their families. The fathers reported either no relationships of any importance or rejected outright the suggestion that there were any. Dyer (1964) found a similar pattern of denial among lower-class men, even though their families displayed a keen perception of the work situation as it affects the father and the family. Kanter (1977) argues that modern bureaucratic organizations, based on the values of rationality and achievement through merit, compete for time, attention, and loyalty with families. The authority structure and values defined by work organizations tend to be at odds with family relationships. It is, perhaps, more comfortable for employees, as well as researchers, to ignore the degree to which one aspect of life spills over into another.

Several authors have developed work typologies that capture dimensions of paternal work status relevant to family life. Aldous (1969) developed a number of distinctive dimensions of paternal work relations, such as the relative salience of work and the degree to which it is synchronized with family schedules, responsibilities, and plans. Rapoport and Rapoport (1971) discuss the isomorphism between family roles and occupational plans. For example, they report that science-oriented technologists have more egalitarian decision-making relationships with their spouses than do technicians who work only with equipment. The reason given is that the science-oriented technologists are more involved with interpersonal relations at work than are the technologists working with machines; however, it is difficult to rule out self-selection as a factor.

In order to examine the impact of paternal occupations and work status on children's achievement levels, it is necessary to conceptualize the process and variables that mediate the effect. The literature is rich in potential theoretical links, but short on empirical results. The majority of studies have focused on values or attitudes as critical conduits. Kohn (1963, 1969) and his associates (Kohn and Carroll, 1960; Schooler, 1972) have studied the degree to which independence training and self-direction are stressed in families, and they trace the source of such values to paternal occupational experiences. The occupational characteristics emphasized by Kohn are the degree of supervision on the job; the intellectual complexity of tasks; whether the worker is principally involved with things, people, or ideas; and the degree of self-reliance required. Working-class fathers are likely to experience demands for conformity on the job, while middle-class fathers enjoy greater autonomy. Child-rearing and discipline patterns are found to parallel the attitudes and values formed on the job; middle-class families emphasize independence, while working-class families expect compliance from children.

Miller and Swanson (1958) point to distinctive clusters of traits that distinguish the child-rearing patterns of fathers employed in bureaucratic organizations rather than entrepreneurial settings. The values attached to "welfare-bureaucratic" homes encourage children to accommodate, express impulses, and seek direction from organizations. In contrast, entrepreneurial families stress self-discipline, control, and mastery of the environment as desirable qualities.

Both studies rely on parental reports regarding attitudes and values, rather than on asking how children are actually raised or how predictable their achievement differences are. There is a large leap of faith involved in assuming that paternal work environment directly affects maternal values and child rearing. Nevertheless, both authors assume mothers are primarily responsible for the transmission of values. Neither study collected data on outcomes for children; yet both studies assume that the traits identified have important consequences for the achievement of children. Kohn's work is often criticized for confusing class differences in child rearing with occupational values, and that of Miller and Swanson has proven difficult to replicate (Hess, 1970).

One dimension of work consistently found to be related to the achievement of children is the relative social standing of the father's occupation. Occupational prestige and the associated factors of income, security of employment, level of authority at the workplace, and the educational credentials required to enter a specific line of work are among the best predictors of a child's performance in school. These interrelated aspects of paternal work are also indicators of socioeconomic status or social class. And as Charters (1963:739-740) observes:

To categorize youth according to the social class position of their parents is to order them on the extent of their participation and degree of "success" in the American educational system. This has been so consistently confirmed by research that it now can be regarded an empirical law. . . . Social class position predicts grades, achievement and intelligence test scores, retentions at grade level, course failures, truancy, suspensions from school, high school drop-outs, plans for college attendance, and total amount of formal schooling. It predicts academic honors and awards in the public school, elective school offices, extent of participation in extracurricular activities and in social affairs.

Studies of the relationship between socioeconomic status and achievement are voluminous. An early quantitative assessment by Neff (1938) reported correlations between parental status and intelligence tests ranging from .21 to .53. A recent review by White (1976) compared 489 analyses of more than 100 separate studies, finding an average correlation of .25 between socioeconomic status variables and various indicators of educational achievement, such as school grades and cognitive achievement tests. Family income was the best predictor of achievement measures among the indicators included, although income is related to the educational attainment of fathers as well.

Studies of the effects of the socioeconomic status of fathers on children's achievement are consistent but difficult to assess. The observed correlations do not reveal the linkages between specific parental behavior or values and the achievement of children. Socioeconomic status is indicative of a host of work-related phenomena that could influence children's achievements and aspirations, but separating the precise determinants of influence appears to be an intractable task. Most of the characteristics of work that have been isolated tend to be highly interrelated; the degree of multicollinearity present tends to prevent researchers from rigorously isolating the effects.

Socioeconomic status, broadly construed, influences the relative stability of families, the life-style and consumption level that can be supported, the division of labor and authority between parents, the degree of marital satisfaction, the patterns of social interaction within and outside the family, and even the modal personalities of family members

(Bernard, 1975; Blood, 1965; Hicks and Platt, 1970; Orden and Bradburn, 1969; Powell, 1961). Moreover, persistent class differences in child rearing, expressive and affective behaviors, language use, parental expectations for children, and the children's perceptions of parents have been identified (Bloom-Feshbach et al., in this volume; Davis and Havighurst, 1946; Havighurst, 1976; Hess, 1970; McKinley, 1964; Pelton, 1978; Zigler, 1970).

Each of these correlates of socioeconomic status, either individually or in concert, may operate as an intervening variable, mediating the influence of family status on the achievement of children. Insofar as the socioeconomic characteristics of work predict measurable differences in family structure that correlate with achievement, it is obligatory to ask how such factors operate, in what combination, and with what effect. Socioeconomic status is conceptually useful because it encompasses many distinctions among families. However, it is virtually impossible to separate and analyze the causal links between work and a child's achievement without considering socioeconomic differences in family structure and organization.

Studies of the effect of socioeconomic status have largely ignored the growing importance of maternal employment on either family status or outcomes for children. The socioeconomic status of a family has traditionally been assumed to derive from the work status of the father. Only recently have efforts been made to incorporate women's work into models of the attainment process (Rosenfeld, 1978; Rosenfeld and Sorensen, 1979; Treiman and Terrell, 1975). Stratification theory and research have lagged behind changes in the commitment of families to work (Barth and Watson, 1964; Haug, 1973). Studies of intergenerational mobility have tended to present intrafamilial processes as a black box, aggregating the contributions of spouses separately. Hence, family income and parental education are viewed as characteristics of the family of origin, irrespective of their source. Contemporary families may garner wages and allocate resources to children in novel ways; the outcomes for children may depend on how these decisions are made, rather than on merely the total amount of resources available.

Finally, we have little evidence on how changes in work patterns influence child rearing and family life. More parents are employed and more children than ever before spend larger portions of their childhood in families in which both parents work (Bane, 1976). The scheduling of work activities directly influences the amount of time available and the spacing of parental contact with children. Working parents provide models of adult behavior that are more immediate and relevant than the stereotyped models available through television. Kanter (1977) has argued that the occupational milieu furnishes a cultural context and a set of relationships that affect family life. But these factors are little studied. Both popular and professional observers have expressed concern about the implications for children of mothers' increased participation in the labor force, yet there are no reasonable estimates of the time fathers spend with their children or the quality of that time when mothers work. The literature on paternal involvement in child rearing is quite recent and still sparse (Aldous, 1969; Berk and Berk, 1979; Fein, 1978; Kamerman, 1980; Lamb, 1979; Levine, 1976; Lynn, 1974; Pleck, 1975, 1979). There have been ethnographic descriptions of "dual-career" families (Bryson and Bryson, 1978; Rapoport and Rapoport, 1971, 1976, 1978) and of "dual-worker" families (Lein et al., 1974), as well as discussion of the coping strategies employed by the two-career family (Angrist et al., 1976). In a more traditional vein, sociologists have studied those families with a "two-person career" (Papenek, 1975), in which the chief breadwinner's occupation dominates the time and attention of the household. However, the effect of these family types on children has been neglected. Systematic research is lacking on how families organize their work and family lives and the impact of such adaptations on children.

In sum, family social status, as measured by paternal occupational prestige and family income, is consistently linked to the achievement of children. The precise mechanisms through which these family attributes operate, however, are not clear. Family status predicts a wide range of social and behavioral differences among families that are correlated to work patterns; however, as family life-styles change and diversify, it is essential to rethink the relationships that predict the achievement of children.

Summer is a period when parents assume the responsibilities of child rearing full time and when the effects of socioeconomic status increase dramatically (Heyns, 1978). In Atlanta it was possible to compare the summer activities of children from a broad spectrum of social backgrounds and to assess the determinants of cognitive growth during the school year and the summer. The most important predictor of achievement was, not surprisingly, socioeconomic differences among families. However, the patterning of activities that mediated and contributed independently to cognitive growth is instructive. Socioeconomic status predicted the number and quality of programs attended, the length of time and distance traveled on family vacations, and the number of hours spent reading, playing with friends, taking athletic or music classes, pursuing hobbies, or going to camp. Each of these was in turn related to achievement growth. Children who attended summer programs farther from home, visited relatives by themselves, or had bicycles of their own were more likely to show achievement gains over and above those predicted by family background.

The activities that contributed to achievement growth independent of background share two characteristics: They require an additional measure of parental time or familial resources, and they imply a special amount of independence from direct parental supervision. In order to attend programs in unfamiliar neighborhoods, children must have parents who are willing to get them there and who trust their competence in a strange setting. A bicycle permits greater mobility and hence independence. Although there was a clear relationship between family income and the probability of owning a bicycle, the children who achieved more than predicted were those who owned one in spite of limited family resources. Similarly, extended vacations were beyond the means of most families, but for those children who went away regardless, and presumably at some family sacrifice, cognitive gains were larger.

Two possible interpretations of these results exist, and either could account for the findings. First, family resources, such as time and money, do influence children, especially when resources are targeted directly to them. Family incomes are important because they enable parents to provide for their children, but families still differ in their willingness to do so. Second, those parents willing to grant greater independence of action and movement to their children are also likely to encourage their achievement. Although middle-class families are more likely to engage in this sort of child rearing, once socioeconomic status is controlled, independence training has an additional effect (Heyns, 1978).

In sum the research on paternal work status and the achievement of children raises more questions than it resolves. The dimensions of paternal work that seem to directly influence children are hierarchic. The major finding is that higher incomes, greater occupational prestige, and more authority on the job are associated with greater cognitive abilities and higher school achievement among children. It is not entirely clear why this is so or how it occurs. Nor can one make an unqualified assumption that these outcomes are related to job characteristics rather than to the traits of the fathers holding them. Maternal employment is conspicuously absent from analyses of the effects of paternal work status on family life. This is the subject of the next section.

MATERNAL EMPLOYMENT AND CHILDREN'S ACHIEVEMENT

Research on the impact of maternal employment on children has been relatively plentiful, and several competent reviews of this literature have been published (Etaugh 1974; Hoffman, 1974, 1980; Hoffman and Nye,

1974; Howrigan, 1973; Maccoby, 1958; Nye and Hoffman, 1963; Salo, 1975; Siegal and Haas, 1963; Stolz, 1960; Taveggia and Thomas, 1974; Wallston, 1973; Yudkin and Holms, 1963). The majority of these reviews, however, share a crucial failing: They tend to review the findings of studies individually and thereby neglect to assess the overall consistency of results. Methodological problems are raised, but only rarely do authors attempt to reconceptualize issues. A typical conclusion is that more research is needed.

In contrast, I argue that the consistency of results is more noteworthy than the limitations of particular studies and that reconsidering the concepts and mechanisms should have higher priority than conducting further research along current lines. To be sure, each study to be discussed has methodological and analytic problems that could be remedied. As Hoffman (1980:320) notes, "there is in fact no study that has properly investigated the connection between maternal employment and the child's academic attitudes or cognitive functioning and abilities." Concentrating on the research flaws of particular studies, however, leads one to overlook the more general finding: Studies of maternal employment have demonstrated, with very few exceptions, that on achievement, the children of working mothers differ very little from the children of nonworking mothers. When they do differ, as in the case of poor or minority children and the sons of middle-class mothers, there are plausible reasons for supposing that other family characteristics are at least as important as employment.

Working mothers differ from nonworking mothers on a variety of dimensions; their family relationships and the organization of their households are different as well. On average, employed mothers spend less time on housework, have a less traditional division of labor with their husbands, have more structured rules for domestic life, and are more likely to share child-care responsibilities with husbands or other adults (Hoffman, 1979). Working mothers tend to be better educated and to have smaller families. They are also more likely to be or to have been divorced (Waite, 1976). When husbands are present, marital relations tend to be egalitarian, and the women report greater satisfaction with their lives. Mothers who work seem to expect more independence from children, and they seem to be a positive role model for daughters (Gerson, 1981; Hoffman, 1979, 1980).

The relationships between these aspects of family life and the achievement of children are, to say the least, complex. To date, the most interesting research on maternal employment concerns family changes and adaptations, not outcomes for children. A good deal of the literature that attempts to trace the effects of mothers' working on children lacks a cogent theoretical focus or a realistic image of family life. It tends to view children not as people but as outcomes. There is an undercurrent of thinly veiled alarm regarding the consequences of maternal employment or social change that rests on the developmental theories of another era. Changes in family life tend to be viewed with foreboding as deviations from a smoothly functioning normalcy. Hence, it behooves any serious scholar reviewing the literature to approach the research with a measure of skepticism.

The following discussion of maternal employment deals with three major topics: minority families, the allocation of time, and job characteristics. Following that discussion, a review of the conceptual and methodological issues and a proposed research agenda will be presented. Each of these topics illuminates the research problems alluded to earlier: (1) Work status consists of a constellation of interrelated indicators; those aspects of work that can be shown to be consistently associated with student achievement cannot be reliably disentangled from other aspects of family life. (2) The empirical linkage between specific indicators and specific achievement outcomes for children and unique effects is difficult to specify. (3) The conceptualization of work, especially for women, is often quite primitive. (4) Correlational analyses based on cross-sectional data ignore the larger issue of the impact of structural change on *all* families and children.

Minority Families: Maternal Employment and Children's Achievement

The recent resurgence of interest in ethnic subcultures has generated several rich ethnographic studies of family life (Stack, 1974) and the determinants of children's achievement (Lightfoot, 1978; Ogbu, 1978) in black families. Moreover, research has been stimulated by concern with the effects on children of the "tangle of pathology," thought to characterize poor, nonwhite families. Studying minority families demonstrates some of the difficulties of trying to disentangle the effects of employment from other aspects of family life, such as the cultural context and economic circumstances. Contemporary trends are found in an exaggerated form in black families. Rates of maternal employment have always been high, as have levels of marital dissolution. More than one-third of all black children under 14 lived in a single-parent family in 1974 (Bane, 1976). The incidence of unemployment, teenage pregnancy, poverty, poor school adjustment, and delinquency are higher than in corresponding white families. Rigorous efforts to relate conditions of work to family life and the achievement of children, however, are few and far between. Hoffman (1980) has noted the paucity of carefully controlled studies that deal with minority families.

The studies of maternal employment among poor and black families have consistently found that a working mother contributes positively to the achievement of children. Woods (1972) studied the fifth-grade children of employed women in a North Philadelphia ghetto school and found that full-time maternal employment was more closely associated with higher IQ scores and better teacher ratings of both boys and girls than part-time employment. The major variable of interest to Woods was quality of the child's supervision during maternal work, rather than work alone. Girls were less likely than boys to be supervised adequately, and tended to show deficits in achievement when supervision was poor. Heyns (1978) found that fifth-grade and sixth-grade black children with working mothers scored better on tests of cognitive achievement than did those with nonworking mothers. Rieber and Womach (1967) found that the children of working mothers in summer Head Start programs showed the most improvement on the Peabody Picture Vocabulary Test. The children studied were drawn from elementary school districts in Houston. More than half the children ranking in the top quartile had working mothers, whereas only 25 percent of the children in the quartile showing the least cognitive growth had employed mothers.

Cherry and Eaton (1977) found that eight-year-old black children who had employed mothers did significantly better on the Illinois test of Psycholinguistic Ability, as long as fathers were present. When fathers were absent, their test scores were lower. Kriesberg (1970) reached the opposite conclusion—maternal employment predicted higher grades, but only when the father was not living at home. Kriesberg's sample consisted entirely of families in poverty and his major comparisons are between families with a husband present and those without. Although close to 40 percent of his sample is white, he does not present tabulations separately by race. For families headed by a male, economic factors are the major determinants of school marks and educational aspirations; maternal employment makes little difference. In contrast, mothers without husbands have higher aspirations for their children and expect better grades despite low family incomes and reliance on public assistance. The children's school marks and aspirations are higher when such mothers are employed, however.

These conflicting results point to the problem of disentangling the effects of economic circumstances from the effects of maternal employment. When one samples poor families, as did Kriesberg, one finds that intact families are likely to be somewhat better off than female-headed ones and impoverished for reasons different from those of families without fathers. A single mother can be poor despite high motivation, a relatively good education, and some employment. Having high educational aspirations for one's children may reflect her background and motivation rather than the conditions of her present life. Families with two adults that qualify as poverty households are likely to have quite different problems.

Cherry and Eaton's sample of 200 lower-class black families included those above the poverty level. Achievement levels were higher for the children of working mothers when fathers were present; that is, when there were two earners. These families were undoubtedly more economically advantaged than single-parent families with only one breadwinner. In the Atlanta study, Heyns (1978) found that differences in family income among black children were strongly associated with achievement; earnings from maternal employment tended to constitute a larger proportion of family income in black families than in white, and the benefits associated with working were correspondingly greater. Once income was controlled, the effects of working were quite small and barely significant.

Black high school daughters report being prepared to work for longer periods of their lives than white students do. Macke and Morgan (1978) argue that modeling, both positive and negative, explains why black seniors have greater work orientations than white seniors. The occupational status of mothers is the major determinant of work modeling; mothers with blue-collar occupations or those who are domestic servants are less likely to inspire high aspirations for work or achievement in their daughters.

Studies of welfare mothers provide another perspective on the effects of employment, or rather the adverse effects of unemployment. On the basis of a variety of personality scales, welfare children were judged to be more psychologically impaired than nonwelfare children (Langner et al., 1969), but then so were their mothers. High school students whose families receive funds from the federal Aid to Families with Dependent Children (AFDC) program are reported to have more problems with school than do children from families who applied for but were denied assistance (Levinson, 1969). Once again, it is difficult to distinguish the conditions and benefits associated with working from the personal and social characteristics that enable mothers to enter the paid labor force. Applicants who are denied welfare assistance may well have had more economic resources available to them than those who received aid. Working mothers are more employable than their counterparts on welfare; perhaps they are more competent and organized as well. At the least, their family income is likely to be higher.

As I have previously noted, examining the effects of maternal employment in black families on children's achievement highlights the difficulty of disentangling casual factors. Black families, particularly those living in or near poverty, tend to be matriarchal and to rely on an extended kinship network for support and child care (Billingsley, 1968; Gutman, 1976; Stack, 1974; Willie, 1970). Mothers' working is a common and respected activity. Despite the relatively large number of children, black families use child care, both formal and informal, more frequently than white families. The financial advantage of employment is substantial; the corresponding benefits for the children's school achievement are apparent. Maternal employment among black families tends to be supported by cultural norms, economic necessity, and the availablity of surrogate parents. It is difficult if not impossible to separate the determinants of a child's performance in school from the constellation of factors that predispose mothers to work and the characteristics of families that enable them to do so.

Black mothers have been more likely to seek and hold paid employment than white mothers for more than a century. In an interesting historical investigation, Pleck (1978) compares the economic, demographic, and cultural factors that predicted maternal employment in black and Italian immigrant families in American cities at the turn of the century. Pleck makes a very persuasive argument that neither the economic nor the demographic explanations are sufficent to account for the observed differences in maternal employment. Kinfolk were important sources of child care for newly emancipated black families; however, Italian immigrant households and neighborhoods were even more likely to include extended families than black ones. Chronic unemployment, low wages, child labor, family instability, and unsupportive attitudes among males were common to both ethnic groups. Families experiencing economic stress were more likely to have mothers employed outside the home. However, regardless of economic conditions, Italian wives were less likely to earn wages or to take in boarders for a fee than black wives. Pleck (1978:502) concludes that one can eliminate a number of economic and demographic explanations; "we are then forced to consider a residual factor: cultural difference."

The cultural factors discussed by Pleck include child-rearing practices and educational aspirations for children. Black children seemed far more independent and likely to help with housework and care of siblings than Italian children. Their caretakers were far less likely to believe that they required constant surveillance, even when small. Young Italians were more likely to drop out of school and get a job, often with parental approval, than black youths. Among blacks, education was highly valued. At every age, black children were substantially more likely to be enrolled in school and to continue their schooling than were Italian youngsters. Maternal employment seems to have helped increase the achievement of black children by keeping them in school longer. Pleck speculates that cultural disparities in educational values and expectations for children help explain heightened rates of maternal employment among blacks. Italian mothers expected children to work in order to support the family, while black mothers invested their work energies outside the family in the hope of providing an education for their children. It may also be that black youth had a more difficult time finding employment.

Cultural explanations for the differences in maternal employment bring the discussion full circle. In order to understand the sources of support for wage earning among black women, one examines the consequences and expected outcomes of work for children as well as other family members. Attitudes and beliefs form a system of social expectations that generate their own fulfillment; within this cultural system, families make choices about mothers' involvement in work and in family. The expectation among blacks that maternal employment benefits the family is thus a cause of both employment and children's attachment to schooling.

In sum, there is consistent evidence to suggest that black maternal employment is positively associated with children's achievement. Several explanations for these findings are plausible: (1) Black mothers may be more employable than other family members. (2) Employed black mothers may be more energetic, competent, and educated than unemployed black mothers. (3) Black maternal employment may be associated with additional adults in the household who contribute time and attention to child care. (4) The black culture seems to support maternal employment more than do other ethnic groups.

Maternal Employment and the Allocation of Time to Work and Family

One important characteristic of work is how much time is spent on work-related activities. No single study has managed to refine the measurement of women's employment or to separate in a convincing fashion the time women spend at work, at home, and on children or family life. Female employment is measured in an arbitrary and rudimentary fashion, if the standard of comparison is male employment statistics. Moreover, since few studies of the effects of maternal employment have tried to replicate previous research, there is an enormous diversity in the way work is defined.

Studies have typically distinguished between working full time, working part time, and not working; however, the definitions of these categories vary widely. Full-time work, for example, has been defined as 40 or more hours per week for pay (Banducci, 1967); 32 hours or more for the last 6-month period (Siegal et al., 1959); 30 or more hours per week for 2 or more years (Frankel, 1963-1964); 28 hours or more for at least 1 year (Yarrow et al., 1962); at least 16 hours per week (Powell, 1961); 40 hours a week for at least 5 years (Dellas et al., 1979). Some authors contrast working full time with not working, thus omitting altogether women who work part time. Others use part-time employment as a residual category for those subjects not classified as either full time or nonworking. The majority of published studies do not contain a definition of the amount of time spent on work at all (Hoffman, 1961; Jones et al., 1967; Keidel, 1970; Kriesberg, 1967, 1970; Macke and Morgan, 1978; Rees and Palmer, 1970; Rieber and Womach, 1967; Roy, 1961); others combine full-time and part-time work (Douvan, 1963; Nelson, 1969; 1971; Nye, 1963).

There are several reasons for the diversity of definitions of maternal employment. Data on the effects of maternal employment have not been gathered systematically, and questions regarding maternal employment often have not been the primary focus of the research study. The sample size has typically been small and regionally specific. In addition most studies have relied on student questionnaires for information about a mother's employment (Almquist and Angrist, 1970; Banducci, 1967; Nelson, 1969; Nye, 1963; Roy, 1961), rather than on official records (Keidel, 1970; Woods, 1972) or parental interviews (Burchinal, 1963; Gold and Andres, 1978a, 1978b; Jones et al., 1967; Kriesberg, 1967). While children's responses may be better than school records or teachers' reports, their information about the hours worked, occupations, or the work history of either parent is likely to be less reliable than data collected from adults (Heyns, 1978).

Early research on maternal employment tended to adopt a relatively loose definition of the amount of time that qualified as full-time employment; later studies were typically more stringent in the criteria imposed.[1] I suspect that as it became easier to identify a reasonable-sized sample of working mothers, analysts raised the standards for what constituted employment. Women with the longest work histories or the

---

[1] An exception in this regard proves the rule. A recent study by Baruch (1972) defined employment as at least one year of paid employment for 10 or more hours a week. Her sample of students, however, was in college; the questions regarding maternal employment referred to their mothers, who were surely older than the mothers of elementary school children who were studied in the seventies.

longest work days became the most strenuous test of the effects of working on children, since they were presumed to be the most committed to the labor force.

The time devoted to working has two discrete components: the amount of time absent from home during specific intervals and the amount of time spent in the labor force during the life cycle. Neither has been measured well in studies of maternal employment. Few studies regard entering or leaving the labor force as a process involving decisions that are reversible over time. Longitudinal data are relatively rare in studies of maternal employment; when they exist, the focus is on the achievement patterns of children over time, rather than changes in the behavior or attitudes of the working mother. When life-cycle factors are deemed relevant, they are defined from the perspective of the child's development, rather than the mother's. For example, a number of studies specified maternal work experiences during the preschool years (Burchinal, 1963; Gold and Andres, 1978a), but neglected to control for the age or career stage of the mother or the presence of older siblings.

Seven studies have looked at changes in the outcomes for children over time (Almquist and Angrist, 1970; Caldwell et al., 1970; Cherry and Eaton, 1977; McCord et al., 1963; Moore, 1975; Rees and Palmer, 1970; Robinson and Robinson, 1971); to my knowledge, however, not one study has examined the outcomes for children in terms of changes in maternal employment over time.[2]

Research on the effects of maternal employment emerged from an explicitly developmental perspective; however, few authors seem aware of the biases introduced by an exclusively child-centered design. Fathers, surrogate caretakers, and siblings recede in importance, while the family context and community life are often simply ignored (Bronfenbrenner, 1979). In the foreground, one finds the mother-child dyad. Maternal behavior, such as holding a job, is presumed to have a powerful and unidirectional impact on the child. The demands or expectations of a child are not assumed to influence in any way a mother's decision to seek employment.

Casual observation suggests the fallacy of this model. Many women postpone their careers or stagger and adjust their work schedules for

---

[2] Caldwell et al. (1970) and Robinson and Robinson (1971) were more concerned about demonstrating the effects of a day-care center in Syracuse (Caldwell) or an experimental day-care program for infants and preschoolers affiliated with the University of North Carolina (Robinson and Robinson) than they were in studying the effects of maternal employment. Although they collected longitudinal data on a number of relevant measures, including the Stanford-Binet, these analyses do not separate working mothers by either the duration of employment or degree of time commitment.

their children. Therefore, the direction of effects is problematic. Perhaps discontinuities in labor force participation are the result of changes in the performance of children, rather than a cause of the change. Instead of being due to maternal employment, perhaps achievement declines or other signs of maladjustment in children lead mothers to quit their jobs. In this event one might find a trivial association between maternal employment and outcomes for children in a cross-sectional study, although a strong reciprocal relationship would be present.

Studies of the work histories of women suggest that the timing of entry and the duration of participation in the work force are substantially different from the patterns observed for men (Bernard, 1971). Ginsberg (1966) and his associates identify six alternative patterns that characterize work during the life span of women: (1) continuous, (2) minor breaks, (3) intermittent, (4) periodic or unstable, (5) terminated temporarily or permanently, (6) minor or none. Not surprisingly, motherhood has a decisive influence on which pattern prevails; the age and spacing of children often are predictably related to a work history that at first glance appears random.

Research on decision making among women also illuminates the complexities of the process (Beckman, 1978; Gerson, 1981). Gerson interviewed a sample of young women in depth about their plans for employment and motherhood; she documents both the search for satisfactory combinations and the difficult and uncertain steps toward full or partial commitments to work and parenting that take place. It is important to remember that few mothers view working as mechanistically as the conventional research classifications portray and that many are ambivalent about the trade-offs and opportunities perceived. Work and family obligations are interdependent, and changes in the salience and priority attached to each are common throughout child rearing. Moreover, these decisions typically involve the presence or absence of other caretakers and their perceived impact on children.

The amount of parental time committed to employment rather than to children is central to an understanding of how work affects family life. We cannot say with certainty whether motherhood takes less time than it used to or whether employment takes more. There are scattered pieces of evidence suggesting that the published figures on maternal employment may be somewhat misleading. Of all women employed in 1977, 56 percent worked for 48 weeks or more; of these, only 79 percent worked more than 35 hours a week (Young, 1979). A random sample of mothers with at least one child between the ages of 5 and 14 was selected in a community near Boston (O'Donnell, 1980). In this sample, 56 percent of the mothers were employed at the time of the interview.

That figure is slightly higher than the national average for all mothers with children under 18. However, only 15 percent of the women were working more than 30 hours a week for any portion of the year. An additional 20 percent worked between 20 and 29 hours on schedules tailored to coincide with the hours their children were in school. The remainder worked less than half time. Unemployment rates increased considerably during the summer months. Even those women with full-time professional jobs were likely to work close to home and to be available to children when needed. O'Donnell (1980:8) concludes: "Paid employment does not necessarily reduce the number of hours a mother is available to school-age children. Rather, the converse appears true. Children's non-school hours cut into the amount of paid employment mothers . . . feel they can maintain."

The timing of work and career choices makes the process of drawing inferences about the effects of maternal employment on children problematic in yet another respect. It is virtually impossible to separate the effects of age, period, and cohort in cross-sectional data. If strong relationships had emerged between a mother working and a child's achievement, interpreting these results would be quite difficult. The propensity to work, even when children are quite young, has increased steadily over time. As Hoffman (1980) notes, the prevailing social norms may have a direct effect on observed differences between working and nonworking mothers. If maternal employment is an accepted fact, rather than a reflection of economic distress or paternal inadequacy, the outcomes for children may be quite different.

The difficulty in interpreting cross-sectional results under conditions of social change is that the historical period confounds effects that may be due to either age or cohort effects. For example, in a personal communication, James Coleman reported that there was a negative correlation between achievement test scores in the 12th grade and student reports that their mothers had worked before they started school. The sample studied was a large national sample of high school seniors; numerous controls were established for family backgrounds, sex, and quality of school attended, although these variables did not diminish the negative effect of early employment. Moreover, two other measures of maternal employment—whether the mother worked when the child was in elementary school and whether she was currently employed—were unrelated to achievement outcomes.

These findings seem to support the conclusion that maternal employment in the early years has long-term adverse effects on children. Developmental psychologists have argued that the age of the child is a factor in assessing the effects of maternal employment (Bronfenbrenner and Crouter, in this volume). However, the age of the child is not the only variable operating.

A single-grade cohort of students, such as those who graduated from high school in 1980, will have mothers who vary considerably in age. Conservatively, the age range could be from 35 to 50. Those who had worked before the children started school could have been working anytime between the ages of 18 and 48; they could have first entered the labor force as early as 1934 or as late as 1968. The younger mothers would be more likely to have more education and to have married later; if the sampled child of a younger mother had siblings, they would tend to be younger. The effects of the historical period, as judged by the time of the mother's entry into the labor force, her age, and correlated attributes that influence her work history could each be the critical factors in predicting achievement differences, as could birth order and other characteristics of the child. Disentangling the individual and structural determinants requires a more complex model of the process than is available from cross-sectional surveys.

A similar difficulty afflicts the life history research. Elder (1974) followed up a sample of children born during 1910 and 1921 to assess the impact of the depression on their lives. The cohort was divided by social-class background and the degree to which their families suffered economically. Deprived children, whose families lost more than half of their income, were different from those growing up in a more stable environment irrespective of social class; they tended to be more security conscious as adults, to have crystalized their vocational plans at an earlier age, and to value their own family ties more highly than did individuals from undeprived families. Their educational and occupational attainments, however, did not seem to be affected; both deprived and undeprived children attained similar levels. Social-class differences in achievement persisted into adulthood, but the effects of deprivation during the depression did not.

At least two inferences from this study are possible. One could conclude that economic dislocation had few enduring effects on the achievement of these children—perhaps, as Bronfenbrenner and Crouter (1981) argue, because a critical developmental phase had passed and the children were sufficiently mature to weather the changing conditions. Alternatively, one could argue that this cohort experienced unique advantages as they entered adulthood. The G.I. Bill and the rapid economic growth after World War II might have boosted their careers and compensated for economic deprivations suffered during late adolescence. The methodological point to be made is that in times of rapid social change, the context can substantially alter the meaning and impact of life-cycle events.

As these observations make clear, the data on maternal employment tend to be poorly conceptualized, inadequately measured, and causally indeterminant. The concept of full-time employment may not have the same meaning to a man or to a career women as it does to the average working mother. The employment status of a mother, whether full-time or part-time, may have only a loose connection to the hours spent away from home or to the time available for children. Mothers may adjust work commitments in response to a child's behavior or in anticipation of negative consequences her absence might entail.

Given the difficulty in specifying hours worked, the complementary dilemma of defining the amount of time not worked becomes problematic as well. Implicitly, analyses of the effects of maternal employment assume that the children of working mothers receive less time and attention than the children of nonworking mothers. The stimulation and encouragement of a mother may well be instrumental to a child's success; however, we know little about the quality of input of mothers or other adults. There is reasonably good evidence that the children of working mothers are not deprived and neglected (Hoffman and Nye, 1974), yet we lack precise estimates of how much time mothers or surrogate mothers spend with children, in what sorts of activities, and with what results.

There is evidence that the actual amount of time spent with children is related to their achievement levels (Benson, 1980; Fleisher, 1977; Hill and Stafford, 1974; Leibowitz, 1974, 1977). However, studies of time use suggest that working mothers spend almost as much time caring for their children as do nonworking mothers. Walker and Woods (1976) estimate that the average nonworking mother spends less than two hours a day caring for all family members. When family size and children's ages are taken into account, the difference between working and nonworking mothers is surprisingly small. The correlation between employment status and time spent in care of family members was $-.05$ when the age of the youngest child was controlled. Although Syracuse, which is where the study was done, may be atypical in certain respects, these data suggest that the distribution of a mother's time is only modestly related to her employment status. Several other studies of time allocation by employed and nonemployed women (Hedges and Barnett, 1972; Vanek, 1980; Walker, 1969) or by husbands and wives in the same household (Pleck and Rustad, 1980) reinforce these results. In general these studies suggest that the amount of time nonworking women spent on housework was roughly constant between 1926 and 1968, although there is evidence that it has declined in recent years (Pleck and Rustad, 1980). The time nonworking women devoted to child care seems to have increased between 1926 and 1968 (Vanek, 1980). Although there has been a dramatic decline in the amount of time the general population spends on housework (Robinson, 1977, 1980), this decline is due to changes in the proportion of women holding jobs. These studies' conclusions are in general agreement—that the time employed husbands spend in family-related work does not change very much when wives are also employed, nor does it seem to have increased over time (Pleck and Rustad, 1980).

The most recent data from family time budgets, summarized by Pleck and Rustad (1980), suggest that in 1975-1976 nonworking wives with at least one child under age 5 spent about 6.5 more hours per week in child care than employed wives. Among wives with children aged 6 to 17, employed wives spent 4.5 fewer hours per week in child care. If one controlled for the number of children, as well as their ages, the discrepancy between working and nonworking mothers would decline further.

These data do not support the notion that working mothers spend substantially less time in child-care activities than nonworking mothers. Nor do they tell us whether the total amount of time adults spend mothering in this society has changed over the years. They do, however, suggest that it is naive to equate increments in labor force participation with decrements in the aggregate time devoted to children.

The literature on the effects of maternal employment has ignored the question of how much time mothers spend with their children; however, some analysts have attempted to distinguish mothers who work during nonschool hours or when the child is very young from other working mothers. Keidel (1970) differentiated between mothers who worked during school hours and those who worked when children were out of school. No significant differences in school grades were reported for his sample of ninth-grade students for either boys or girls.

Burchinal (1963) analyzed the effects of maternal employment during different periods of a child's life. He gathered data on work histories for 1,824 families in Cedar Rapids, Iowa, by means of a mail questionnaire. Five different measures of maternal employment were constructed: (1) the number of months the mother worked during the first three years of the child's life, (2) the number of months she worked during the second three years, (3) the total months worked during the first six years, (4) the number of months employed during the previous 30 months, and (5) the total months worked throughout the life of the child. Although these data cannot encompass sporadic employment or part-time work, they are substantially more detailed than the data generally available. Seven different measures of school achievement were calculated (intelligence, achievement scores, grades in school, days absent, days tardy, extracurricular activities, and the perception of being liked by classmates), along with 23 selected personality characteristics for each child. For each measure of maternal employment, the correlation was calculated separately by sex for seventh-grade and eleventh-grade children. Among these 140 correlations, only one was significant after controlling for the social status of the family. This correlation, between grades and recent employment for eleventh-grade boys, was −.17 before social status was introduced, and −.12 afterward. Interestingly, this single correlation is often the only finding reported for the study. For the complete analysis, 600 correlations were calculated; 49 of the zero-order relationships attained significance. That is, 92 percent of the observed correlations were insignificant, whether or not socioeconomic status was controlled. The author also notes that there were no discernible patterns among the correlations and that the single largest correlation was .20.

Two recent studies of maternal employment (Gold and Andres, 1978a, 1978b) defined the measures relatively clearly and presented results separately for sex, social class, and linguistic background. Working mothers were defined as those who had been employed since the child's birth 10 years before, while nonworking mothers were those who had not been employed since the birth of the child 10 years before. The academic outcomes, including test scores on the Canadian Test of Basic Skills, grades, and attitudes toward school, were not significantly different for children with working and nonworking mothers.

To sum up, one major difficulty with the literature on maternal employment is the definition of work. At best, the connection between employment status and the time spent working is ambiguous. Little attention is paid to the duration of work, its proximity to home, or the time involved. The definitions adopted are arbitrary and lack theoretical specificity; few studies consider the number of hours worked as more than a classification device. No study has dealt adequately with the diversity of employment patterns prevalent among mothers during the course of the family life cycle. The possibility that mothers may withdraw from active participation in the labor force as a consequence of the behavior or performance of their children seems not to have been considered. Cross-sectional studies do not, and probably cannot, determine the direction of causality. These difficulties are straightforward; even more complicated interpretation problems would ensue if analysts worried about the quality, as well as the quantity, of time spent with children.

It seems fair to conclude that the operational definitions of maternal employment are conceptually weak and poorly measured. Nevertheless, the results of the vast majority of studies are clear—the children of working mothers generally do not differ significantly from the children of nonworking mothers, irrespective of how employment is defined. This finding, coupled with the following assessment of the effects of maternal employment characteristics on children's achievement, makes it clear that better data are less important than a reconceptualization of the issue.

Maternal Employment and the Characteristics of Work

As we have seen, few studies have defined the characteristics of women's work very carefully or have attempted to examine the relationship between changes in rates of labor force participation and changes in the labor force. For example, we do not know to what extent work or family life has changed. Have the demands and responsibilities of motherhood lessened? Have work roles evolved to the point of permitting more part-time or intermittent participation in the labor force? To some extent, both have happened. Families are smaller and more closely spaced; at the same time, mother's participation in the labor force has increased irrespective of age or number of children. Yet it would be useful to know precisely how the competing demands of work and motherhood are balanced, both in society as a whole and in the individual lives of women.

Hardly any data exist on how achievement outcomes for children relate to the type of employment or occupational status of mothers; the little there are suggest that professional employment is more positively associated with school achievement than nonprofessional work. Keidel (1970) and Jones and his associates (1967) both report such a finding. Frankel (1960, 1963-1964) presents data that might be interpreted in this way. He divided a select group of intellectually gifted high school boys into high and low achievers after matching by intelligence. Although the mothers of high-achieving sons were less likely to work than other mothers, when they did they were more likely to hold professional positions.

Among women college students, their occupational aspirations, although not their grades or self-esteem, seem to be related to having an employed mother (Almquist and Angrist, 1970; Baruch, 1972; Tangri, 1972). College women are more likely to admire their mothers when they are employed than when they are not. Tangri reported that college women whose mothers were employed in occupations numerically dominated by men were more likely to aspire to nontraditional careers themselves. The relationship persisted when socioeconomic status, mother's education, and the number of years the mother had worked after marriage were controlled. Highly educated mothers are more likely both to work and to have children who perform well in school (Hutner, 1972).

These occupational differences are difficult to interpret. Just as in the case of fathers, high occupational prestige is associated with above-average earnings, advanced educational degrees, and greater job satisfaction. Each of these factors seems to contribute to a family environment that promotes achievement. However, this constellation of interrelated factors is difficult to disentangle. The fact of maternal employment may be less relevant to children's achievement than the attributes of parents that lead them to hold a particular sort of job. The incumbents of high-prestige occupations tend to have high-achieving children, regardless of the sex of the parent.

One aspect of maternal employment that has been shown to relate to outcomes for children is the mother's attitude toward work and job satisfaction. Hoffman (1961) found that children of mothers who enjoyed their work had higher levels of intellectual performance than children of mothers who did not, although the children of nonworking mothers outperformed both groups. As Hoffman argues, job satisfaction is a function of job status, and higher-status jobs tend to be well liked. Yarrow et al. (1962) present similar findings: Working mothers who were dissatisfied had children with more signs of poor adjustment than did satisfied working mothers. Yarrow and her associates complicate these results by also showing that the children of satisfied homemakers are better adjusted than those of discontented homemakers. The central question is whether employment is the factor influencing children or whether the mother's satisfaction, regardless of employment status, is crucial.

The qualitative aspects of maternal employment and their potential effect on children's achievement have not been well explored. We know that the occupational structure is bifurcated by sex and that, to a considerable degree, men and women occupy different roles and work in different contexts. Despite the increase in labor force participation of women, occupational segregation persists (Gross, 1968; Snyder et al., 1973), and the great majority of women still work in traditionally female jobs.

Female employment is concentrated in the service sector and women's jobs often reinforce traditional patterns of role differentiation by sex (Bernard, 1971). There is evidence that the occupational preferences of students were almost as sex-typed in 1975 as they were in 1964 (Lueptow,

1981). In addition the ratio of a wife's earnings to those of her husband has scarcely changed during the last quarter century (Hayghe, 1976), although families with two earners spend income in different ways (Strober, 1977).

The point to be made here is that female employment may not alter female roles very much in the short term. If one expected work experiences to alter family life and child rearing so that the achievement of children was affected, one would first have to show that such experiences somehow changed the conventional role definitions of mothers. There is little evidence to suggest, however, that women's increased participation in the labor force has been accompanied by a shift in the types of work chosen or the roles performed. Although a larger number of women participate in every occupational sphere, the distribution of women's work roles has remained relatively constant.

What, then, can be inferred regarding the impact of maternal employment on children? First, the achievement outcomes for children seem largely unrelated to the fact of employment. Second, when there are consistent positive effects, as in the case of low-income families and professional mothers, a parsimonious explanation would be that maternal earnings materially benefitted the family. Alternatively, it is possible that other maternal traits, such as educational background or general competence, that are associated with choosing to work, enjoying that work, and achieving some success at it, are the underlying factors.

These conclusions are vulnerable to the extent that the studies on which they are based are flawed methodologically. An inventory of the conceptual and methodological difficulties afflicting research on maternal employment would conclude, as did Hoffman (1980), that there is no altogether satisfactory study. Since research on this topic is enormously important, it is worth summarizing in some detail the intractable methodological problems besetting it. I do that in the next section; in the final section, I argue that reconceptualizing the problem of maternal employment should have higher priority than pursuing the tactics that have been used in the past.

AN OVERVIEW OF METHODOLOGICAL ISSUES

Several methodological issues that have been raised regarding research on the effects of maternal employment deserve particular attention. First, the classification of working, as well as of not working, deserves more conceptual and theoretical refinement, particularly with respect to time allocation. Second, cross-sectional studies do not capture the dynamics of change, nor can they resolve the thorny issue of causality.

Third, the critical links between maternal employment and school achievement have not been systematically explored; moreover, there are reasons for believing that the most consistent findings are overdetermined. Finally, despite the fact that there have been large transformations in the nature of work and family life in the last 30 years, we have not developed the conceptual tools for understanding the structural change.

Work is inherently a global construct when it is defined as all activities that earn a salary during some part of a person's day or life span. As such, one must abstract more meaningful distinctions between the kinds of activities and the periods of time to which work refers. Moreover, the characteristics of women's jobs and careers may be quite different from those of men. Simply borrowing the conceptual typologies used to describe male employment may not be adequate to describe the effects of maternal employment on children. This paper has discussed at length the importance of maternal time commitments as they mediate the effects of employment on children. Yet, the quality of time spent with children is undoubtedly an even more critical factor; our ability to measure quality, however, is problematic (Benson, 1980; Benson et al., 1980).

The conceptual difficulty, however, cannot be remedied solely by a more careful specification of the variables. Analyses that document an association between patterns of work and children's achievement also must posit a credible causal sequence. Changing work patterns generate family adaptations that can substantially change relationships and child-rearing practices, but the dynamics of such change are not well understood. The adaptations may compensate for adverse effects or may have an independent effect. Alternative child care, whether by fathers, neighbors, or the local nursery school, is both an adaptation to maternal employment and a new developmental context for children. Observing an association between maternal work characteristics and the behavior of children may tell us something about the effects of maternal employment, something about the effects of family adaptation, or something about the effects of alternative contexts for development. Even the allocation of time, as we have seen, is not a direct function of employment. A host of intervening variables and conditions could mediate the impact of maternal work on children. Among them are the values and attitudes of parents, child-care patterns, the division of labor in the home, linguistic and cultural factors, and the use of family resources for educational purposes. Such factors may be a result of work conditions or a response to the needs of children. However, such adaptations surely confound the original relationship. These relationships are hopelessly entangled in correlational studies with single observations over time.

Two specific findings regarding the determinants of achievement can be given as examples. Birth order and family size are associated with student achievement (Adams, 1972; Clausen and Clausen, 1973) as well as maternal employment. Large families tend to be more tightly organized and to have more rules than smaller families. Moreover, they require a larger contribution of time and assistance from both fathers and siblings. In addition, relationships within the family tend to be more structured and autocratic than in smaller families (Clausen and Clausen, 1973; Elder and Bowerman, 1963). Families in which both parents are employed tend to be smaller than average, but they may make similar demands on members' time and require forms of domestic organization similar to those of larger families. Structured families have been shown to have higher-achieving children, irrespective of social class (McKinley, 1964). Classifying families by size, age, composition, and quality of relationships is an enormous but necessary task, since the effect of employment may be inseparable from such structural features.

A consequence of increased maternal employment may be a decline in the geographic mobility of families. Long (1973) has shown that families with an employed wife tend to move long distances or between states less frequently than those with a nonworking wife, although within-county mobility rates are higher. His interpretation of these differences suggests that families with two earners are more likely to move to a better neighborhood, but less likely to change jobs or communities. Children's achievement is linked to disruptions in schooling; children in families that move a great deal have lower IQ scores than those in stable families, even when family status is controlled (Street, 1969). Perhaps one unintended consequence of two-career families is that children will change schools and classmates less often and that this stability will enhance their achievement.

As these examples illustrate, work may have a direct impact on family organization and mobility; however, it is also possible that these adaptations exert their own influence on children. When one observes correlated factors in cross-sectional research, it is usually not possible to disentangle and interpret causation. Both of these examples would suggest a positive relationship between maternal employment and achievement; however, most studies would not be able to separate the effects of family structure or mobility from the impact of maternal employment.

The examples could be multiplied; the dilemma remains. When work status differs between families, a large number of other differences are also likely to be found. In research, a significant association between work and children's achievement will be overdetermined because a large number of family attributes and characteristics are correlated and, hence, difficult to separate. In addition, a significant pattern of associations among correlated factors is difficult to interpret because, as I have previously noted, the direction of causality cannot be inferred from cross-sectional research. Should family organization or the propensity to move be considered an adaptation to work, or a family characteristic that precedes choice of work roles and sites? Families have been observed to structure the rules for homework or to change neighborhoods and schools in response to a child's achievement. There are plausible reasons for supposing that at least some families make decisions regarding the organization of family life and the desirability of relocating on the basis of their children's school performance. At the very least, a large number of parents have persuaded both themselves and their children that large sacrifices and major decisions were made for the sake of their children's education.

Textbooks on research design provide insight, if not solutions, for these problems. The dilemma of correlated determinants can be resolved, at least in part, if one has a very large sample or a very tightly controlled design. The issue of causal direction requires a series of observations taken before and after the behavior of interest or a strong theoretical rationale for assuming a specific ordering. Both strategies are, however, relatively costly in terms of time and resources. Without a cogent theoretical agenda, the prospects for systematic research in these areas seem dim.

Finally, the historical patterns of increasing employment by women reflect dramatic changes in both the nature of work and the expectations of families. Later marriage means a longer period of time in which to gain work experience before childbearing, and previous work experience predicts continuous participation in the labor force. Smaller families are associated with higher rates of maternal employment (Presser and Baldwin, 1980). The increase in the demand for women's work has been documented (Oppenheimer, 1974). We do not have systematic studies of how changes in the timing and sequencing of family life have facilitated maternal employment, nor do we know how the work context has changed or adjusted to the needs of mothers. It is not unreasonable to argue that structural changes in the nature of work have enabled mothers to work, while family and life-style changes have accommodated to the demands of work. Studies of such changes require different models and assumptions than are common in social research; in particular, they cannot be studied in depth by analyzing cross-sectional patterns.

These methodological problems are not new to analysts in the field. However, they imply different strategies for both data collection and analysis than have been common in the past. In the final section of this paper, I suggest several ways in which research can contribute to a better conceptualization of the issues and linkages present.

WHITHER RESEARCH? THE CASE FOR INTENSIVE STUDIES OF SPECIAL GROUPS

The methodological issues involved in linking work, family life, and achievement are so broad and multifaceted it seems somewhat paradoxical to conclude with the recommendation that intensive research should be initiated on special groups through small-scale in-depth interviews. The advantages of such studies, however, seem to outweigh the disadvantages. From exploratory studies one can begin to reconceptualize the linkages between work and family life, observe families changing over time, and simultaneously interview several members of a family or participants in a work environment.

In order to study how changes in work patterns affect families, it is necessary to study families in the process of change. Longitudinal data is one clear necessity, but it is also possible to frame interviews and select samples strategically so as to maximize the information available regarding change. Studies of the effect of first births on parents (Dyer, 1963; Hobbs, 1965; LeMasters, 1963) or of divorce on children yield a wealth of insight about family dynamics under stress. Research on families in which work patterns have changed or are changing would help our efforts to conceptualize how work intersects with family life.

From a policy perspective, certain groups demand particular attention. In 1978, 78 percent of all children under 14 lived with both parents. That figure is roughly 10 percent lower than the proportion reported for 1960. More than half of the children in single-parent households live below the poverty line. Although both the number of children and their proportion in the population have declined steadily since 1960, their number and proportion in poverty have risen since 1969. The number of single-parent families is growing two and one-half times faster than all families; yet we have very little systematic information about the integration of work and child rearing in such families, the extent and impact of supportive community networks, or how the children are affected (Schorr and Moen, 1979). Single-parent families constitute an extreme case of the consolidation of work and parenting roles in one person; therefore, the impact of work on family life can be seen with stark clarity in such families. While it is true that many of these families are poor or distressed in other ways, many are not. Large numbers of such families are found in every socioeconomic stratum. Single parenthood is, for most families, a period of transition rather than a permanent status (Bane, 1976); yet longitudinal research on the process of family formation, dissolution, and reformation is difficult to find. Such research would contribute to our understanding of the challenges and problems in combining work and family life and the potential impact on children. At present a large part of the literature on these topics consists of self-help paperbacks filled with anecdotes and case studies drawn from the files of marriage counselors.

The impact of work roles on women and their families is another area of research that deserves more systematic clarification than it has received. Job satisfaction influences the effectiveness of mothering and the activity of children (Hoffman, 1980), yet we do not know what aspects of a job lead to satisfaction. The content and meaning of women's work as it relates to children has largely escaped analysis (Gerson, 1981). There are, to my knowledge, no ethnographic studies of the workplace or the employment context for women that link specific aspects of work to family or child-rearing patterns and outcomes.

Finally, few studies have examined the outcomes for children by comparing children within the same family. In recent studies of the impact of socioeconomic status on children, the strategy of comparing siblings has been used well. We know that sex and birth order are related to achievement differences between children (Adams, 1972), yet there are no studies that ask whether work influences the family dynamics among children. If one found that children had consistent reactions to parental work patterns, one would feel somewhat more confident in attributing them to the effect of common experiences. Moreover, by ignoring siblings one cannot ask how the employment of other family members contributes to family life and to outcomes for children still in school. In the context of explaining these linkages, it would be important to develop an integrated view of work in the life of the entire family, not just the relationship between the work of one parent and school outcomes for one child.

Small-scale ethnographic studies with intensive interviews have limitations: It is difficult to generalize without adequate baseline data and it is important to select samples carefully so that critical variations can be observed without confounding. Panel studies that promise partially to solve both problems are, however, now in progress. Subsamples can be selected for special study and one can compare the characteristics of groups of families with national data. Although large-scale replication ultimately would be desirable, the first priority is a better conceptualization of the problem.

REFERENCES AND BIBLIOGRAPHY

Aberle, D. F., and Naegele, K. (1952) Middle-class fathers' occupational role and attitudes toward children. *American Journal of Orthopsychiatry* 22(April):366-378.

Adams, B. N. (1972) Birth order: a critical review. *Sociometry* 35(3):411-439.

Adams, R. G. (1981) Adult Household Composition and Mother's Employment in a Black Community. Paper presented at the American Sociological Association meeting, Toronto, Ontario.

Aldous, J. (1969) Occupational characteristics and males' role performance in the family. *Journal of Marriage and the Family* 37:707-712.

Almquist, E. M. (1971) Role modeling influences on college women's career aspirations. *Merrill-Palmer Quarterly* 17(3):263-279.

Almquist, E. M., and Angrist, S. S. (1970) Career salience and atypicality of occupational choice among college women. *Journal of Marriage and the Family* 32:242-249.

Angrist, S. S., Love, J., and Mickelson, R. (1976) How working mothers manage: socioeconomic differences in work, child care and household tasks: *Social Science Quarterly* 56(4):631-637.

Banducci, R. (1967) The effect of mother's employment on the achievement, aspirations, and expectations of the child. *Personnel and Guidance Journal* 46:263-267.

Bane, M. J. (1976) *Here to Stay: American Families in the Twentieth Century*. New York: Basic Books.

Barth, E. A. T., and Watson, W. B. (1974) Questionable assumptions in the theory of social stratification. *Pacific Sociological Review* 7 (Spring):11-16.

Baruch, G. K. (1972) Maternal influences upon college women's attitudes toward women and work. *Developmental Psychology* 6:32-37.

Beckman, L. J. (1978) The relative rewards and costs of parenthood and employment for employed women. *Psychology of Women Quarterly* 2 (Spring):215-234.

Benson, C. S. (1980) *Household Production of Human Capital: Time Uses of Parents and Children as Inputs*. Children's Time Study. Berkeley: University of California, Schools of Law and Education.

Benson, C. S., Buckley, S., and Medrich, E. A. (1980) A new view of school efficiency: household time contributions to school achievement. Pp. 169-204 in J. Guthrie, ed., *School Finance Policy in the 1980's: A Decade of Conflict*. Cambridge, Mass.: Ballinger.

Berk, R., and Berk, S. F. (1979) *Labor and Leisure at Home: Content and Organization of the Household Day*. Beverly Hills, Calif.: Sage Publications.

Bernard, J. (1971) *Women and the Public Interest*. Chicago: Aldine.

Bernard, J. (1975) *Women, Wives, Mothers: Values and Options*. Chicago: Aldine.

Billingsley, A. (1968) *Black Families in White America*. Englewood Cliffs, N.J.: Prentice-Hall.

Billingsley, A., and Billingsley, A. (1979) *Black Families in White America*. Englewood Cliffs, N.J.: Prentice-Hall.

Blau, Z. A. (1972) Maternal aspiration, socialization, and achievement of boys and girls in the working class. *Journal of Youth and Adolescence* 1:35-57.

Blood, R. O., Jr. (1965) Long-range causes and consequences of the employment of married women. *Journal of Marriage and the Family* 27:43-47.

Brim, O. G. (1975) Macro-structural influences on child development and the need for childhood and social indicators. *American Journal of Orthopsychiatry* 45:516-524.

Bronfenbrenner, U., (1979) *The Ecology of Human Development.* Cambridge, Mass.: Harvard University Press.

Bryson, J. B., and Bryson, R., eds. (1978) *Dual-Career Couples.* New York: Human Sciences Press.

Burchinal, L. G. (1963) Personality characteristics of children. Pp. 106-121 in F. I. Nye and L. W. Hoffman, eds., *The Employed Mother in America.* Chicago: Rand McNally.

Caldwell, B., Wright, C. M., Honig, A. S., and Tannenbaum, J. (1970) Infant day care and attachment. *American Journal of Orthopsychiatry* 40:397-412.

Charters, W. W., Jr. (1963) The social background of teaching. Pp. 715-813 in N. L. Gage, ed., *Handbook of Research on Teaching.* Chicago: Rand McNally.

Cherry, F. F., and Eaton, E. L. (1977) Physical and cognitive development in children of low-income mothers working in the child's early years. *Child Development* 48:158-166.

Clausen, J. A., and Clausen, S. R. (1973) The effects of family size on parents and children. In J. Fawcett, ed., *Psychological Perspectives on Fertility.* New York: Basic Books.

Davis, A., and Havighurst, R. J. (1946) Social class and color differences in child-rearing. *American Sociological Review* 11:698-710.

Dellas, M., Gaier, E. L., and Emihovich, C. A. (1979) Maternal employment and selected behaviors and attitudes of pre-adolescents and adolescents. *Adolescence* 14(15):579-589.

Department of Labor (1977) *Working Mothers and Their Children.* Washington, D.C.: U.S. Department of Labor.

Douvan, E. (1963) Employment and the adolescent. Pp. 142-164 in F. I. Nye and L. W. Hoffman, eds., *The Employed Mother in America.* Chicago: Rand McNally.

Dyer, E. D. (1963) Parenthood as crisis: a re-study. *Marriage and Family Living* 25:196-201.

Dyer, W. G. (1956) The interlocking of work and family social systems among lower occupational families. *Social Forces* 34(March):230-233.

Dyer, W. G. (1964) Family reactions to the father's job. Pp. 86-91 in A. Shostak and W. Gomberg, eds., *Blue-Collar World: Studies of the American Worker.* Englewood Cliffs, N.J.: Prentice-Hall.

Elder, G. (1974) *Children of the Great Depression.* Chicago: University of Chicago Press.

Elder, G. H., and Bowerman, C. E. (1963) Family structure and child-rearing patterns: the effect of family size and sex composition. *American Sociological Review* 28(6):891-905.

Essig, H., and Morgan, D. H. (1945) Adjustment of adolescent daughters of employed mothers to family life. *Journal of Educational Psychology* 37:219-233.

Etaugh, C. (1974) Effects of maternal employment on children: a review of recent research. *Merrill-Palmer Quarterly* 20(2):71-98.

Farley, J. (1968) Maternal employment and child behavior. *Cornell Journal of Social Relations* 3:58-71.

Fein, R. A. (1978) Research on fathering: social policy and an emergent perspective. *Journal of Social Issues* 34(1):122-135.

Fleisher, B. M. (1977) Mother's home time and the production of child quality. *Demography* 14:197-212.

Frankel, E. (1960) A comparative study of achieving and underachieving high school boys of high intellectual ability. *Journal of Educational Research* 53:172-180.

✓Frankel, E. (1963-1964) Characteristics of working and non-working mothers among intellectually gifted high and low achievers. *The Personnel and Guidance Journal* 42:776-780.

Furstenberg, F. F., Jr. (1974) Work experience and family life. Pp. 341-360 in J. O'Toole, ed., *Work and the Quality of Life*. Cambridge, Mass.: MIT Press.

Gerson, K. (1981) Hard Choices: How Women Decide About Work, Career and Family. Ph.D. dissertation, University of California, Berkeley.

Ginsberg, E. (1966) *Life Styles of Educated Women*. New York: Columbia University Press.

Gold, D., and Andres, D. (1978a) Developmental comparisons between ten-year-old children with employed and nonemployed mothers. *Child Development* 49:75-84.

Gold, D., and Andres, D. (1978b) Comparisons of adolescent children with employed and nonemployed mothers. *Merrill-Palmer Quarterly* 24:75-84.

Gold, A., Andres, D., and Glorieux, J. (1979) The development of Francophone nursery-school children with employed and nonemployed mothers. *Canadian Journal of Behavioural Science* 11:169-173.

Gross, E. (1968) Plus ca change...? The sexual structure of occupations over time. *Social Problems* 16:198-208.

Gutman, H. G. (1976) *The Black Family in Slavery and Freedom*. New York: Pantheon.

Hareven, T. K. (1975) Family time and industrial time: family and work in a planned corporation town, 1900-1924. *Monthly Labor Review* 98(2):46-53.

Haug, M. R. (1973) Social class measurement and women's occupational roles. *Social Forces* 52(September):86-98.

Havighurst, R. J. (1976) The relative importance of social class and ethnicity in human development. *Human Development* 19:56-64.

Hayghe, H. (1976) Families and the rise of working wives: an overview. *Monthly Labor Review* 99:12-19.

Hayghe, H. (1981) Husbands and wives as earners: an analysis of family data. *Monthly Labor Review* 104(2):46-53.

Hedges, J. N., and Barnett, J. K. (1972) Working women and division of household tasks. *Monthly Labor Review* 95:9-14.

Hess, R. D. (1970) Social class and ethnic influences upon socialization Pp. 457-556 in P. H. Mussen, ed., *Carmichael's Manual of Child Psychology*, vol. 2, 3rd ed. New York: John Wiley and Sons.

Heyns, B. (1978) *Summer Learning and the Effects of Schooling*. New York: Academic Press.

Hicks, M., and Platt, M. (1970) Marital happiness and stability: a review of the research in the sixties. *Journal of Marriage and Family* 32:553-575.

Hill, R., and Stafford, F. (1974) Time inputs to children. Pp. 319-344 in J. N. Morgan, ed., *Five Thousand American Families: Patterns of Economic Progress*, vol. 2. Ann Arbor, Mich: Institute for Social Research.

Hobbs, D. F., Jr. (1965) Parenthood as crisis: a third study. *Journal of Marriage and the* ✓ *Family* 27:367-372.

✓Hoffman, L. W. (1961) Effects of maternal employment on the child. *Child Development* 32:187-197.

✓Hoffman, L. W. (1974) Effects of maternal employment on the child—a review of the research. *Developmental Psychology* 10:204-228.

Hoffman, L. W. (1979) Maternal employment: 1979. *American Psychologist* 34(10):859-865.

Hoffman, L. W. (1980) The effects of maternal employment on the academic attitudes and performance of school-aged children. *School Psychology Review* 9:319-335.

Hoffman, L. W., and Nye, I. F. (1974) *Working Mothers*. San Francisco: Jossey-Bass.

Howrigan, G. (1973) The effects of working mothers on children. Cambridge, Mass.: Center for the Study of Public Policy.

Hutner, F. D. (1972) Mother's education and working: effect on the school child. *Journal of Psychology* 82:27-37.

Jones, J. B., Lundsteen, S. W., and Michael, M. B. (1967) The relationship of the professional employment status of mothers to reading achievement of sixth grade children. *California Journal of Educational Research* 18:102-108.

Kahne, H. (1978) Economic research on work and families. *Signs: Journal of Women in Culture and Society* 3(3):652-665.

Kamerman, S. B. (1980) *Parenting in an Unresponsive Society: Managing Work and Family Life*. New York: The Free Press.

Kanter, R. M. (1977) *Work and Family in the United States: A Critical Review and Agenda for Research and Policy*. Social Science Frontiers. New York: Russell Sage Foundation.

Keidel, K. (1970) Maternal employment and ninth grade achievement in Bismark, North Dakota. *The Family Co-Ordinator* 19:95-97.

Kohn, M. L. (1963) Social class and parent-child relationships: an interpretation. *American Journal of Sociology* 68:471-480.

Kohn, M. L. (1969) *Class and Conformity: A Study in Values*. Homewood, Ill.: Dorsey.

Kohn, M. L., and Carroll, E. E. (1960) Social class and the allocation of parental responsibilities. *Sociometry* 23:372-392.

Kriesberg, L. (1967) Rearing children for educational achievement in fatherless families. *Journal of Marriage and the Family* 29:288-301.

Kriesberg, L. (1970) *Mothers in Poverty: A Study of Fatherless Families*. Chicago: Aldine.

Lamb, M. E., ed. (1979) *The Role of the Father in Child Development*. New York: John Wiley and Sons.

Langner, T., Green, E., Herson, J., James, J., Goff, J., Rostkowski, J., and Zykorie, D. (1969) Psychiatric impairment in welfare and nonwelfare children. *Welfare in Review* 7(March-April):10-21.

Laslett, B. (1978) Family membership, past and present. *Social Problems* 25(5):476-490.

Leibowitz, A. (1974) Home investments in children. *Journal of Political Economy* 82(March-April):S111-S135.

Leibowitz, A. (1977) Parental inputs and children's achievement. *Journal of Human Resources* 12(2):247-250.

Lein, L., et al. (1974) *Work and Family Life*. Final report to the National Institute of Education. Cambridge, Mass.: Center for the Study of Public Policy.

LeMasters, E. E. (1963) Parenthood as crisis. *Marriage and Family Living* 25:196-201.

Levine, J. A. (1976) *Who Will Raise the Children?: New Options for Fathers (and Mothers)*. Philadelphia, Pa.: Lippincott.

Levinson, P. (1969) The next generation: a study of children in AFDC families. *Welfare in Review* 7(March-April):1-9.

Lightfoot, S. L. (1978) *Worlds Apart: Relationships Between Family and Schools*. New York: Basic Books.

Lloyd, C. B., ed. (no date) *Sex, Discrimination, and the Division of Labor*. New York: Columbia University Press.

Long, L. (1973) Women's labor force participation and the residential mobility of families. *Social Forces* 52(3):342-348.

Lueptow, L. B. (1981) Sex-typing and change in the occupational choices of high school seniors: 1964-1975. *Sociology of Education* 54(January):16-24.

Lynn, D. B. (1974) *The Father: His Role in Child Development*. Monterey, Calif.: Brooks and Cole.

Maccoby, E. E. (1958) Effects upon children of mothers' outside employment. Pp. 150-172 in *Work in the Lives of Married Women*. New York: Columbia University Press.

Macke, A. S., and Morgan, W. R. (1978) Maternal employment, race, and work orientation of high school girls. *Social Forces* 57:187-204.

McCord, J., McCord, W., and Thurber, E. (1963) Effects of maternal employment on lower-class boys. *Journal of Abnormal and Social Psychology* 67:177-182.

McKinley, D. G. (1964) *Social Class and Family Life*. New York: The Free Press.

Miller, D. R., and Swanson, G. E. (1958) *The Changing American Parent: A Study in the Detroit Area*. New York: John Wiley and Sons.

Miller, S. M. (1975) Effects of maternal employment on sex-role perception, interests, and self-esteem in kindergarten girls. *Developmental Psychology* 11:405-406.

Moore, T. W. (1975) Exclusive early mothering and its alternatives. *Scandinavian Journal of Psychology* 16:256-272.

Neff, W. S. (1938) Socioeconomic status and intelligence: a critical survey. *Psychological Bulletin* 35:727-757.

Nelson, D. D. (1969) A study of school achievement among adolescent children with working and nonworking mothers. *Journal of Educational Research* 62:456-457.

Nelson, D. D. (1971) A study of personality adjustment among adolescent chidren with working and nonworking mothers. *Journal of Educational Research* 64:328-330.

Nolan, F. L. (1963) Effects on rural children. Pp. 122-124 in F. Nye and L. Hoffman, eds., *The Employed Mother in America*. Chicago: Rand McNally.

Nye, F. I. (1963) The adjustment of adolescent children. Pp. 133-141 in F. I. Nye and L. W. Hoffman, eds., *The Employed Mother in America*. Chicago: Rand McNally.

Nye, F. I., and Hoffman, L. W., eds. (1963) *The Employed Mother in America*. Chicago: Rand McNally.

O'Donnell, L., (1980) Extensions of Mothering: Maternal Involvement in Volunteer Work and Children's Activities. Mimeo, Center for Research on Women, Wellesley College.

O'Donnell, L., and Stueve, A. (1980) Employed Women: Mothers and Good Neighbors. Mimeo, Center for Research on Women, Wellesley College.

Ogbu, J. U. (1974) *The Next Generation: An Ethnography of Education in an Urban Neighborhood*. New York: Academic Press.

Ogbu, J. U. (1978) *Minority Education and Caste: The American System in Cross Cultural Perspective*. New York: Academic Press.

Oppenheimer, V. K. (1974) Women's economic role in the family. *American Sociological Review* 42(June):387-406.

Orden, S. R., and Bradburn, N. N. (1969) Working wives and marriage happiness. *American Journal of Sociology* 78(January):853-872.

Papenek, H. (1975) Men, women, and work: reflections on the two-person career. *American Journal of Sociology* 78(January):853-872.

Pelton, L. H. (1978) Child abuse and neglect: the myth of classlessness. *American Journal of Orthopsychiatry* 48:608-617.

Perry, J. B., Jr. (1961) The mother substitutes of employed mothers: an exploratory inquiry. *Marriage and Family Living* 23:362-367.

Peterson, E. T. (1961) The impact of maternal employment on the mother-daughter relationship. *Marriage and Family Living* 23:355-361.

Pleck, E. (1976) Two worlds in one: work and family. *Journal of Social History* 10:178-195.

Pleck, E. (1978) A mother's wages: income earning among married Italian and black women, 1896-1911. Pp. 490-510 in G. Michael, ed., *American Family in Social Historical Perspective*, New York: St Martins Press.

Pleck, J. H. (1975) Work and Family Roles: From Sex Patterned Segregation to Integration. Paper presented at the meeting of the American Sociological Association, San Francisco, Calif.

Pleck, J. H. (1977) The work-family role system. *Social Problems* 24:417-427.

Pleck, J. H. (1979), Men's family work: three perspectives and some data. *Family Coordinator* 28:431-488.

Pleck, J. H., and Rustad, M. (1980) Husbands' and Wives' Time in Family Work and Paid Work in the 1975-76 Study of Time Use. Working Paper No. 63. Center for Research on Women, Wellesley College.

Pleck, J. H., Staines, G. L., and Lang, L. (1980) Conflicts between work and family life. *Monthly Labor Review* 3:29-32.

Plunkett, M. W. (1980) Working Mothers of Young Children: A Study of Conflict and Integration. Ph.D. dissertation, University of Michigan.

Powell, K. S. (1961) Maternal employment in relation to family life. *Marriage and Family Living* 23:350-355.

Presser, H. B., and Baldwin, W. (1980) Child care as a constraint on employment: prevalence, correlates, and bearing on work and fertility nexus. *American Journal of Sociology* 85(5):1202-1213.

Rapoport, R., and Rapoport, R. (1971) *Dual-Career Families*. London: Penguin Books.

Rapoport, R., and Rapoport, R. (1976) *Dual-Career Families Re-Examined* New York: Harper and Row.

Rapoport, R., and Rapoport, R. (1978) Dual-career families: progress and prospects. *Marriage and Family Review* 1(5):1-12.

Rees, A. N., and Palmer, F. H. (1970) Factors related to change in mental test performance. *Developmental Psychology Monograph* 3(2):Part 2, 1-57.

Rieber, M., and Womach, M. (1967) The intelligence of preschool children as related to ethnic and demographic variables. *Exceptional Children* 34:609-614.

Robinson, J. H., and Robinson, N. M. (1971) Longitudinal development of very young children in a comprehensive day care program. *Child Development* 42:1673-1684.

Robinson, J. P. (1977) *How Americans Use Time: A Social-Psychological Analysis*. New York: Praeger.

Robinson, J. P. (1980) Housework technology and household work. Pp. 53-67 in S. F. Berk, ed., *Women and Household Labor*. Beverly Hills, Calif: Sage Publications.

Rosenberg, M. (1956) *Occupations and Values*. New York: The Free Press.

Rosenfeld, C., and Parrella, V. C. (1965) Why women start and stop working: a study in mobility. *Monthly Labor Review* 85(9):1077-1082.

Rosenfeld, R. A. (1978) Women's intergenerational occupational mobility. *American Sociological Review* 48:36-42.

Rosenfeld, R. A., and Sorensen, A. (1979) Sex differences in patterns of career mobility. *Demography* 16(February):89-101.

Roy, P. (1961) Maternal employment and adolescent roles: rural-urban differentials. *Marriage and Family Living* 23:340-349.

Salo, K. E. (1975) *Maternal Employment and Children's Behavior: A Review of the Literature*. Ms. No. 1007, Selected Documents in Psychology. Washington, D.C.: American Psychological Association.

Sawhill, I. V. (1977) Economic perspectives on the family. *Daedalus* 106:115-125.

Scanzoni, J. (1978) *Sex Roles, Women's Work, and Marital Conflict*. Lexington, Mass.: Lexington Books.

Schooler, C. (1972) Childhood family structure and adult characteristics. *Sociometry* 35:255-269.

Schoor, A. L., and Moen, P. (1979) The single parent and public policy. *Social Policy* 9(5):15-21.

Siegel, A. E., and Curtis, E. A. (1963) Familial correlates of orientation towards employment among college women. *Journal of Educational Psychology* 54(1):33-37.

Siegel, A. E., and Haas, M. B. (1963) The working mother: a review of the research. *Child Development* 34:513-542.

Siegel, A. E., Stoltz, L. M., Hitchcock, E. A., and Adamson, J. (1959) Dependence and independence on the children of working mothers. *Child Development* 30:533-546.

Skard, A. G. (1965) Maternal deprivation: the research and its implications. *Journal of Marriage and the Family* 27:333-343.

Snyder, D., Hayward, M. D., and Hudis, P. M. (1973) The location of change in the sexual structure of occupations, 1950-1970. *American Journal of Sociology* 84:706-717.

Stack, C. B. (1974) *All Our Kin*. New York: Harper and Row.

Stolz, L. M. (1960) Effects of maternal employment on children: evidence from research. *Child Development* 31(December):749-782.

Street, D., ed. (1969) *Innovations in Mass Education*. New York: Wiley Interscience.

Strober, M. H. (1977) Wives' labor force behavior and family consumption patterns. *American Economic Review* 67(1):410-417.

Sussman, M. B. (1961) Needed research on the employed mother. *Marriage and Family Living* 23:368-373.

Sweet, J. A. (1973) *Women in the Labor Force*. New York: Seminar Press.

Sweet, J. A. (1979a) Changes in the Allocation of Time by Young Women Among Schooling, Marriage, Work and Childrearing: 1960-1976. Working Paper 79-15. Center for Demography and Ecology, University of Wisconsin, Madison.

Sweet, J. A. (1979b) Changes in the Allocation of Time of Young Men Among Schooling, Marriage, Work and Childrearing: 1960-1976. Working Paper 79-28. Center for Demography and Ecology, University of Wisconsin, Madison.

Taeuber, K. A., and Sweet, J.A. (1976) Family and work: the social life cycle of women. In J. M. Kreps, ed., *Women and the American Economy: A Look at the 1980s*. Englewood Cliffs, N.J.: Prentice-Hall.

Tangri S. S. (1972) Determinants of occupational role innovation among college women. *Journal of Social Issues* 23(2):177-199.

Taveggia, T. C., and Thomas, E. M. (1974) Latchkey children. *Pacific Sociological Review* 17(1):27-34.

Tilly, L. A., and Scott, J. W. (1978) *Women, Work, and Family*. New York: Holt, Rinehart and Winston.

Treiman, D., and Terrell, K. (1975) Sex and the process of status attainment: a comparison of working women and men. *American Sociological Review* 40 (April):174-200.

Uhlenberg, P. R. (1974) Cohort variations in family life cycle experiences of U.S. females. *Journal of Marriage and the Family* 36:284-292.

Vanek, J. (1980) Time spent in housework. Pp. 82-90 in A. H. Amsden, ed., *The Economics of Women and Work*. New York: St. Martin's Press.

Vogel, S. R., Broverman, I. K., Broverman, D. M., Clarkson, F., and Rosenkrantz, P. S. (1970) Maternal employment and perception of sex roles among college students. *Developmental Psychology* 3:384-391.

Wade, M. (1973) *Flexible Working Hours in Practice*. New York: Halstead Press.

Waite, L. (1976) Working wives: 1940-1960. *American Sociological Review* 41(February):65-80.

Walker, K. E. (1969) Time spent in household work by homemakers. *Family Economics Review* 3(September):5-6.

Walker, K. E. (1970) Time spent by husbands in household work. *Family Economics Review* 4:8-11.

Walker, K. E., and Woods, M. (1966) *Time Use: A Measure of Household Production of Family Goods and Services*. Washington, D.C.: American Home Economics Association.

Wallston, B. (1973) The effects of maternal employment on children. *Journal of Child Psychology and Psychiatry and Applied Disciplines* 14:81-95.

Walters, J., and Stinett, N. (1971) Parent-child relationships: a decade of review of research. *Journal of Marriage and the Family* 33(1):70-111.

White, K. R. (1976) The Relationship Between Socioeconomic Status and Academic Achievement. Ph.D. dissertation, University of Colorado, Boulder.

Wijting, J. P., Arnold, C. R., and Conrad, K. A. (1978) Generational differences in work values between parents and children and between boys and girls across grade levels 6, 9, 10, and 12. *Journal of Vocational Behavior* 2:245-260.

Willie, C. V. (1970) *The Family Life of Black People*. Columbus, Ohio: Charles E. Merrill.

Woods, M. B. (1972) The unsupervised child of the working mother. *Developmental Psychology* 6:14-25.

Yarrow, M. R. (1961) Maternal employment and child-rearing. *Children* 8(November-December):223-228.

Yarrow, M. R., Scott, P. deLeeuw, L., and Heinig, C. (1962) Childrearing in families of working and non-working mothers. *Sociometry* 25:122-140.

Young, A. M. (1979) Work experience of the population in 1977. *Monthly Labor Review* 102(3):53-57.

Yudkin, S., and Holms, A. (1963) *Working Mothers and their Children*. London: Michael Joseph.

Zigler, E. (1970) Social class and the socialization process. *Review of Educational Research* 40(1):87-110.

8

Work, Family, and Children's Perceptions of the World

Sally Bloom-Feshbach, *National Research Council*, Jonathan Bloom Feshbach, *Counseling Center, Georgetown University,* and Kirby A. Heller, *National Research Council*

INTRODUCTION

At the center of children's lives are their perceptions of the world. What is more fundamental than the child's sense of self-worth, views of family members, and basic feelings about what possibilities life may hold? This paper considers these and other child-size views that relate to the worlds of work and family life. Our primary focus is the influence of parents' work experiences on children's perceptions and the impact of adolescents' work experiences on the teenagers themselves.

We emphasize the interlocking life experiences that influence the developmental path of the child. The world of work, for example, must be viewed through the prism of family experience. As the reader will discover, the research literature on this topic is limited. Therefore, in order to answer some important questions, we must consider nonreplicated and exploratory investigations.

Before entering this sometimes muddy realm of research, we have to clarify certain basic assumptions. First, we discuss the importance of the child's perspective of the world. Next, we outline our conceptual approach to understanding children's views, examining the entire ecological context in which they develop. Then, we discuss briefly a very complex and pervasive issue—the many ways in which socioeconomic status is used in research and how it is used in this paper. Following this section is a comprehensive review of research on work, family, and children's perceptions of the world. We end with a discussion of meth-

268

odological concerns and a list of recommendations to guide future investigation.

THE IMPORTANCE OF STUDYING CHILDREN'S PERCEPTIONS

Emphasizing the child's *perception* of the world—rather than adjustment, achievement, or other behavioral indices—is an approach receiving increasing attention. In the past, social scientists often have neglected the importance and influential power of the individual's subjective experience (Hudson, 1972). Currently, various social science perspectives on childhood socialization (Berger and Luckman, 1967; Harré, 1974), on the effects of socioeconomic status (Rubin, 1976; Sennett and Cobb, 1973), and on the individual's competence or efficacy (Lazarus et al., 1974), give considerable weight to the impact of the phenomenological world (Schutz, 1972). "Phenomenological" is used here to refer to the world as experienced by the individual, rather than as it may exist from a more objective standpoint. For example, the availability of government services or community resources may be quite different in *fact* than in *perception*. Further, the American ethos of choice, of a free society in which hard work brings prosperity, may be perceived differently by children living in varying social and economic environments. The literature on "locus of control" (e.g., Lefcourt, 1976; Rotter, 1966) demonstrates how a wide range of behaviors depends on people's generalized expectations about whether they can influence the world or whether world events are thought to inevitably carry them along. Other research has found that subjective, phenomenological impressions or attributions affect the developing child's reactions to school and achievement experiences (Dweck, et al., 1978; Weiner and Peter, 1973).

Thus, our understanding of child development, family life, and community institutions is incomplete unless we add a subjective, experiential dimension. Further, perceptions of the same experience frequently differ even among family members. Concrete facts about child care, health, and educational attainment are enriched by knowing the child's perspective. In an article addressing the need for social indicators in developing informed social policies for children, Orville Brim (1975:520) noted, "The absence of reports *from* children *about* children is a striking deficiency in current survey research on the quality of life in America. Adults are interviewed about their attitudes and values, their 'hopes and fears,' and the 'perceived quality' of their lives." In order to answer basic questions about the interwoven worlds of work and family, the child's own perspective must be determined as well.

AN ECOLOGICAL APPROACH TO CHILDREN'S PERCEPTIONS OF THE
WORLD

Rather than studying children within a scientific laboratory, the ecological approach to child development focuses on children in their natural environment (Bronfenbrenner, 1979; Kelly, 1968; Lewin, 1935,
1936, 1951; Moos, 1976; Trickett et al., 1972). The ecological principle
of *interdependence* assumes that all family members influence the developing child (Bloom-Feshbach et al., 1980; Bryant, 1979; Kellam et
al., 1977). In addition the family functions as an interacting system, a
coordinated team, and any one player's actions affect the team as a
whole. Thus, children's perceptions of family life are linked to their
place within the system (for example, as eldest child), as well as to
chains of events. For instance, parental work experience may influence
the parent's approach to child rearing, or the father's support of the
mother's employment may facilitate positive marital communication.
Inevitably, the child's perception of family life will be determined by,
and will also mediate, the mix of many factors such as these.

Children and their complex family units are in contact with other
important systems, such as neighborhoods, government programs, religious organizations, schools, and child-care settings. On an even larger
scale, macrostructural variables such as the family's place in society and
cultural (or subcultural) customs and beliefs also shape children's ways
of perceiving themselves and their opportunities.

Another ecological principle central to understanding children's views
is the concept of succession—of *development* or *history* (Trickett et al.,
1972). The child's capacity to comprehend the world shifts qualitatively
throughout development. The young infant is only able to experience
the world in a primitive somatic fashion, using touch, taste, and smell
to learn about the environment. Parental employment at this stage, for
example, is not comprehensible for the child; only the very physical
event of parental separation is experienced. The kindergarten child is
able to understand the world in a more differentiated way. Thinking in
concrete terms, the child at this age understands that parental work
determines whether the parent is home or not home, that parental work
is how money is obtained, and so forth. Similar to and intertwined with
the continued development of the child's cognitive world is a progression
in affective maturity, as the child's egocentric orientation gradually shifts
toward a greater capacity to experience other people's perspectives and
needs. A 10-year-old may not only experience the frustration of an
absent parent, but may also understand the reasons for this absence,
such as financial necessity or even the intrinsic motivation provided by

a fulfilling job. In the years between the start of school and adolescence, children become exposed to the wider world of peers and adults outside the family, such as teachers and community leaders. It is during this stage that they experiment with different ways of acting upon the world and in general learn a great deal more about how the world operates. It is only the adolescent, however, who has available the highest-level cognitive structure of "formal operations"—the ability to abstract and utilize thoughts in acting upon other thoughts. Such adult cognitive processes permit comparison and integration of such concepts as how parental occupational experience might relate to one's own vocational aspirations.

This suggestive sketch of cognitive and affective change is provided simply to remind the reader of the complex qualitative differences in the capacity to perceive the world that accompany normal development.[1] In addition the child's cognitive and affective development occurs within a particular period in the family's life course. On a broader level the family itself exists within a given historical context. Dominant historical events such as war, economic hardship, or cultural conflict shape the many factors that in turn influence children's perceptions of the world.

SOCIOECONOMIC STATUS

There are few dimensions of life more ubiquitous in influence than a person's socioeconomic status or social standing (Bernstein, 1964; Havighurst, 1976; Hess, 1970; Miller and Swanson, 1958; Rubin, 1976; Sennett and Cobb, 1973). An individual's place in the stratification of society's resources and rewards is based on a wide spectrum of factors, including the more typical indices of education, occupation, and income, and less readily quantifiable variables such as "moral standards, family history, community participation, social skills, speech and physical appearance" (Coleman and Rainwater, 1978:22).

Thus, children's views of the world clearly are shaped by the social standing of the families in which they grow up. But research on children's families employs a variety of indices to measure socioeconomic status. And, typically, the fine-grained continuum of social position is oversimplified into such categories as professional, middle, lower, or working classes, or is based upon the educational and occupational status of only one parent. While acknowledging these limitations, we present findings in terms of the class categories selected by investigators themselves.

---

[1] See Furth (1980) for a more complete presentation of the Piagetian approach to children's views of society.

ORGANIZATION OF THE RESEARCH LITERATURE

Our presentation of the research literature is organized around several major work patterns: Maternal employment, paternal employment, unemployment and low-income jobs, and teenage employment are discussed in turn as we examine what is known about how these variations in labor force participation influence children's perceptions of the world. The section on unemployment and low-income work departs from a focus on the experience of work per se and emphasizes job instability and the effects of financial stress.

To ease the reader's task of sifting through often complicated research findings, each section begins with a brief list of highlighted conclusions. In addition, each section ends with a summary of the most important generalizations emerging from the literature. It should be noted that few investigations to date have utilized the ecological approach emphasized here and that a variety of other limitations flaw the research literature. However, in an heuristic spirit, we review existing findings to pinpoint issues for future exploration. Following the literature review, a section on methodology discusses what future researchers must consider in studying the relationship between work and family life.

RESEARCH ON MATERNAL EMPLOYMENT

Popular debate about working mothers and their children has inspired a large body of research. Before the late 1960s when the image of the employed mother gained wider visibility and acceptance, research focused on potential problems created by maternal employment. More recently, investigators have addressed both the benefits and pitfalls of having a working mother. There has been growing recognition that characteristics of the mother's work and her satisfaction with it may be as important as whether she works. Further, the notion that how the children will fare depends on mother alone is no longer widely accepted.

The research literature examining the effects of maternal employment on children's views roughly falls into the following four areas: (1) children's views of their parents; (2) children's views of themselves (self-concept or self-esteem); (3) children's vocational, occupational, or educational expectations or aspirations; and (4) children's sex-role attitudes and perceptions of men and women. First, we highlight briefly what we know about each of these aspects of children's perceptions of the world. Then we review the supporting literature in each area in somewhat more detail. Where possible, we focus on preschool children first and move along a developmental continuum to adolescence.

Children's Views of Their Parents

• Maternal employment has different effects on the perceptions of girls and boys. Daughters hold their mothers in higher esteem when mothers are employed. Sons from families lower in the socioeconomic spectrum view their fathers more negatively when mothers work.

• When mothers work because of personal choice, their daughters view both parents with more admiration.

• When mothers are employed, their children's perceptions of parental child-rearing roles differ only in the area of authority and discipline.

Research evidence supports the popular assumption that having a mother who works outside the home influences how a child perceives both father and mother. Not surprisingly, maternal employment appears to have a greater effect on feelings about the parent of the same sex as the child (i.e., on girls' perceptions of their mothers and on boys' perceptions of their fathers). Daughters' admiration for their mothers is heightened when their mothers are employed. This finding has been noted for kindergarten girls (S. M. Miller, 1975), as well as for girls between the ages of 9 and 16 (Kappel and Lambert, 1972). Thus, participation in the labor force appears to enhance the mother's image, making her a more positive role model for her daughter. In contrast a son's esteem for his mother does not appear to depend upon her work status.

Maternal employment is more likely to affect boys' evaluations of their fathers. However, for boys the impact differs on the basis of the family's standing in the socioeconomic spectrum. Boys from lower-class families evaluate their fathers more negatively when their mothers are employed. In contrast, boys from families higher on the socioeconomic ladder view their fathers similarly whether or not their mothers work outside the home. This finding has been replicated in several studies of preadolescents and adolescents (Douvan, 1963; Kappel and Lambert, 1972; McCord et al., 1963; Propper, 1972). One possible explanation is that in less affluent families, sons may regard maternal employment as a reflection of their father's inability to provide adequate support and thus a violation of the traditional stereotype of the father as breadwinner.

Even when no social-class effects are noted, mothers' motivations for working may affect their children's perceptions. For example, Kappel and Lambert (1972) found that when mothers chose to work for self-oriented reasons (i.e. because they wanted to work), their daughters viewed both parents more positively than when mothers' motivations were family-oriented, (i.e., because of financial reasons). The element of personal choice in the decision to work may cause a mother less tension between work and family roles. That lack of tension may be reflected in more positive parent-child and marital relationships. Another possible explanation is that the mother who chooses to work for its intrinsic satisfaction may provide a more competent and hence more admirable model of adulthood. Similarly, the father whose wife chooses to work may present a more secure and flexible parental image.

Having a mother who is employed affects not only how children feel about their parents but also how they view their parents' behavior. One striking conclusion is that children of employed and nonemployed mothers differ in their perceptions of only one aspect of child-rearing behavior—parental authority and discipline. For example, nursery-school-age sons of employed mothers saw their fathers as more punitive than all other groups of children did (Gold and Andres, 1978a). Elementary- and junior-high-school-age children of varying racial and socioeconomic backgrounds viewed their employed mothers as more consistent (Woods, 1972) and more severe (Franke, 1972) in their discipline. While the explanation for these findings remains speculative, it appears that maternal employment affects children's role perceptions in a domain that has traditionally been regarded as paternal—discipline. As mothers deviate from traditional roles outside the home, it is not surprising that their child-rearing role also changes.

Our discussion of children's perceptions of their parents concludes with an important cautionary note: A child's family status—whether parents are married, separated, or divorced—will likely affect how parents and family are viewed. For example, Rosenthal's (1979) study of junior high school students found that fathers in two-parent families were seen as more loving and casual, divorced fathers were viewed as less demanding, and separated fathers were seen as more rejecting than fathers in other family conditions. Because children's achievement, occupational aspirations, and self-concept are all related to their perceptions of parents, family status appears to have far-reaching effects. Therefore, although the Rosenthal study does not find differences attributable to parental work, it nonetheless illustrates the need to consider employment effects within the context of family structure. The growing body of research on the perceptions of children in divorced and nondivorced families (e.g., Camara, 1980; Kurdek and Siesky, 1980) is potentially relevant here, although links to the world of work have yet to be made explicit.

Children's Views of Themselves

- For preschool-age children of both sexes, there are no differences in self-concept based on maternal employment status.
- For older children of employed mothers, self-concept depends upon mothers' type of work, reasons for working, and work satisfaction.

Children's self-concept or self-esteem is difficult to assess, as there is much disagreement about what it is and how best to measure it (see Harter, 1981; Rosenberg, 1979). Even when self-concept is considered apart from the effects of parental work status, there are conflicting findings on the effects of race, socioeconomic status, sex, and age (see Maccoby and Jacklin, 1974, and Wylie, 1979, for reviews of the literature).

Nevertheless, some researchers have attempted to disentangle the effects of maternal labor force participation on the self-esteem of children of various ages. For the preschool child, having a mother who works does not appear either to enhance or diminish self-esteem (Al-Timini, 1977; S. M. Miller, 1975). For older children, however, conclusions are harder to draw. Not surprisingly, the way children feel about themselves seems to depend more on the *nature* of mother's work and how mother *feels* about working than on the simple fact that she is employed. For example, Kappel and Lambert (1972) found that 9- to 16-year-old daughters with full-time working mothers had more positive views of themselves than did daughters whose mothers were not employed. However, this link between maternal work and daughters' positive self-esteem was limited to employed mothers who were self-motivated in seeking work, satisfied with working, or whose work was professional in nature.

Although T. W. Miller's (1975) study of maternal employment and children's self-esteem does not focus explicitly on the nature of work, his comparison of black inner-city and white suburban samples may, in fact, have tapped differences in work motivation and satisfaction. Miller found that the self-esteem of 12- to 15-year-old black inner-city boys and girls was lower when their mothers worked full time, while the self-esteem of white suburban children was not affected by maternal employment. One might surmise that in the former group, mothers work because of harsh economic reality, most likely at low-status jobs that offer meager wages and few other rewards. We can only speculate about the complex chain of influence that extends from these characteristics of the mother's work to the child's poor self-image. Although Miller's findings do not shed light on these intervening factors, they suggest the need for further research on how parents' reasons for working and the characteristics of their jobs affect children's views.

Children's Vocational Aspirations

• In general, girls of all ages whose mothers are employed seek to combine work and family life when they reach adulthood. However, employment plans also depend upon mothers' values and the characteristics of mothers' jobs.
• The educational aspirations of adolescent boys and girls with employed mothers depend upon the nature of fathers' work and community characteristics.

It is commonly assumed that a person's hopes and goals for the future begin taking shape in childhood and are molded at least in part by family experience. One important question is whether growing up with a mother who works affects children's future plans. Researchers have attempted to answer this question, focusing on two areas: vocational and educational aspirations.

Since the fact of maternal employment reflects a shift in the female role model, daughters' vocational goals have received the most attention. Across the age spectrum, daughters of employed mothers aspire, like their mothers, to combine work and family life (Hartley, 1960, elementary school girls; Banducci, 1967, high school seniors).

There are some intriguing exceptions to this tendency for girls to model themselves after their mothers. Klecka and Hiller (1977) and Macke and Morgan (1978) describe a "negative modeling" process. The theory is that when mothers appear dissatisfied or inadequate in their roles, whether employed or unemployed, their daughters no longer strive to emulate them. Macke and Morgan's study of black and white high school girls demonstrates this process. They found that black girls did *not* aspire to work when their mothers were employed in blue collar, low-status jobs, such as cleaning or housekeeping. Thus, a simple view of maternal employment status—participation or nonparticipation in the work force—obscures the complicated context in which children view the meaning of their mothers' work.

Macke and Morgan's results also reflect the complex factors involved in the shaping of a child's goals. Both black and white girls whose mothers worked were especially likely to plan to work themselves when their mothers held traditional values. The authors explain that when employed mothers hold traditional values, this family-centeredness leads them to spend more time with their daughters. When the employed mother is more available, she becomes a more positive role model.

Regardless of whether or not one agrees with Macke and Morgan's modeling conclusions, their data eloquently highlight the dynamic interweaving of cultural, familial, and occupational characteristics underlying children's attitudes and aspirations. Even when maternal employment status is not considered, differences between the views of black and white teenage girls are noteworthy. Black girls were more work-oriented ("planning to work all the time") than white girls ("planning to work after the children enter grade school")(Macke and Morgan, 1978:192). These differences reflect experiences with and attitudes toward working mothers with young children. White girls also were more likely to indicate that they had not given much prior consideration to issues of combining work and family roles. Those whites who did plan to seek employment had career ambitions; they expected to attend college or graduate school in preparation for their careers. For black girls, employment plans were not necessarily linked to careers.

In contrast to the research on vocational plans, studies of educational aspirations have included children of both sexes. The implication that maternal employment may affect the strivings of boys as well as girls may have arisen from early indications that, in some circumstances, mothers' work is associated with decrements in sons' achievement (See Chapter 5 by Bronfenbrenner and Crouter in this volume for more details).

Two large-scale studies of high school students provide most of what we know about maternal employment and children's educational aspirations. Roy's (1963) research points out the need to consider the community in which the family lives before drawing conclusions. He found that in a rural community both sons and daughters whose mothers were employed were more likely to plan on attending college than children of nonemployed mothers. In contrast, sons and daughters of employed mothers living in an urban area had lower educational aspirations than their counterparts whose mothers were not employed. Whether this finding reflects the particular communities sampled or more general urban-rural differences is not yet known.

The family's position in society also has significance for children's aspirations. For example, Banducci (1967) found that when fathers were laborers or skilled workers, their high-school-age sons and daughters had *higher* educational goals, as long as mothers also worked. In contrast, when fathers' work was professional in nature, their sons and daughters had *lower* educational goals if mothers were employed as well. It is possible that the diminished educational aspirations of sons of employed mothers in professional families reflect a cohort phenomenon. In the 1960s many children of upper middle-class nontraditional families eschewed college, choosing instead to pursue careers calling for craftsmanship or proximity to the land. Another possibility is that the lower educational expectations of daughters of employed women in the professional class reflect an identification with the mother's status relative to that of the father. In other words, in contrast to the high prestige and status of the father's profession, the mother's occupation, with its lesser rewards, may present an unattractive goal. Baruch (1976) also draws this status-differential conclusion. These speculative explanations for Banducci's counter-intuitive but provocative findings call for further investigation.

It is important for the reader to recognize that research on children's aspirations would be enriched by including both a developmental perspective and knowledge of the mother's employment history at various points in the child's life. Choices for schooling, such as subjects to be pursued or extracurricular activities, often are made before the child reaches adolescence, thus providing a basis for further achievement. Hence, *when* a mother enters the labor force, as well as her motivations and other factors, may help shape her children's views of their vocational and educational futures.

Children's Sex-Role Perceptions and Attitudes

• In general, boys and girls of all ages are more egalitarian in their sex-role attitudes when their mothers are employed. However, the effects of maternal employment also depend upon the mother's work satisfaction and the family's socioeconomic position.

• Older children and children from middle-class or upper-class families have broader sex-role perceptions.

Children of different ages, ethnic backgrounds, and socioeconomic circumstances differ in their perceptions of how each sex behaves. In general, younger children, who think in concrete terms, are more likely than older children to hold rigid sex-role stereotypes. Older children benefit from the flexibility permitted by abstract reasoning; they have the tools for understanding how family life styles differ. As they grow closer to their peers, children also gain greater access to the world beyond the family. Adolescents in particular are exposed to a range of alternative models and social norms (Cicone and Ruble, 1978; Marantz and Mansfield, 1977). Like their parents, children of families at the lower end of the economic spectrum tend to hold more traditional sex-role definitions, with greater differentiation between male and female roles, than their middle-class counterparts (Kohn, 1963). In addition, ethnic differences in sex-role perceptions have been widely noted, although these may be confounded by the effects of social class (Romer and Cherry, 1980).

Because an employed mother provides a nontraditional role model, her children's definitions of sex roles and beliefs about males and females may be less traditional as well. The evidence supporting this notion is quite striking, regardless of the child's age. For example, Gold and Andres (1978a) found that in middle-class two-parent families, preschool sons whose mothers were employed had broader sex-role conceptions; they were less likely than sons of nonemployed mothers to indicate a preference for traditionally masculine activities. Daughters of employed mothers made longer lists than any other group of children of activities that they considered appropriate for each sex, also suggesting a broadening of sex-role beliefs. In another nursery school group, Gold et al. (1979) found that both sons and daughters of employed mothers were more likely than children of nonemployed mothers to list the same activities as appropriate for both sexes. Similarly, S. M. Miller (1975) found that kindergarten girls whose mothers were employed held less traditional sex-role perceptions in general, as well as less stereotyped views of their parents' roles. All these studies suggest the conclusion that maternal employment fosters broader sex-role conceptions.

With elementary school children the pattern of results remains consistent: Children of employed mothers hold fewer sex-role stereotypes. This conclusion holds true for whites as well as blacks (Brookins, 1978: 6- to 8-year-olds; Hartley, 1960: 5-, 8- and 11-year-olds). In general, when an employed mother feels happy about her role, her children are even more egalitarian in their sex-role beliefs; when a working mother is dissatisfied with her role—as is often the case for working-class mothers of sons—her children hold more sex-role stereotypes (Gold and Andres, 1978b). Subjective experience is important from the child's perspective as well; daughters who feel more positively about their mother's life style, whatever that may be, show less sex-role stereotyping (Marantz and Mansfield, 1977: 5- to 11-year-old girls).

It is also interesting to note that children of employed mothers are less likely than children of nonemployed mothers to believe that women find going to work unpleasant (Hartley, 1960). In contrast, having an employed mother seems to foster the belief that men find work unpleasant. However, once again there is evidence that the *nature* of parents' work affects children's views; children from families higher in the socioeconomic spectrum view work as more pleasant for both men and women. Presumably, the parents of these children do indeed hold more rewarding jobs.

While the results of the Hartley study are two decades old, a more recent study by Dellas et al. (1979) further supports the conclusion that socioeconomic differences as well as developmental factors help shape children's attitudes toward parental work. Dellas and colleagues found that preadolescents (aged 9 to 11) whose fathers held professional jobs felt positively toward maternal employment regardless of whether their mothers worked. For children whose fathers held managerial positions, the picture was more complicated: Those with employed mothers favored maternal employment, while those with nonemployed mothers were divided in their beliefs. Differences in attitudes were once again more clear-cut in children whose fathers held working-class jobs: Children from these families favored the work status held by their own mothers. Regardless of the kind of jobs their fathers held, children of employed mothers cited financial factors and women's rights to choose their life styles as reasons why women should or should not choose to work. In contrast, children from families in which mothers were not employed were more likely to offer the traditional view that mothers belong at home with their children.

Interestingly, when Dellas et al. repeated their study with adolescents, they no longer found differences in attitudes between children of employed and nonemployed mothers. The authors concluded that attitudes of preadolescent children were more affected by maternal behavior because developmentally linked concrete reasoning made it difficult to go beyond their own family experiences. In contrast, adolescents were able to consider sex roles more objectively. Dellas et al. hypothesized that preadolescents from professional families were an exception to this general rule because they may have a broader notion of what work means; these children likely had greater social opportunity and exposure as well as experience with mothers who work in a volunteer capacity. We might hypothesize that these children may hold more positive views of work life in general, given the extent of rewards and resources such as pay and status that accompany their father's job.

Although Dellas et al. suggest that maternal employment has little if any effect on the sex-role beliefs of adolescents, Gold and Andres (1978c) found that 14- to 16-year-olds whose mothers are employed do hold less traditional views. Consistent with the data based on younger children, Gold and Andres note that adolescent girls generally have less traditional attitudes than boys, with boys from working-class families retaining the most traditional views of all. Thus, the fact that a mother works, along with other job and family characteristics such as work satisfaction and the family's social standing, shapes the development of the sex-role perceptions of both boys and girls.

Research on Maternal Employment: Summary

The literature on all four aspects of children's views suggests that the effects of maternal employment are mediated by a complex network of variables, ranging from characteristics of the individual (sex, developmental level) to characteristics of family (family status, values) and work (job prestige, job satisfaction, motivation for working) to larger societal dimensions (socioeconomic status, nature of the community, race). With the exception of sex-role beliefs, which are consistent across age groups, developmental differences have received scant attention. In particular we know little about younger children's views of work and the processes through which occupational goals, so crucial for adult achievement, are shaped.

Nevertheless, some interesting trends do emerge from this review. Maternal employment appears to have more clear-cut positive effects for daughters than for sons, in terms of the child's self-concept and the esteem in which parents are held. In addition, girls whose mothers are employed are more likely to aspire to combine work and family life, except when their mothers hold low-status jobs or are unhappy in their roles. Indeed, several conflicting findings about maternal employment effects can be sorted out when mothers' reasons for and satisfaction with working are considered. The issues of work motivation and nature of job are inextricably intertwined with the family's position in society. In poorer families, in which mothers are more likely to work for financial reasons in low-prestige and often unrewarding jobs, children, especially sons, appear to have diminished views of themselves and their fathers.

This review also highlights the importance of further examining children's perceptions of parental discipline when their mothers are employed and raises the question of whether *perceptions* of parental discipline are accompanied by actual changes in the disciplinary practices of employed mothers and their spouses. This is only one of many interesting questions about the effects of maternal employment that await additional study.

RESEARCH ON PATERNAL EMPLOYMENT

Only in the last decade have social scientists begun actively to consider the father's influence on child development and family functioning. It is not surprising, then, that there are no studies that span the entire set of linkages from paternal work to family process to the child's perceptions. However, some research linking paternal employment to family functioning suggests that the father and his work help shape the child's views. The major findings of this line of inquiry are highlighted below, followed by a fuller discussion of the research evidence:

• Little is known about the direct effects of paternal labor force participation on children's views.
• The father's child-rearing style is influenced by the degree of occupational self-direction and substantive complexity in his job.
• When fathers are supportive, mothers function better as parents and are more satisfied with their work.

Research by Melvin Kohn and his colleagues (Kohn, 1969, 1977; Kohn and Carroll, 1960; Kohn and Schooler, 1973) indicates how characteristics of the father's job (notably, the degree of occupational self-direction and substantive complexity it offers) are linked to his child-rearing style. Self-directed, complex jobs are more challenging and offer opportunities for flexible thought and independent action, in contrast to highly supervised jobs that require the completion of repetitive, simple tasks. The findings demonstrate that fathers with self-directed, complex jobs value independent thinking in their children and rely on reason in their disciplinary techniques. Fathers with jobs affording less self-direction and substantive complexity tend to disregard the intent behind the child's misbehavior when meting out discipline (Gecas and Nye, 1974). It is important to note here that low-autonomy, low-complexity jobs are not limited to the world of blue-collar work. Many white-collar, middle-class jobs also meet these criteria. In addition it might be noted that while certain characteristics will attract or qualify men for a given job, over time the job itself has a shaping influence on the man and affects his child-rearing style. In sum, while Kohn's research demonstrates that paternal occupational experience significantly influences family relationships, it unfortunately does not include the final link that is relevant to our paper: how paternal work experience affects the child's perception of the world.

The Kohn approach to studying work and family emphasizes the connection between parental work and patterns of child rearing. The father also influences the interplay between work and family in other ways. Carew (1978) has shown that the father's support of maternal employment is a crucial factor in the mother's job satisfaction and feelings about combining work and family life. Bloom-Feshbach (1979) reported that new fathers with more autonomy in their jobs and hence more flexible work schedules experienced less conflict in their coordination of employment and family responsibilities. Pleck and Lang (1978) have found that, contrary to expectation, men derive a great deal of satisfaction from their participation in family activities, in fact more satisfaction than they derive from work. Some jobs, because of long hours, night shifts, or travel, may keep fathers from fully engaging in family life. This may not only diminish the father's life satisfaction, but may also make it difficult for him to provide adequate support for the mother. Several studies have indicated that wives make better mothers (e.g., their caretaking and feeding improves) when their husbands are supportive (Lewis and Feiring, 1978; Pederson et al., 1977).

One approach to the study of the father's role in child development has been the research on father-absence effects. Many of these effects are deleterious, although researchers have frequently confounded the loss of the father's financial contribution with the loss of his emotional support. One exception is a study by Reuter and Biller (1973), which found that the father's perceived *psychological* absence may be as problematic in its impact on the child as his actual physical absence. This suggests the possibility that the work-absent father may have a negative influence on children's views of the world—a hypothesis that future research can test.

Research on Paternal Employment Effects: Summary

Although we know little about how paternal work directly affects children's views, increased research attention is beginning to focus on the father's impact on family functioning. Research has also shown that self-directed, complex jobs foster less authoritarian modes of child rearing. As yet we can only infer the impact this has on children's views. Studies of the father's role in the family system indicate how paternal support of the mother helps her perform effectively both at home and at work. Because the father's role has been a comparatively neglected area of family research, it is a promising direction for future investigation.

UNEMPLOYMENT AND LOW-INCOME WORK

Parental job loss and family poverty unquestionably influence children's views of the world. The research that addresses this issue differs substantially from the more experimental studies on the effects of parental employment. In some instances a case-study approach is used (e.g., Rubin, 1976), while other research employs historical analyses (e.g., Elder, 1974, 1979). The commonality across studies is an interest in underlying attitudes and in placing the child within a broad social context. Such factors are sometimes ignored in the literature on parental employment. The major conclusions of the literature on economic deprivation are listed below:

- In general, good family relationships may mitigate the effects of economic hardship.
- Children who live in extreme poverty may develop negative views of themselves and the world.
- The psychological experience of feeling poor may be as important a determinant of children's perceptions as actual poverty.

The most dramatic and informative body of research in this area is the work of Glen Elder and his colleagues on the impact of the Great Depression (Elder, 1974, 1979; Elder and Rockwell, 1979). Using longitudinal archival data, Elder has gleaned a great deal of information about how families were affected by the privations of the depression. By comparing the experiences of different age groups of children during the depression years, Elder has produced data highlighting the importance of the child's sex, developmental level, and family relationships in determining the impact of stressful economic conditions.

Elder found that psychological health suffered most when children were exposed to economic hardship from infancy; those who were adolescents during the depression generally fared better. Adverse effects were especially strong for boys. These children saw their families as insecure and lacking warmth (Elder, cited in Runck, 1979:48): "Their world view was distinguished by a sense of victimization and meaninglessness." They had less confidence in themselves as well as a more passive, less goal-oriented attitude toward achievement and life in general.

However, Elder also found that predepression family relationships usually moderated the impact of the Great Depression. For example, a good marital relationship prior to the depression strengthened a father's relationships with children of both sexes. In contrast a poor marital relationship drew daughters closer to their mothers but increased the distance between fathers and sons. Other researchers also describe how unemployed husbands sometimes lost the respect of family members (e.g., Cavan, 1959). Furstenberg (1973:353) elaborates: "While occupational failure did not guarantee loss of the father's esteem within the family, unless efforts were made to explain, discount, or neutralize the misfortune of the breadwinner, children were likely to resent his economic failure."

Research on families in the 1960s and 1970s supports the findings of the depression studies. Schwartz and Henderson (1964) interviewed adolescent boys (aged 13 to 19) from intact black families in which fathers had been unemployed for at least six months. They found that roughly half the sample of 130 teenagers viewed their mothers as the dominant parent and their fathers as weak, while the other half perceived their fathers as strong, despite the fact that they were not providing economic support for the family. Teenagers with "strong" fathers considered themselves more obedient and attended church more regularly. In contrast, boys from mother-dominant families saw themselves as relatively powerless and believed that their own prospects for securing and maintaining steady employment were bleak. Results from a small-scale participant observational study of black families living in public housing again highlights how family relationships affect children's perceptions of paternal unemployment. Schulz (1968, 1969) distinguishes three paternal patterns in these intact, economically deprived families: (1) monogamous fathers who provide respectable family models for their children; (2) fathers who are emotionally expressive and gain authority by virtue of their success at manipulating the environment through gambling or discreet extramarital affairs, for example; and (3) fathers who are blatantly sporadic in their family allegiance and thus unsuccessful both at home and in the outside world. The first two types of fathers are perceived favorably by their children, and their current inability to support the family economically is understood and accepted. The third type of father, however, is viewed as weak, and when unemployed, he is resented, especially by his teenage sons.

A more recent study by David Caplovitz (1979) looks at families across the economic spectrum. Caplovitz's major investigation of the 1974-1975 recession focuses on how families were affected by the recession and by rising inflation in general. Economic pressures resulted in both positive and negative effects, with some spouses pulling together (1979:136): "Some 19% reported a mixture of good and bad consequences for their marriage, and 14 percent reported only bad consequences. Those most vulnerable to inflation crunch and the recession were those whose marriages were likely to be affected, and chiefly for the worse." Caplovitz (1979:137) found that the parent-child relationship was also affected by economic strain as "many parents (43 percent of the total) were forced to deny their children things they wanted because of the economic pinch."

The effects of such denial on children's views likely depend on several mediating factors. If the degree of deprivation is not excessive, then the child may develop coping mechanisms to deal with these problems. This in turn may foster positive views of parents, self, and the world in general. However, when children's needs are denied excessively, it may diminish the prestige and authority of the father (or mother) and also deprive the family of positive shared activities. Young children may not understand the reasons their needs are being frustrated and may be less able to cope than older children, who can comprehend explanations. Again, the quality of relationships in the family system will affect the impact of poverty and job loss, but pressures nevertheless are greatest for families on the lower end of the socioeconomic spectrum. Children from such families generally marry at younger ages, which can diminish marital stability. And they obtain jobs with fewer rewards and resources, which can foster marital tension. Thus, the family of low socioeconomic status has fewer financial and psychological resources with which to cope with economic strain (Furstenberg, 1973).

Rubin's (1976) analysis of working-class life distinguishes two separate family patterns—the stable, comparatively economically sound group and the unstable, more unpredictable, and more impoverished group. Children in this latter group are most vulnerable to the negative effects of poverty and job loss. Rubin (1976:32) interviewed one mother about her childhood: "My father did so many things, I can't tell you his occupation. I guess he was a painter, but he did a lot of other stuff, too. It seemed like most of the time he was out of work." In many cases joblessness led to drinking, unstable family relations, and violence, as the same woman reported (1976:32): "When my father got drunk, he'd get mean and pick on whoever was around. When I was about twelve, he came home roaring drunk one night and picked me up like a sack of potatoes and threw me right across the room. My mother stood there and watched, and she never did a thing."

Anecdotal reports such as these are buttressed by statistical evidence. Child abuse is much more common in low-socioeconomic-status groups, especially among those under economic strain (Garbarino, 1976; Pelton, 1978). In a study of fathers whose children's mean age was only 11 months, Bloom-Feshbach (1979) found a strong correlation between verbally and physically harsh paternal behavior and lack of income, even after the variance due to educational and occupational status was partialled out. Thus, financial stress, quite apart from social standing, may strain the parent-child relationship. The effects of physical and emotional abuse and neglect on children's views of the world have been studied by clinicians, as well as researchers. Abusive experiences have negative influences on children's self-concept, their sense of efficacy, and their attitudes toward parents and family life (Martin and Rode-heffer, 1976; Reidy et al., 1980; Segal, 1979).

The effects of economic stress on children need not be as extreme as physical maltreatment to affect children's views negatively. Lefkowitz et al. (1979) reported that children suffering economic deprivation are more depressed—they are unhappier and have a more passive stance toward the world. Further, these children are higher on the external side of locus of control, perceiving life as governed by external events over which they have little potential influence.

The distinction between consequences following from objective states of unemployment and low income and the psychological interpretation of these events (in other words, *being* poor versus *feeling* poor) has been emphasized in much of the research on poverty and family life. Caplovitz stresses these two dimensions throughout his book and, for example, finds that (1979:155) "our measure of subjective inflation crunch, the degree of hurting caused by inflation, was even more strongly related to these measures of mental stress than the objective fact of keeping up with or falling behind rising prices." Similarly, children of seasonal workers who expect periodic parental unemployment will not be so adversely affected—the family system is prepared to cope with the event.

In addition to psychological and family factors, the duration of job loss or poverty is also crucial. Indeed, the long-term effects of job loss are noteworthy. Ferman (cited in Blehar, 1979:421) noted that "job loss in many cases is only mildly traumatic compared to what follows— searching for new jobs, dashing of hopes that the old employer will call again, being rebuffed by new prospective employers. These are the events that try the patience and sanity of most workers." In order to assess the effects of job loss and poverty on children, we must consider their degree and duration within the overall context of the family's economic and psychological resources.

Unemployment and Low-Income Work: Summary

The studies reviewed in this section address the effects of unemployment and poverty on children's views. Historical studies of the Great Depression and recent research on the 1974-1975 recession show that parental job instability and low-income conditions may have either positive or negative effects on children's views. In meeting the challenge of economic privation, families may draw together and children may develop a greater capacity for self-reliance. On the other hand, especially with chronic poverty, family tension may increase and children may develop depressed, victimized views of self and world. In these studies the *psychological* experience of poverty or job instability was crucial, as was the influence of supportive family ties.

Unemployment and inflation rates currently are increasing at an alarming pace, so that burdens previously experienced by low-socioeconomic-status families soon may be shared by many others. These trends underscore the importance of studying the effects of unemployment and low-income work on children and their perceptions of the world.

CHILDREN AS WORKERS

Having seen how parents' work and unemployment can shape children's views, we now turn our focus to children as workers. More teenagers than ever before are combining school with part-time employment. In 1940 only 4 percent of 16-year-old boys and 17 percent of 16-year-old girls attending school also worked part time. By 1970 these figures increased to 27 percent for boys and 16 percent for girls. Current estimates are that 50 percent of all high school juniors and seniors and 30 percent of all ninth- and tenth-grade students work for pay at some time during the school year. Also, students are working longer hours: 56 percent of 16-year-old working males and 46 percent of 16-year-old working females spent more than 14 hours a week at their jobs in 1970.

For many years, interest in adolescent behavior and attitudes has centered on the worlds of family, school, and peers. How does participation in a fourth setting—the workplace—affect adolescents' attitudes? Despite the attention that teenage work and rising youth unemployment have received from national commissions, such as the President's Science Advisory Committee, and from the general public, little systematic research examines how employment and unemployment shape teenagers' views of the world. Instead, studies have focused on how working affects adolescents' grades and their likelihood of obtaining employment after high school. Several other important questions arise out of our interest in the overlapping worlds of work and family life. How do parental work status and work history affect children's employment practices? What are the effects of children's participation in the work force on their views of themselves, their parents, peers, and coworkers? In addition, how does teenage employment or unemployment affect perceptions of school and work itself?

The relationship between parents' and children's work patterns has received scant attention. We learned from a study conducted two decades ago that adolescent daughters of employed mothers are more likely to work than daughters of nonemployed mothers and from a more recent longitudinal investigation that teenage sons aspire to jobs like those their fathers hold (Parnes et al., 1970). It is also interesting to speculate about links between parental employment and the teenager's actual work status. It is possible that the work patterns of parents and adolescents are relatively independent; all teenagers who want or need extra money and have an opportunity to obtain a part-time job may actually work, regardless of their parents' employment status. More likely, however, the family's means of earning a living influences the teenager's work status. For example, families who own their own businesses or work on farms may rely on their children's help, with or without pay. Single-parent families or dual-worker families may rely on the oldest child for the care of younger siblings, precluding this child from participation in the paid labor force. Schulz (1969) vividly portrays the experience of eldest daughters of working mothers in poor ghetto families. These girls assume major child-care and household responsibility at a young age, often experiencing pride and self-efficacy at being trusted, along with resentment of the burden and loss of their own childhood freedoms. At the other end of the economic spectrum, teenagers with large allowances also may be less likely to work, since they already can afford to buy whatever they need or want. Parents' own experience as adolescents may be an additional factor; parents whose schooling suffered because they had to work during their teenage years might encourage their children to devote full time to studies. In contrast, in families in which the father is absent, or one or both parents is either unemployed or employed for very low wages, the teenager may play quite a central role in the family economy. Indeed, with the rise in teenage pregnancy, teenagers themselves may function as household heads, responsible for supporting the family. In these situations, adolescent work becomes a necessity, and unemployment may have serious consequences. These issues are addressed in more detail toward the end of our discussion of children as workers. (See the subsection "Minority and Low-Income Youth.")

One ongoing research effort, the "Project for the Study of Adolescent Work" at the University of California, Irvine, provides much of what we know about the impact of work experience on teenagers' views of the world (Greenberger and Steinberg, 1980; Greenberger et al., 1980). This pioneering inquiry into the relatively unexplored field of adolescent employment has some methodological limitations and has not been replicated by other investigators. Therefore, although we discuss this series of studies in some detail, the generalizations emerging from it must be considered tentative.

In the "Project for the Study of Adolescent Work," tenth and eleventh graders were divided into three groups: students who were working in their first paid part-time jobs (Group 1), students who had not worked but were looking for jobs (Group 2), and students who had neither worked nor were looking for jobs (Group 3). This design separates effects due to working (Group 1 versus Groups 2 and 3) from effects due to motivation for seeking work (Groups 1 and 2 versus Group 3). Adolescents in all three groups were asked about their attitudes toward school and work, their educational plans, and the quantity and quality of their relationships with parents, peers, and co-workers. In addition some students were observed at work and others were interviewed along with their parents. Generalizations emerging from the studies by Greenberger and her colleagues are listed below. These findings are then discussed in three categories: (1) perceptions of parents and others, (2) perceptions of self, and (3) perceptions of school and work.

- In general, a more advanced understanding of relationships at work may develop from teenage employment experience.
- Few differences have been found between teenage workers and nonworkers in the quality of family and peer relationships, although the sex of the worker may be important to consider.
- Relationships with co-workers are not as intimate as those with peers from school or with parents.
- Little is known about how adolescent work affects self-concept.
- Teenage workers tend to enjoy school less than students who are not employed.
- Youngsters who work feel they display different competencies at school and on the job.

Perceptions of Parents and Others

The investigators were interested in whether interactions with different types of people as well as the necessity constantly to switch roles from student to child to employee and back again would help the teenage worker develop a more advanced social understanding in the workplace (Steinberg et al., 1980). Anecdotal evidence from interviews with the teenage workers suggests that they were more sensitive to the needs of others, better able to communicate effectively, and more aware of the effects of social institutions on interpersonal interactions. Employed students seemed to appreciate the complex dynamics underlying interactions between workers and supervisors, workers and clients or customers, and among co-workers. Additional research will be needed to determine whether this sensitivity to others was indeed a result of the teenagers' employment, or a factor in helping them secure work to begin with. It also will be interesting to determine whether this enhanced social understanding extends beyond the workplace.

Another question addressed by Greenberger and her colleagues was how teenage work affects family relations and perceptions of parents. Although, in general, few differences between workers and nonworkers were noted, the results suggest that adolescents' perceptions of family relations may depend at least in part on whether the worker is male or female. For example, female workers and those seeking jobs reported spending less time in family-related activities and feeling less close to their parents than girls who had never worked. In contrast, male workers were more likely to discuss their personal problems with their fathers than were boys who were not employed (Greenberger et al., 1980). Parents of adolescent workers of both sexes still controlled the spending decisions of their children and were influential in determining how much of the teenager's salary should be saved. Thus, it appears that teenage workers do not perceive themselves as any more financially independent from their parents than nonworkers.

The "Project for the Study of Adolescent Work" also suggests that employment has little effect on peer relationships (Greenberger et al., 1980). Employed and nonemployed teenagers spent roughly the same amount of time with friends and reported similar feelings about peer relationships. In addition those adolescents who worked felt that relationships formed on the job were less significant than relationships formed in other settings. Thus, employed adolescents were able to maintain friendships with peers outside the workplace; relationships with co-workers seemed unlikely to replace or compete with longstanding friendships.

Several interesting hypotheses about adolescent workers and their parents were not addressed by Greenberger et al. For example, one possible beneficial effect of adolescent work on perceptions of parents is a sharing of the work role. That is, teenagers may have a better understanding of how work affects their parents' behavior at home. They also may feel closer to their parents because they participate in similar types of activities. In addition, more frequent interactions with many other adults may help teenagers realize that their parents are not the only representatives of the adult world. Hence, the teenage worker may gain a more realistic understanding of the diversity in adult behavior, values, and standards. These hypotheses about adolescent workers' views clearly warrant systematic study.

Perceptions of Self

One could imagine profound influences of work on the self-concept of the teenager. Juggling home life, peer relations, school, and work requires an assessment of goals and priorities. The adolescent who is able to meet the challenges of various competing demands may develop a sense of competence and positive self-esteem. However, the self-esteem of working teenagers may suffer if grades decline or if they feel cheated out of valued leisure time. The student's perceived ability on the job may also affect self-concept. Competency in the workplace may compensate for or complement performance in school. Earning a steady salary may afford adolescents a feeling of independence from their parents and a sense of internal control over events in their lives. Future investigations will help clarify these issues and raise additional questions.

Perceptions of School and Work

Unfavorable attitudes toward school may be either a cause or an effect of teenage employment. That is, students who dislike school may choose to work part time as an escape. Or the perceived benefits, both financial and personal, accrued from work may lead adolescents to devalue their school experiences. Greenberger and Steinberg (1980) found that workers were more likely than both groups of nonworkers to report that they did not enjoy school and were less likely to view school as a place where their competencies were expressed. In a comparison of the work and the school setting, employed teenagers thought that they were more able to help others, meet new people, and earn money at work, but that they were more able to learn new things and make their own decisions at school. Each setting, therefore, seems to offer unique advantages. The workplace seems to complement rather than replace school as a context in which certain needs can be satisfied. In addition, the lack of differences between unemployed job seekers and those not seeking jobs suggests that *actual* work, rather than the desire to seek work, leads to changes in attitudes toward school.

Minority and Low-Income Youth

Media attention to unemployment and underemployment among minority and low-income adolescents in the United States has brought these chronic problems before the public eye. In academic circles, considerable debate has centered around the question of whether economically disadvantaged youth reject the work ethic and achievement orientation of the larger society or whether they share the aspirations and values of more privileged teenagers; does high unemployment among teenagers from low-income families reflect a lack of striving or a lack of equal opportunity? Clearly, for teenagers from poor families entry into the world of work holds particular significance as well as stress. The earnings of many such youngsters form a necessary part of the family economy. How do these adolescents' educational and occupational goals correspond to the realities of joblessness and low-income work that they observe in their communities? Some general conclusions emerge:

• Minority and low-income teenagers share the high educational and occupational goals of other adolescents.
• Teenagers with work experience are more optimistic about their chances to reach their goals and are more realistic in setting educational and occupational goals.
• Minority adolescents may opt for unemployment or work in the street economy rather than accept low-level work.
• Adolescents who perceive the labor market more accurately are more successful in the labor market as young adults.

Several studies indicate that minority and low-income adolescents hold values and goals that are quite similar to their more well-to-do counterparts. In an investigation of nearly 600 black and Chicano young men (aged 16 to 19 and 20 to 24) from low-income families in Los Angeles, Bullock (1973) found that most youths aspire to graduate from school and find full-time employment; 48 percent of blacks and 42 percent of Chicanos hope to finish college before taking a job. Regardless of their family income, these young men want white-collar or professional work. However, those youths who are higher on the socioeconomic ladder and those who already have had some work experience are consistently more optimistic about their chances to actually achieve these goals; they not only aspire to high goals but expect to reach them.

Another study of male youths between the ages of 14 and 24, this one longitudinal, nationwide, and very large-scale, also notes the similarity in educational and occupational aspirations between black and white adolescents (Parnes et al., 1970). Parnes and his colleagues find some racial differences that are of interest: White youths who feel more positively about their high school experience are more likely to want professional or technical jobs. For black youths such career aspirations are unrelated to their perceptions of high school. Indeed, Bullock notes that although black teenagers in particular feel that job opportunities will depend on their educational background, they are decidedly pessimistic about developing successful careers. Bullock (1973:55) describes the youngsters' attitudes:

. . . pessimism is often related to a perception that their existing schooling is inadequate and that they may never have an opportunity to fill the gap. They suspect that their education has little or no substance in it and largely because they *do* associate prospects for success with a good education, they can become even more deeply pessimistic as they enter the labor market.

   While only a small proportion of teenagers cite economic motivation as the reason for their work goals, black youths are twice as likely as white youths to do so. Kohen and Parnes (1971) also note that while low-income white adolescents lowered their educational goals during the high school years, low-income black adolescents maintained high goals that were unrealistic because of the actual employment picture. Further, the longer white youths were out of school, the more stable their long-range career goals became; for black youths no longer in school, career goals grew more variable (Kohen and Andrisani, 1974). Regardless of racial background, however, high school students with more experience in the world of work were more likely to hold educational and occupational goals that were congruent with one another (Kohen et al., 1977). Thus, actual work experience appears related not only to a teenager's optimism about life prospects but also to realism in setting goals.

   It is also noteworthy, although not surprising, that black and Chicano youths, unlike whites, show little desire to follow in their fathers' career footsteps (Bullock, 1973). This finding parallels research on black teenage girls, which shows that when mothers hold low-status jobs, daughters do not plan to seek employment when they reach adulthood (Macke and Morgan, 1978). Minority teenagers also are generally less satisfied with their jobs and less attached to their current work than white adolescents (Parnes et al., 1970). Young blacks may wait for what they consider a good job, refusing low-level work, and opting instead for unemployment (Bullock, 1973; Schulz, 1969). Another attractive alternative for youths who are disenchanted with the traditional labor market is the street economy. According to Bullock (1973:99), "the subeconomy is probably the greatest single source of market income for young men in the central city." Gambling, drug traffic, illegal numbers, pimping, or prostitution may be seen as the most viable route through which economically disadvantaged adolescents can fulfill the high aspirations for money and prestige that they share with the rest of American youth.

   Both the Bullock study and the longitudinal effort by Parnes and his colleagues highlight the importance of adolescents' perceptions of the labor market. Indeed, the teenager with a more accurate understanding of the work world is likely to have higher earnings, a more prestigious job, and more rapid occupational advancement in young adulthood (Kohen et al., 1977). In general, however, knowledge of the world of work increases with age and with socioeconomic standing. Further, 14- to 17-year-olds with a clearer grasp of labor market information also have more specific career goals and higher work aspirations (Parnes et al., 1970). Bullock found that Chicano youths perceive the nature of job tasks and earnings more accurately than blacks. He speculates that this difference is attributable to the Chicanos' greater work experience.

Information about the world of work is likely more limited for children growing up in families with parents who are either unemployed or working in low-paying, unsatisfying jobs. Such parents themselves may lack a differentiated understanding of educational and job options, as well as job contacts that could help their children negotiate the ladder of opportunity. Thus far, there is little to indicate that school or government programs are successfully serving this function either. The disparity between the hopes of low-income teenagers and their realistic job possibilities remains distressing to contemplate.

Children as Workers: Summary

Despite the increasing prevalance of adolescents in the workplace, research has barely addressed the effects of this trend on the lives and views of the teenage worker. There is some indication that a better understanding of interpersonal relationships, at least in the workplace, may develop from the teenager's work experience. A finding that is more difficult to interpret is that school is less satisfying for the employed student. These findings from the "Project for the Study of Adolescent Work" clearly need to be supplemented by results from other studies.

In addition, future research must consider broader issues related to teenage employment. Adolescents, especially those from minority groups and low-income families, have difficulty obtaining jobs when they seek work. An important question is how early experiences of unemployment or of jobs that offer few rewards affect teenagers' future aspirations. Further, the social policy context of adolescent work is in flux, with the dismantling of federal job training programs, and with proposals to permit a subminimum wage for teenagers. Such macro issues as government policies, ethnic and socioeconomic differences, and demographic trends also deserve research attention.

METHODOLOGICAL ISSUES IN STUDYING WORK AND CHILDREN'S VIEWS

As our ecological framework suggests and our literature review illustrates, the myriad factors that combine to determine how parental work affects children's views are very difficult to disentangle. Few research investigations attempt to address the complex process through which children's perceptions develop by taking into consideration how the child lives within both the family system and society as a whole. All too frequently either work or family is treated as a unidimensional construct or placed within a limited cause and effect model, obscuring important qualifying factors and reciprocal influences.

Another problem affecting research in this area is the traditionally accepted limits of inquiry within individual social-scientific disciplines. Hence, sociologists have been apt to examine social roles and institutions, while psychologists traditionally have explored individual behavior and inner experience. Rarely have the internal and external perspectives of human life and child development been studied in concert. When attempts have been made, there have typically been losses in breadth or rigor. Consider, for example, the single case study, which sacrifices scientific rigor for depth. In contrast, more circumscribed studies of maternal employment utilize control groups, self-esteem scales, and so forth, but often fail to consider the broader social context.

Further, much of the research reviewed here does not place the meaning of parental employment, unemployment, and nonemployment within a cultural (or subcultural) context. The subculture within which the child grows helps determine values and attitudes about work and family life and even future aspirations. Surely ghetto children who observe the limited employment options of elders are restricted in their own hopes for the future (e.g., Ogbu, 1974, 1978).

In addition to considering the cultural context, research on work-family interactions often obscures social standing and family status (whether there are one or two parents). Although research designs cannot and need not systematically vary all these dimensions, some previous investigators have failed to even gather these very relevant basic demographic facts. Further, many studies in this field, notably studies of maternal work, focus solely on the mother without considering the father's behavior and views. As Kanter (1977:63) so aptly states, this body of research suffers from the "implication that a woman creates her marriage and raises her children alone."

Another important limitation in research on children's views of the world is the paucity of measures designed specifically for children. Many of the methods for assessing the child's self-concept or perceptions of the social world are derived from measures originally designed for adults. Further, those measures that have been adapted for children often do not take sufficient account of the qualitatively different cognitive capacities of children of different ages. Future investigators may need to consider utilizing different instruments to measure the same phenomenon in children at different developmental stages. Whereas an open-ended interview strategy may be appropriate for adolescents who can reflect on their experience, young children may require projective or other innovative techniques. For example, youngsters may be able to arrange pictures of family members to express their views of family relationships, while teenagers may be able to report family communication patterns. Clearly the development of new methods for assessing children's perceptions will be an important component of future research efforts.

Other methodological issues that primarily pertain to research on maternal employment effects deserve brief mention here (also see Hoffman, 1974). By definition, research on maternal employment compares children of employed mothers to children of nonemployed mothers. Some studies lack actual comparison groups and instead include only sons and daughters of employed mothers, or use maternal employment status as a variable within a correlational design. Without control groups, findings may be difficult to interpret. However, in this field, control groups are not easy to select, because the population of employed mothers differs from that of nonemployed mothers on demographic characteristics and perhaps personality and attitudinal dimensions as well. In their review of the literature, Siegel and Haas (1963) highlight the problem of finding matched pairs of employed and nonemployed mothers. Maternal employment is itself a value-laden issue about which most people in our society have formulated opinions. Personal biases on the part of both researchers and subjects, who may hold either favorable or unfavorable attitudes toward maternal employment, are a complicating factor in interpreting results. This is especially true when studying attitudes and perceptions, which are largely self-reported.

Studies on the effects of maternal employment are difficult to compare because definitions of work status vary considerably. In some research, criteria for inclusion in the employed group are undefined; presumably the mothers in this group are working for pay at the time of data collection. There is a similar problem with the definition of nonemployed mothers; too often this group becomes merely a residual category in which employment history remains unspecified. As we stress throughout this paper, other dimensions of the mother's work life may intervene in determining effects on the child. These work-related variables, which apply to research on paternal employment as well, include aspects of the job itself (e.g., job versus career, kind of work, level of autonomy or variety, prestige, location inside or outside the home, work schedule, employer adaptations to family status); aspects of the mother's employment history (the interval during which she has worked and age of child when she worked); and personal characteristics of the mother (work satisfaction, motivations for working, feelings about being an employed mother, etc.).

The mother's employment history and how it coincides with the child's changing developmental capacities is especially important to take into consideration. For example, a cross-sectional research strategy with a sample of employed mothers of elementary school children obscures the possible implications of the child's age at different points in the mother's employment history. The child's perceptions may differ depending on whether the mother has been employed full time since the child's birth, part time since birth, or whether she entered the labor force only after the child began attending school. For example, the mother's return to work may coincide with a critical transition for the child, such as the move from elementary school to junior high school, which is typically accompanied by a drop in self-esteem. This expectable developmental change in the child's perception of self may be mistakenly attributed to the mother's entry into the labor force. Alternatively, the two life changes—mother's and child's—may interact to alter the child's views. Better specification of employment history would help make sense out of research findings.

One final issue applies not only to studies of maternal work but to the entire body of research on parental employment effects. Because trends in labor force participation are so clearly in flux, we must be sensitive to possible historical (cohort) effects in evaluating research findings. The same research study conducted a decade later may yield very different data, especially when measuring attitudes and perceptions. The reader must, therefore, ask when a study was done in order to fairly evaluate its conclusions. At the same time, certain effects, such as the negative world views engendered by extreme poverty, may be evident regardless of historical context.

RECOMMENDATIONS FOR FUTURE RESEARCH

While some information is known about the effects of work patterns on children's views of the world, this area of inquiry is relatively uncharted, and further research must address many unanswered questions. In this final section, we suggest some new directions and particular methodological approaches for future research. Our list is not exhaustive; it offers selected examples that have emerged from the focus of the Panel on Work, Family, and Community and the literature reviewed here.

Research Agenda: Selected Ideas

(1)   We know very little about how variations in parental work affect children's views of school, work, and other community institutions and services. Parental labor force participation must be examined in relationship to

  (a) the effects of government services on educational and vocational aspirations,

  (b) the effects of schools as caretaking as well as educational institutions on attitudes toward authority and achievement,

  (c) the function of school as a preparation for work.

(2)   Although we are beginning to develop a more complete understanding of how maternal labor force participation affects children's self-concepts, questions remain about how work affects the development of other aspects of the self, such as locus of control, social competence, and vocational aspirations.

(3)   The existing research suggests that living in extreme poverty has a variety of negative effects on children's views of the world. Research might investigate the constellation of variables that cause children to feel impoverished and might identify family, community, and government supports that make it easier to cope with economic hardship.

(4)   The large body of literature on the absence of the father might be complemented by research on the effects of living with parents (father, mother, or both) who are absent due to work demands. Similarly, parents who are very career-oriented may be psychologically absent from their children; how does this state of affairs affect the child at various ages and in various family constellations?

(5)   There have been several recent studies of the relationship between parents' vocational attitudes and children's attitudes toward work (e.g., Blau, 1972; Goodale and Hall, 1976; Wijting et al., 1978). However, the effects of the parents' *actual* job status and work characteristics on children's attitudes toward work await further investigation.

(6)   Researchers might compare families who are experiencing severe work-family conflict with those who are managing well. Through intensive study, a set of coping strategies could be identified for investigation in a larger sample. Such data might help in the design of interventions that attempt to ease work-family strains and enhance the positive effects on children that emanate from their parents' work lives.

(7)   The area of children's participation in the work world deserves extensive study. Many research questions remain, including the following:

    (a) how work experiences affect children's views of themselves and of relations with authority figures;

    (b) how children are affected by unpaid work, such as caring for siblings because of parental employment demands;

    (c) what it means for a child to work with parents or other family members, as in family-owned businesses or seasonal migrant work;

    (d) how the limited range of jobs available to teenagers affects their attitudes about future work.

    (8)   A number of natural experiments have been created by changes in parental labor force participation. Investigators could use these natural laboratories to evaluate effects on children's perceptions of self, others, and the world of work. Situations in which children's views might be studied include

    (a) job-related family relocation, often necessitating changes in child care, school, etc.;

    (b) parental career shifts that span diverse areas of vocational interest;

    (c) Aid to Families with Dependent Children programs that provide benefits to father-present families versus those that do not;

    (d) employer-provided work site child care.

Research Agenda: Methodology

    (1)   Longitudinal research designs are needed to trace developmental shifts in children's perceptions. In addition, such designs would help disentangle the many effects due to such parental work changes as a mother's entry or reentry into the work force and a father's temporary unemployment. Long-term as well as more immediate consequences could be determined. Although cross-sectional designs are useful, they obscure the crucial relationship between parents' work history and the development of the child.

    (2) Cross-sectional designs can yield important information about historical differences in children's views, such as whether the effects of maternal employment change as the phenomenon gains acceptance in various segments of society. In addition, cross-sectional research might identify universal patterns that are not cohort-specific. Such research could, for example, examine continuities in the views of children who are affected by economic recessions in different historical contexts. Schaie's (1965) general developmental model utilizes both cross-sectional and

longitudinal designs. This model allows for the disentangling of effects of historical change by comparing subjects of the same age born in different years; effects due to age, by comparing subjects of different ages; and effects due to development, by comparing the behavior or views of subjects at two points in time.

(3) Small-scale, qualitative studies of the complex family conditions that influence children's perceptions are needed to supplement more rigorous large-sample data. Such accounts would offer valuable information about the interactive processes of daily life that shape how children view the world.

(4) In future research, the independent variable of employment status must not be defined as simple participation or nonparticipation in the labor force. Rather, the operational definition of work status must include subjective factors, such as reasons for and satisfaction with working, as well as a better differentiation of objective factors like type of job, work scheduling, and benefits. The Kohn research on work-family interaction is an excellent model, given the specification of job characteristics, the selection of relevant socializaton variables, and the theoretical and statistical treatment of reciprocal influences and causal relations between work and family life. This research model clearly should be extended to include direct observation of children's behavior and perceptions of the world.

(5) Family status and composition should be defined and reported in all future research, so that findings about the effects of parental labor force participation are easier to interpret. For example, specification of family status would disentangle the effects of maternal work on children in father-present as compared to father-absent families. In addition, it would help chart how the prevalence of alternative family types, such as single-parent and multigenerational families, interacts with changing patterns in the world of work.

(6) In studying the effects of work and family responsibilities, researchers must attend to each family member's contributions, including those of fathers and children. This approach could address questions such as

(a) how diversified experiences with working adults affect children's views of work;

(b) how parental selection of shift work to better accommodate child-care responsibilities affects sex-role attitudes;

(c) how each member's participation in family and work life changes when the family is under economic stress.

(7) As mentioned throughout our literature review, research designs

that include information about the father—his work life and his relationship to wife and children—would add considerably to knowledge in a field that has long focused disproportionately on the mother.

(8) Information about socioeconomic standing should be noted in future research, even in nonexperimental designs. The standard information about income, occupation, and education should be gathered about both parents, not just the father. Different methods of calculating socioeconomic status, including the use of variables that tap characteristics of the mother, may reveal different effects on children.

(9) Future investigators must be more careful to specify which respondents serve as sources of data. For example, fathers and mothers often provide conflicting reports of their children's behavior (Eron et al., 1961). Ideally, multiple observers would provide information on each behavior of interest.

(10) Finally, we need to evaluate existing methods and develop new age-appropriate means of studying children's perceptions. In accomplishing this task, we face the long-standing difficulty of determining how subjective reports relate to actual behavior, as well as further complications posed by the changing nature of the child's developing cognitive and affective capacities.

REFERENCES AND BIBLIOGRAPHY

Al-Timini, S. (1977) Self-Concepts of Young Children with Working and Non-Working Mothers. Ph.D. dissertation, George Peabody College for Teachers.
Banducci, R. (1967) The effect of mother's employment on the achievement, aspirations and expectations of the child. *Personnel and Guidance Journal* 46:263-267.
Baruch, G. K. (1976) Girls who perceive themselves as competent: some antecedents and correlates. *Psychology of Women Quarterly* 1:38-48.
Berger, P. L., and Luckman, T. (1967) *The Social Construction of Reality*. London: Allen Lane.
Bernstein, B. (1964) Elaborated and restricted codes: their social origins and some consequences. *American Anthropology* 66:55-69.
Blau, Z. S. (1972) Maternal aspiration, socialization, and achievement of boys and girls in the white working class. *Journal of Youth and Adolescence* 1:35-57.
Blehar, M. (1979) Family adjustment to unemployment. Pp. 413-439 in E. Corfman, ed., *Families Today*, vol. 1. NIMH Science Monographs. Rockville, Md.: U.S. Department of Health, Education, and Welfare.
Bloom-Feshbach, J. (1979) The Beginnings of Fatherhood. Ph.D. dissertation, Yale University.
Bloom-Feshbach, S., Bloom-Feshbach, J., and Gaughran, J. (1980) The child's tie to both parents: separation patterns and nursery school adjustment. *American Journal of Orthopsychiatry* 50:505-521.
Brim, O. G. (1975) Macro-structural influences on child development and the need for childhood and social indicators. *American Journal of Orthopsychiatry* 45:516-524.

Bronfenbrenner, U. (1979) *The Ecology of Human Development: Experiments by Nature and Design.* Cambridge, Mass.: Harvard University Press.

Brookins, G. K. (1978) Maternal employment: its impact on the sex roles and occupational choices of middle and working class black children. Ph.D. dissertation, Harvard University.

Bryant, B. K. (1979) Siblings as Caretakers. Paper presented at the annual meeting of the American Psychological Association, New York.

Bullock, P. (1973) *Aspiration vs. Opportunity: "Careers" in the Inner City.* Ann Arbor, Mich.: Institute of Labor and Industrial Relations, University of Michigan and Wayne State University.

Camara, K. A. (1980) Children's construction of social knowledge: concepts of family and the experience of parental divorce. Ph.D. dissertation, Stanford University.

Caplovitz, D. (1979) *Making Ends Meet: How Families Cope with Inflation and Recession.* Beverly Hills, Calif.: Sage Publications.

Carew, M. C. (1978) Employment and Mothers' Emotional States: A Psychological Study of Women Reentering the Work Force. Ph.D. dissertation, Yale University.

Cavan, R. S. (1959) Unemployment: crisis of the common man. *Marriage and Family Living* 21:139-146.

Cicone, M. V., and Ruble, D. N. (1978) Beliefs about males. *Journal of Social Issues* 34:5-16.

Coleman, R., and Rainwater, L. (1978) *Social Standing in America.* New York: Basic Books.

Dellas, M., Gaier, E. L., and Emihovich, C. A. (1979) Maternal employment and selected behaviors and attitudes of preadolescents and adolescents. *Adolescence* 14:579-589.

Douvan, E. (1963) Employment and the adolescent. Pp. 142-164 in F. I. Nye and L.W. Hoffman, eds., *The Employed Mother in America.* Chicago: Rand McNally.

Dweck, C. S., Davidson, W., Nelson, S., and Enna B. (1978) Sex differences in learned helplessness. II: the contingencies of evaluative feedback in the classroom. III: an experimental analysis. *Developmental Psychology* 14:268-276.

Elder, G. (1974) *Children of the Great Depression.* Chicago: University of Chicago Press.

Elder, G. (1979) Historical change in life patterns and personality. Pp. 117-159 in P. Baltes and O. Brim, Jr., eds., *Life-Span Development and Behavior*, vol. 2. New York: Academic Press.

Elder, G. H., and Rockwell, R. C. (1979) The depression experience in men's lives. Pp. 95-118 in A. J. Lichtman and J. R. Challinor, eds., *Kin and Communities: Families in America.* Washington, D.C.: Smithsonian Press.

Eron, L. D., Banta, T. J., Walder, L. O., and Laulicht, J. H. (1961) Comparison of data obtained from mothers and fathers on child-rearing practices and their relation to aggression. *Child Development* 32:457-472.

Franke, H. (1972) A comparison of perceived parental behavior characteristics of 8th-grade children of working and non-working mothers. Ph.D. dissertation, University of Florida.

Furstenberg, F. F., Jr. (1973) Work experience and family life. Pp. 341-360 in J. O'Toole, ed., *Work and the Quality of Life.* Cambridge, Mass: MIT Press.

Furth, H. G. (1980) *The World of Grown-ups: Children's Conceptions of Society.* New York: Elsevier.

Garbarino, J. (1976) A preliminary study of some ecological correlates of child abuse: the impact of socioeconomic stress on mothers. *Child Development* 47:178-185.

Gecas, V., and Nye, F. I. (1974) Sex and class differences in parent-child interaction: a test of Kohn's hypothesis. *Journal of Marriage and the Family* 36:742-749.

Gold, D., and Andres, D. (1978a) Relations between maternal employment and development of nursery school children. *Canadian Journal of Behavioural Science* 10:116-129.

Gold, D., and Andres, D. (1978b) Developmental comparisons between ten-year-old children with employed and nonemployed mothers. *Child Development* 49:75-84.

Gold, D., and Andres, D. (1978c) Comparisons of adolescent children with employed and nonemployed mothers. *Merrill-Palmer Quarterly* 24: 243-254.

Gold, A., Andres, D., and Glorieux, J. (1979) The development of Francophone nursery-school children with employed and nonemployed mothers. *Canadian Journal of Behavioural Science* 11:169-173.

Goodale, J. G., and Hall, D. T. (1976) Inheriting a career: the influence of sex, values, and parents. *Journal of Vocational Behavior* 18:19-30.

Greenberger, E., and Steinberg, L. D. (1980) Part-time employment of in-school youth: a preliminary assessment of costs and benefits. In *A Review of Youth Employment Problems, Programs and Policies, Vol. 1, The Youth Employment Problem: Causes and Dimensions.* The Vice President's Task Force on Youth Employment. Washington, D.C.: U.S. Department of Labor.

Greenberger, E., Steinberg, L. D., Vaux, A., and McAuliffe, S. (1980) Adolescents who work: effects of part-time employment on family and peer relations. *Journal of Youth and Adolescence* 9:189-202.

Harré, R. (1974) The conditions for a social psychology of childhood. Pp. 245-262 in M. P. Richards, ed., *The Integration of a Child into a Social World.* London: Cambridge University Press.

Harter, S. (1981) Developmental perspectives on the self system. In M. Hetherington, ed., *Carmichael's Manual of Child Psychology, Volume on Social and Personality Development.* New York: John Wiley and Sons.

Hartley, R. E. (1960) Children's concepts of male and female roles. *Merrill-Palmer Quarterly* 6:83-91.

Havighurst, R. J. (1976) The relative importance of social class and ethnicity in human development. *Human Development* 19:56-64.

Hess, R. D. (1970) Social class and ethnic influences on socialization. Pp. 457-557 in P. H. Musson, ed., *Carmichael's Manual of Child Psychology,* vol. II. 3rd ed. New York: John Wiley and Sons.

Hoffman, L. W. (1974) Effects of maternal employment on the child—a review of the research. *Developmental Psychology* 10:204-228.

Hudson, L. (1972) *The Cult of the Fact.* New York: Harper and Row.

Kanter, R. M. (1977) *Work and Family in the United States: A Critical Review and Agenda for Research and Policy.* New York: Russell Sage Foundation.

Kappel, B. E., and Lambert, R. D. (1972) *Self Worth among the Children of Working Mothers.* Unpublished ms. University of Waterloo, Ontario.

Kellam, S. G., Ensminger, M. E., and Turner, R. J. (1977) Family structure and the mental health of children. *Archives of General Psychiatry* 34:1012-1022.

Kelly, J. G. (1968) Towards an ecological conception of preventive interventions. Pp. 76-99 in J. W. Carter, Jr., ed., *Research Contributions from Psychology to Community Mental Health.* New York: Behavioral Publications.

Klecka, C. O., and Hiller, D. V. (1977) Impact of mothers' life style on adolescent gender-role socialization. *Sex Roles* 3:241-255.

Kohen, A. I., and Andrisani, P. (1974) *Career Thresholds: A Longitudinal Study of the Education and Labor Market Experience of Male Youth.* U.S. Department of Labor

Manpower Research Monograph No. 16, Vol. 4. Washington, D.C.: U.S. Government Printing Office.

Kohen, A. I., Grasso, J. T., Myers, S. C., and Shields, P. M. (1977) *Career Thresholds: A Longitudinal Study of the Education and Labor Market Experience of Male Youth*. U.S. Department of Labor Manpower Research Monograph No. 16, Vol. 6. Washington, D.C.: U.S. Government Printing Office.

Kohen, A. I., and Parnes, H. S. (1971) *Career Thresholds: A Longitudinal Study of the Educaton and Labor Market Experience of Male Youth*. U.S. Department of Labor Manpower Research Monograph No. 16, Vol. 3. Washington, D.C.: U.S. Government Printing Office.

Kohn, M. L. (1963) Social class and parent-child relationships: an interpretation. *American Journal of Sociology* 68: 471-480.

Kohn, M. L. (1969, 1977) *Class and Conformity: A Study in Values*. Homewood, Ill.: Dorsey.

Kohn, M. L., and Carroll, E. E. (1960) Social class and the allocation of parental responsibilities. *Sociometry* 23:372-392.

Kohn, M. L., and Schooler, C. (1973) Occupational experience and psychological functioning: an assessment of reciprocal effects. *American Sociological Review* 38:97-118.

Kurdek, L. A., and Siesky, A. E. (1980) Sex role self-concepts of single divorced parents and their children. *Journal of Divorce* 3:249-261.

Lazarus, R. S., Averill, J. R., and Opton, E. M. (1974) The psychology of coping: issues of research and assessment. Pp. 249-315 in G. Coelho, D. Hamburg, and J. Adams, eds., *Coping and Adaptation*. New York: Basic Books.

Lefcourt, H. M. (1976) *Locus of Control: Current Trends in Theory and Research*. Hillsdale, N.J.: Lawrence Erlbaum.

Lefkowitz, M. M., Tesing, E. P., and Gordon, N. H. (1979) Childhood Depression, Family Income, and Locus of Control. Paper presented at the annual meeting of the American Psychological Association, New York.

Lewin, K. (1935) *A Dynamic Theory of Personality*. New York: McGraw-Hill.

Lewin, K. (1936) *Problems of Topological Psychology*. New York: McGraw-Hill.

Lewin, K. (1951) *Field Theory in Social Science*. New York: McGraw-Hill.

Lewis, M., and Feiring, C. (1978) The child's social world. Pp. 47-69 in R. M. Lerner and G. B. Spanier, eds., *Child Influences on Marital and Family Interaction*. New York: Academic Press.

Maccoby, E. E., and Jacklin, C. N. (1974) *The Psychology of Sex Differences*. Stanford, Calif.: Stanford University Press.

Macke, A. S., and Morgan, W. R. (1978) Maternal employment, race, and work orientation of high school girls. *Social Forces* 57:187-204.

Marantz, S. A., and Mansfield, A. F. (1977) Maternal employment and the development of sex-role stereotyping in five- to eleven-year-old girls. *Child Development* 48:668-673.

Martin, H. P., and Rodeheffer, M. A. (1976) The psychological impact of abuse on children. *Journal of Pediatric Psychology* 1:12-15.

McCord, J., McCord, W., and Thurber, E. (1963) Effects of maternal employment on lower-class boys. *Journal of Abnormal and Social Psychology* 67:177-182.

Miller, D. R., and Swanson, G. E. (1958) *The Changing American Parent: A Study in the Detroit Area*. New York: John Wiley and Sons.

Miller, S. M. (1975) Effects of maternal employment on sex-role perception, interests, and self-esteem in kindergarten girls. *Developmental Psychology* 11:405-406.

Miller, T. W. (1975) Effects of maternal age, education, and employment status on the self-esteem of the child. *Journal of Social Psychology* 95:141-142.

Moos, R. H. (1976) *The Human Context: Environmental Determinations of Behavior.* New York: John Wiley and Sons.

Ogbu, J. (1974) *The Next Generation: An Ethnography of Education in an Urban Neighborhood.* New York: Academic Press.

Ogbu, J. (1978) *Minority Education and Caste.* New York: Academic Press.

Parnes, H. S., Miljus, R. C., Spitz, R. S., and Associates (1970) *Career Thresholds: A Longitudinal Study of the Education and Labor Market Experience of Male Youth 14-24 Years of Age.* U.S. Department of Labor Manpower Research Monograph No. 16, Vol. 1. Washington, D.C.: U.S. Government Printing Office.

Pederson, F. A., Anderson, B. J., and Cain, R. L. (1977) An Approach to Understanding Linkages Between the Parent-Infant and Spouse Relationships. Paper presented at the Society for Research in Child Development Meeting, New Orleans.

Pelton, L. H. (1978) Child abuse and neglect: the myth of classlessness. *American Journal of Orthopsychiatry* 48:608-617.

Pleck, J. H., and Lang, L. (1978) Men's family role: its nature and consequences. Unpublished manuscript. Center for Research on Women, Wellesley College, Wellesley, Mass.

Propper, A. M. (1972) The relationship of maternal employment to adolescent roles, activities and parental relationships. *Journal of Marriage and the Family* 34:417-431.

Reidy, J. J., Anderegg, T. R., Tracy, R. J., and Cotler, S. (1980) Abused and neglected children: the cognitive, social and behavioral correlates. Pp. 284-290 in G. J. Williams and J. Money, eds., *Traumatic Abuse and Neglect of Children at Home.* Baltimore, Md.: The Johns Hopkins University Press.

Reuter, M. W., and Biller, H. B. (1973) Perceived paternal nurturance-availability and personality adjustment among college males. *Journal of Consulting and Clinical Psychology* 40:339-342.

Romer, N., and Cherry, D. (1980) Ethnic and social class difference in children's sex-role concepts. *Sex Roles* 6:245-263.

Rosenberg, M. (1979) *Conceiving the Self.* New York: Basic Books.

Rosenthal, D. (1979) Working and Nonworking Mothers in Intact and Non-Intact Families and Effects on Child's Perception of the Parent Child Relation, Educational Achievement, Self Concept, Occupational Aspiration and Vocational Maturity. Ph.D. dissertation, State University of New York at Buffalo.

Rotter, J. B. (1966) Generalized expectancies for internal versus external control of reinforcement. *Psychological Monographs* 80, no. 609.

Roy, P. (1963) Adolescent roles: rural-urban differentials. Pp. 165-181 in F. I. Nye and L. W. Hoffman, eds., *The Employed Mother in America.* Chicago: Rand McNally.

Rubin, L. B. (1976) *Worlds of Pain: Life in the Working-Class Family.* New York: Basic Books.

Runck, B. R. (1979) Families in hard times—a legacy. Pp. 29-65 in E. Corfman, ed., *Families Today*, vol. 1. NIMH Science Monographs. Rockville, Md.: U.S. Department of Health, Education, and Welfare.

Schaie, K. W. (1965) A general model for the study of developmental problems. *Psychological Bulletin* 64:92-107.

Schulz, D. A. (1968) Variations in the father role in complete families of the Negro lower class. *Social Science Quarterly* 49:651-659.

Schulz, D. A. (1969) *Coming Up Black: Patterns of Ghetto Socialization.* Englewood Cliffs, N.J.: Prentice-Hall.

Schutz, A. (1972) *The Phenomenology of the Social World.* London: Heinemann.

Schwartz, M., and Henderson, G. (1964) The culture of unemployment: some notes on

Negro children. Pp. 459-468 in A. B. Shostak and W. Gomberg, eds., *Blue Collar World: Studies of the American Worker*. Englewood Cliffs, N.J.: Prentice-Hall.

Segal, J. (1979) Child abuse: a review of research. Pp. 577-606 in E. Corfman, ed., *Families Today*, vol. 2. NIMH Science Monographs. Rockville, Md.: U.S. Department of Health, Education, and Welfare.

Sennett, R., and Cobb, J. (1973) *The Hidden Injuries of Class*. New York: Vintage Books.

Siegel, A. E., and Haas, M. B. (1963) The working mother: a review of research. *Child Development* 34:513-542.

Steinberg, L. D., Greenberger, E., Jacobi, M., and Garduque, L. (1980) Early Work Experience: A Partial Antidote for Adolescent Egocentrism. Unpublished manuscript. University of California, Irvine.

Trickett, E. J., Kelly, J. G., and Todd, P. M. (1972) The social environment of the high school: guidelines for individual change and organizational redevelopment. Pp. 331-406 in S. Golann and C. Eisdorfer, eds., *Handbook of Community Mental Health*. New York: Appleton Century Crofts.

Weiner, B., and Peter, N. A. (1973) A cognitive-developmental analysis of achievement and moral judgment. *Developmental Psychology* 3: 290-309.

Wijting, J. P., Arnold, C. R., and Conrad, K. A. (1978) Generational differences in work values between parents and children and between boys and girls across grade levels 6, 9, 10, and 12. *Journal of Vocational Behavior* 12:245-260.

Woods, M. B. (1972) The unsupervised child of the working mother. *Developmental Psychology* 6:14-25.

Wylie, R. (1979) *The Self Concept: Theory and Research on Selected Topics*, vol. 2. Lincoln, Neb.: University of Nebraska Press.

PART III
The State of Knowledge

9
The Known and the Unknown

The Panel on Work, Family, and Community was established to explore significant policy and research issues associated with changing patterns of work and family structure as they affect children's socialization and education. In particular we focused on how families, employers, and various formal and informal community institutions have adapted and the consequences for children. In this study, we have sought (1) to document the nature and extent of change in children's lives, (2) to review the status of existing knowledge concerning the effects of change on children's experiences and development, and (3) to suggest promising directions for future research intended to influence public-sector and private-sector policies toward working families and their children. What have we learned?

Work cannot be viewed as a single uniform condition. The nature of the work experience and the meaning of work may lead to different consequences for children and families in different circumstances.
    A fundamental conclusion of our study that underlies all others is that work (i.e., paid employment) cannot be viewed as a single uniform condition experienced the same way by all parents with consistent effects on all children. It is instead the distinctive characteristics of work, such as the nature of the job, the workplace, work scheduling, earnings, work history, and the meaning of work, that determine how parents' employment affects the well-being of their children. Contrary to strong popular opinion on both sides of the issue, there is no compelling evi-

311

dence to suggest that mothers' or fathers' labor force participation has only good or only bad consequences for all children in all social, economic, and cultural circumstances. It seems to have varying effects (some good and some bad) depending on how the conditions of work interact with family processes and the roles of formal and informal community institutions (e.g., schools, churches, social service agencies, recreation centers, and neighborhood groups). There is no simple, predictable, linear relationship, for example, between parents' work status and children's academic achievement and their attitudes about work. It is therefore not work alone but the complex links between and among work, family, and community as they directly and indirectly influence children's daily experiences that determine whether parental employment—mothers' or fathers' or both parents'—will produce positive, negative, or neutral outcomes in children.

Existing research paradigms are generally inadequate and inappropriate for understanding the complex effects of work on children and their families. Heretofore, many researchers have viewed parental employment as a simple, dichotomous variable. Most studies have concentrated on maternal employment and ignored paternal or parental employment, as well as work by children themselves. Furthermore, from our review it is clear that most studies have focused on discrete aspects of the dynamic relationships and interactions among work, family, and community without taking into account a variety of intervening variables. For example, studies of the effects of maternal employment on school achievement among boys and girls have generally concluded that there are neglible differences between children with working and nonworking mothers when there is a control for socioeconomic level. However, work may have significant effects on such things as spousal relationships and mothers' sense of happiness, which may significantly affect family functioning and, in turn, children's performance in the classroom. As Bronfenbrenner and Crouter (Chapter 3 in this volume) point out "Studies that are limited to searching for differences in the characteristics of children solely as a function of the mother's employment status have clearly reached the point of diminishing returns. The focus of investigation must shift to the exploration of intervening processes both within and outside the family. This shift, in turn, requires the use of more complex research paradigms. . . ."

There is growing evidence that men and women work for similar reasons and that income alone is not the only motivating factor. Depending on the conditions and the meaning of work to the parent or parents, employment may carry with it status, prestige, a sense of competence, independence, and higher self-esteem, or the reverse. Jobs may provide important peer relationships. Parental employment may offer new and positive role models for children. As the review by Bloom-Feshbach, Bloom-Feshbach, and Heller (Chapter 8 in this volume) suggests, there is some evidence that how parents, especially mothers, feel about their work may affect how they feel about themselves and their children. In turn it may affect children's attitudes about themselves and their parents and their educational and career aspirations. Race, ethnicity, and religious background, as well as educational attainment, socioeconomic status, and age, may be significant determinants of mothers' attitudes about work. In general, however, research has not explored the extent and ways in which the varying conditions and meaning of work for both mothers and fathers influence child outcomes as well as parents' perceptions of their children.

Existing research has also largely failed to account for the fact that the consequences of the parental work experience may be different for parents and children. For example, immediately following divorce, working outside the home may be essential to the mother's adjustment and well-being. On the other hand it may have negative consequences for her children, who may feel doubly abandoned, especially if the mother did not work before the divorce. These types of consequences may vary for children of different ages and sexes.

In sum, as several papers in this volume have shown, work is a complex variable and its effects on children are intricately related to a variety of other factors, such as the age and sex of the child, socioeconomic level, family income, race and ethnicity, family structure, presence and age of siblings, parent education and job satisfaction, parent-child relationships, and peer relationships, to name just a few. Inevitably therefore, it is difficult to identify the distinctive characteristics of children whose sole parent or whose mother and father are in the paid labor force. Moreover, as more children grow up in families in which one or both parents are working on a full-time or part-time basis, the meaning of the work experience for parents and the consequences for their children may become almost as diverse as the families and children themselves. Indeed, to try to isolate the effects of parental employment, as a single variable, on children is like trying to identify the consequences of industrialization or urbanization.

Although we have identified no single overall effect on children that results from their parents working, we know that paid employment creates or adds to family income and decreases family time.

From our review of the existing literature a major conclusion is that the simple fact of parents working outside the home has no universally predictable direct effect on children. It does, however, ensure that children will be materially better off and will have less time together with their employed parent or parents.

As we have previously noted, the social and economic environments in which children are reared are generally agreed to be the most significant indicator of their overall well-being—health, educational achievement, later employment, and earnings. In terms of family income, children are better off if both parents or a sole parent are in the paid labor force. Children in single-parent families are more likely to be poor, particularly if the parent is not working. Thus for example in 1979 (the most recent year for which we have complete data) of the 9.7 million children who lived in families with income below the poverty level, 5.5 million, almost 57 percent lived in female-headed families (Bureau of the Census, 1981). Almost 85 percent of the 3.3 million children in single-parent families whose mothers did not work lived in poverty, in contrast to 31 percent of those whose mothers worked at least some time during the year and 12 percent of those whose mothers worked full time all year round. Of the 3.8 million poor children living in husband-wife families, 65 percent had nonworking mothers. Only 2.2 percent of those children whose fathers worked full time all year and whose mothers worked at some time during the year were poor. (Although the Census Bureau's measure of poverty does not include such noncash benefits as food stamps, most of these children would still be living in poverty regardless of whether their families received such benefits.)

Economic well-being is not *necessarily* correlated with positive child outcomes nor does it *necessarily* maximize the well-being of all family members. However, as noted in the reviews by Bronfenbrenner and Crouter (Chapter 3 in this volume) and by Heyns (Chapter 7 in this volume), lack of income is *frequently* correlated with negative cognitive, social, and developmental outcomes in children and often with family stress and related problems. Although the value of work and related earnings varies for families at different income levels (i.e., depending on the extent to which taxes, day-care expenses, transportation expenses, etc., reduce net earnings gains), parental employment clearly enhances families' economic well-being (Ferber and Birnbaum, Chapter 4 in this volume). Paid employment is essential for most families headed by women if income is to be above the poverty threshold. (Obviously, wage levels and hours worked are also important.) It may mean the difference between adequate and inadequate housing, nutrition, clothing, and health care. Although the number and proportion of poor two-parent families is substantially smaller regardless of whether one or both parents work, poverty is almost negligible when both parents work. Among moderate-income and upper-income families, earnings that result when both parents work may contribute to a more comfortable standard of living and thereby provide children with opportunities that enhance their development, such as extracurricular programs, summer programs, and family vacations.

From our review of the existing data and research literature, we also conclude that children of working parents spend less time each day with their mothers, fathers, or both and more time in settings away from their homes and in the care of other adults. Increasing numbers of preschool children are spending some portion of their day in day-care centers, in preschool programs (in and outside of schools), or in family day-care homes. Many other very young children who remain at home are cared for by family members or nonrelatives while their parent or parents are at work, or are cared for by other parents who share responsibilities on a cooperative basis. School-age children are spending more of their nonschool time in a variety of settings (e.g., recreation centers, extended day programs in schools, after-school care arrangements) about which there is little systematic information. Although data do not exist, there are also undoubtedly a significant number of children, both preschool and school age, who are left alone without any formal care arrangement during the hours when their parent or parents are working.

There is little firm evidence of the effects of various care arrangements or lack of care arrangements on children, although we do know that children cared for in groups tend to get more colds and flu than other children. Some emerging studies seem to suggest negative effects on cognitive and personality development among middle-class boys whose mothers work full time, although these findings are not firm. The effects of substitute care or the lack of organized, supervised arrangements on outcomes such as maternal attachment and peer orientation seem to depend largely on the quality of that care, the characteristics of the child (e.g., age, health, sex), and the attitudes of the working parents about their jobs and their children.

Working mothers in both single-parent and two-parent families spend approximately as much time each day in the direct physical care of their children as mothers who are housewives do. Evidence also suggests that at all socioeconomic levels, fathers in two-parent families in which the mother works spend some more time in child care than do husbands with nonworking wives (Moore and Hofferth, 1979). Nevertheless, as Ferber and Birnbaum (Chapter 4 in this volume) suggest, the overall difference in the level of father's participation is relatively insignificant.

Mothers continue to carry primary responsibility for child and home even when they work full time. As a result, working mothers generally carry a large responsibility for home-related tasks in addition to their jobs. This burden is increased if the father travels frequently in connection with his work. It is even greater for single mothers. Research generally has not addressed the particular circumstances of single fathers, although the popular media have recently highlighted them. It is reasonable to assume that single fathers share many of the problems of single mothers who are combining work and parenting responsibilities; however, they are likely to have more income available to solve such problems than do women who head families.

There is some evidence that working parents, especially working mothers, are likely to spend much of their nonwork time with their children rather than in other pursuits. We have found no evidence, however, that parents whose work schedules are somewhat more flexible than the standard nine-to-five work day (e.g., those working flexitime schedules or off-peak shifts), spend more time with their children. Except for complaints by parents about time constraints and a sense of pressure, the consequent effects of the time crunch for their children are also unclear. In addition the implications for the quantity and quality of parent-child interactions among parents who work full time as opposed to part time are not fully understood.

Families are making their own personal adaptations to changing work patterns. Parents seem to be responding and coping in a variety of ways, but some circumstances permit more successful adaptation than others.

As work patterns and related patterns of family structure continue to change, there is increasing evidence that families are adapting in a variety of ways—some more, some less successfully. Parents, for example, are making greater use of private preschool and nursery school programs, of commercial child care services, and of public- and private-school extended day-care programs for child care. Working parents are also more frequently choosing private-school alternatives to public education, although it is unclear whether parents, in particular mothers, go to work in order to afford private education or whether having additional income leads them to choose private schools. Parents are arranging carpools to manage their own and their children's transportation needs. Some parents in two-earner families are opting to work alternate shifts in order to meet their child-care needs. Others are organizing multiple care arrangements, including schools, formal or informal family day care, and care by relatives, to ensure adequate coverage during the hours they are at work. Although the proportion of women who are working part time has decreased over the last decade, some mothers still choose part-time employment in order to manage family and work responsibilities simultaneously; others may choose jobs that permit greater flexibility of work scheduling and work site.

Little systematic information exists concerning the types of arrangements that families, especially families with school-age children, make to accommodate parental work roles and family responsibilities. Little is known as well about the extent to which such arrangements create or alleviate family stress, which in turn affects parent-child relations, spousal relations, and mothers' and fathers' sense of coping. Nor is it clearly understood which parents cope most successfully and why, or which fail and why. Indeed, both working families and those with an at-home parent, especially a mother, are changing their life-styles in important ways. Although a mother's employment status may be a significant variable in determining the goods and services that families purchase, income level may be more important. Moreover, the spillover effects occurring as a result of changes initiated by working families have consequences for traditional families as well.

Changes are also occurring in the roles of the workplace, schools, and other community institutions, but conceptualization and measurement are not well developed.

In our review of existing data sources and the research literature we also discovered evidence of changes that are occurring in other institutions in our society outside the family—in the workplace, in schools, and in other community institutions. The extent of these changes is difficult to determine, however, because systematic data are not available. Moreover, it is difficult to assess what factors account for these developments and to determine the direct and indirect causes as well as the consequences for children, families, and the institutions themselves.

As noted in the Kamerman and Kingston review (Chapter 5 in this volume), both voluntarily and as a result of federal mandate many employers are beginning to adopt innovative policies and practices to meet the needs of a changing work force. In 1978 for example, Congress passed the Pregnancy Discrimination Act (P.L. 95-555), which requires that health insurance, disability, and sick leave benefits be paid for pregnancy and related absences on the same basis as any illness or disability. Similarly, from 1971, when the concept of flexitime was first introduced by an American company, to 1977 the proportion of the labor force covered by this provision rose to 6 percent. It rose to an estimated 10 percent by 1980.

With regard to schools, elementary and secondary school enrollments declined by almost 20 percent during the 1970s as a result of a significant decrease in the size of the eligible cohort. At the same time, nursery school enrollment more than doubled despite a significant decrease in the number of children in this age group. Many new public schools that were opened in the late 1960s and early 1970s are now closing, while private-school alternatives appear to be burgeoning.

With regard to other community institutions, a variety of changes are becoming evident. Public and private day-care arrangements, for example, have developed rapidly. The number of children in federally funded day-care and preschool programs increased from about 300,000 in 1971 (200,000 in programs funded under the Social Security Act and 100,000 in Head Start) to 1.8 million in 1978 (more than 1 million in Social-Security-funded programs and more than 700,000 almost equally divided between Head Start and programs sponsored under Title I of the Elementary and Secondary Education Act). Market responses to the child-care needs of working parents increased similarly, especially in the last half of the decade. Proprietary (for-profit) child-care chains, for example, were first established in the United States in the early 1970s. By 1980 there were 10 such commercial chains across the country accounting for about 5 percent of all of the country's 19,000 licensed centers. It is important to note that the majority of these public and private care arrangements are for very young children.

Other changes among public and private community institutions include the rapid growth of various self-help groups, such as those for parents without partners, those to counsel prospective parents on methods of childbirth, those for parents of children with particular disabilities and handicaps, and those for working parents with very young children. Similarly, a variety of counseling and homemaker services have emerged, some publicly supported, others privately sponsored, and still others available in the marketplace.

As the Kamerman-Kingston and Bell reviews (Chapters 5 and 6, respectively, in this volume) suggest, however, little systematic research has been done on workplace conditions, policies, and practices as they affect the personal-familial roles and relationships of employees; on the variations among employers; or on the factors accounting for, or effects of, these variations. Nor has attention been paid to the fit between supports provided by employers and those provided by other public or private, formal or informal institutions. Similarly, the role of the workplace in mediating (or exacerbating) the effects of inadequacies in existing community institutions and supports has been largely overlooked in existing studies.

Given the limited range of institutions we have studied, the most significant—and the most obvious—lack of information regarding any type of response is about the community institutions: schools; informal supports, including kin, neighbors, friends; formal service systems; religious institutions; small businesses; and neighborhoods. We believe that more is actually occurring than appears in the literature. We conclude therefore that either the data are unavailable or the research has addressed the wrong questions.

Most of the studies of those institutions impinging directly on children (family, neighborhood, school) or indirectly through their parents (the workplace) do not address family and child outcomes in a systematic way, nor do they take account of work patterns and work status as significant variables. Efforts at understanding the nature, extent, and consequences of adaptations by community institutions and responses to the changes we have described are limited by the lack of a conceptual framework that includes attention to these phenomena. Thus far researchers have not viewed the changing employment status of parents or of adults likely to become parents as salient to the study of schools or of other formal or informal community institutions. The extensive efforts we have made to review existing research from this perspective have been frustrated by (1) the absence of an appropriate conceptual framework among researchers working in the field and (2) the failure of most researchers to pay attention to the phenomenon.

Little systematic research on community institutions exists. Most research views community institutions as serving very narrow, specialized functions (e.g., schools) or as responding to pathologies or problems rather than to ordinary or normal needs (e.g. social agencies). Some obvious exceptions exist, including several excellent studies of child-care services (e.g. Abt Associates, 1978); a national study of family services, including both formal and informal, market and nonmarket, religious and secular, practical and therapeutic services (Kahn and Kamerman, 1982); an in-depth study of social networks in one community and a subsequent study in four communities (Lein, 1977; Lein et al., in progress); and a replication of an earlier, major study of a midwestern community (Caplow et al., 1982). Apart from these and a few others, most existing research on community institutions has largely addressed formal and informal institutions as discrete entities. The configurations of formal service institutions—public and private—and informal organizations and helping networks have not been studied from the perspective of how they interrelate with one another. Nor has attention been paid to how market services fit or to the role such institutions may play in mediating the effects of different parental work patterns on children.

To date, the greatest concentration of research and program resources devoted to understanding and improving the effectiveness of children's education has largely been targeted on schools on the grounds that public policy for education can operate only on and through these institutions. A significant literature concerning those attributes of schools and schooling that effectively contribute to education has developed in recent years (Rutter et al., 1979; Averch et al., 1972), as has a body of research on the implemention of innovative curricular and extracurricular programs by schools (McLaughlin and Berman, 1975; Elmore, 1978; 1979-1980). An important conclusion of this literature is that a complex interaction of external factors—including emerging social, demographic, and economic trends; family functioning; workplace policies and practices; and the roles of other formal and informal community institutions—influences what goes on in schools and the resultant effects on children. We conclude therefore that a better understanding is needed of the direct and indirect roles of these other institutions and their interrelationships to see how they support, fail to support, and/or mediate the outcomes of school programs.

Little is known about the consequences for children of parental employment or unemployment. Simple propositions regarding the positive or negative consequences of parents' work cannot be demonstrated and sophisticated ones have generally not been investigated. Child outcomes, where they have been addressed, are conceived very narrowly.

Much of the research on child outcomes ignores parental employment, or treats it as a global, uniform variable. Similarly, many of the studies we reviewed ignore the mediating role played by other institutions impinging on children and the other-than-family settings where children spend much of their time. Thus, we have found that the data on children and child outcomes are largely inadequate to explain variance.

Most of the research on child outcomes is concentrated on cognitive and achievement measures narrowly defined. We know little about social and emotional outcomes for children; values and attitudes; peer relationships; problem-solving abilities; or behavioral outcomes such as dropping out of school, teenage employment, or family formation. We also know little about the effects of work on family processes that may in turn have consequences for children. Our measures for some of these outcomes are still relatively crude. More importantly, we do not know with any certainty to what factors we should attribute differences.

Although it is clear that parental work is by itself neither helpful nor harmful to families and children, there is some evidence that the outcomes for children may vary depending on a variety of child and parent characteristics, parental work characteristics, and a host of other factors. Among those factors that may make a difference are the age and sex of the child; the income, marital status, race, or ethnicity of the parents; the nature of the parent's job; and the meaning work has to that parent. In addition the extent and availability of supportive services, such as child care, relatives' help, and job flexibility, may play an important role. Given the multiplicity of antecedent and intervening variables, it may be very difficult to sort out differences in child outcomes and to account for them in any clear and consistent fashion. Certainly, current knowledge does not permit us to do so.

As the Heyns review (Chapter 7 in this volume) suggests, most existing research on child outcomes in schools is narrowly focused on curriculum issues and cognitive outcomes or other types of test scores. Yet education goes well beyond this narrow view of schooling to include the family, the community, and changes in the world of work. Singly or in combination, they all influence children's education and life chances. The role of schools has evolved over time to accommodate the predominant needs and values of families in our society. At times in our history, schools have provided a variety of services, courses, and programs in addition to traditional curricular programs. At other times they have been more circumscribed in their functions, reflecting a strong societal value on maintaining child-rearing functions as a family matter (Cuban, 1980). Nevertheless, there has been no systematic attention paid to these evolutions and the consequences of particular developments for children, for their families, and for the capacity of the schools to perform their traditional educational role.

As the reviews by Bronfenbrenner and Crouter (Chapter 3 in this volume) and by Bloom-Feshbach, Bloom-Feshbach, and Heller (Chapter 8 in this volume) indicate, most existing research is also focused on middle-class families. Only a few studies examine the coping behavior of black and other minority families, although black families have by far the longest history of maternal employment, particularly among mothers in married-couple families. Working families have been a dominant type in the black community for years and offer a much longer time frame in which to study the phenomenon, yet they have received little systematic analysis. The lower labor force participation rate of black single mothers compared to white mothers in the same situation raises a different set of questions that also has not been adequately addressed thus far.

Similarly, we have found no existing research directed toward the study of such special families as migrant families, immigrant families, refugee families, native American families, or military families.

As several of the reviews in the preceding section of this report point out, most studies have addressed maternal employment only. For the most part they have ignored the effects of paternal employment and/or the interrelated consequences of maternal and paternal employment. Although there is a growing body of research that documents the importance of the father in the socialization and psychological growth of children from early infancy onward, little attention has been devoted to the family as a system in which change in any one part inevitably affects others.

Finally, our review of the existing literature suggests that much of the research on single-parent families has failed to disentangle single-parent status and family income from the nature and characteristics of mother's work and the presence or absence of formal and informal external supports such as kin networks, neighborhood child-care facilities, and transportation arrangements.

REFERENCES AND BIBLIOGRAPHY

Abt Associates (1978) *National Day Care Study: Preliminary Findings and Their Implications*. Prepared for Administration for Children, Youth, and Families, Day Care Division, Department of Health, Education, and Welfare. Cambridge, Mass.: Abt Associates.

Averch, H., Carroll, S., Donaldson, T., Kiesling, H., and Pincus, J. (1972) *How Effective is Schooling? A Critical Review and Synthesis of Research Findings*. Santa Monica, Calif.: Rand Corporation.

Bureau of the Census (1981) Money income and poverty status of families and persons in the United States: 1980. *Current Population Reports*, Series P-60, No. 127. Washington, D.C.: U.S. Department of Commerce.

Caplow, T., Bahr, H., Chadwick, B. A., Hill, R., and Williamson, M. H. (1982) *Middletown Families: Fifty Years of Change and Continuity*. Minneapolis, Minn.: University of Minnesota Press.

Cuban, L. (1980) Schools as a community support system. Pp. 55-60 in C. Hayes, ed., *Work, Family, and Community: Summary Proceedings of an Ad Hoc Meeting*. Washington, D.C.: National Academy Press.

Elmore, R. (1978) Organizational models of social program implementation. *Public Policy* 26(Spring):185-228.

Elmore, R. (1979-1980) Backward mapping: implementation research and policy decisions. *Political Science Quarterly* 94(Winter):601-616.

Kahn, A., and Kamerman, S. (1982) *Helping America's Families*. Philadelphia, Pa.: Temple University Press.

Lein, L. (1977) Working Family Project: Family and Social Ties. Final unpublished report. U.S. Public Health Service, National Institute of Mental Health, Rockville, Md.

Lein, L. et al. (in progress) Families and Communities: Helping Networks.

McLaughlin, M., and Berman, P. (1975) *Macro and Micro Implementation*. Santa Monica, Calif.: Rand Corporation.

Moore, K., and Hofferth, S. (1979) Women and their children. Pp. 125-158 in R. E. Smith, ed., *The Subtle Revolution: Women at Work*. Washington, D.C.: The Urban Institute.

Rutter, M., Maughan, B., Mortimore, P., Ouston, J., with Smith, A. (1979) *Fifteen Thousand Hours: Secondary Schools and Their Effects on Children*. London: Open Books.

10
A Research Agenda

Implicit in our summary of what is known and what remains to be known about the effects of changing patterns of work and family on children's experiences and development is an agenda for future research. In addition, each of the topical research reviews presented in Part II includes the authors' more focused suggestions for further study. A lengthly shopping list of additional studies, highlighting what we do not know but want to know, could certainly be added. Such a miscellaneous listing seems inappropriate, however, in light of our objective of proposing a new paradigm for studying the consequences of social change for children's socialization and education.

Instead therefore, we pose a limited number of suggestions that both illustrate the approach presented in the previous chapter and are aimed at filling gaps in existing knowledge when the findings could significantly influence public- and private-sector decision making, public opinion, and/or popular beliefs.

The major finding of this study is that employment by mothers, fathers, or both is neither universally good nor bad for children. To address questions concerning the effect of parental work on children, one must take account of the mediating forces of various adaptations (both successful and unsuccessful) by individuals, by families, and by other formal and informal institutions in our society. Understanding the capacity of children and their families to cope with changing work patterns and work status requires more and better structural analyses (e.g., studies of changes in the nature of work, child-care patterns, policies, and services). But such studies must be premised on a conceptual framework that includes the role and impact of intervening factors. It requires an understanding of the dynamic psychosocial interaction of a family or similar families (for example, racial and ethnic minorities; families sharing the same social, cultural, and economic characteristics; or perhaps geographical location) within primary (i.e., family, kin, and close friends), secondary (i.e., people, policies, and practices in local community institutions), and tertiary (i.e., people, policies, and practices of the larger society) social systems. It depends on what psychosocial adaptive mechanisms families and others in the primary social system develop in response to social, cultural, and economic environmental conditions and then transmit to subsequent generations. Finally, the outcomes depend on how the individual family and child integrate and act on experiences from the environment in which they live and manage. In short, our first and most fundamental recommendation is the need to base future research on a concept of individual and family adaptation that includes interaction with larger social systems and conditions in our society.

In proposing further directions for future research that derive from this conceptualization, we would particularly stress the following:

• Improving the existing data base on children and on the work situation and the work history of their parents
• Obtaining insights and knowledge concerning the kinds of adaptations (successful and unsuccessful) now being made by working families, employers, schools, and other community institutions
• Evaluating the direct and indirect outcomes of government policies, employment policies, and community services
• Improving the state of knowledge about the effects of employment, unemployment, and welfare on children's well-being.

These suggestions are discussed in greater detail in the remainder of this chapter.

IMPROVING THE EXISTING DATA BASE ON CHILDREN AND ON THE
WORK SITUATION AND WORK HISTORY OF THEIR PARENTS

The panel recommends that the existing data base on children in working families be improved (1) to pay more attention to the child and child outcomes and (2) to be more sensitive to the complexity of the parental work dimension and to the range of intervening variables we have identified as significant. Examples of alternative approaches to accomplishing this include the development of better childhood social indicators;

continued maintenance of selected data series; the conduct of secondary analyses of existing large-scale data sets; and the development of new, well-designed cross-sectional and longitudinal studies. Illustrations of each are presented below.

Childhood Social Indicators

At present, our knowledge of what is happening to children as a consequence of major social changes occurring in the society, including changing work patterns and related changes in family life-styles, is limited both by the inadequacy of existing research and the brevity of the time period in which these phenomena have taken place and received scholarly attention. Undoubtedly, many children will adapt to these changes as their parents make necessary adjustments in their daily lives. Some will experience stress. Others, who are more fragile or who are reared in more vulnerable families (e.g., those who are poor) under difficult circumstances, may have more serious problems. Given the nature, extent, and pace of change in family structure and functioning, schools, peer groups, and neighborhoods, it is essential that researchers begin to assess what the consequences are for children's social, emotional, physical, and intellectual development.

Childhood social indicators—quantitative or statistical measures of specified conditions of children's lives—are now beginning to be developed in order to assess what is happening to children over time. These indicators represent new ways of measuring key aspects of children's development, including their physical health, social and intellectual competence, ethical and moral values, attitudes, and aspirations, as well as other aspects of their well-being. If our goal is to be able to better assess the impact of social change on children, to focus social science research more directly on the consequences for children, then improving the quantity and quality of statistical data on children and improving measures of child development are important research priorities. Included here are the maintenance of basic national statistical series, the conduct of periodic surveys of children, and the development of new methods for measuring family functioning and child development.

Maintenance of Existing Data Sources Containing Information on the Socialization and Education of Children in a Changing Context

Children are growing up in a rapidly changing society with everyday experiences seemingly different from those of children who grew up a generation ago. They are more likely than ever before to live for at least some period of time in a single-parent family, and they will probably have only one or two siblings. As adults, they are likely to live in a very different world, one in which men as well as women will be active participants in child rearing and related parental responsibilities, as well as active participants in the labor force. Accordingly, it is important to know whether current patterns of socialization and education are preparing children for their future roles in society. Implicitly, there is a shift from concentrating on the effects of parental employment per se to a study of the conditions under which children grow and prosper, given a changed reality. Which antecedent and intervening variables matter? Which familial and nonfamilial characteristics and supports make a difference?

What views do children (preadolescents and adolescents) hold of adult roles at work and at home? How realistic are children in assessing what they are likely to be and to do when they are grown up? Do girls see themselves as workers outside the home or as homemakers who' care for their own children? Do boys see themselves as married to working women or to women who are at home during the day doing housework and preparing elaborate meals for their return at night? Do boys see themselves as fathers diapering a baby, feeding a toddler, picking up a child after school, or is this all viewed as women's work?

Which children, with what characteristics, from which types of families, with what parental characteristics seem best prepared for these changing realities? What other attributes do they possess as regards school achievement, occupational aspirations, peer relationships, leadership capacities, values, and attitudes? Can we, for example, use surveys that include retrospective data to account for different outcomes by backward mapping, unraveling the multiple variables described earlier related to parental work status, family interaction, and the presence and type of institutional supports? What is the role played by school, television, employers, and other formal and informal institutions in the shaping of children's views and behavior, and which are most significant, how are they significant, and why?

At the very least we believe existing data series containing information of these types should be maintained and indeed enriched in order to provide data on family and institutional responses as well as child outcomes. Where such information does not already exist, efforts should be made to begin to collect it, preferably as added features of existing surveys. The purpose here is to begin to develop a data base that will permit the monitoring of changes over time. Given the monetary and time costs involved in carrying out new studies, especially longitudinal studies, continued maintenance of certain existing data series becomes enormously important. Several now exist (e.g., Panel Study of Income Dynamics, The National Longitudinal Surveys, the National Survey of Children, The National Survey of Family Growth, the Children's Time Study, and the new Survey of Income and Program Participation), and extensive prior investment has begun to generate, or could generate, significant findings. Funding for several of these is currently in jeopardy. Nevertheless, they provide unusually valuable potential for secondary analyses.

Secondary Analyses of Existing Data

One immediate possibility is to explore those large-scale data sets, both cross-sectional and longitudinal, that include at least some data on parental employment, child outcomes, and selected intervening variables. Researchers might test hypotheses concerning how various support systems (directly or indirectly, individually or collectively) influence how changing patterns of labor force participation affect children. Independent variables would include factors such as work status of parents and youth (e.g., hours, occupation), socioeconomic level, family structure, and age and sex of the child. Dependent variables would be child outcomes of various types, such as school achievement, the formation of values and attitudes toward work, education, family formation, peer interactions, and parent and sibling relationships. The intervening variables would include those support systems that influence children's socialization, such as schools, community social services, television, and the other media. The purpose of such secondary analyses would be to examine the extent to which existing data (that correlate family structure and the work status of parents and youths with various outcomes among children of different sexes, at different ages, and in families with different structures and work patterns) also yield an understanding of the role of various support systems (e.g., schools, workplace policies and practices, other formal and informal institutions), and what accounts for variations in outcomes among children.

Existing data sets which lend themselves to such analyses include the surveys mentioned above as well as the Seattle-Denver Income Maintenance Study.

Cross-Sectional Studies

Cross-sectional studies continue to yield important information. Any new studies of the consequences of changing patterns of work and family on children should provide greater specificity with regard to parent, child, and workplace characteristics, as well as the presence or absence of alternative support systems. Similarly, institutional studies—of schools, community services, and the workplace—should include attention to the family and employment characteristics of adults and where possible to some child outcomes as well.

Particular attention should be paid to the role of such factors as the age of the child when the parent commenced working (or stopped working) and the child's age at the time of the study; the sex of the child; family structure, income, and race and ethnicity; parents' education and occupation; parents' job and salary, hours, and place of work; commuting time to the workplace; parents' attitude toward work and work history; and type and continuity of child care. All these factors seem to influence how parental employment affects children. Of special importance where young children are concerned is how parents view these arrangements, what their preferences might be, and what other support systems (e.g., friends, neighbors, workplace, kin) exist and what role they play.

Some indication of who provides the data is also important. For example, in reports of children's attitudes and behavior, whether mother, father, or child is the source of the information obviously could make a significant difference, as it would for parent or teacher reports, or for employer and employee reports.

Longitudinal Studies

Most relevant research has been cross-sectional. By definition such methodology precludes any possibility of assessing long-term effects and changes over time. Since the long-term consequences of the major social changes we are highlighting cannot be discerned from a snapshot in time, existing research has not adequately explored (1) changing employment patterns over the course of the family life cycle; (2) changing aspects of the family system as adaptations are made, or not made, to new patterns of work and family structure; (3) evolving roles and relationships among community institutions (e.g., the schools, social service agencies, churches, neighborhood groups); and (4) changes in child outcomes as children develop and mature.

A major recommendation of several of the papers included in Part II of this volume, therefore, is that future studies should include more opportunity for obtaining data on long-term effects. Ideally, longitudinal studies would include attention to the changing characteristics of children, of the family system, and of the context and content of the experiences in which children and their families are exposed over the life course. Of particular importance is the extent to which norms and expectations are changing with regard to the participation of husbands and wives in work and family life. An alternative to launching new and expensive longitudinal studies might be to piggyback questions onto such existing studies as the Panel Study of Income Dynamics and the National Longitudinal Survey and to do special studies on subpopulations, such as low-income single parents.

OBTAINING INSIGHTS AND KNOWLEDGE CONCERNING THE KINDS OF
ADAPTATIONS (SUCCESSFUL AND UNSUCCESSFUL) NOW BEING MADE
BY WORKING FAMILIES, EMPLOYERS, SCHOOLS, AND OTHER
COMMUNITY INSTITUTIONS

The objective here is to learn more about (1) the experience of individual family members (parents and children) within the family itself, in their neighborhoods, and in peer groups; which families cope well with the demands of the two worlds of work and family life, which have difficulty, and with what consequences for children; (2) how different types of institutions (large and small firms, formal and informal organizations, market and nonmarket services) are responding to the changes now being experienced by employers, employees, consumers, and client groups; (3) how different countries at comparable levels of development are responding, and what their experiences have been, with what results. Surveys, case studies, ethnographic studies, natural experiments, and cross-national studies offer alternative approaches to gathering this information. Illustrations follow below.

Adaptations by Different Types of Working Families

Everything we know about how social change occurs and how society functions suggests that families—parents and children—must be making all sorts of adaptations on an individual basis. As we have suggested, parents are coping in a variety of ways, some more, some less successfully. How they cope—the methods they use and their effectiveness— have implications for them, for their children, and for a variety of institutions. How widespread are the kinds of adaptations we observe among some families? What exactly are they doing and what do they view as helpful, for whom, under what circumstances, and why?

Researchers know very little about the daily life experiences of children and parents in working families (or for that matter in families with an at-home mother). For example, exactly where and how do children spend their days? How do they and their parents use their time? What kinds of community services and institutions do working families of different types use, for what purposes, with what consequences? How are these experienced? Do working parents make different choices concerning schools, and do they view schools differently than do nonworking parents? What does work provide in the way of in-kind benefits, to which families, with what results? What are the implications for the significant differential that exists among those receiving and those not receiving these benefits?

In many families the major burden or adaptation may be carried by the parents themselves as they perform their primary child-caring and child-rearing responsibilities despite significantly less time and with less or different kinds of outside help. Among married-couple families, to what extent are husbands and wives making different personal adjustments in order to cope with these new realities? For example, which parents are choosing to work different shifts or different hours in order to ensure the presence of at least one parent at home all or most of the time? Are these choices made because the parents prefer caring for their children themselves or because the alternative resources for child care are nonexistent or inadequate? What are the consequences of such patterns for the family system (e.g., spouse relations, parent-child relations) and for parents' capacity to monitor and supervise their children's activities, as well as for children's development?

Life-cycle events affect work and family interactions, too. If marriage or the decision to have a child can alter a person's decision to have a career (or the kind of career to have), a new job, a promotion, or a transfer can affect parents' use of time; their patterns of familial, social, and community relationships; and their attitudes and behavior toward their children. What is not known, however, is what differentiates those families and work organizations in which events are constructively handled from those in which the effects are deleterious. Yet this kind of information is important for families in managing their own affairs and for employers in developing policies.

Which parents with what characteristics are coping well, which are not, and by what criteria? Are parents, for example, experiencing more stress even though in the short run they seem to be managing adequately? Are they experiencing more stress that is leading to identifiable problems for themselves or their families (e.g., marital problems, somatic problems, work problems, behavior problems toward children)? Are those families that are usually viewed as especially vulnerable (low-income families, single-parent families, black or Hispanic families) more likely to experience difficulties as a consequence of both parents working? To what extent do class, race, and family structure so overwhelm all other factors that the work status of parents may be impossible to isolate as a significant variable? Or in contrast, is the income effect so strong as to overwhelm all else for low-income families?

How do parents think others are managing and how do they view the consequences for their children? Who do they think should be responsible for facilitating whatever adaptations and responses need to be made? What does coping well mean? Does it mean that parents do not say they are experiencing undue stress, that they do not attribute any problems to their children as a consequence of the changes in their own life-style, or that by some objective criteria, no such problems can be identified?

Among those parents who seem to be coping successfully, which institutions (e.g., employers, neighbors, friends, kin, schools, community services) do they view as helpful, why, and in what ways?

Institutional Adaptations

All that we know about society would indicate that those community institutions serving families and children will be responding to the changes in their client-consumer groups, although there may be a time lag before such adaptations emerge and are recognized. Thus far what has been learned from existing research suggests very limited responses.

It would seem that where community institutions are concerned (formal and informal service systems, market and nonmarket services, and so forth), one major problem has been the lack of an adequate conceptualization of the domain and a concomitant failure to ask questions relating what these organizations do or do not provide, and why, to changes in their client-user population and the effects on children. For example, to what extent is the market responding to these new needs? Which families use the market and which are excluded from obtaining such help through the market, with what consequences? Could more cash and personal disposable income ensure access to private services or goods, and would they provide an adequate substitute or equivalent for collective goods?

Are existing social service agencies designed to serve only those with identifiable problems? If so, where do families go who do not view themselves as having problems but want some help managing complicated routines, such as regular child care, care of a temporarily ill child, and care of a child when school is closed?

As suggested in the Bell review (Chapter 6 in this volume), in some ways it might be helpful to view small firms as a kind of community institution, too. To what extent do small employers provide a kind of intimacy, an opportunity for personal relationships, greater flexibility in work hours, and more autonomy that may outweigh the more concrete benefits offered by larger firms? More specifically, there is a need for community and social network studies that would focus on the inter-relationship of schools, community services (market and nonmarket, religious and secular), informal supports, and small firms and would analyze the ways in which these institutions are or are not reponding to new family life-styles. Once again, a new conceptualization, a way of seeing connections among the relevant institutions and of collecting and assessing data, is needed.

Given the growing evidence on the significance of environmental fac-tors in accounting for differences in child and family functioning, there is a need to learn which services and institutions are viewed as supportive and which are not and what the effects are of their presence and avail-ability. Where are responses emerging, why, and what could or should be done to facilitate their development where none have emerged yet? Why are certain responses likely to emerge in certain institutions? Which families benefit, and with what consequences? For example, some schools provide preschool programs and extended day programs for preschool and primary school children during the hours when schools are usually closed but parents are at work. Learning which schools provide such services, why, and with what results could lead to some conclusions about what other schools should do or could do. Large firms and unionized firms are likely to provide more generous fringe benefits—pensions, health insurance, vacations, sick leaves, and so forth. Women, minorities, and youth are much less likely to work in such firms, how-ever. What are the actual family consequences of differential treatment with regard to such potentially valuable in-kind benefits? Apart from compensation policies, which other employee policies and practices are important for worker-parents, why, and in what ways? Both public and private policy responses could be more informed if systematic data re-garding these developments and their consequences were available.

Adaptations in Elementary and Secondary School Programs

Clearly, there is need for a new approach to studying schools as com-munity institutions. Ultimately, any study of schools as they are adapting to these changes must pay attention to the school as a community service facility and to the family and the community as major intervening var-iables in education, as centers of learning themselves. The family must

be addressed, also, as a significant, if not the most significant, determinant of how children make use of school.

Schools in the United States are going through a period of immense
challenge and change. Declining enrollments have led to closings and
teacher layoffs. Voter resistance to bond issues and property tax increases has produced financial difficulties for schools in some areas and
restructuring of school budgets in others. Other changes in elementary
schools are being produced by state and federal antidiscrimination laws
and by the political movements that led to the passage of these laws.
For example, Public Law 94-142, the Education for All Handicapped
Children Act of 1975, mandated that all handicapped children are entitled to a free and appropriate public education in the least restrictive
environment possible. The Bilingual Education Act of 1968 called for
recognition of the needs of children from non-English-speaking backgrounds. Similarly, vouchers and tuition tax credits that allegedly will
provide parents and their children with a broader educational choice,
loom large as possible future changes that will affect the role and operations of U.S. schools. Traditional school practices have also been
challenged by legislation and litigation dealing with sex discrimination.

There has been considerable publicity and debate about the decline
over time in average College Board scores and to other indicators of
declining academic achievement. Yet no one has questioned the continuing deficiencies in the academic achievement of minority group children in comparison with their middle-class nonminority counterparts.
Some observers have questioned the validity of the comparisons over
time. After years of searching for scapegoats, such as television, family
background, and other forces external to the educatonal system, there
is a growing inclination to hold the schools accountable for the failure
of students to master fundamental skills. Yet this new accountability is
occurring at the same time that the resources for schools are becoming
still more scarce, the regulatory constraints are continuing, major changes
in how children are reared are extending to a lárger portion of the
population, and there is growing recognition of the complexity of factors
which affect the ultimate outcomes for children. The impact on schools
must be examined within this larger context.

No systematic profile of changes over time in the policies and practices
of U.S. schools is now available. While there are promising beginnings,
there is little systematic information on which aspects of the curriculum
seem to be critical in bolstering student achievement and fostering other
educational goals. Children spend more of their daily lives in school
than they do in any other single institution other than their families.
Moreover, given the trends we have described for nursery and other

preschools, exposure to school is beginning earlier for some and may be covering more time each weekday, too.

There is need for research that would monitor what is occurring in the schools, with a particular focus on the impact of these changes on children. Despite the plethora of educational research studies done in the United States each year, there is no current survey program that provides a national picture of educational policies and practices broadly defined in a representative sample of schools. Such a survey, focusing on the whole range of school activities, not just narrowly defined academic curricula, could provide a systematic picture of the variety of extracurricular programs (including special programs provided in some schools linking parents and school, the workplace and the school, and local social service organizations and the school) and the role these play in the ultimate consequences for children. Such information would be of use to parents; teachers; school adminstrators; policy makers at local, state, and federal levels; and researchers. Monitoring changes in elementary and secondary school programs should be aimed at (1) developing a systematic picture of what schools are now providing and how they relate to other formal and informal community institutions; and (2) assessing the factors accounting for differences in school policies and practices as well as the consequences for children's education and socialization.

Natural Experiments

Given the extensiveness of the social changes under discussion and the likelihood that the adaptation process is already occurring in families and in all other related institutions, the process may have been accelerated in some cases. Unusual and interesting adaptations may have emerged. Parents are coping in various ways; some employers appear to have responded in modest ways; some schools and other community institutions have developed new programs as well. Attempts at studying a selected group of interesting policies or programs designed to provide help or support to families and children experiencing these changes could offer insights into what is happening, what might be helpful, and why. The findings of such natural experiments could provide the basis for formulating more refined hypotheses for subsequent testing.

Cross-National Research

Cross-national transfers of data and findings would add an important dimension to the study of societal adaptations to changes in parental work patterns and the consequences for children. While we did not conduct a systematic review of international research on changing patterns of parental employment, the nature of institutional responses, and the effects on children, there is an extensive literature on the experiences of several industrialized countries. The patterns of change are similar, the changes occurring earlier in some countries, which are therefore farther along already (e.g., Sweden, the German Democratic Republic, Hungary); or concurrently (e.g., France); or slightly later in others (e.g., Federal Republic of Germany). Far more extensive and deliberate government policy responses have already emerged in many of these countries, including substantial provision of out-of-home child-care services as well as work-related benefits for employees who are parents. The experiences of several European countries offer the opportunity for study in a natural laboratory in which one can hold constant parental employment (by the characteristics of the parents) while studying the effects of diverse institutional responses on a variety of outcomes for children. One such study compared the policies and programs of five European countries in addition to those of the United States, examining the nature of the policies, those factors accounting for differences among them, and their costs and benefits (Kamerman and Kahn, 1981). A recent Danish survey of the care of children from birth to age five (Gronhoj, 1981) includes data on parents, their employment status, and selected child outcomes. Research comparing selected outcomes for children in different countries could provide important insights into the consequences of alternative experiences for children, even though these would have to be placed in the context of the individual countries.

EVALUATING THE DIRECT AND INDIRECT OUTCOMES OF
GOVERNMENT POLICIES, EMPLOYMENT POLICIES, AND COMMUNITY
SERVICES

The panel recommends greater investment in evaluating the direct and indirect outcomes (including the costs and the benefits) of (1) the influence of government policies at different levels (federal, state, local) and of different types (tax, transfer, grant) on institutions (schools, employers, social service agencies, and family members); (2) employment policies and practices (benefits, services, alternative work schedules); and (3) community services and programs (formal and informal, public and private, market and nonmarket). Illustations follow.

The Role and Impact of Government Policies

Federal, state, and local government policies play an important role in influencing the nature and extent of these changes as well as the responses to them. Federal policies affect employment and unemployment rates; income tax policies may influence wives' work decisions; income transfer policies may affect the decisions of both single and married mothers by providing either incentives or disincentives for working. Federal policies affect employer policies through direct legislation, tax incentives, and regulation.

The federal government has been the major funder of publicly subsidized child care and related services. It also provides an extensive subsidy to parents through the child-care tax credit, which helps some parents in the purchase of whatever type of care they wish at a somewhat lower cost to themselves. The federal government has significantly supplemented the funding available to schools through such means as direct grants for special programs. It has imposed a variety of regulations on schools, adding to their administrative costs. The federal government has also provided subsidies to employers through tax deductions for the provision of certain benefits and services and to employees by attaching a tax-free status to the receipt of such services as pensions, health insurance, child care, and counseling.

To what extent have federal funds provided an incentive for schools to do more? To what extent have such funds (and the regulations accompanying them) impeded greater responsiveness by the schools, or influenced them to emphasize only certain kinds of services, or in other ways skewed their policies or practices? Similarly, learning how federal policies influence employers' decisions to provide benefits and employees' choice of benefits over cash wages could contribute to our understanding of the factors influencing the development of new responses by employers. How are the current changes in federal funding and regulations affecting school functioning and child outcomes?

Federal funds for social services, including much of the public funds for child-care services, have been substantially reduced. Funds for Title 20 of the Social Security Act are no longer required to be spent on specific groups (e.g., Aid to Families with Dependent Children recipients). To what extent this will affect the quantity and quality of child care remains to be seen.

State and local governments contribute to local social service agencies and often impose regulations and constraints on what they can do. More important, they are the major source of funding of primary and secondary school programs and the major enunciator of educational policies and practices. And during the past decade there has been an enormous increase in the states' regulation of schools.

What has been the role of state policies (e.g., funding, regulations) in influencing what schools do? To what extent have federal, state, and local government policies been interrelated? As tax revenues dwindle, these questions become all the more salient. There is growing interest on the part of many state legislatures in linking schools to other institutions within the community, such as employers and social service agencies. What types of government policies might facilitate such linkages, for what kinds of children and families, with what consequences? In addition, what will be the effects on these institutions of proposed policies, such as the federal tuition tax credit?

Institutional Supports as Contributors to Family and Individual Autonomy or Dependency

To the extent that work creates additional needs for families, new institutional supports are likely to emerge over time. Indeed, we are increasingly aware of how strongly these supports can affect the ultimate outcomes for parents and for children. As already indicated we clearly believe it is important to study those types of supports (e.g., extended school day, cooperative child-care services, paid maternity and paternity leaves) that emerge or do not emerge, what factors account for their development or their lack of development, and what the likely consequences are for children. However, it is also important to develop some understanding of the consequences of different types of supports for family functioning. For example, there is a frequently expressed concern that those supportive benefits and services provided directly by government—or even indirectly through extensive public subsidy—foster dependency on the part of those families who benefit. It would be important to know whether, in fact, such provision does make families more dependent and what dependency means in this context, or whether family members can retain their autonomy despite the availability and use of such supports. What are the consequences for children? And how do they view their capacity for leadership, for stability in their lives, for autonomy? Does it matter, for example, whether provision is direct or indirect; that is, whether service auspices are public rather than private? Does it matter if the subsidy is given directly to the parent rather than funneled through the provider? If the services are purchased in the market, are the consequences for dependency or autonomy different, and if so, how, in what ways, and why? When employers are the providers of benefits and services, do such practices create dependency among employees who are parents? If so, is there a difference between the effects of public provision and the effects of private provision? What is the relationship between government-provided and employer-provided benefits and services? Such knowledge could make an important difference in the nature of public- and private-policy responses.

IMPROVING THE STATE OF KNOWLEDGE ABOUT THE EFFECTS
OF EMPLOYMENT, UNEMPLOYMENT, AND WELFARE ON CHILDREN'S
WELL-BEING

For years, work and its effects on families have been studied as if paternal unemployment and maternal employment were potential problems for families and children. Over time the perspective has shifted somewhat, toward a partial redefinition of the issue. Now there are those who view maternal employment, like paternal employment, as a positive force for the development of children, just as there are those who view maternal unemployment, like paternal unemployment, as a problem. As we have pointed out repeatedly, most existing research views paternal and maternal employment status as discrete and distinctive phenomena and most view employment as a single, undifferentiated variable. The basic theme underlying all our findings has been a complete rejection of this approach. Instead, we urge a holistic and systemic view of a very complex set of phenomena, in which many intervening variables play a potentially significant roles in influencing child outcomes.

Ultimately, it may be discovered that it is the availability of a job for parents—at a decent wage and with adequate benefits—that is the single most critical factor affecting children and how they develop. We have not here reviewed the consequences of unemployment (sole parent, sole wage earner in a married-couple family, one of two working parents). Yet it seems clear that this is an important topic for study. While the effects of current federal policies and the high and possibly still higher levels of unemployment are cushioned to some extent by unemployment insurance and related benefits, there are many economic, social, and psychological problems that may result from prolonged unemployment. Moreover, although some families may find the economic impact of a father's unemployment attenuated by the presence of a mother's earnings (even if at a lower level than the father's), other families have long integrated both parents' earnings into the family budget. Thus, the family economy can be as much disrupted by the loss of either parent's earnings as it was earlier when only the father worked and he became unemployed.

How do families cope with prolonged unemployment? What are the consequences of the loss of one paycheck if there is only one earner in the family, and what difference does it make if the unemployed wage earner is the father or the mother? There is some evidence that the unemployment rate for low-income, married women is higher for those in families with unemployed husbands. How do families alter their role perceptions so that it is acceptable for wives to work when husbands are unemployed and for men to become more involved with home and family tasks? Are families more or less mobile when the wife is working and the husband becomes unemployed, and what are the consequences of this mobility or lack of it?

What is the impact of parental unemployment on children of different ages: on their diets, health, and physical development; on their school achievement; on their attitudes toward their parents; on their self-perceptions; on their relationships with their peers; on their orientations to work and to family formation?

Such information could be of major importance to policy makers and to the public at large. To provide answers to these questions, we need systematic studies of different types of families with different numbers of workers at different educational, occupational, and wage levels; with children of different ages at the time of parental unemployment; with different types of benefits entitlements for parents living in different kinds of communities; with different types of familial and nonfamilial supports available.

TOWARD A POLICY AGENDA

In response to the growing concern about how changing patterns of work and family structure affect the ways in which children develop, we have systematically reviewed the research on this subject and concluded that employment—paid work—has no single, overall, uniform effect except to add to family income and decrease the amount of time parents have available for family tasks. Clearly, income is very important, especially to parents. Indeed, income may be more important than ever to individual parents, given the growing number of single parents who are the sole source of support for their families, the increasing likelihood of single-parent status for women, and the need on the part of many low-income or moderate-income families for two paychecks in order to ensure a desired standard of living. Moreover, work and a job may carry with it concomitants other than money that are significant and potentially beneficial for adults and their children. Such concomitants include a sense of achievement, self-esteem, peer relationships, new role models, and so forth. If one were to conclude that work and what work brings with it are so important that the availability of a job for all those wanting one is an essential policy goal, we would still be faced with the critical tasks of knowledge building that we have laid out in this last chapter:

(1) to identify those families in which work has had a beneficial impact on the family system, including the children; to explore which institutions have been supportive and how, the circumstances under which family and nonfamily adaptations have been effective and why, and the consequences for children—and ways to encourage those institutions;

(2) to identify those families and children for whom problems have emerged, exploring why these have occurred and how they could be avoided.

Ultimately, therefore, this catalog becomes both a research and a policy agenda.

REFERENCES AND BIBLIOGRAPHY

Gronhoj, B. (1981) *Day Care of Preschool Children: A Problem for Parents and Local Authorities*. Danish National Institute of Social Research Publication 103. Copenhagen: I Kommission Hos Teknisk Forlag Kobenhaven.

Kamerman, S. B., and Kahn, A. J. (1981) *Child Care, Family Benefits, and Working Parents*. New York: Columbia University Press.